RSMeans Residential Square Foot Costs

CONTRACTOR'S PRICING GUIDE

Senior Editor
Bob Mewis, CCC

Contributing Editors
Christopher Babbitt
Ted Baker
Barbara Balboni
Robert A. Bastoni
John H. Chiang, PE
Gary W. Christensen
David G. Drain, PE
Cheryl Elsmore
Robert J. Kuchta
Robert C. McNichols
Melville J. Mossman, PE
Jeannene D. Murphy
Stephen C. Plotner
Eugene R. Spencer
Marshall J. Stetson
Phillip R. Waier, PE

Book Design
Norman R. Forgit

President & CEO
Iain Melville

**Vice President,
Product & Development**
Richard Remington

**Vice President of
Operations**
David C. Walsh

Vice President of Sales
Thomas Kesler

Director, Cost Products
Daimon Bridge

Marketing Director
John M. Shea

Engineering Manager
Bob Mewis, CCC

Cover Design
Paul Robertson
Wayne Engebretson

Production Manager
Michael Kokernak

Production Coordinator
Jill Goodman

Production
Paula Reale-Camelio
Sheryl A. Rose
Jonathan Forgit
Debbie Panarelli
Mary Lou Geary

Technical Support
A.K. Dash
Tom Dion
Roger Hancock
Gary L. Hoitt
Genevieve Medeiros
Kathryn S. Rodriguez
Sharon Proulx

PRINTED WITH SOY INK

RSMeans
Residential
Square Foot Costs

2010
CONTRACTOR'S PRICING GUIDE

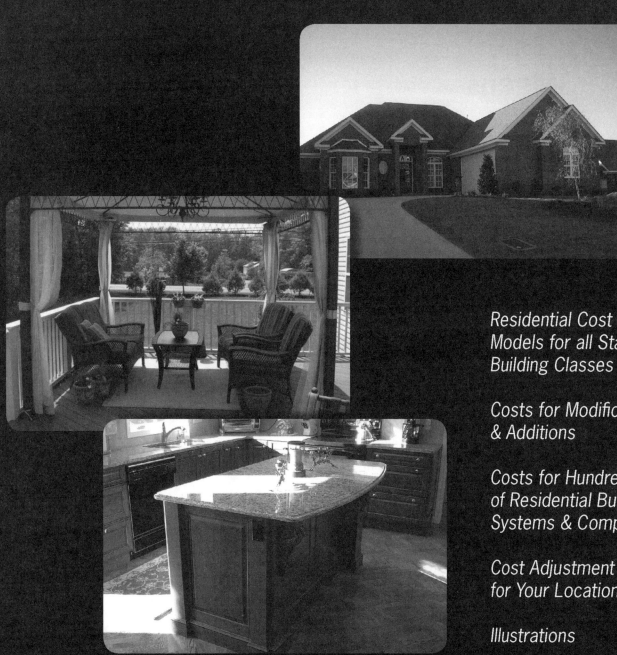

Residential Cost Models for all Standard Building Classes

Costs for Modifications & Additions

Costs for Hundreds of Residential Building Systems & Components

Cost Adjustment Factors for Your Location

Illustrations

$39.95 per copy (in United States)
Price subject to change without prior notice.

RS**Means**

Copyright © 2009
A division of Reed Construction Data
Construction Publishers & Consultants
63 Smiths Lane
Kingston, MA 02364-3008
781-422-5000
www.rsmeans.com

Printed in the United States of America

ISSN 1074-0481

ISBN 978-0-87629-831-2

This book is printed on recycled paper, using soy-based printing ink. This book is recyclable.

Foreword

Our Mission

Since 1942, RSMeans has been actively engaged in construction cost publishing and consulting throughout North America.

Today, more than 65 years after RSMeans began, our primary objective remains the same: to provide you, the construction and facilities professional, with the most current and comprehensive construction cost data possible.

Whether you are a contractor, owner, architect, engineer, facilities manager, or anyone else who needs a reliable construction cost estimate, you'll find this publication to be a highly useful and necessary tool.

With the constant flow of new construction methods and materials today, it's difficult to find the time to look at and evaluate all the different construction cost possibilities. In addition, because labor and material costs keep changing, last year's cost information is not a reliable basis for today's estimate or budget.

That's why so many construction professionals turn to RSMeans. We keep track of the costs for you, along with a wide range of other key information, from city cost indexes . . . to productivity rates . . . to crew composition . . . to contractors' overhead and profit rates.

RSMeans performs these functions by collecting data from all facets of the industry and organizing it in a format that is instantly accessible to you. From the preliminary budget to the detailed unit price estimate, you'll find the data in this book useful for all phases of construction cost determination.

The Staff, the Organization, and Our Services

When you purchase one of RSMeans' publications, you are, in effect, hiring the services of a full-time staff of construction and engineering professionals.

Our thoroughly experienced and highly qualified staff works daily at collecting, analyzing, and disseminating comprehensive cost information for your needs. These staff members have years of practical construction experience and engineering training prior to joining the firm. As a result, you can count on them not only for accurate cost figures, but also for additional background reference information that will help you create a realistic estimate.

The RSMeans organization is always prepared to help you solve construction problems through its variety of data solutions, including online, CD, and print book formats, as well as cost estimating expertise available via our business solutions, training, and seminars.

Besides a full array of construction cost estimating books, RSMeans also publishes a number of other reference works for the construction industry. Subjects include construction estimating and project and business management, special topics such as green building and job order contracting, and a library of facility management references.

In addition, you can access all of our construction cost data electronically using *Means CostWorks*® CD or on the Web using **MeansCostWorks.com.**

What's more, you can increase your knowledge and improve your construction estimating and management performance with an RSMeans construction seminar or in-house training program. These two-day seminar programs offer unparalleled opportunities for everyone in your organization to become updated on a wide variety of construction-related issues.

RSMeans is also a worldwide provider of construction cost management and analysis services for commercial and government owners.

In short, RSMeans can provide you with the tools and expertise for constructing accurate and dependable construction estimates and budgets in a variety of ways.

Robert Snow Means Established a Tradition of Quality That Continues Today

Robert Snow Means spent years building RSMeans, making certain he always delivered a quality product.

Today, at RSMeans, we do more than talk about the quality of our data and the usefulness of our books. We stand behind all of our data, from historical cost indexes to construction materials and techniques to current costs.

If you have any questions about our products or services, please call us toll-free at 1-800-334-3509. Our customer service representatives will be happy to assist you. You can also visit our Web site at **www.rsmeans.com.**

Table of Contents

How the Book is Built: An Overview

A Powerful Construction Tool

You have in your hands one of the most powerful construction tools available today. A successful project is built on the foundation of an accurate and dependable estimate. This book will enable you to construct just such an estimate.

For the casual user the book is designed to be:

- quickly and easily understood so you can get right to your estimate.
- filled with valuable information so you can understand the necessary factors that go into the cost estimate.

For the regular user, the book is designed to be:

- a handy desk reference that can be quickly referred to for key costs.
- a comprehensive, fully reliable source of current construction costs so you'll be prepared to estimate any project.
- a source book for preliminary project cost, product selections, and alternate materials and methods.

To meet all of these requirements we have organized the book into the following clearly defined sections.

Square Foot Cost Section

This section lists Square Foot costs for typical residential construction projects. The organizational format used divides the projects into basic building classes. These classes are defined at the beginning of the section. The individual projects are further divided into ten common components of construction. A Table of Contents, an explanation of square foot prices, and an outline of a typical page layout are located at the beginning of the section.

Assemblies Cost Section

This section uses an Assemblies (sometimes referred to as systems) format grouping all the functional elements of a building into nine construction divisions.

At the top of each Assemblies cost table is an illustration, a brief description, and the design criteria used to develop the cost. Each of the components and its contributing cost to the system is shown.

Material: These cost figures include a standard 10% markup for profit. They are national average material costs as of January of the current year and include delivery to the job site.

Installation: The installation costs include labor and equipment, plus a markup for the installing contractor's overhead and profit.

For a complete breakdown and explanation of a typical Assemblies page, see "How to Use the Assemblies Section" at the beginning of the Assemblies Section.

Location Factors: You can adjust total project costs to over 900 locations throughout the U.S. and Canada by using the data in this section.

Abbreviations: A listing of the abbreviations used throughout this book, along with the terms they represent, is included in this section.

Index

A comprehensive listing of all terms and subjects in this book to help you find what you need quickly.

The Scope of This Book

This book is designed to be as comprehensive and as easy to use as possible. To that end we have made certain assumptions and limited its scope in three key ways:

1. We have established material prices based on a national average.

2. We have computed labor costs based on a seven major-region average of residential wage rates.

Project Size/Type

The material prices in Means data cost books are "contractor's prices." They are the prices that contractors can expect to pay at the lumberyards, suppliers/distributers warehouses, etc. Small orders of speciality items would be higher than the costs shown, while very large orders, such as truckload lots, would be less. The variation would depend on the size, timing, and negotiating power of the contractor. The labor costs are primarily for new construction or major renovations rather than repairs or minor alterations. With reasonable exercise of judgment, the figures can be used for any building work.

How to Use the Book: The Details

What's Behind the Numbers? The Development of Cost Data

The staff at RSMeans continuously monitors developments in the construction industry in order to ensure reliable, thorough, and up-to-date cost information.

While *overall* construction costs may vary relative to general economic conditions, price fluctuations within the industry are dependent upon many factors. Individual price variations may, in fact, be opposite to overall economic trends. Therefore, costs are continually monitored and complete updates are published yearly. Also, new items are frequently added in response to changes in materials and methods.

Costs – $ (U.S.)

All costs represent U.S. national averages and are given in U.S. dollars. The RSMeans Location Factors can be used to adjust costs to a particular location. The Location Factors for Canada can be used to adjust U.S. national averages to local costs in Canadian dollars. No exchange rate conversion is necessary.

Material Costs

The RSMeans staff contacts manufacturers, dealers, distributors, and contractors all across the U.S. and Canada to determine national average material costs. If you have access to current material costs for your specific location, you may wish to make adjustments to reflect differences from the national average. Included within material costs are fasteners for a normal installation. RSMeans engineers use manufacturers' recommendations, written specifications, and/or standard construction practice for size and spacing of fasteners. Adjustments to material costs may be required for your specific application or location. Material costs do not include sales tax.

Labor Costs

Labor costs are based on the average of residential wages from across the U.S. for the current year. Rates, along with overhead and profit markups, are listed on the inside back cover of this book.

- If wage rates in your area vary from those used in this book, or if rate increases are expected within a given year, labor costs should be adjusted accordingly.

Labor costs reflect productivity based on actual working conditions. In addition to actual installation, these figures include time spent during a normal workday on tasks such as, as material receiving and handling, mobilization at site, site movement, breaks, and cleanup.

Productivity data is developed over an extended period so as not to be influenced by abnormal variations and reflects a typical average.

Equipment Costs

Equipment costs include not only rental, but also operating costs for equipment under normal use. Equipment and rental rates are obtained from industry sources throughout North America—contractors, suppliers, dealers, manufacturers, and distributers.

Factors Affecting Costs

Costs can vary depending upon a number of variables. Here's how we have handled the main factors affecting costs.

Quality—The prices for materials and the workmanship upon which productivity is based represent sound construction work. They are also in line with U.S. government specifications.

Overtime—We have made no allowance for overtime. If you anticipate premium time or work beyond normal working hours, be sure to make an appropriate adjustment to your labor costs.

Productivity—The productivity, daily output, and labor-hour figures for each line item are based on working an eight-hour day in daylight hours in moderate temperatures. For work that extends beyond normal work hours or is performed under adverse conditions, productivity may decrease.

Size of Project—The size, scope of work, and type of construction project will have a significant impact on cost. Economies of scale can reduce costs for large projects. Unit costs can often run higher for small projects. Costs in this book are intended for the size and type of project as previously described in "How the Book Is Built: An Overview." Costs for projects of a significantly different size or type should be adjusted accordingly.

Location—Material prices in this book are for metropolitan areas. However, in dense urban areas, traffic and site storage limitations may increase costs. Beyond a 20-mile radius of large cities, extra trucking or transportation charges may also increase the material costs slightly. On the other hand, lower wage rates may be in effect. Be sure to consider both of these factors when preparing an estimate, particularly if the job site is located in a central city or remote rural location.

In addition, highly specialized subcontract items may require travel and per-diem expenses for mechanics.

Other Factors–

- season of year
- contractor management
- weather conditions
- local union restrictions
- building code requirements
- availability of:
    - adequate energy
    - skilled labor
    - building materials
- owner's special requirements/ restrictions
- safety requirements
- environmental considerations

Overhead & Profit—The "Assemblies" section of this book uses costs that include the installing contractor's overhead and profit (O&P). An allowance covering the general contractor's markup must be added to these figures. The general contractor can include this price in the bid with a normal markup ranging from 5% to 15%. The markup depends on economic conditions plus the supervision and troubleshooting expected by the general contractor. For purposes of this book, it is best for a general contractor to add an allowance of 10% to the figures in the Assemblies section.

General Conditions

General Conditions, or General Requirements, of the contract should also be added to the Total Cost including O&P when applicable. General Conditions for the *Installing Contractor* may range from 0% to 10% of the Total Cost including O&P. For the *General or Prime Contractor*, costs for General Conditions may range from 5% to 15% of the Total Cost including O&P, with a figure of 10% as the most typical allowance.

Unpredictable Factors—General business conditions influence "in-place" costs of all items. Substitute materials and construction methods may have to be employed. These may affect the installed cost and/or life cycle costs. Such factors may be difficult to evaluate and cannot necessarily be predicted on the basis of the job's location in a particular section of the country. Thus, where these factors apply, you may find significant but unavoidable cost variations for which you will have to apply a measure of judgment to your estimate.

Rounding of Costs

In general, all unit prices in excess of $5.00 have been rounded to make them easier to use and still maintain adequate precision of the results. The rounding rules we have chosen are in the following table.

Prices from . . .	Rounded to the nearest . . .
$.01 to $5.00	$.01
$5.01 to $20.00	$.05
$20.01 to $100.00	$.50
$100.01 to $300.00	$1.00
$300.01 to $1,000.00	$5.00
$1,000.01 to $10,000.00	$25.00
$10,000.01 to $50,000.00	$100.00
$50,000.01 and above	$500.00

Final Checklist

Estimating can be a straightforward process provided you remember the basics. Here's a checklist of some of the steps you should remember to complete before finalizing your estimate.

Did you remember to . . .

- factor in the Location Factor for your locale?
- take into consideration which items have been marked up and by how much?
- mark up the entire estimate sufficiently for your purposes?
- include all components of your project in the final estimate?
- double check your figures for accuracy?
- call RSMeans if you have any questions about your estimate or the data you've found in our publications?

Remember, RSMeans stands behind its publications. If you have any questions about your estimate, about the costs you've used from our books—or even about the technical aspects of the job that may affect your estimate—feel free to call the RSMeans editors at 1-800-334-3509.

Square Foot Cost Section

Table of Contents

How to Use the Square Foot Cost Pages

Introduction: This section contains costs per square foot for four classes of construction in seven building types. Costs are listed for various exterior wall materials which are typical of the class and building type. There are cost tables for wings and ells with modification tables to adjust the base cost of each class of building. Non-standard items can easily be added to the standard structures.

Accompanying each building type in each class is a list of components used in a typical residence. The components are divided into ten primary estimating divisions. The divisions correspond with the "Assemblies" section of this manual.

Cost estimating for a residence is a three-step process:
(1) Identification
(2) Listing dimensions
(3) Calculations

Guidelines and a sample cost estimating form are shown on the following pages.

Identification: To properly identify a residential building, the class of construction, type, and exterior wall material must be determined. Located at the beginning of this section are drawings and guidelines for determining the class of construction. There are also detailed specifications accompanying each type of building, along with additional drawings at the beginning of each set of tables, to further aid in proper building class and type identification.

Sketches for seven types of residential buildings and their configurations are shown along with definitions of living area next to each sketch. Sketches and definitions of garage types follow the residential buildings.

Living Area: Base cost tables are prepared as costs per square foot of living area. The living area of a residence is that area which is suitable and normally designed for full-time living. It does not include basement recreation rooms or finished attics, although these areas are often considered full-time living areas by owners.

Living area is calculated from the exterior dimensions without the need to adjust for exterior wall thickness. When calculating the living area of a 1-1/2-story, two-story, three-story or tri-level residence, overhangs and other differences in size and shape between floors must be considered.

Only the floor area with a ceiling height of six feet or more in a 1-1/2 story residence is considered living area. In bi-levels and tri-levels, the areas that are below grade are considered living area, even when these areas may not be completely finished.

Base Tables and Modifications: Base cost tables show the base cost per square foot without a basement, with one full bath and one full kitchen. Adjustments for finished and unfinished basements are part of the base cost tables. Adjustments for multi-family residences, additional bathrooms, townhouses, alternative roofs, and air conditioning and heating systems are listed in Modifications, Adjustments, and Alternatives tables below the base cost tables.

The component list for each residence type should also be consulted when preparing an estimate. If the components listed are not appropriate, modifications can be made by consulting the "Assemblies" section of this manual.

Costs for other modifications, adjustments, and alternatives, including garages, breezeways, and site improvements, are in the modification tables at the end of this section.

Listing of Dimensions: To use this section of the manual, only the dimensions used to calculate the horizontal area of the building and additions and modifications are needed. The dimensions, normally the length and width, can come from drawings or field measurements. For ease in calculation, consider measuring in tenths of feet, i.e., 9 ft. 6 in. = 9.5 ft., 9 ft. 4 in. = 9.3 ft.

In all cases, make a sketch of the building. Any protrusions or other variations in shape should be noted on the sketch with dimensions.

Calculations: The calculations portion of the estimate is a two-step activity:
(1) The selection of appropriate costs from the tables
(2) Computations

Selection of Appropriate Costs: To select the appropriate cost from the base tables the following information is needed:
(1) Class of construction
(2) Type of residence
(3) Occupancy
(4) Building configuration
(5) Exterior wall construction
(6) Living area

Consult the tables and accompanying information to make the appropriate selections. Modifications, adjustments, and alternatives are classified by class, type and size. Further modifications can be made using the "Assemblies" Section.

Computations: The computation process should take the following sequence:
(1) Multiply the base cost by the area
(2) Add or subtract the modifications
(3) Apply the location modifier

When selecting costs, interpolate or use the cost that most nearly matches the structure under study. This applies to size, exterior wall construction, and class.

How to Use the Square Foot Cost Pages

Exterior wall system

Basement additions

Specification highlights

Class of construction

Type of residence

Living areas used to compute costs per square foot. (Living areas explained on pages 6–12.)

Base cost per square foot of living area for a 2 story wood sided residence without basement with total living area of 2,000 square feet. A detailed breakdown of this cost, typical for all residences of this class and type, appears on the facing page

Addition for unfinished basement

Modifications for typical alternates in roof cover, air conditioning and heating systems

Multiplier for Townhouse/Rowhouse (Adjustments for common wall).

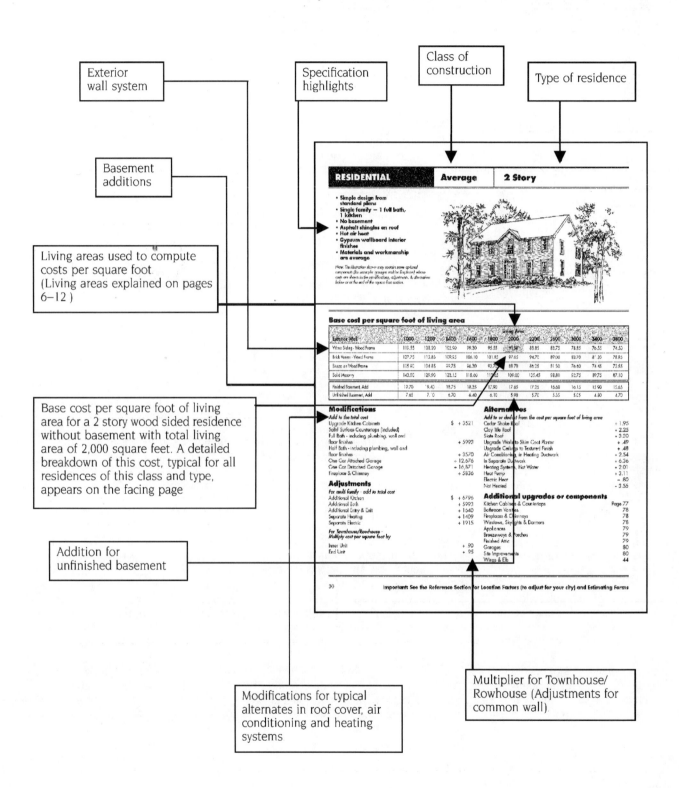

RESIDENTIAL — Average — 2 Story

- Simple design from standard plans
- Single family — 1 full bath, 1 kitchen
- No basement
- Asphalt shingles on roof
- Hot air heat
- Gypsum wallboard interior finishes
- Materials and workmanship are average

Note: The illustration above may contain some optional components (for example garages and/or fireplaces) whose costs are shown in the specifications, adjustments, & alternatives below or at the end of the square foot section.

Base cost per square foot of living area

Exterior Wall	1000	1200	1400	1600	1800	2000	2200	2600	3000	3400	3800
Wood Siding - Wood Frame	119.55	108.20	102.50	99.30	95.55	91.95	88.85	83.75	78.85	76.55	74.50
Brick Veneer - Wood Frame	127.75	113.85	109.55	106.10	101.85	97.65	94.70	89.00	83.70	81.20	78.95
Stucco on Wood Frame	115.90	104.85	99.75	96.30	92.70	88.70	86.25	81.50	76.60	74.45	72.55
Solid Masonry	143.00	129.90	123.15	118.60	113.65	109.00	105.45	98.80	92.75	89.75	87.10
Finished Basement, Add	19.70	19.40	18.75	18.35	17.90	17.65	17.25	16.60	16.15	15.90	15.65
Unfinished Basement, Add	7.65	7.10	6.70	6.40	6.10	5.09	5.70	5.35	5.05	4.80	4.70

Modifications
Add to the total cost

Upgrade Kitchen Cabinets	$ + 3521
Solid Surface Countertops (Included)	
Full Bath - including plumbing, wall and floor finishes	+ 5993
Half Bath - including plumbing, wall and floor finishes	+ 3570
One Car Attached Garage	+ 12,676
One Car Detached Garage	+ 16,871
Fireplace & Chimney	+ 5836

Adjustments
For multi family - add to total cost

Additional Kitchen	$ + 6796
Additional Bath	+ 5993
Additional Entry & Exit	+ 1640
Separate Heating	+ 1409
Separate Electric	+ 1915

For Townhouse/Rowhouse -
Multiply cost per square foot by

Inner Unit	+ .90
End Unit	+ .95

Alternatives
Add to or deduct from the cost per square foot of living area

Cedar Shake Roof	+ 1.95
Clay Tile Roof	+ 2.25
Slate Roof	+ 3.20
Upgrade Walls to Skim Coat Plaster	+ .49
Upgrade Ceilings to Textured Finish	+ .48
Air Conditioning, in Heating Ductwork	- 2.54
In Separate Ductwork	+ 6.36
Heating Systems, Hot Water	+ 2.01
Heat Pump	+ 3.11
Electric Heat	- .80
Not Heated	- 3.56

Additional upgrades or components

Kitchen Cabinets & Countertops	Page 77
Bathroom Vanities	78
Fireplaces & Chimneys	78
Windows, Skylights & Dormers	78
Appliances	79
Breezeways & Porches	79
Finished Attic	79
Garages	80
Site Improvements	80
Wings & Ells	44

30   Important: See the Reference Section for Location Factors (to adjust for your city) and Estimating Forms

Components
This page contains the ten components needed to develop the complete square foot cost of the typical dwelling specified. All components are defined with a description of the materials and/or task involved. Use cost figures from each component to estimate the cost per square foot of that section of the project.

Specifications
The parameters for an example dwelling from the facing page are listed here. Included are the square foot dimensions of the proposed building. LIVING AREA takes into account the number of floors and other factors needed to define a building's TOTAL SQUARE FOOTAGE. Perimeter and partition dimensions are defined in terms of linear feet.

Average 2 Story
Living Area - 2000 S.F.
Perimeter - 135 L.F.

		Cost Per Square Foot Of Living Area			% of Total
		Mat.	Inst.	Total	(room)
1	Site Work — Site preparation for slab; 4' deep trench excavation for foundation wall.		.72	.72	0.8%
2	Foundation — Continuous reinforced concrete footing 8" deep x 18" wide; dampproofed and insulated reinforced concrete foundation wall, 8" thick, 4' deep, 4" concrete slab on 4" crushed stone base and polyethylene vapor barrier, trowel finish.	2.97	3.73	6.70	7.3%
3	Framing — Exterior walls - 2" x 4" wood studs, 16" O.C.; 1/2" plywood sheathing; 2" x 6" rafters 16" O.C. with 1/2" plywood sheathing, 4 in 12 pitch; 2" x 6" ceiling joists 16" O.C.; 2" x 8" floor joists 16" O.C. with 5/8" plywood subfloor; 1/2" plywood subfloor on 1" x 2" wood sleepers 16" O.C.	4.96	8.27	13.23	14.5%
4	Exterior Walls — Beveled wood siding and building paper on insulated wood frame walls; 6" attic insulation; double hung windows; 3 flush solid core wood exterior doors with storms.	12.67	5.25	17.92	19.6%
5	Roofing — 25 year asphalt shingles; #15 felt building paper; aluminum gutters, downspouts, drip edge and flashings.	.96	1.11	2.07	2.3%
6	Interiors — Walls and ceilings, 1/2" taped and finished gypsum wallboard, primed and painted with 2 coats; painted baseboard and trim, finished hardwood floor 40%, carpet with 1/2" underlayment 40%, vinyl tile with 1/2" underlayment 15%, ceramic tile with 1/2" underlayment 5%; hollow core and louvered doors.	12.71	13.38	26.09	28.5%
7	Specialties — Average grade kitchen cabinets - 14 L.F. wall and base with solid surface counter top and kitchen sink; 40 gallon electric water heater.	2.26	.83	3.09	3.4%
8	Mechanical — 1 lavatory, white, wall hung; 1 water closet, white; 1 bathtub with shower; enameled steel, white; gas fired warm air heat.	3.02	2.68	5.70	6.2%
9	Electrical — 200 Amp. service; romex wiring; incandescent lighting fixtures, switches, receptacles.	1.13	1.54	2.67	2.9%
10	Overhead — Contractor's overhead and profit and plans.	6.92	6.39	13.31	14.5%
	Total	47.60	43.90	91.50	

31

Line Totals
The extreme right-hand column lists the sum of two figures. Use this total to determine the sum of MATERIAL COST plus INSTALLATION COST. The result is a convenient total cost for each of the ten components.

Installation
The labor rates included here incorporate the overhead and profit costs for the installing contractor. The average markup used to create these figures is 68.8 % over and above BARE LABOR COST including fringe benefits.

Bottom Line Total
This figure is the complete square foot cost for the construction project. To determine TOTAL PROJECT COST, multiply the BOTTOM LINE TOTAL times the LIVING AREA. (TOTAL PROJECT COST = BOTTOM LINE TOTAL x LIVING AREA).

Materials
This column gives the unit needed to develop the COST OF MATERIALS. Note: The figures given here are not BARE COSTS. Ten percent has been added to BARE MATERIAL COST to cover handling.

*NOTE
The components listed on this page are typical of all the sizes of residences from the facing page. Specific quantities of components required would vary with the size of the dwelling and the exterior wall system.

Building Classes

Given below are the four general definitions of building classes. Each building — Economy, Average, Custom and Luxury — is common in residential construction. All four are used in this book to determine costs per square foot.

Economy Class

An economy class residence is usually mass-produced from stock plans. The materials and workmanship are sufficient only to satisfy minimum building codes. Low construction cost is more important than distinctive features. Design is seldom other than square or rectangular.

Average Class

An average class residence is simple in design and is built from standard designer plans. Material and workmanship are average, but often exceed the minimum building codes. There are frequently special features that give the residence some distinctive characteristics.

Custom Class

A custom class residence is usually built from a designer's plans which have been modified to give the building a distinction of design. Material and workmanship are generally above average with obvious attention given to construction details. Construction normally exceeds building code requirements.

Luxury Class

A luxury class residence is built from an architect's plan for a specific owner. It is unique in design and workmanship. There are many special features, and construction usually exceeds all building codes. It is obvious that primary attention is placed on the owner's comfort and pleasure. Construction is supervised by an architect.

Residential Building Types

One Story

This is an example of a one-story dwelling. The living area of this type of residence is confined to the ground floor. The headroom in the attic is usually too low for use as a living area.

One-and-a-half Story

The living area in the upper level of this type of residence is 50% to 90% of the ground floor. This is made possible by a combination of this design's high-peaked roof and/or dormers. Only the upper level area with a ceiling height of 6' or more is considered living area. The living area of this residence is the sum of the ground floor area plus the area on the second level with a ceiling height of 6' or more.

Residential Building Types

Two Story

This type of residence has a second floor or upper level area which is equal or nearly equal to the ground floor area. The upper level of this type of residence can range from 90% to 110% of the ground floor area, depending on setbacks or overhangs. The living area is the sum of the ground floor area and the upper level floor area.

Two-and-one-half Story

This type of residence has two levels of equal or nearly equal area and a third level which has a living area that is 50% to 90% of the ground floor. This is made possible by a high peaked roof, extended wall heights and/or dormers. Only the upper level area with a ceiling height of 6 feet or more is considered living area. The living area of this residence is the sum of the ground floor area, the second floor area and the area on the third level with a ceiling height of 6 feet or more.

Three Story

This type of residence has three levels which are equal or nearly equal. As in the 2 story residence, the second and third floor areas may vary slightly depending on the setbacks or overhangs. The living area is the sum of the ground floor area and the two upper level floor areas.

Bi-Level

This type of residence has two living areas, one above the other. One area is about 4 feet below grade and the second is about 4 feet above grade. Both are equal in size. The lower level in this type of residence is originally designed and built to serve as a living area and not as a basement. Both levels have full ceiling heights. The living area is the sum of the lower level area and the upper level area.

Tri-Level

This type of residence has three levels of living area. One is at grade level, the second is about 4 feet below grade, and the third is about 4 feet above grade. All levels are originally designed to serve as living areas. All levels have full ceiling heights. The living area is the sum of the areas of each of the three levels.

Exterior Wall Construction

Wood Studs
Baseboard
Shoe
Sub & Finish Floor
Exterior Sheathing
Solid Blocking
Floor Joists
Plate
Wood Strapping & Finish Ceiling
Exterior Siding
Interior Sheathing
Insulation
Building Paper

Typical Frame Construction

Typical wood frame construction consists of wood studs with insulation between them. A typical exterior surface is made up of sheathing, building paper and exterior siding consisting of wood, vinyl, aluminum or stucco over the wood sheathing.

1" Air Space
Wood Studs
Baseboard
Shoe
Sub & Finish Floor
Brick Veneer
Solid Blocking
Floor Joists
Metal Ties
Plate
Wood Strapping & Finish Ceiling
Sheathing
Interior Sheathing
Insulation
Building Paper

Brick Veneer

Typical brick veneer construction consists of wood studs with insulation between them. A typical exterior surface is sheathing, building paper, and an exterior of brick tied to the sheathing with metal strips.

Furring Channels
Interior Sheathing
Base
Sub Finish Floor
Stone Face
Fire Cut End of Joists
Floor Joists
Conc. Block Back-up
Wood Strapping & Finish Ceiling
Metal Ties
Solid Blocking

Stone

Typical solid masonry construction consists of a stone or block wall covered on the exterior with brick, stone, or other masonry.

Residential Configurations

Detached House

This category of residence is a freestanding separate building with or without an attached garage. It has four complete walls.

Town/Row House

This category of residence has a number of attached units made up of inner units and end units. The units are joined by common walls. The inner units have only two exterior walls. The common walls are fireproof. The end units have three walls and a common wall. Town houses/row houses can be any of the five types.

Semi-Detached House

This category of residence has two living units side-by-side. The common wall is a fireproof wall. Semi-detached residences can be treated as a row house with two end units. Semi-detached residences can be any of the five types.

Residential Garage Types

Attached Garage

Shares a common wall with the dwelling. Access is typically through a door between dwelling and garage.

Built-In Garage

Constructed under the second floor living space and above basement level of dwelling. Reduces gross square feet of living area.

Basement Garage

Constructed under the roof of the dwelling but below the living area.

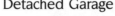

Detached Garage

Constructed apart from the main dwelling. Shares no common area or wall with the dwelling.

RESIDENTIAL
COST ESTIMATE

OWNER'S NAME: _____

APPRAISER: _____

RESIDENCE ADDRESS: _____

PROJECT: _____

CITY, STATE, ZIP CODE: _____

DATE: _____

CLASS OF CONSTRUCTION	RESIDENCE TYPE	CONFIGURATION	EXTERIOR WALL SYSTEM
☐ ECONOMY	☐ 1 STORY	☐ DETACHED	☐ WOOD SIDING - WOOD FRAME
☐ AVERAGE	☐ 1-1/2 STORY	☐ TOWN/ROW HOUSE	☐ BRICK VENEER - WOOD FRAME
☐ CUSTOM	☐ 2 STORY	☐ SEMI-DETACHED	☐ STUCCO ON WOOD FRAME
☐ LUXURY	☐ 2-1/2 STORY		☐ PAINTED CONCRETE BLOCK
	☐ 3 STORY	OCCUPANCY	☐ SOLID MASONRY (AVERAGE & CUSTOM)
	☐ BI-LEVEL	☐ ONE FAMILY	☐ STONE VENEER - WOOD FRAME
	☐ TRI-LEVEL	☐ TWO FAMILY	☐ SOLID BRICK (LUXURY)
		☐ THREE FAMILY	☐ SOLID STONE (LUXURY)
		☐ OTHER _____	

* LIVING AREA (Main Building)		* LIVING AREA (Wing or Ell) ( )		* LIVING AREA (WING or ELL) ( )	
First Level	_____ S.F.	First Level	_____ S.F.	First Level	_____ S.F.
Second level	_____ S.F.	Second level	_____ S.F.	Second level	_____ S.F.
Third Level	_____ S.F.	Third Level	_____ S.F.	Third Level	_____ S.F.
Total	_____ S.F.	Total	_____ S.F.	Total	_____ S.F.

* Basement Area is not part of living area.

MAIN BUILDING	COSTS PER S.F. LIVING AREA
Cost per Square Foot of Living Area, from Page _____	$
Basement Addition: _____ % Finished, _____ % Unfinished	+
Roof Cover Adjustment: _____ Type, Page _____ (Add or Deduct)	( )
Central Air Conditioning: ☐ Separate Ducts ☐ Heating Ducts, Page _____	+
Heating System Adjustment: _____ Type, Page _____ (Add or Deduct)	( )
Main Building: Adjusted Cost per S.F. of Living Area	$

MAIN BUILDING TOTAL COST	$ _____ /S.F. Cost per S.F. Living Area	X	_____ S.F. Living Area	X	_____ Town/Row House Multiplier (Use 1 for Detached)	=	$ _____ TOTAL COST

WING OR ELL ( ) _____ STORY	COSTS PER S.F. LIVING AREA
Cost per Square Foot of Living Area, from Page _____	$
Basement Addition: _____ % Finished, _____ % Unfinished	+
Roof Cover Adjustment: _____ Type, Page _____ (Add or Deduct)	( )
Central Air Conditioning: ☐ Separate Ducts ☐ Heating Ducts, Page _____	+
Heating System Adjustment: _____ Type, Page _____ (Add or Deduct)	( )
Wing or Ell ( ): Adjusted Cost per S.F. of Living Area	$

WING OR ELL ( ) TOTAL COST	$ _____ /S.F. Cost per S.F. Living Area	X	_____ S.F. Living Area	X	_____	=	$ _____ TOTAL COST

WING OR ELL ( ) _____ STORY	COSTS PER S.F. LIVING AREA
Cost per Square Foot of Living Area, from Page _____	$
Basement Addition: _____ % Finished, _____ % Unfinished	+
Roof Cover Adjustment: _____ Type, Page _____ (Add or Deduct)	( )
Central Air Conditioning: ☐ Separate Ducts ☐ Heating Ducts, Page _____	+
Heating System Adjustment: _____ Type, Page _____ (Add or Deduct)	( )
Wing or Ell ( ): Adjusted Cost per S.F. of Living Area	$

WING OR ELL ( ) TOTAL COST	$ _____ /S.F. Cost per S.F. Living Area	X	_____ S.F. Living Area	X	_____	=	$ _____ TOTAL COST

TOTAL THIS PAGE _____

RESIDENTIAL
COST ESTIMATE

Total Page 1					$
			QUANTITY	UNIT COST	
Additional Bathrooms: _____ Full _____ Half					
Finished Attic: _____ Ft. x _____ Ft.			S.F.		+
Breezeway: ☐ Open ☐ Enclosed _____ Ft. x _____ Ft.			S.F.		+
Covered Porch: ☐ Open ☐ Enclosed _____ Ft. x _____ Ft.			S.F.		+
Fireplace: ☐ Interior Chimney ☐ Exterior Chimney					
☐ No. of Flues ☐ Additional Fireplaces					+
Appliances:					+
Kitchen Cabinets Adjustments: (±)					
☐ Garage ☐ Carport: _____ Car(s) Description _____ (±)					
Miscellaneous:					+

ADJUSTED TOTAL BUILDING COST | $ |

REPLACEMENT COST	
ADJUSTED TOTAL BUILDING COST	$ _____
Site Improvements	
(A) Paving & Sidewalks	$ _____
(B) Landscaping	$ _____
(C) Fences	$ _____
(D) Swimming Pools	$ _____
(E) Miscellaneous	$ _____
TOTAL	$ _____
Location Factor	x _____
Location Replacement Cost	$ _____
Depreciation	- $ _____
LOCAL DEPRECIATED COST	$ _____

INSURANCE COST	
ADJUSTED TOTAL BUILDING COST	$ _____
Insurance Exclusions	
(A) Footings, Site work, Underground Piping	- $ _____
(B) Architects Fees	- $ _____
Total Building Cost Less Exclusion	$ _____
Location Factor	x _____
LOCAL INSURABLE REPLACEMENT COST	$ _____

SKETCH AND ADDITIONAL CALCULATIONS

1 Story

1-1/2 Story

2 Story

Bi-Level

Tri-Level

©Design Basics, Inc.

- **Mass produced from stock plans**
- **Single family — 1 full bath, 1 kitchen**
- **No basement**
- **Asphalt shingles on roof**
- **Hot air heat**
- **Gypsum wallboard interior finishes**
- **Materials and workmanship are sufficient to meet codes**

Note: The illustration shown may contain some optional components (for example: garages and/or fireplaces) whose costs are shown in the modifications, adjustments, & alternatives below or at the end of the square foot section.

©Home Planners, Inc.

Base cost per square foot of living area

Exterior Wall	Living Area										
	600	800	1000	1200	1400	1600	1800	2000	2400	2800	3200
Wood Siding - Wood Frame	113.20	102.25	94.05	87.30	81.50	77.80	75.95	73.45	68.45	64.80	62.30
Brick Veneer - Wood Frame	118.40	106.90	98.30	91.10	85.00	81.05	79.10	76.40	71.15	67.30	64.55
Stucco on Wood Frame	106.90	96.65	89.00	82.75	77.35	73.90	72.20	69.95	65.25	61.85	59.50
Painted Concrete Block	112.10	101.25	93.15	86.50	80.75	77.10	75.30	72.85	67.90	64.30	61.80
Finished Basement, Add	27.90	26.30	25.10	24.00	23.20	22.60	22.30	21.85	21.15	20.70	20.25
Unfinished Basement, Add	12.30	10.95	10.05	9.15	8.45	8.00	7.80	7.40	6.90	6.50	6.15

Modifications

Add to the total cost

Upgrade Kitchen Cabinets	$ + 803
Solid Surface Countertops	+ 576
Full Bath - including plumbing, wall and floor finishes	+ 4775
Half Bath - including plumbing, wall and floor finishes	+ 2845
One Car Attached Garage	+ 11,273
One Car Detached Garage	+ 14,630
Fireplace & Chimney	+ 5267

Adjustments

For multi family - add to total cost

Additional Kitchen	$ + 3709
Additional Bath	+ 4775
Additional Entry & Exit	+ 1640
Separate Heating	+ 1409
Separate Electric	+ 1066

For Townhouse/Rowhouse - Multiply cost per square foot by

Inner Unit	+ .95
End Unit	+ .97

Alternatives

Add to or deduct from the cost per square foot of living area

Composition Roll Roofing	– 1.05
Cedar Shake Roof	+ 4.20
Upgrade Walls and Ceilings to Skim Coat Plaster	+ .65
Upgrade Ceilings to Textured Finish	+ .48
Air Conditioning, in Heating Ductwork	+ 4.05
In Separate Ductwork	+ 7.72
Heating Systems, Hot Water	+ 2.11
Heat Pump	+ 2.56
Electric Heat	– 1.81
Not Heated	– 4.56

Additional upgrades or components

Kitchen Cabinets & Countertops	Page 77
Bathroom Vanities	78
Fireplaces & Chimneys	78
Windows, Skylights & Dormers	78
Appliances	79
Breezeways & Porches	79
Finished Attic	79
Garages	80
Site Improvements	80
Wings & Ells	24

Living Area - 1200 S.F.
Perimeter - 146 L.F.

			Cost Per Square Foot Of Living Area			% of Total
			Mat.	Inst.	Total	(roun
1	**Site Work**	Site preparation for slab; 4' deep trench excavation for foundation wall.		1.17	1.17	1.4%
2	**Foundation**	Continuous reinforced concrete footing, 8" deep x 18" wide; dampproofed and insulated 8" thick reinforced concrete block foundation wall, 4' deep; 4" concrete slab on 4" crushed stone base and polyethylene vapor barrier, trowel finish.	5.39	6.67	12.06	14.6%
3	**Framing**	Exterior walls - 2" x 4" wood studs, 16" O.C.; 1/2" insulation board sheathing; wood truss roof frame, 24" O.C. with 1/2" plywood sheathing, 4 in 12 pitch.	3.97	5.73	9.70	11.7%
4	**Exterior Walls**	Metal lath reinforced stucco exterior on insulated wood frame walls; 6" attic insulation; sliding sash wood windows; 2 flush solid core wood exterior doors with storms.	6.73	6.05	12.78	15.4%
5	**Roofing**	20 year asphalt shingles; #15 felt building paper; aluminum gutters, downspouts, drip edge and flashings.	1.85	2.16	4.01	4.8%
6	**Interiors**	Walls and ceilings, 1/2" taped and finished gypsum wallboard, primed and painted with 2 coats; painted baseboard and trim; rubber backed carpeting 80%, asphalt tile 20%; hollow core wood interior doors.	8.32	11.18	19.50	23.6%
7	**Specialties**	Economy grade kitchen cabinets - 6 L.F. wall and base with plastic laminate counter top and kitchen sink; 30 gallon electric water heater.	2.36	.89	3.25	3.9%
8	**Mechanical**	1 lavatory, white, wall hung; 1 water closet, white; 1 bathtub, enameled steel, white; gas fired warm air heat.	4.06	3.16	7.22	8.7%
9	**Electrical**	100 Amp. service; romex wiring; incandescent lighting fixtures, switches, receptacles.	.89	1.38	2.27	2.7%
10	**Overhead**	Contractor's overhead and profit.	5.03	5.76	10.79	13.0%
	Total		38.60	44.15	**82.75**	

- **Mass produced from stock plans**
- **Single family — 1 full bath, 1 kitchen**
- **No basement**
- **Asphalt shingles on roof**
- **Hot air heat**
- **Gypsum wallboard interior finishes**
- **Materials and workmanship are sufficient to meet codes**

Note: The illustration shown may contain some optional components (for example: garages and/or fireplaces) whose costs are shown in the modifications, adjustments, & alternatives below or at the end of the square foot section.

Base cost per square foot of living area

Exterior Wall	Living Area										
	600	800	1000	1200	1400	1600	1800	2000	2400	2800	3200
Wood Siding - Wood Frame	129.30	107.15	95.65	90.25	86.40	80.55	77.65	74.60	68.45	66.00	63.50
Brick Veneer - Wood Frame	136.55	112.45	100.60	94.85	90.80	84.50	81.40	78.15	71.60	69.00	66.25
Stucco on Wood Frame	120.50	100.80	89.80	84.80	81.15	75.80	73.10	70.30	64.65	62.45	60.20
Painted Concrete Block	127.75	106.05	94.65	89.30	85.45	79.70	76.85	73.85	67.75	65.40	62.90
Finished Basement, Add	21.55	18.25	17.45	16.80	16.35	15.70	15.35	15.00	14.30	14.00	13.65
Unfinished Basement, Add	10.90	8.30	7.65	7.15	6.80	6.25	6.00	5.70	5.15	4.95	4.60

Modifications

Add to the total cost

Upgrade Kitchen Cabinets	$ + 803
Solid Surface Countertops	+ 576
Full Bath - including plumbing, wall and floor finishes	+ 4775
Half Bath - including plumbing, wall and floor finishes	+ 2845
One Car Attached Garage	+ 11,273
One Car Detached Garage	+ 14,630
Fireplace & Chimney	+ 5267

Adjustments

For multi family - add to total cost

Additional Kitchen	$ + 3709
Additional Bath	+ 4775
Additional Entry & Exit	+ 1640
Separate Heating	+ 1409
Separate Electric	+ 1066

For Townhouse/Rowhouse - Multiply cost per square foot by

Inner Unit	+ .95
End Unit	+ .97

Alternatives

Add to or deduct from the cost per square foot of living area

Composition Roll Roofing	– .70
Cedar Shake Roof	+ 3.05
Upgrade Walls and Ceilings to Skim Coat Plaster	+ .66
Upgrade Ceilings to Textured Finish	+ .48
Air Conditioning, in Heating Ductwork	+ 3.03
In Separate Ductwork	+ 6.79
Heating Systems, Hot Water	+ 2.01
Heat Pump	+ 2.82
Electric Heat	– 1.44
Not Heated	– 4.20

Additional upgrades or components

Kitchen Cabinets & Countertops	Page 77
Bathroom Vanities	78
Fireplaces & Chimneys	78
Windows, Skylights & Dormers	78
Appliances	79
Breezeways & Porches	79
Finished Attic	79
Garages	80
Site Improvements	80
Wings & Ells	24

Economy 1-1/2 Story

Living Area - 1600 S.F.
Perimeter - 135 L.F.

			Cost Per Square Foot Of Living Area			% of Total
			Mat.	Inst.	Total	(roun
1	**Site Work**	Site preparation for slab; 4' deep trench excavation for foundation wall.		.88	.88	1.1%
2	**Foundation**	Continuous reinforced concrete footing, 8" deep x 18" wide; dampproofed and insulated 8" thick reinforced concrete block foundation wall, 4' deep; 4" concrete slab on 4" crushed stone base and polyethylene vapor barrier, trowel finish.	3.61	4.53	8.14	10.1%
3	**Framing**	Exterior walls - 2" x 4" wood studs, 16" O.C.; 1/2" insulation board sheathing; 2" x 6" rafters, 16" O.C. with 1/2" plywood sheathing, 8 in 12 pitch; 2" x 8" floor joists 16" O.C. with bridging and 5/8" plywood subfloor.	3.91	6.43	10.34	12.8%
4	**Exterior Walls**	Beveled wood siding and building paper on insulated wood frame walls; 6" attic insulation; double hung windows; 2 flush solid core wood exterior doors with storms.	11.54	4.79	16.33	20.3%
5	**Roofing**	20 year asphalt shingles; #15 felt building paper; aluminum gutters, downspouts, drip edge and flashings.	1.16	1.35	2.51	3.1%
6	**Interiors**	Walls and ceilings, 1/2" taped and finished gypsum wallboard, primed and painted with 2 coats; painted baseboard and trim; rubber backed carpeting 80%, asphalt tile 20%; hollow core wood interior doors.	9.34	11.85	21.19	26.3%
7	**Specialties**	Economy grade kitchen cabinets - 6 L.F. wall and base with plastic laminate counter top and kitchen sink; 30 gallon electric water heater.	1.77	.67	2.44	3.0%
8	**Mechanical**	1 lavatory, white, wall hung; 1 water closet, white; 1 bathtub, enameled steel, white; gas fired warm air heat.	3.33	2.83	6.16	7.6%
9	**Electrical**	100 Amp. service; romex wiring; incandescent lighting fixtures, switches, receptacles.	.81	1.24	2.05	2.5%
10	**Overhead**	Contractor's overhead and profit.	5.33	5.18	10.51	13.0%
	Total		40.80	39.75	**80.55**	

17

- **Mass produced from stock plans**
- **Single family — 1 full bath, 1 kitchen**
- **No basement**
- **Asphalt shingles on roof**
- **Hot air heat**
- **Gypsum wallboard interior finishes**
- **Materials and workmanship are sufficient to meet codes**

Note: The illustration shown may contain some optional components (for example: garages and/or fireplaces) whose costs are shown in the modifications, adjustments, & alternatives below or at the end of the square foot section.

Base cost per square foot of living area

Exterior Wall	Living Area										
	1000	1200	1400	1600	1800	2000	2200	2600	3000	3400	3800
Wood Siding - Wood Frame	101.65	91.80	87.20	84.10	80.90	77.30	74.90	70.40	66.05	64.05	62.30
Brick Veneer - Wood Frame	107.30	97.00	92.10	88.70	85.30	81.55	78.95	74.05	69.45	67.20	65.30
Stucco on Wood Frame	94.95	85.55	81.35	78.50	75.65	72.25	70.05	66.05	62.05	60.25	58.65
Painted Concrete Block	100.45	90.75	86.20	83.10	80.00	76.40	74.05	69.65	65.35	63.35	61.65
Finished Basement, Add	14.65	14.05	13.50	13.20	12.80	12.60	12.35	11.85	11.50	11.25	11.05
Unfinished Basement, Add	6.70	6.15	5.75	5.50	5.25	5.05	4.85	4.45	4.15	4.00	3.80

Modifications

Add to the total cost

Upgrade Kitchen Cabinets	$ + 803
Solid Surface Countertops	+ 576
Full Bath - including plumbing, wall and floor finishes	+ 4775
Half Bath - including plumbing, wall and floor finishes	+ 2845
One Car Attached Garage	+ 11,273
One Car Detached Garage	+ 14,630
Fireplace & Chimney	+ 5820

Adjustments

For multi family - add to total cost

Additional Kitchen	$ + 3709
Additional Bath	+ 4775
Additional Entry & Exit	+ 1640
Separate Heating	+ 1409
Separate Electric	+ 1066

For Townhouse/Rowhouse - Multiply cost per square foot by

Inner Unit	+ .93
End Unit	+ .96

Alternatives

Add to or deduct from the cost per square foot of living area

Composition Roll Roofing	− .50
Cedar Shake Roof	+ 2.10
Upgrade Walls and Ceilings to Skim Coat Plaster	+ .67
Upgrade Ceilings to Textured Finish	+ .48
Air Conditioning, in Heating Ductwork	+ 2.45
In Separate Ductwork	+ 6.21
Heating Systems, Hot Water	+ 1.96
Heat Pump	+ 3
Electric Heat	− 1.26
Not Heated	− 3.96

Additional upgrades or components

Kitchen Cabinets & Countertops	Page 77
Bathroom Vanities	78
Fireplaces & Chimneys	78
Windows, Skylights & Dormers	78
Appliances	79
Breezeways & Porches	79
Finished Attic	79
Garages	80
Site Improvements	80
Wings & Ells	24

		Cost Per Square Foot Of Living Area			% of Total
		Mat.	Inst.	Total	(roun
1 Site Work	Site preparation for slab; 4' deep trench excavation for foundation wall.		.70	.70	0.9%
2 Foundation	Continuous reinforced concrete footing, 8" deep x 18" wide; dampproofed and insulated 8" thick reinforced concrete block foundation wall, 4' deep; 4" concrete slab on 4" crushed stone base and polyethylene vapor barrier, trowel finish.	2.89	3.63	6.52	8.4%
3 Framing	Exterior walls - 2" x 4" wood studs, 16" O.C.; 1/2" insulation board sheathing; wood truss roof frame, 24" O.C. with 1/2" plywood sheathing, 4 in 12 pitch; 2" x 8" floor joists 16" O.C. with bridging and 5/8" plywood subfloor.	3.94	6.77	10.71	13.9%
4 Exterior Walls	Beveled wood siding and building paper on insulated wood frame walls; 6" attic insulation; double hung windows; 2 flush solid core wood exterior doors with storms.	11.90	4.89	16.79	21.7%
5 Roofing	20 year asphalt shingles; #15 felt building paper; aluminum gutters, downspouts, drip edge and flashings.	.93	1.08	2.01	2.6%
6 Interiors	Walls and ceilings, 1/2" taped and finished gypsum wallboard, primed and painted with 2 coats; painted baseboard and trim; rubber backed carpeting 80%, asphalt tile 20%; hollow core wood interior doors.	9.24	11.87	21.11	27.3%
7 Specialties	Economy grade kitchen cabinets - 6 L.F. wall and base with plastic laminate counter top and kitchen sink; 30 gallon electric water heater.	1.42	.53	1.95	2.5%
8 Mechanical	1 lavatory, white, wall hung; 1 water closet, white; 1 bathtub, enameled steel, white; gas fired warm air heat.	2.88	2.63	5.51	7.1%
9 Electrical	100 Amp. service; romex wiring; incandescent lighting fixtures; switches, receptacles.	.76	1.16	1.92	2.5%
10 Overhead	Contractor's overhead and profit.	5.09	4.99	10.08	13.0%
Total		39.05	38.25	**77.30**	

- **Mass produced from stock plans**
- **Single family — 1 full bath, 1 kitchen**
- **No basement**
- **Asphalt shingles on roof**
- **Hot air heat**
- **Gypsum wallboard interior finishes**
- **Materials and workmanship are sufficient to meet codes**

Note: The illustration shown may contain some optional components (for example: garages and/or fireplaces) whose costs are shown in the modifications, adjustments, & alternatives below or at the end of the square foot section.

Base cost per square foot of living area

Exterior Wall	Living Area										
	1000	1200	1400	1600	1800	2000	2200	2600	3000	3400	3800
Wood Siding - Wood Frame	94.20	84.90	80.75	77.85	75.10	71.70	69.60	65.55	61.60	59.80	58.25
Brick Veneer - Wood Frame	98.40	88.80	84.40	81.40	78.35	74.85	72.60	68.25	64.10	62.20	60.50
Stucco on Wood Frame	89.15	80.15	76.35	73.70	71.15	67.85	65.95	62.30	58.55	56.90	55.50
Painted Concrete Block	93.30	84.05	79.95	77.15	74.40	71.00	68.95	65.00	61.10	59.30	57.75
Finished Basement, Add	14.65	14.05	13.50	13.20	12.80	12.60	12.35	11.85	11.50	11.25	11.05
Unfinished Basement, Add	6.70	6.15	5.75	5.50	5.25	5.05	4.85	4.45	4.15	4.00	3.80

Modifications

Add to the total cost

Upgrade Kitchen Cabinets	$ + 803
Solid Surface Countertops	+ 576
Full Bath - including plumbing, wall and floor finishes	+ 4775
Half Bath - including plumbing, wall and floor finishes	+ 2845
One Car Attached Garage	+ 11,273
One Car Detached Garage	+ 14,630
Fireplace & Chimney	+ 5267

Adjustments

For multi family - add to total cost

Additional Kitchen	$ + 3709
Additional Bath	+ 4775
Additional Entry & Exit	+ 1640
Separate Heating	+ 1409
Separate Electric	+ 1066

*For Townhouse/Rowhouse -
Multiply cost per square foot by*

Inner Unit	+ .94
End Unit	+ .97

Alternatives

Add to or deduct from the cost per square foot of living area

Composition Roll Roofing	– .50
Cedar Shake Roof	+ 2.10
Upgrade Walls and Ceilings to Skim Coat Plaster	+ .63
Upgrade Ceilings to Textured Finish	+ .48
Air Conditioning, in Heating Ductwork	+ 2.45
In Separate Ductwork	+ 6.21
Heating Systems, Hot Water	+ 1.96
Heat Pump	+ 3
Electric Heat	– 1.26
Not Heated	– 3.96

Additional upgrades or components

Kitchen Cabinets & Countertops	Page 77
Bathroom Vanities	78
Fireplaces & Chimneys	78
Windows, Skylights & Dormers	78
Appliances	79
Breezeways & Porches	79
Finished Attic	79
Garages	80
Site Improvements	80
Wings & Ells	24

Economy Bi-Level

Living Area - 2000 S.F.
Perimeter - 135 L.F.

		Cost Per Square Foot Of Living Area			% of Total
		Mat.	Inst.	Total	(roun
1 Site Work	Excavation for lower level, 4' deep. Site preparation for slab.		.70	.70	1.0%
2 Foundation	Continuous reinforced concrete footing, 8" deep x 18" wide; dampproofed and insulated 8" thick reinforced concrete block foundation wall, 4' deep; 4" concrete slab on 4" crushed stone base and polyethylene vapor barrier, trowel finish.	2.89	3.63	6.52	9.1%
3 Framing	Exterior walls - 2" x 4" wood studs, 16" O.C.; 1/2" insulation board sheathing; wood truss roof frame, 24" O.C. with 1/2" plywood sheathing, 4 in 12 pitch; 2" x 8" floor joists 16" O.C. with bridging and 5/8" plywood subfloor.	3.73	6.36	10.09	14.1%
4 Exterior Walls	Beveled wood siding and building paper on insulated wood frame walls; 6" attic insulation; double hung windows; 2 flush solid core wood exterior doors with storms.	9.25	3.84	13.09	18.3%
5 Roofing	20 year asphalt shingles; #15 felt building paper; aluminum gutters, downspouts, drip edge and flashings.	.93	1.08	2.01	2.8%
6 Interiors	Walls and ceilings, 1/2" taped and finished gypsum wallboard, primed and painted with 2 coats; painted baseboard and trim, rubber backed carpeting 80%, asphalt tile 20%; hollow core wood interior doors.	9.04	11.49	20.53	28.6%
7 Specialties	Economy grade kitchen cabinets - 6 L.F. wall and base with plastic laminate counter top and kitchen sink; 30 gallon electric water heater.	1.42	.53	1.95	2.7%
8 Mechanical	1 lavatory, white, wall hung; 1 water closet, white; 1 bathtub, enameled steel, white; gas fired warm air heat.	2.88	2.63	5.51	7.7%
9 Electrical	100 Amp. service; romex wiring; incandescent lighting fixtures; switches, receptacles.	.76	1.16	1.92	2.7%
10 Overhead	Contractor's overhead and profit.	4.65	4.73	9.38	13.1%
Total		35.55	36.15	**71.70**	

- **Mass produced from stock plans**
- **Single family — 1 full bath, 1 kitchen**
- **No basement**
- **Asphalt shingles on roof**
- **Hot air heat**
- **Gypsum wallboard interior finishes**
- **Materials and workmanship are sufficient to meet codes**

Note: The illustration shown may contain some optional components (for example: garages and/or fireplaces) whose costs are shown in the modifications, adjustments, & alternatives below or at the end of the square foot section.

©Design Basics, Inc.

Base cost per square foot of living area

Exterior Wall	Living Area										
	1200	1500	1800	2000	2200	2400	2800	3200	3600	4000	4400
Wood Siding - Wood Frame	86.90	79.75	74.35	72.15	69.00	66.45	64.50	61.80	58.55	57.45	55.00
Brick Veneer - Wood Frame	90.75	83.25	77.50	75.15	71.90	69.15	67.10	64.20	60.80	59.65	57.05
Stucco on Wood Frame	82.30	75.50	70.50	68.50	65.50	63.20	61.35	58.85	55.90	54.85	52.55
Solid Masonry	86.10	78.95	73.65	71.50	68.35	65.90	63.95	61.20	58.05	57.05	54.60
Finished Basement, Add*	17.50	16.70	16.00	15.70	15.40	15.05	14.80	14.45	14.10	13.95	13.70
Unfinished Basement, Add*	7.30	6.70	6.15	5.85	5.60	5.35	5.15	4.85	4.60	4.50	4.30

*Basement under middle level only.

Modifications

Add to the total cost

Upgrade Kitchen Cabinets	$ + 803
Solid Surface Countertops	+ 576
Full Bath - including plumbing, wall and floor finishes	+ 4775
Half Bath - including plumbing, wall and floor finishes	+ 2845
One Car Attached Garage	+ 11,273
One Car Detached Garage	+ 14,630
Fireplace & Chimney	+ 5267

Adjustments

For multi family - add to total cost

Additional Kitchen	$ + 3709
Additional Bath	+ 4775
Additional Entry & Exit	+ 1640
Separate Heating	+ 1409
Separate Electric	+ 1066

For Townhouse/Rowhouse - Multiply cost per square foot by

Inner Unit	+ .93
End Unit	+ .96

Alternatives

Add to or deduct from the cost per square foot of living area

Composition Roll Roofing	– .70
Cedar Shake Roof	+ 3.05
Upgrade Walls and Ceilings to Skim Coat Plaster	+ .57
Upgrade Ceilings to Textured Finish	+ .48
Air Conditioning, in Heating Ductwork	+ 2.10
In Separate Ductwork	+ 5.78
Heating Systems, Hot Water	+ 1.88
Heat Pump	+ 3.11
Electric Heat	– 1.09
Not Heated	– 3.84

Additional upgrades or components

Kitchen Cabinets & Countertops	Page 77
Bathroom Vanities	78
Fireplaces & Chimneys	78
Windows, Skylights & Dormers	78
Appliances	79
Breezeways & Porches	79
Finished Attic	79
Garages	80
Site Improvements	80
Wings & Ells	24

Living Area - 2400 S.F.
Perimeter - 163 L.F.

		Cost Per Square Foot Of Living Area			% of Total
		Mat.	Inst.	Total	(roun
1 Site Work	Site preparation for slab; 4' deep trench excavation for foundation wall, excavation for lower level, 4' deep.		.58	.58	0.9%
2 Foundation	Continuous reinforced concrete footing, 8" deep x 18" wide; dampproofed and insulated 8" thick reinforced concrete block foundation wall, 4' deep; 4" concrete slab on 4" crushed stone base and polyethylene vapor barrier, trowel finish.	3.26	3.94	7.20	10.8%
3 Framing	Exterior walls - 2" x 4" wood studs, 16" O.C.; 1/2" insulation board sheathing; wood truss roof frame, 24" O.C. with 1/2" plywood sheathing, 4 in 12 pitch; 2" x 8" floor joists 16" O.C. with bridging and 5/8" plywood subfloor.	3.61	5.71	9.32	14.0%
4 Exterior Walls	Beveled wood siding and building paper on insulated wood frame walls; 6" attic insulation; double hung windows; 2 flush solid core wood exterior doors with storms.	7.98	3.33	11.31	17.0%
5 Roofing	20 year asphalt shingles; #15 felt building paper; aluminum gutters, downspouts, drip edge and flashings.	1.23	1.44	2.67	4.0%
6 Interiors	Walls and ceilings, 1/2" taped and finished gypsum wallboard, primed and painted with 2 coats; painted baseboard and trim, rubber backed carpeting 80%, asphalt tile 20%; hollow core wood interior doors.	7.97	10.21	18.18	27.4%
7 Specialties	Economy grade kitchen cabinets - 6 L.F. wall and base with plastic laminate counter top and kitchen sink; 30 gallon electric water heater.	1.17	.45	1.62	2.4%
8 Mechanical	1 lavatory, white, wall hung; 1 water closet, white; 1 bathtub, enameled steel, white; gas fired warm air heat.	2.60	2.49	5.09	7.7%
9 Electrical	100 Amp. service; romex wiring; incandescent lighting fixtures, switches, receptacles.	.72	1.10	1.82	2.7%
10 Overhead	Contractor's overhead and profit.	4.26	4.40	8.66	13.0%
Total		32.80	33.65	**66.45**	

1 Story   Base cost per square foot of living area

Exterior Wall	Living Area							
	50	100	200	300	400	500	600	700
Wood Siding - Wood Frame	157.10	119.20	102.75	84.95	79.60	76.35	74.25	74.80
Brick Veneer - Wood Frame	170.25	128.60	110.65	90.15	84.30	80.75	78.40	78.85
Stucco on Wood Frame	141.35	107.95	93.40	78.70	74.00	71.10	69.15	69.95
Painted Concrete Block	154.35	117.20	101.15	83.90	78.60	75.40	73.35	73.90
Finished Basement, Add	42.80	34.90	31.55	26.05	24.95	24.30	23.85	23.55
Unfinished Basement, Add	23.70	17.55	14.95	10.70	9.80	9.30	8.95	8.70

1-1/2 Story   Base cost per square foot of living area

Exterior Wall	Living Area							
	100	200	300	400	500	600	700	800
Wood Siding - Wood Frame	124.70	99.95	84.90	75.60	71.05	68.85	66.10	65.30
Brick Veneer - Wood Frame	136.45	109.35	92.75	81.70	76.70	74.15	71.05	70.25
Stucco on Wood Frame	110.60	88.70	75.50	68.25	64.35	62.50	60.05	59.30
Painted Concrete Block	122.15	98.00	83.20	74.35	69.90	67.75	64.95	64.20
Finished Basement, Add	28.55	25.25	23.00	20.60	19.95	19.50	19.10	19.05
Unfinished Basement, Add	14.50	11.95	10.25	8.35	7.80	7.50	7.15	7.15

2 Story   Base cost per square foot of living area

Exterior Wall	Living Area							
	100	200	400	600	800	1000	1200	1400
Wood Siding - Wood Frame	127.10	94.10	79.70	65.30	60.65	57.75	55.90	56.70
Brick Veneer - Wood Frame	140.25	103.50	87.55	70.55	65.35	62.20	60.10	60.75
Stucco on Wood Frame	111.35	82.85	70.35	59.05	55.00	52.55	50.90	51.85
Painted Concrete Block	124.35	92.10	78.10	64.20	59.65	56.90	55.05	55.85
Finished Basement, Add	21.45	17.45	15.85	13.10	12.55	12.20	12.00	11.80
Unfinished Basement, Add	11.90	8.80	7.50	5.35	4.95	4.70	4.45	4.35

Base costs do not include bathroom or kitchen facilities. Use Modifications/Adjustments/Alternatives on pages 77–80 where appropriate.

1 Story

1-1/2 Story

2 Story

2-1/2 Story

Bi-Level

Tri-Level

- **Simple design from standard plans**
- **Single family — 1 full bath, 1 kitchen**
- **No basement**
- **Asphalt shingles on roof**
- **Hot air heat**
- **Gypsum wallboard interior finishes**
- **Materials and workmanship are average**

Note: The illustration shown may contain some optional components (for example: garages and/or fireplaces) whose costs are shown in the modifications, adjustments, & alternatives below or at the end of the square foot section.

eHome Planners, Inc.

Base cost per square foot of living area

Exterior Wall	Living Area										
	600	800	1000	1200	1400	1600	1800	2000	2400	2800	3200
Wood Siding - Wood Frame	135.60	122.45	112.70	104.85	98.30	94.05	91.75	88.85	83.15	78.95	76.10
Brick Veneer - Wood Frame	152.80	138.85	128.50	120.05	112.95	108.35	105.95	102.75	96.70	92.20	89.10
Stucco on Wood Frame	141.80	129.05	119.55	112.00	105.65	101.50	99.35	96.50	91.05	86.95	84.20
Solid Masonry	166.85	151.40	139.85	130.30	122.25	117.10	114.35	110.65	103.95	98.90	95.30
Finished Basement, Add	33.95	32.80	31.25	29.85	28.75	27.95	27.60	27.00	26.10	25.50	24.90
Unfinished Basement, Add	13.90	12.50	11.55	10.65	9.95	9.50	9.20	8.85	8.30	7.90	7.60

Modifications

Add to the total cost

Upgrade Kitchen Cabinets	$ + 3521
Solid Surface Countertops (Included)	
Full Bath - including plumbing, wall and floor finishes	+ 5993
Half Bath - including plumbing, wall and floor finishes	+ 3570
One Car Attached Garage	+ 12,676
One Car Detached Garage	+ 16,871
Fireplace & Chimney	+ 5234

Adjustments

For multi family - add to total cost

Additional Kitchen	$ + 6796
Additional Bath	+ 5993
Additional Entry & Exit	+ 1640
Separate Heating	+ 1409
Separate Electric	+ 1915

For Townhouse/Rowhouse - Multiply cost per square foot by

Inner Unit	+ .92
End Unit	+ .96

Alternatives

Add to or deduct from the cost per square foot of living area

Cedar Shake Roof	+ 3.85
Clay Tile Roof	+ 4.55
Slate Roof	+ 6.65
Upgrade Walls to Skim Coat Plaster	+ .41
Upgrade Ceilings to Textured Finish	+ .48
Air Conditioning, in Heating Ductwork	+ 4.19
In Separate Ductwork	+ 8.02
Heating Systems, Hot Water	+ 2.16
Heat Pump	+ 2.66
Electric Heat	– 1.01
Not Heated	– 3.80

Additional upgrades or components

Important: See the Reference Section for Location Factors (to adjust for your city) and Estimating Forms

Average 1 Story

Living Area - 1600 S.F.
Perimeter - 163 L.F.

			Cost Per Square Foot Of Living Area			% of Total
			Mat.	Inst.	Total	(roun
1	**Site Work**	Site preparation for slab; 4' deep trench excavation for foundation wall.		.90	.90	1.0%
2	**Foundation**	Continuous reinforced concrete footing 8" deep x 18" wide; dampproofed and insulated reinforced concrete foundation wall, 8" thick, 4' deep; 4" concrete slab on 4" crushed stone base and polyethylene vapor barrier, trowel finish.	5.02	6.07	11.09	11.8%
3	**Framing**	Exterior walls - 2" x 4" wood studs, 16" O.C.; 1/2" plywood sheathing; 2" x 6" rafters 16" O.C. with 1/2" plywood sheathing, 4 in 12 pitch; 2" x 6" ceiling joists 16" O.C.; 1/2" plywood subfloor on 1" x 2" wood sleepers 16" O.C.	4.39	8.56	12.95	13.8%
4	**Exterior Walls**	Beveled wood siding and building paper on insulated wood frame walls; 6" attic insulation; double hung windows; 3 flush solid core wood exterior doors with storms.	10.53	4.51	15.04	16.0%
5	**Roofing**	25 year asphalt shingles; #15 felt building paper; aluminum gutters, downspouts, drip edge and flashings.	1.90	2.22	4.12	4.4%
6	**Interiors**	Walls and ceilings, 1/2" taped and finished gypsum wallboard, primed and painted with 2 coats; painted baseboard and trim, finished hardwood floor 40%, carpet with 1/2" underlayment 40%, vinyl tile with 1/2" underlayment 15%, ceramic tile with 1/2" underlayment 5%; hollow core and louvered doors.	11.16	11.93	23.09	24.6%
7	**Specialties**	Average grade kitchen cabinets - 14 L.F. wall and base with solid surface counter top and kitchen sink; 40 gallon electric water heater.	2.83	1.05	3.88	4.1%
8	**Mechanical**	1 lavatory, white, wall hung; 1 water closet, white; 1 bathtub with shower, enameled steel, white; gas fired warm air heat.	3.50	2.87	6.37	6.8%
9	**Electrical**	200 Amp. service; romex wiring; incandescent lighting fixtures, switches, receptacles.	1.25	1.68	2.93	3.1%
10	**Overhead**	Contractor's overhead and profit and plans.	6.92	6.76	13.68	14.5%
	Total		47.50	46.55	**94.05**	

- Simple design from standard plans
- Single family — 1 full bath, 1 kitchen
- No basement
- Asphalt shingles on roof
- Hot air heat
- Gypsum wallboard interior finishes
- Materials and workmanship are average

Note: The illustration shown may contain some optional components (for example: garages and/or fireplaces) whose costs are shown in the modifications, adjustments, & alternatives below or at the end of the square foot section.

©By Designer

Base cost per square foot of living area

Exterior Wall	Living Area										
	600	800	1000	1200	1400	1600	1800	2000	2400	2800	3200
Wood Siding - Wood Frame	151.70	126.70	113.30	106.95	102.40	95.75	92.40	88.90	82.05	79.25	76.35
Brick Veneer - Wood Frame	162.30	134.35	120.45	113.60	108.75	101.55	97.85	94.10	86.60	83.60	80.35
Stucco on Wood Frame	146.95	123.20	110.15	103.95	99.55	93.15	89.95	86.60	79.95	77.30	74.50
Solid Masonry	181.90	148.55	133.55	125.90	120.45	112.20	107.95	103.70	95.10	91.65	87.80
Finished Basement, Add	27.80	24.25	23.20	22.40	21.85	20.95	20.45	20.10	19.15	18.80	18.30
Unfinished Basement, Add	12.10	9.45	8.70	8.20	7.85	7.30	7.00	6.75	6.20	5.90	5.65

Modifications

Add to the total cost

Upgrade Kitchen Cabinets	$ + 3521
Solid Surface Countertops (Included)	
Full Bath - including plumbing, wall and floor finishes	+ 5993
Half Bath - including plumbing, wall and floor finishes	+ 3570
One Car Attached Garage	+ 12,676
One Car Detached Garage	+ 16,871
Fireplace & Chimney	+ 5234

Adjustments

For multi family - add to total cost

Additional Kitchen	$ + 6796
Additional Bath	+ 5993
Additional Entry & Exit	+ 1640
Separate Heating	+ 1409
Separate Electric	+ 1915

For Townhouse/Rowhouse - Multiply cost per square foot by

Inner Unit	+ .92
End Unit	+ .96

Alternatives

Add to or deduct from the cost per square foot of living area

Cedar Shake Roof	+ 2.80
Clay Tile Roof	+ 3.30
Slate Roof	+ 4.80
Upgrade Walls to Skim Coat Plaster	+ .47
Upgrade Ceilings to Textured Finish	+ .48
Air Conditioning, in Heating Ductwork	+ 3.19
In Separate Ductwork	+ 7.01
Heating Systems, Hot Water	+ 2.05
Heat Pump	+ 2.96
Electric Heat	- .91
Not Heated	- 3.67

Additional upgrades or components

Kitchen Cabinets & Countertops	Page 77
Bathroom Vanities	78
Fireplaces & Chimneys	78
Windows, Skylights & Dormers	78
Appliances	79
Breezeways & Porches	79
Finished Attic	79
Garages	80
Site Improvements	80
Wings & Ells	44

			Cost Per Square Foot Of Living Area			% of Total
			Mat.	Inst.	Total	(roun
1	**Site Work**	Site preparation for slab; 4' deep trench excavation for foundation wall.		.80	.80	0.9%
2	**Foundation**	Continuous reinforced concrete footing 8" deep x 18" wide; dampproofed and insulated reinforced concrete foundation wall, 8" thick, 4' deep; 4" concrete slab on 4" crushed stone base and polyethylene vapor barrier, trowel finish.	3.57	4.46	8.03	8.7%
3	**Framing**	Exterior walls - 2" x 4" wood studs, 16" O.C.; 1/2" plywood sheathing; 2" x 6" rafters 16" O.C. with 1/2" plywood sheathing, 8 in 12 pitch; 2" x 8" floor joists 16" O.C. with 5/8" plywood subfloor; 1/2" plywood subfloor on 1" x 2" wood sleepers 16" O.C.	4.67	7.99	12.66	13.7%
4	**Exterior Walls**	Beveled wood siding and building paper on insulated wood frame walls; 6" attic insulation; double hung windows; 3 flush solid core wood exterior doors with storms.	11.59	4.83	16.42	17.8%
5	**Roofing**	25 year asphalt shingles; #15 felt building paper; aluminum gutters, downspouts, drip edge and flashings.	1.19	1.39	2.58	2.8%
6	**Interiors**	Walls and ceilings, 1/2" taped and finished gypsum wallboard, primed and painted with 2 coats; painted baseboard and trim, finished hardwood floor 40%, carpet with 1/2" underlayment 40%, vinyl tile with 1/2" underlayment 15%, ceramic tile with 1/2" underlayment 5%; hollow core and louvered doors.	12.87	13.38	26.25	28.4%
7	**Specialties**	Average grade kitchen cabinets - 14 L.F. wall and base with solid surface counter top and kitchen sink; 40 gallon electric water heater.	2.52	.93	3.45	3.7%
8	**Mechanical**	1 lavatory, white, wall hung; 1 water closet, white; 1 bathtub with shower, enameled steel, white; gas fired warm air heat.	3.24	2.76	6.00	6.5%
9	**Electrical**	200 Amp. service; romex wiring; incandescent lighting fixtures, switches, receptacles.	1.18	1.61	2.79	3.0%
10	**Overhead**	Contractor's overhead and profit and plans.	6.92	6.50	13.42	14.5%
	Total		47.75	44.65	**92.40**	

- Simple design from standard plans
- Single family — 1 full bath, 1 kitchen
- No basement
- Asphalt shingles on roof
- Hot air heat
- Gypsum wallboard interior finishes
- Materials and workmanship are average

Note: The illustration shown may contain some optional components (for example: garages and/or fireplaces) whose costs are shown in the modifications, adjustments, & alternatives below or at the end of the square foot section.

Base cost per square foot of living area

Exterior Wall	Living Area										
	1000	1200	1400	1600	1800	2000	2200	2600	3000	3400	3800
Wood Siding - Wood Frame	119.55	108.20	102.90	99.30	95.55	91.50	88.85	83.75	78.85	76.55	74.50
Brick Veneer - Wood Frame	127.75	115.85	109.95	106.10	101.85	97.65	94.70	89.00	83.70	81.20	78.95
Stucco on Wood Frame	115.90	104.85	99.75	96.30	92.70	88.70	86.25	81.30	76.60	74.45	72.55
Solid Masonry	143.00	129.90	123.15	118.60	113.65	109.00	105.45	98.80	92.75	89.75	87.10
Finished Basement, Add	19.70	19.40	18.75	18.35	17.90	17.65	17.25	16.60	16.15	15.90	15.65
Unfinished Basement, Add	7.65	7.10	6.70	6.40	6.10	5.90	5.70	5.35	5.05	4.80	4.70

Modifications

Add to the total cost

Upgrade Kitchen Cabinets	$ + 3521
Solid Surface Countertops (Included)	
Full Bath - including plumbing, wall and floor finishes	+ 5993
Half Bath - including plumbing, wall and floor finishes	+ 3570
One Car Attached Garage	+ 12,676
One Car Detached Garage	+ 16,871
Fireplace & Chimney	+ 5836

Adjustments

For multi family - add to total cost

Additional Kitchen	$ + 6796
Additional Bath	+ 5993
Additional Entry & Exit	+ 1640
Separate Heating	+ 1409
Separate Electric	+ 1915

For Townhouse/Rowhouse - Multiply cost per square foot by

Inner Unit	+ .90
End Unit	+ .95

Alternatives

Add to or deduct from the cost per square foot of living area

Cedar Shake Roof	+ 1.95
Clay Tile Roof	+ 2.25
Slate Roof	+ 3.30
Upgrade Walls to Skim Coat Plaster	+ .49
Upgrade Ceilings to Textured Finish	+ .48
Air Conditioning, in Heating Ductwork	+ 2.54
In Separate Ductwork	+ 6.36
Heating Systems, Hot Water	+ 2.01
Heat Pump	+ 3.11
Electric Heat	− .80
Not Heated	− 3.55

Additional upgrades or components

Kitchen Cabinets & Countertops	Page 77
Bathroom Vanities	78
Fireplaces & Chimneys	78
Windows, Skylights & Dormers	78
Appliances	79
Breezeways & Porches	79
Finished Attic	79
Garages	80
Site Improvements	80
Wings & Ells	44

Average 2 Story

Living Area - 2000 S.F.
Perimeter - 135 L.F.

			Cost Per Square Foot Of Living Area			% of Total
			Mat.	Inst.	Total	(roun
1	**Site Work**	Site preparation for slab; 4' deep trench excavation for foundation wall.		.72	.72	0.8%
2	**Foundation**	Continuous reinforced concrete footing 8" deep x 18" wide; dampproofed and insulated reinforced concrete foundation wall, 8" thick, 4' deep, 4" concrete slab on 4" crushed stone base and polyethylene vapor barrier, trowel finish.	2.97	3.73	6.70	7.3%
3	**Framing**	Exterior walls - 2" x 4" wood studs, 16" O.C.; 1/2" plywood sheathing; 2" x 6" rafters 16" O.C. with 1/2" plywood sheathing, 4 in 12 pitch; 2" x 6" ceiling joists 16" O.C.; 2" x 8" floor joists 16" O.C. with 5/8" plywood subfloor; 1/2" plywood subfloor on 1" x 2" wood sleepers 16" O.C.	4.96	8.27	13.23	14.5%
4	**Exterior Walls**	Beveled wood siding and building paper on insulated wood frame walls; 6" attic insulation; double hung windows; 3 flush solid core wood exterior doors with storms.	12.67	5.25	17.92	19.6%
5	**Roofing**	25 year asphalt shingles; #15 felt building paper; aluminum gutters, downspouts, drip edge and flashings.	.96	1.11	2.07	2.3%
6	**Interiors**	Walls and ceilings, 1/2" taped and finished gypsum wallboard, primed and painted with 2 coats; painted baseboard and trim, finished hardwood floor 40%, carpet with 1/2" underlayment 40%, vinyl tile with 1/2" underlayment 15%, ceramic tile with 1/2" underlayment 5%; hollow core and louvered doors.	12.71	13.38	26.09	28.5%
7	**Specialties**	Average grade kitchen cabinets - 14 L.F. wall and base with solid surface counter top and kitchen sink; 40 gallon electric water heater.	2.26	.83	3.09	3.4%
8	**Mechanical**	1 lavatory, white, wall hung; 1 water closet, white; 1 bathtub with shower; enameled steel, white; gas fired warm air heat.	3.02	2.68	5.70	6.2%
9	**Electrical**	200 Amp. service; romex wiring; incandescent lighting fixtures, switches, receptacles.	1.13	1.54	2.67	2.9%
10	**Overhead**	Contractor's overhead and profit and plans.	6.92	6.39	13.31	14.5%
	Total		47.60	43.90	**91.50**	

- **Simple design from standard plans**
- **Single family — 1 full bath, 1 kitchen**
- **No basement**
- **Asphalt shingles on roof**
- **Hot air heat**
- **Gypsum wallboard interior finishes**
- **Materials and workmanship are average**

Note: The illustration shown may contain some optional components (for example: garages and/or fireplaces) whose costs are shown in the modifications, adjustments, & alternatives below or at the end of the square foot section.

Base cost per square foot of living area

Exterior Wall	Living Area										
	1200	1400	1600	1800	2000	2400	2800	3200	3600	4000	4400
Wood Siding - Wood Frame	118.55	111.25	101.50	99.60	95.95	90.20	85.75	81.10	78.80	74.55	73.25
Brick Veneer - Wood Frame	127.20	119.10	108.75	106.90	102.80	96.40	91.65	86.50	83.85	79.25	77.85
Stucco on Wood Frame	114.60	107.75	98.25	96.35	92.90	87.45	83.10	78.75	76.45	72.45	71.20
Solid Masonry	143.45	133.70	122.15	120.35	115.45	107.85	102.55	96.35	93.20	88.05	86.25
Finished Basement, Add	16.70	16.30	15.75	15.70	15.25	14.65	14.35	13.85	13.60	13.30	13.15
Unfinished Basement, Add	6.35	5.80	5.50	5.40	5.15	4.75	4.55	4.25	4.10	3.90	3.85

Modifications

Add to the total cost

Upgrade Kitchen Cabinets	$ + 3521
Solid Surface Countertops (Included)	
Full Bath - including plumbing, wall and floor finishes	+ 5993
Half Bath - including plumbing, wall and floor finishes	+ 3570
One Car Attached Garage	+ 12,676
One Car Detached Garage	+ 16,871
Fireplace & Chimney	+ 6634

Adjustments

For multi family - add to total cost

Additional Kitchen	$ + 6796
Additional Bath	+ 5993
Additional Entry & Exit	+ 1640
Separate Heating	+ 1409
Separate Electric	+ 1915

*For Townhouse/Rowhouse -
Multiply cost per square foot by*

Inner Unit	+ .90
End Unit	+ .95

Alternatives

Add to or deduct from the cost per square foot of living area

Cedar Shake Roof	+ 1.70
Clay Tile Roof	+ 1.95
Slate Roof	+ 2.90
Upgrade Walls to Skim Coat Plaster	+ .47
Upgrade Ceilings to Textured Finish	+ .48
Air Conditioning, in Heating Ductwork	+ 2.31
In Separate Ductwork	+ 6.14
Heating Systems, Hot Water	+ 1.81
Heat Pump	+ 3.19
Electric Heat	– 1.40
Not Heated	– 4.15

Additional upgrades or components

Kitchen Cabinets & Countertops	Page 77
Bathroom Vanities	78
Fireplaces & Chimneys	78
Windows, Skylights & Dormers	78
Appliances	79
Breezeways & Porches	79
Finished Attic	79
Garages	80
Site Improvements	80
Wings & Ells	44

Important: See the Reference Section for Location Factors (to adjust for your city) and Estimating Forms

Average 2-1/2 Story

Living Area - 3200 S.F.
Perimeter - 150 L.F.

			Cost Per Square Foot Of Living Area			% of Total
			Mat.	Inst.	Total	(roun
1	**Site Work**	Site preparation for slab; 4' deep trench excavation for foundation wall.		.45	.45	0.6%
2	**Foundation**	Continuous reinforced concrete footing 8" deep x 18" wide, dampproofed and insulated reinforced concrete foundation wall, 8" thick, 4' deep; 4" concrete slab on 4" crushed stone base and polyethylene vapor barrier, trowel finish.	2.14	2.65	4.79	5.9%
3	**Framing**	Exterior walls - 2" x 4" wood studs, 16" O.C.; 1/2" plywood sheathing; 2" x 6" rafters 16" O.C. with 1/2" plywood sheathing, 4 in 12 pitch; 2" x 6" ceiling joists 16" O.C.; 2" x 8" floor joists 16" O.C. with 5/8" plywood subfloor; 1/2" plywood subfloor on 1" x 2" wood sleepers 16" O.C.	5.00	8.08	13.08	16.1%
4	**Exterior Walls**	Beveled wood siding and building paper on insulated wood frame walls; 6" attic insulation; double hung windows; 3 flush solid core wood exterior doors with storms.	10.71	4.41	15.12	18.6%
5	**Roofing**	25 year asphalt shingles; #15 felt building paper; aluminum gutters, downspouts, drip edge and flashings.	.73	.85	1.58	1.9%
6	**Interiors**	Walls and ceilings, 1/2" taped and finished gypsum wallboard, primed and painted with 2 coats; painted baseboard and trim, finished hardwood floor 40%, carpet with 1/2" underlayment 40%, vinyl tile with 1/2" underlayment 15%, ceramic tile with 1/2" underlayment 5%; hollow core and louvered doors.	12.44	12.93	25.37	31.3%
7	**Specialties**	Average grade kitchen cabinets - 14 L.F. wall and base with solid surface counter top and kitchen sink; 40 gallon electric water heater.	1.42	.51	1.93	2.4%
8	**Mechanical**	1 lavatory, white, wall hung; 1 water closet, white; 1 bathtub with shower, enameled steel, white; gas fired warm air heat.	2.33	2.38	4.71	5.8%
9	**Electrical**	200 Amp. service; romex wiring; incandescent lighting fixtures, switches, receptacles.	.97	1.35	2.32	2.9%
10	**Overhead**	Contractor's overhead and profit and plans.	6.06	5.69	11.75	14.5%
	Total		41.80	39.30	**81.10**	

- **Simple design from standard plans**
- **Single family — 1 full bath, 1 kitchen**
- **No basement**
- **Asphalt shingles on roof**
- **Hot air heat**
- **Gypsum wallboard interior finishes**
- **Materials and workmanship are average**

Note: The illustration shown may contain some optional components (for example: garages and/or fireplaces) whose costs are shown in the modifications, adjustments, & alternatives below or at the end of the square foot section.

Base cost per square foot of living area

Exterior Wall	Living Area										
	1500	1800	2100	2500	3000	3500	4000	4500	5000	5500	6000
Wood Siding - Wood Frame	109.85	99.65	95.10	91.60	85.00	82.05	77.95	73.60	72.25	70.55	68.85
Brick Veneer - Wood Frame	118.00	107.30	102.20	98.40	91.15	87.90	83.25	78.50	77.00	75.10	73.15
Stucco on Wood Frame	106.20	96.30	91.95	88.60	82.30	79.45	75.55	71.40	70.10	68.50	67.00
Solid Masonry	133.25	121.30	115.35	110.90	102.55	98.65	93.05	87.55	85.70	83.55	81.10
Finished Basement, Add	14.35	14.20	13.80	13.50	13.05	12.70	12.40	12.00	11.95	11.75	11.60
Unfinished Basement, Add	5.15	4.80	4.55	4.35	4.05	3.85	3.60	3.40	3.30	3.25	3.15

Modifications

Add to the total cost

Upgrade Kitchen Cabinets	$ + 3521
Solid Surface Countertops (Included)	
Full Bath - including plumbing, wall and floor finishes	+ 5993
Half Bath - including plumbing, wall and floor finishes	+ 3570
One Car Attached Garage	+ 12,676
One Car Detached Garage	+ 16,871
Fireplace & Chimney	+ 6634

Adjustments

For multi family - add to total cost

Additional Kitchen	$ + 6796
Additional Bath	+ 5993
Additional Entry & Exit	+ 1640
Separate Heating	+ 1409
Separate Electric	+ 1915

*For Townhouse/Rowhouse -
Multiply cost per square foot by*

Inner Unit	+ .88
End Unit	+ .94

Alternatives

Add to or deduct from the cost per square foot of living area

Cedar Shake Roof	+ 1.30
Clay Tile Roof	+ 1.50
Slate Roof	+ 2.20
Upgrade Walls to Skim Coat Plaster	+ .49
Upgrade Ceilings to Textured Finish	+ .48
Air Conditioning, in Heating Ductwork	+ 2.31
In Separate Ductwork	+ 6.14
Heating Systems, Hot Water	+ 1.81
Heat Pump	+ 3.19
Electric Heat	– 1.09
Not Heated	– 3.85

Additional upgrades or components

Kitchen Cabinets & Countertops	Page 77
Bathroom Vanities	78
Fireplaces & Chimneys	78
Windows, Skylights & Dormers	78
Appliances	79
Breezeways & Porches	79
Finished Attic	79
Garages	80
Site Improvements	80
Wings & Ells	44

			Cost Per Square Foot Of Living Area			% of Total
			Mat.	Inst.	Total	(roun
1	**Site Work**	Site preparation for slab; 4' deep trench excavation for foundation wall.		.48	.48	0.6%
2	**Foundation**	Continuous reinforced concrete footing 8" deep x 18" wide, dampproofed and insulated reinforced concrete foundation wall, 8" thick, 4' deep; 4" concrete slab on 4" crushed stone base and polyethylene vapor barrier, trowel finish.	1.99	2.49	4.48	5.3%
3	**Framing**	Exterior walls - 2" x 4" wood studs, 16" O.C.; 1/2" plywood sheathing; 2" x 6" rafters 16" O.C. with 1/2" plywood sheathing, 4 in 12 pitch; 2" x 6" ceiling joists 16" O.C.; 2" x 8" floor joists 16" O.C. with 5/8" plywood subfloor; 1/2" plywood subfloor on 1" x 2" wood sleepers 16" O.C.	5.18	8.36	13.54	15.9%
4	**Exterior Walls**	Horizontal beveled wood siding; building paper; 3-1/2" batt insulation; wood double hung windows; 3 flush solid core wood exterior doors; storms and screens.	12.21	5.04	17.25	20.3%
5	**Roofing**	25 year asphalt shingles; #15 felt building paper; aluminum gutters, downspouts, drip edge and flashings.	.64	.74	1.38	1.6%
6	**Interiors**	Walls and ceilings, 1/2" taped and finished gypsum wallboard, primed and painted with 2 coats; painted baseboard and trim, finished hardwood floor 40%, carpet with 1/2" underlayment 40%, vinyl tile with 1/2" underlayment 15%, ceramic tile with 1/2" underlayment 5%; hollow core and louvered doors.	12.88	13.38	26.26	30.9%
7	**Specialties**	Average grade kitchen cabinets - 14 L.F. wall and base with solid surface counter top and kitchen sink; 40 gallon electric water heater.	1.53	.57	2.10	2.5%
8	**Mechanical**	1 lavatory, white, wall hung; 1 water closet, white; 1 bathtub with shower, enameled steel, white; gas fired warm air heat.	2.42	2.41	4.83	5.7%
9	**Electrical**	200 Amp. service; romex wiring; incandescent lighting fixtures, switches, receptacles.	.98	1.37	2.35	2.8%
10	**Overhead**	Contractor's overhead and profit and plans.	6.42	5.91	12.33	14.5%
	Total		44.25	40.75	85.00	

- **Simple design from standard plans**
- **Single family — 1 full bath, 1 kitchen**
- **No basement**
- **Asphalt shingles on roof**
- **Hot air heat**
- **Gypsum wallboard interior finishes**
- **Materials and workmanship are average**

Note: The illustration shown may contain some optional components (for example: garages and/or fireplaces) whose costs are shown in the modifications, adjustments, & alternatives below or at the end of the square foot section.

Base cost per square foot of living area

Exterior Wall	Living Area										
	1000	1200	1400	1600	1800	2000	2200	2600	3000	3400	3800
Wood Siding - Wood Frame	111.50	100.75	95.90	92.60	89.25	85.40	83.10	78.45	74.00	72.00	70.10
Brick Veneer - Wood Frame	117.65	106.45	101.25	97.70	94.00	90.00	87.50	82.45	77.70	75.45	73.45
Stucco on Wood Frame	108.75	98.20	93.50	90.30	87.05	83.35	81.15	76.75	72.35	70.40	68.70
Solid Masonry	129.05	117.00	111.05	107.10	102.80	98.50	95.60	89.80	84.45	81.85	79.60
Finished Basement, Add	19.70	19.40	18.75	18.35	17.90	17.65	17.25	16.60	16.15	15.90	15.65
Unfinished Basement, Add	7.65	7.10	6.70	6.40	6.10	5.90	5.70	5.35	5.05	4.80	4.70

Modifications

Add to the total cost

Upgrade Kitchen Cabinets	$ + 3521
Solid Surface Countertops (Included)	
Full Bath - including plumbing, wall and floor finishes	+ 5993
Half Bath - including plumbing, wall and floor finishes	+ 3570
One Car Attached Garage	+ 12,676
One Car Detached Garage	+ 16,871
Fireplace & Chimney	+ 5234

Adjustments

For multi family - add to total cost

Additional Kitchen	$ + 6796
Additional Bath	+ 5993
Additional Entry & Exit	+ 1640
Separate Heating	+ 1409
Separate Electric	+ 1915

For Townhouse/Rowhouse - Multiply cost per square foot by

Inner Unit	+ .91
End Unit	+ .96

Alternatives

Add to or deduct from the cost per square foot of living area

Cedar Shake Roof	+ 1.95
Clay Tile Roof	+ 2.25
Slate Roof	+ 3.30
Upgrade Walls to Skim Coat Plaster	+ .45
Upgrade Ceilings to Textured Finish	+ .48
Air Conditioning, in Heating Ductwork	+ 2.54
In Separate Ductwork	+ 6.36
Heating Systems, Hot Water	+ 2.01
Heat Pump	+ 3.11
Electric Heat	– .80
Not Heated	– 3.55

Additional upgrades or components

Kitchen Cabinets & Countertops	Page 77
Bathroom Vanities	78
Fireplaces & Chimneys	78
Windows, Skylights & Dormers	78
Appliances	79
Breezeways & Porches	79
Finished Attic	79
Garages	80
Site Improvements	80
Wings & Ells	44

Important: See the Reference Section for Location Factors (to adjust for your city) and Estimating Forms

			Cost Per Square Foot Of Living Area			% of Total
			Mat.	Inst.	Total	(roun
1	**Site Work**	Excavation for lower level, 4' deep. Site preparation for slab.		.72	.72	0.8%
2	**Foundation**	Continuous reinforced concrete footing 8" deep x 18" wide, dampproofed and insulated reinforced concrete foundation wall, 8" thick, 4' deep; 4" concrete slab on 4" crushed stone base and polyethylene vapor barrier, trowel finish.	2.97	3.73	6.70	7.8%
3	**Framing**	Exterior walls - 2" x 4" wood studs, 16" O.C.; 1/2" plywood sheathing; 2" x 6" rafters 16" O.C. with 1/2" plywood sheathing, 4 in 12 pitch; 2" x 6" ceiling joists 16" O.C.; 2" x 8" floor joists 16" O.C. with 5/8" plywood subfloor; 1/2" plywood subfloor on 1" x 2" wood sleepers 16" O.C.	4.75	7.84	12.59	14.7%
4	**Exterior Walls**	Horizontal beveled wood siding; building paper; 3-1/2" batt insulation; wood double hung windows; 3 flush solid core wood exterior doors; storms and screens.	9.83	4.11	13.94	16.3%
5	**Roofing**	25 year asphalt shingles; #15 felt building paper; aluminum gutters, downspouts, drip edge and flashings.	.96	1.11	2.07	2.4%
6	**Interiors**	Walls and ceilings, 1/2" taped and finished gypsum wallboard, primed and painted with 2 coats; painted baseboard and trim, finished hardwood floor 40%, carpet with 1/2" underlayment 40%, vinyl tile with 1/2" underlayment 15%, ceramic tile with 1/2" underlayment 5%; hollow core and louvered doors.	12.51	12.99	25.50	29.9%
7	**Specialties**	Average grade kitchen cabinets - 14 L.F. wall and base with solid surface counter top and kitchen sink; 40 gallon electric water heater.	2.26	.83	3.09	3.6%
8	**Mechanical**	1 lavatory, white, wall hung; 1 water closet, white; 1 bathtub with shower, enameled steel, white; gas fired warm air heat.	3.02	2.68	5.70	6.7%
9	**Electrical**	200 Amp. service; romex wiring; incandescent lighting fixtures, switches, receptacles.	1.13	1.54	2.67	3.1%
10	**Overhead**	Contractor's overhead and profit and plans.	6.37	6.05	12.42	14.5%
	Total		43.80	41.60	**85.40**	

- **Simple design from standard plans**
- **Single family — 1 full bath, 1 kitchen**
- **No basement**
- **Asphalt shingles on roof**
- **Hot air heat**
- **Gypsum wallboard interior finishes**
- **Materials and workmanship are average**

Note: The illustration shown may contain some optional components (for example: garages and/or fireplaces) whose costs are shown in the modifications, adjustments, & alternatives below or at the end of the square foot section.

©Design Basics, Inc.

Base cost per square foot of living area

Exterior Wall	Living Area										
	1200	1500	1800	2100	2400	2700	3000	3400	3800	4200	4600
Wood Siding - Wood Frame	105.90	97.55	91.35	86.00	82.50	80.50	78.35	76.25	72.80	70.00	68.65
Brick Veneer - Wood Frame	111.55	102.70	95.95	90.20	86.45	84.25	81.90	79.70	76.05	73.00	71.55
Stucco on Wood Frame	103.35	95.25	89.25	84.10	80.75	78.80	76.75	74.70	71.40	68.60	67.35
Solid Masonry	122.00	112.15	104.55	97.95	93.70	91.30	88.55	86.10	82.00	78.55	76.90
Finished Basement, Add*	22.50	22.10	21.15	20.35	19.95	19.65	19.25	19.00	18.60	18.25	18.10
Unfinished Basement, Add*	8.40	7.75	7.20	6.70	6.40	6.25	6.00	5.80	5.55	5.35	5.25

*Basement under middle level only.

Modifications

Add to the total cost

Upgrade Kitchen Cabinets	$ + 3521
Solid Surface Countertops (Included)	
Full Bath - including plumbing, wall and floor finishes	+ 5993
Half Bath - including plumbing, wall and floor finishes	+ 3570
One Car Attached Garage	+ 12,676
One Car Detached Garage	+ 16,871
Fireplace & Chimney	+ 5234

Adjustments

For multi family - add to total cost

Additional Kitchen	$ + 6796
Additional Bath	+ 5993
Additional Entry & Exit	+ 1640
Separate Heating	+ 1409
Separate Electric	+ 1915

For Townhouse/Rowhouse - Multiply cost per square foot by

Inner Unit	+ .90
End Unit	+ .95

Alternatives

Add to or deduct from the cost per square foot of living area

Cedar Shake Roof	+ 2.80
Clay Tile Roof	+ 3.30
Slate Roof	+ 4.80
Upgrade Walls to Skim Coat Plaster	+ .39
Upgrade Ceilings to Textured Finish	+ .48
Air Conditioning, in Heating Ductwork	+ 2.14
In Separate Ductwork	+ 6
Heating Systems, Hot Water	+ 1.94
Heat Pump	+ 3.23
Electric Heat	– .65
Not Heated	– 3.43

Additional upgrades or components

Kitchen Cabinets & Countertops	Page 77
Bathroom Vanities	78
Fireplaces & Chimneys	78
Windows, Skylights & Dormers	78
Appliances	79
Breezeways & Porches	79
Finished Attic	79
Garages	80
Site Improvements	80
Wings & Ells	44

			Cost Per Square Foot Of Living Area			% of Total
			Mat.	Inst.	Total	(roun
1	**Site Work**	Site preparation for slab; 4' deep trench excavation for foundation wall, excavation for lower level, 4' deep.		.60	.60	0.7%
2	**Foundation**	Continuous reinforced concrete footing 8" deep x 18" wide; dampproofed and insulated reinforced concrete foundation wall, 8" thick, 4' deep; 4" concrete slab on 4" crushed stone base and polyethylene vapor barrier, trowel finish.	3.35	4.05	7.40	9.0%
3	**Framing**	Exterior walls - 2" x 4" wood studs, 16" O.C.; 1/2" plywood sheathing; 2" x 6" rafters 16" O.C. with 1/2" plywood sheathing, 4 in 12 pitch; 2" x 6" ceiling joists 16" O.C.; 2" x 8" floor joists 16" O.C. with 5/8" plywood subfloor; 1/2" plywood subfloor on 1" x 2" wood sleepers 16" O.C.	4.35	7.37	11.72	14.2%
4	**Exterior Walls**	Horizontal beveled wood siding: building paper; 3-1/2" batt insulation; wood double hung windows; 3 flush solid core wood exterior doors; storms and screens.	8.49	3.57	12.06	14.6%
5	**Roofing**	25 year asphalt shingles; #15 felt building paper; aluminum gutters, downspouts, drip edge and flashings.	1.26	1.48	2.74	3.3%
6	**Interiors**	Walls and ceilings, 1/2" taped and finished gypsum wallboard, primed and painted with 2 coats; painted baseboard and trim, finished hardwood floor 40%, carpet with 1/2" underlayment 40%, vinyl tile with 1/2" underlayment 15%, ceramic tile with 1/2" underlayment 5%; hollow core and louvered doors.	12.97	12.72	25.69	31.1%
7	**Specialties**	Average grade kitchen cabinets - 14 L.F. wall and base with solid surface counter top and kitchen sink; 40 gallon electric water heater.	1.89	.70	2.59	3.1%
8	**Mechanical**	1 lavatory, white, wall hung; 1 water closet, white; 1 bathtub with shower, enameled steel, white; gas fired warm air heat.	2.65	2.53	5.18	6.3%
9	**Electrical**	200 Amp. service; romex wiring; incandescent lighting fixtures, switches, receptacles.	1.06	1.46	2.52	3.1%
10	**Overhead**	Contractor's overhead and profit and plans.	6.13	5.87	12.00	14.5%
	Total		42.15	40.35	**82.50**	

- Post and beam frame
- Log exterior walls
- Simple design from standard plans
- Single family — 1 full bath, 1 kitchen
- No basement
- Asphalt shingles on roof
- Hot air heat
- Gypsum wallboard interior finishes
- Materials and workmanship are average

Note: The illustration shown may contain some optional components (for example: garages and/or fireplaces) whose costs are shown in the modifications, adjustments, & alternatives below or at the end of the square foot section.

Base cost per square foot of living area

Exterior Wall	Living Area										
	600	800	1000	1200	1400	1600	1800	2000	2400	2800	3200
6" Log - Solid Wall	152.60	138.45	128.00	119.40	112.20	107.60	105.10	101.85	95.75	91.20	88.05
8" Log - Solid Wall	143.40	130.20	120.50	112.65	106.15	101.85	99.55	96.65	90.95	86.80	84.00
Finished Basement, Add	33.95	32.80	31.25	29.85	28.75	27.95	27.60	27.00	26.10	25.50	24.90
Unfinished Basement, Add	13.90	12.50	11.55	10.65	9.95	9.50	9.20	8.85	8.30	7.90	7.60

Modifications

Add to the total cost

Upgrade Kitchen Cabinets	$ + 3521
Solid Surface Countertops (Included)	
Full Bath - including plumbing, wall and floor finishes	+ 5993
Half Bath - including plumbing, wall and floor finishes	+ 3570
One Car Attached Garage	+ 12,676
One Car Detached Garage	+ 16,871
Fireplace & Chimney	+ 5234

Adjustments

For multi family - add to total cost

Additional Kitchen	$ + 6796
Additional Bath	+ 5993
Additional Entry & Exit	+ 1640
Separate Heating	+ 1409
Separate Electric	+ 1915

For Townhouse/Rowhouse - Multiply cost per square foot by

Inner Unit	+ .92
End Unit	+ .96

Alternatives

Add to or deduct from the cost per square foot of living area

Cedar Shake Roof	+ 3.85
Air Conditioning, in Heating Ductwork	+ 4.19
In Separate Ductwork	+ 8
Heating Systems, Hot Water	+ 2.16
Heat Pump	+ 2.65
Electric Heat	– 1.04
Not Heated	– 3.80

Additional upgrades or components

Kitchen Cabinets & Countertops	Page 77
Bathroom Vanities	78
Fireplaces & Chimneys	78
Windows, Skylights & Dormers	78
Appliances	79
Breezeways & Porches	79
Finished Attic	79
Garages	80
Site Improvements	80
Wings & Ells	44

Solid Wall 1 Story

Living Area - 1600 S.F.
Perimeter - 163 L.F.

			Cost Per Square Foot Of Living Area			% of Total
			Mat.	Inst.	Total	(roun
1 Site Work		Site preparation for slab; 4' deep trench excavation for foundation wall.		.90	.90	0.8%
2 Foundation		Continuous reinforced concrete footing 8" deep x 18" wide; dampproofed and insulated reinforced concrete foundation wall, 8" thick, 4' deep; 4" concrete slab on 4" crushed stone base and polyethylene vapor barrier, trowel finish.	5.02	6.07	11.09	10.3%
3 Framing		Exterior walls - Precut traditional log home. Handcrafted white cedar or pine logs. Delivery included.	20.33	13.19	33.52	31.2%
4 Exterior Walls		Wood double hung windows, solid wood exterior doors.	5.26	2.61	7.87	7.3%
5 Roofing		25 year asphalt shingles; #15 felt building paper; aluminum gutters, downspouts, drip edge and flashings.	1.90	2.22	4.12	3.8%
6 Interiors		Walls and ceilings, 1/2" taped and finished gypsum wallboard, primed and painted with 2 coats; painted baseboard and trim, finished hardwood floor 40%, carpet with 1/2" underlayment 40%, vinyl tile with 1/2" underlayment 15%, ceramic tile with 1/2" underlayment 5%, hollow core and louvered doors.	10.53	10.74	21.27	19.8%
7 Specialties		Average grade kitchen cabinets - 14 L.F. wall and base with solid surface counter top and kitchen sink; 40 gallon electric water heater.	2.83	1.05	3.88	3.6%
8 Mechanical		1 lavatory, white, wall hung; 1 water closet, white; 1 bathtub with shower, enameled steel, white; gas fired warm air heat.	3.50	2.87	6.37	5.9%
9 Electrical		200 Amp. service; romex wiring; incandescent lighting fixtures, switches, receptacles.	1.25	1.68	2.93	2.7%
10 Overhead		Contractor's overhead and profit and plans.	8.63	7.02	15.65	14.5%
Total			59.25	48.35	**107.60**	

- Post and beam frame
- Log exterior walls
- Simple design from standard plans
- Single family — 1 full bath, 1 kitchen
- No basement
- Asphalt shingles on roof
- Hot air heat
- Gypsum wallboard interior finishes
- Materials and workmanship are average

Note: The illustration shown may contain some optional components (for example: garages and/or fireplaces) whose costs are shown in the modifications, adjustments, & alternatives below or at the end of the square foot section.

Base cost per square foot of living area

Exterior Wall	Living Area										
	1000	1200	1400	1600	1800	2000	2200	2600	3000	3400	3800
6" Log-Solid	135.50	123.40	117.50	113.50	109.20	104.90	101.95	96.10	90.70	88.20	85.90
8" Log-Solid	125.50	114.20	108.85	105.25	101.45	97.40	94.85	89.70	84.75	82.55	80.50
Finished Basement, Add	19.70	19.40	18.75	18.35	17.90	17.65	17.25	16.60	16.15	15.90	15.65
Unfinished Basement, Add	7.65	7.10	6.70	6.40	6.10	5.90	5.70	5.35	5.05	4.80	4.70

Modifications

Add to the total cost

Upgrade Kitchen Cabinets	$ + 3521
Solid Surface Countertops (Included)	
Full Bath - including plumbing, wall and floor finishes	+ 5993
Half Bath - including plumbing, wall and floor finishes	+ 3570
One Car Attached Garage	+ 12,676
One Car Detached Garage	+ 16,871
Fireplace & Chimney	+ 5836

Adjustments

For multi family - add to total cost

Additional Kitchen	$ + 6796
Additional Bath	+ 5993
Additional Entry & Exit	+ 1640
Separate Heating	+ 1409
Separate Electric	+ 1915

For Townhouse/Rowhouse - Multiply cost per square foot by

Inner Unit	+ .92
End Unit	+ .96

Alternatives

Add to or deduct from the cost per square foot of living area

Cedar Shake Roof	+ 2.80
Air Conditioning, in Heating Ductwork	+ 2.54
In Separate Ductwork	+ 6.36
Heating Systems, Hot Water	+ 2.01
Heat Pump	+ 3.11
Electric Heat	– .80
Not Heated	– 3.55

Additional upgrades or components

Kitchen Cabinets & Countertops	Page 77
Bathroom Vanities	78
Fireplaces & Chimneys	78
Windows, Skylights & Dormers	78
Appliances	79
Breezeways & Porches	79
Finished Attic	79
Garages	80
Site Improvements	80
Wings & Ells	44

		Cost Per Square Foot Of Living Area			% of Total
		Mat.	Inst.	Total	(roun
1 Site Work	Site preparation for slab; 4' deep trench excavation for foundation wall.		.72	.72	0.7%
2 Foundation	Continuous reinforced concrete footing 8" deep x 18" wide; dampproofed and insulated reinforced concrete foundation wall, 8" thick, 4' deep, 4" concrete slab on 4" crushed stone base and polyethylene vapor barrier, trowel finish.	2.97	3.73	6.70	6.4%
3 Framing	Exterior walls - Precut traditional log home. Handcrafted white cedar or pine logs. Delivery included.	22.72	13.68	36.40	34.7%
4 Exterior Walls	Wood double hung windows, solid wood exterior doors.	5.81	2.79	8.60	8.2%
5 Roofing	25 year asphalt shingles; #15 felt building paper; aluminum gutters, downspouts, drip edge and flashings.	.96	1.11	2.07	2.0%
6 Interiors	Walls and ceilings, 1/2" taped and finished gypsum wallboard, primed and painted with 2 coats; painted baseboard and trim, finished hardwood floor 40%, carpet with 1/2" underlayment 40%, vinyl tile with 1/2" underlayment 15%, ceramic tile with 1/2" underlayment 5%; hollow core and louvered doors.	11.89	11.83	23.72	22.6%
7 Specialties	Average grade kitchen cabinets - 14 L.F. wall and base with solid surface counter top and kitchen sink; 40 gallon electric water heater.	2.26	.83	3.09	2.9%
8 Mechanical	1 lavatory, white, wall hung; 1 water closet, white; 1 bathtub with shower; enameled steel, white; gas fired warm air heat.	3.02	2.68	5.70	5.4%
9 Electrical	200 Amp. service; romex wiring; incandescent lighting fixtures, switches, receptacles.	1.13	1.54	2.67	2.5%
10 Overhead	Contractor's overhead and profit and plans.	8.64	6.59	15.23	14.5%
Total		59.40	45.50	**104.90**	

1 Story — Base cost per square foot of living area

Exterior Wall	Living Area							
	50	100	200	300	400	500	600	700
Wood Siding - Wood Frame	178.60	136.90	118.75	99.85	93.95	90.35	88.00	88.90
Brick Veneer - Wood Frame	188.10	140.95	120.55	97.85	91.15	87.10	84.45	85.10
Stucco on Wood Frame	169.85	130.55	113.40	96.30	90.65	87.30	85.05	86.05
Solid Masonry	233.15	175.90	151.20	121.50	113.45	108.50	106.90	106.95
Finished Basement, Add	54.20	44.95	40.45	32.90	31.40	30.55	29.90	29.50
Unfinished Basement, Add	25.55	19.20	16.60	12.20	11.30	10.80	10.40	10.15

1-1/2 Story — Base cost per square foot of living area

Exterior Wall	Living Area							
	100	200	300	400	500	600	700	800
Wood Siding - Wood Frame	144.50	115.95	98.90	88.95	83.75	81.35	78.20	77.25
Brick Veneer - Wood Frame	198.15	147.90	122.45	106.90	99.25	95.15	90.70	89.05
Stucco on Wood Frame	173.40	128.05	105.95	94.10	87.40	83.95	80.10	78.60
Solid Masonry	229.75	173.15	143.55	123.40	114.45	109.45	104.25	102.50
Finished Basement, Add	36.60	33.10	30.15	26.80	25.95	25.30	24.75	24.65
Unfinished Basement, Add	16.00	13.30	11.60	9.60	9.10	8.75	8.40	8.40

2 Story — Base cost per square foot of living area

Exterior Wall	Living Area							
	100	200	400	600	800	1000	1200	1400
Wood Siding - Wood Frame	144.30	107.80	91.75	76.45	71.25	68.05	66.00	67.10
Brick Veneer - Wood Frame	201.90	140.70	112.80	90.45	82.90	78.25	75.25	75.70
Stucco on Wood Frame	174.20	120.90	96.25	79.50	73.00	69.10	66.50	67.25
Solid Masonry	237.35	165.95	133.90	104.50	95.50	90.05	86.50	86.55
Finished Basement, Add	29.05	24.45	22.15	18.45	17.65	17.25	16.95	16.75
Unfinished Basement, Add	13.00	9.80	8.45	6.25	5.80	5.55	5.40	5.25

Base costs do not include bathroom or kitchen facilities. Use Modifications/Adjustments/Alternatives on pages 77–80 where appropriate.

1 Story

1-1/2 Story

2 Story

2-1/2 Story

Bi-Level

Tri-Level

- **A distinct residence from designer's plans**
- **Single family — 1 full bath, 1 half bath, 1 kitchen**
- **No basement**
- **Asphalt shingles on roof**
- **Forced hot air heat/air conditioning**
- **Gypsum wallboard interior finishes**
- **Materials and workmanship are above average**

Note: The illustration shown may contain some optional components (for example: garages and/or fireplaces) whose costs are shown in the modifications, adjustments, & alternatives below or at the end of the square foot section.

©Design Basics, Inc.

Base cost per square foot of living area

Exterior Wall	Living Area										
	800	1000	1200	1400	1600	1800	2000	2400	2800	3200	3600
Wood Siding - Wood Frame	161.95	146.65	134.40	124.60	117.80	114.15	109.80	101.65	95.70	91.55	87.25
Brick Veneer - Wood Frame	180.80	164.70	151.65	141.15	133.95	130.10	125.30	116.75	110.45	105.90	101.30
Stone Veneer - Wood Frame	185.65	169.10	155.60	144.80	137.35	133.35	128.40	119.55	113.05	108.35	103.55
Solid Masonry	190.20	173.15	159.30	148.15	140.50	136.45	131.25	122.10	115.45	110.55	105.60
Finished Basement, Add	50.70	50.50	48.40	46.60	45.50	44.85	43.90	42.60	41.60	40.75	39.95
Unfinished Basement, Add	20.90	19.65	18.50	17.60	17.00	16.65	16.20	15.50	14.95	14.50	14.10

Modifications

Add to the total cost

Upgrade Kitchen Cabinets	$	+ 1108
Solid Surface Countertops (Included)		
Full Bath - including plumbing, wall and floor finishes		+ 7102
Half Bath - including plumbing, wall and floor finishes		+ 4230
Two Car Attached Garage		+ 21,916
Two Car Detached Garage		+ 25,336
Fireplace & Chimney		+ 5760

Adjustments

For multi family - add to total cost

Additional Kitchen	$	+ 14,160
Additional Full Bath & Half Bath		+ 11,332
Additional Entry & Exit		+ 1640
Separate Heating & Air Conditioning		+ 6271
Separate Electric		+ 1915

For Townhouse/Rowhouse - Multiply cost per square foot by

Inner Unit	+ .90
End Unit	+ .95

Alternatives

Add to or deduct from the cost per square foot of living area

Cedar Shake Roof	+ 3.45
Clay Tile Roof	+ 4.10
Slate Roof	+ 6.20
Upgrade Ceilings to Textured Finish	+ .48
Air Conditioning, in Heating Ductwork	Base System
Heating Systems, Hot Water	+ 2.21
Heat Pump	+ 2.64
Electric Heat	− 2.95
Not Heated	− 4.77

Additional upgrades or components

Kitchen Cabinets & Countertops	Page 77
Bathroom Vanities	78
Fireplaces & Chimneys	78
Windows, Skylights & Dormers	78
Appliances	79
Breezeways & Porches	79
Finished Attic	79
Garages	80
Site Improvements	80
Wings & Ells	60

Custom 1 Story

Living Area - 2400 S.F.
Perimeter - 207 L.F.

			Cost Per Square Foot Of Living Area			% of Total
			Mat.	Inst.	Total	(roun
1	**Site Work**	Site preparation for slab; 4' deep trench excavation for foundation wall.		.71	.71	0.7%
2	**Foundation**	Continuous reinforced concrete footing 8" deep x 18" wide; dampproofed and insulated reinforced concrete foundation wall, 8" thick, 4' deep, 4" concrete slab on 4" crushed stone base and polyethylene vapor barrier, trowel finish.	5.60	6.71	12.31	12.1%
3	**Framing**	Exterior walls - 2" x 6" wood studs, 16" O.C.; 1/2" plywood sheathing; 2" x 8" rafters 16" O.C. with 1/2" plywood sheathing, 4 in 12 pitch; 2" x 6" ceiling joists 16" O.C.; 5/8" plywood subfloor on 1" x 3" wood sleepers 16" O.C.	2.92	6.21	9.13	9.0%
4	**Exterior Walls**	Horizontal beveled wood siding; building paper; 6" batt insulation; wood double hung windows; 3 solid core wood exterior doors; storms and screens.	9.13	3.14	12.27	12.1%
5	**Roofing**	30 year asphalt shingles; #15 felt building paper; aluminum gutters, downspouts and drip edge; copper flashings.	4.66	3.25	7.91	7.8%
6	**Interiors**	Walls and ceilings - 5/8" gypsum wallboard, skim coat plaster, painted with primer and 2 coats; hardwood baseboard and trim, sanded and finished; hardwood floor 70%, ceramic tile with underlayment 20%, vinyl tile with underlayment 10%; wood panel interior doors, primed and painted with 2 coats.	12.54	11.77	24.31	23.9%
7	**Specialties**	Custom grade kitchen cabinets - 20 L.F. wall and base with solid surface counter top and kitchen sink; 4 L.F. bathroom vanity; 75 gallon electric water heater, medicine cabinet.	5.04	1.18	6.22	6.1%
8	**Mechanical**	Gas fired warm air heat/air conditioning; one full bath including: bathtub, corner shower, built in lavatory and water closet; one 1/2 bath including: built in lavatory and water closet.	6.04	2.96	9.00	8.9%
9	**Electrical**	200 Amp. service; romex wiring; fluorescent and incandescent lighting fixtures, switches, receptacles.	1.19	1.66	2.85	2.8%
10	**Overhead**	Contractor's overhead and profit and design.	9.43	7.51	16.94	16.7%
	Total		56.55	45.10	**101.65**	

- **A distinct residence from designer's plans**
- **Single family — 1 full bath, 1 half bath, 1 kitchen**
- **No basement**
- **Asphalt shingles on roof**
- **Forced hot air heat/air conditioning**
- **Gypsum wallboard interior finishes**
- **Materials and workmanship are above average**

Note: The illustration shown may contain some optional components (for example: garages and/or fireplaces) whose costs are shown in the modifications, adjustments, & alternatives below or at the end of the square foot section.

©Donald A. Gardner Architects, Inc.

Base cost per square foot of living area

	Living Area										
Exterior Wall	1000	1200	1400	1600	1800	2000	2400	2800	3200	3600	4000
Wood Siding - Wood Frame	145.30	135.10	127.80	119.10	114.10	109.20	99.85	95.55	91.55	88.55	84.30
Brick Veneer - Wood Frame	154.60	143.80	136.15	126.65	121.25	115.90	105.80	101.25	96.85	93.65	89.00
Stone Veneer - Wood Frame	159.75	148.60	140.65	130.80	125.15	119.70	109.10	104.35	99.70	96.45	91.60
Solid Masonry	164.50	153.05	144.90	134.60	128.75	123.10	112.15	107.25	102.35	99.00	94.00
Finished Basement, Add	33.65	33.90	32.95	31.60	30.90	30.15	28.80	28.15	27.50	27.05	26.50
Unfinished Basement, Add	14.15	13.45	13.05	12.30	11.90	11.55	10.85	10.50	10.15	9.95	9.60

Modifications

Add to the total cost

Upgrade Kitchen Cabinets	$ + 1108
Solid Surface Countertops (Included)	
Full Bath - including plumbing, wall and floor finishes	+ 7102
Half Bath - including plumbing, wall and floor finishes	+ 4230
Two Car Attached Garage	+ 21,916
Two Car Detached Garage	+ 25,336
Fireplace & Chimney	+ 5760

Adjustments

For multi family - add to total cost

Additional Kitchen	$ + 14,160
Additional Full Bath & Half Bath	+ 11,332
Additional Entry & Exit	+ 1640
Separate Heating & Air Conditioning	+ 6271
Separate Electric	+ 1915

For Townhouse/Rowhouse - Multiply cost per square foot by

Inner Unit	+ .90
End Unit	+ .95

Alternatives

Add to or deduct from the cost per square foot of living area

Cedar Shake Roof	+ 2.50
Clay Tile Roof	+ 2.95
Slate Roof	+ 4.50
Upgrade Ceilings to Textured Finish	+ .48
Air Conditioning, in Heating Ductwork	Base System
Heating Systems, Hot Water	+ 2.10
Heat Pump	+ 2.77
Electric Heat	- 2.60
Not Heated	- 4.40

Additional upgrades or components

Kitchen Cabinets & Countertops	Page 77
Bathroom Vanities	78
Fireplaces & Chimneys	78
Windows, Skylights & Dormers	78
Appliances	79
Breezeways & Porches	79
Finished Attic	79
Garages	80
Site Improvements	80
Wings & Ells	60

			Cost Per Square Foot Of Living Area			% of Total
			Mat.	Inst.	Total	(roun
1	**Site Work**	Site preparation for slab; 4' deep trench excavation for foundation wall.		.61	.61	0.6%
2	**Foundation**	Continuous reinforced concrete footing 8" deep x 18" wide; dampproofed and insulated reinforced concrete foundation wall, 8" thick, 4' deep, 4" concrete slab on 4" crushed stone base and polyethylene vapor barrier, trowel finish.	3.91	4.78	8.69	9.1%
3	**Framing**	Exterior walls - 2" x 6" wood studs, 16" O.C.; 1/2" plywood sheathing; 2" x 8" rafters 16" O.C. with 1/2" plywood sheathing, 8 in 12 pitch; 2" x 10" floor joists 16" O.C. with 5/8" plywood subfloor; 5/8" plywood subfloor on 1" x 3" wood sleepers 16" O.C.	3.80	6.54	10.34	10.8%
4	**Exterior Walls**	Horizontal beveled wood siding; building paper; 6" batt insulation; wood double hung windows; 3 solid core wood exterior doors; storms and screens.	9.17	3.18	12.35	12.9%
5	**Roofing**	30 year asphalt shingles; #15 felt building paper; aluminum gutters, downspouts and drip edge; copper flashings.	2.92	2.03	4.95	5.2%
6	**Interiors**	Walls and ceilings - 5/8" gypsum wallboard, skim coat plaster, painted with primer and 2 coats; hardwood baseboard and trim, sanded and finished; hardwood floor 70%, ceramic tile with underlayment 20%, vinyl tile with underlayment 10%; wood panel interior doors, primed and painted with 2 coats.	13.81	12.80	26.61	27.8%
7	**Specialties**	Custom grade kitchen cabinets - 20 L.F. wall and base with solid surface counter top and kitchen sink; 4 L.F. bathroom vanity; 75 gallon electric water heater, medicine cabinet.	4.32	1.01	5.33	5.6%
8	**Mechanical**	Gas fired warm air heat/air conditioning; one full bath including: bathtub, corner shower, built in lavatory and water closet; one 1/2 bath including: built in lavatory and water closet.	5.25	2.78	8.03	8.4%
9	**Electrical**	200 Amp. service; romex wiring; fluorescent and incandescent lighting fixtures, switches, receptacles.	1.12	1.60	2.72	2.8%
10	**Overhead**	Contractor's overhead and profit and design.	8.85	7.07	15.92	16.7%
	Total		53.15	42.40	**95.55**	

- A distinct residence from designer's plans
- Single family — 1 full bath, 1 half bath, 1 kitchen
- No basement
- Asphalt shingles on roof
- Forced hot air heat/air conditioning
- Gypsum wallboard interior finishes
- Materials and workmanship are above average

Note: The illustration shown may contain some optional components (for example: garages and/or fireplaces) whose costs are shown in the modifications, adjustments, & alternatives below or at the end of the square foot section.

Base cost per square foot of living area

Exterior Wall	Living Area										
	1200	1400	1600	1800	2000	2400	2800	3200	3600	4000	4400
Wood Siding - Wood Frame	135.85	127.55	121.75	116.70	111.20	103.20	96.50	92.00	89.40	86.55	84.20
Brick Veneer - Wood Frame	145.80	136.90	130.60	125.10	119.25	110.45	103.10	98.15	95.30	92.15	89.55
Stone Veneer - Wood Frame	151.25	141.95	135.45	129.60	123.65	114.45	106.70	101.55	98.60	95.20	92.55
Solid Masonry	156.35	146.70	140.00	133.90	127.70	118.10	110.05	104.70	101.65	98.05	95.30
Finished Basement, Add	27.05	27.25	26.50	25.75	25.35	24.25	23.40	22.85	22.45	22.00	21.75
Unfinished Basement, Add	11.30	10.80	10.45	10.05	9.85	9.25	8.80	8.50	8.35	8.10	7.95

Modifications

Add to the total cost

Upgrade Kitchen Cabinets	$ + 1108
Solid Surface Countertops (Included)	
Full Bath - including plumbing, wall and floor finishes	+ 7102
Half Bath - including plumbing, wall and floor finishes	+ 4230
Two Car Attached Garage	+ 21,916
Two Car Detached Garage	+ 25,336
Fireplace & Chimney	+ 6502

Adjustments

For multi family - add to total cost

Additional Kitchen	$ + 14,160
Additional Full Bath & Half Bath	+ 11,332
Additional Entry & Exit	+ 1640
Separate Heating & Air Conditioning	+ 6271
Separate Electric	+ 1915

For Townhouse/Rowhouse - Multiply cost per square foot by

Inner Unit	+ .87
End Unit	+ .93

Alternatives

Add to or deduct from the cost per square foot of living area

Cedar Shake Roof	+ 1.70
Clay Tile Roof	+ 2.05
Slate Roof	+ 3.10
Upgrade Ceilings to Textured Finish	+ .48
Air Conditioning, in Heating Ductwork	Base System
Heating Systems, Hot Water	+ 2.05
Heat Pump	+ 3.08
Electric Heat	– 2.60
Not Heated	– 4.16

Additional upgrades or components

Kitchen Cabinets & Countertops	Page 77
Bathroom Vanities	78
Fireplaces & Chimneys	78
Windows, Skylights & Dormers	78
Appliances	79
Breezeways & Porches	79
Finished Attic	79
Garages	80
Site Improvements	80
Wings & Ells	60

Custom 2 Story

Living Area - 2800 S.F.
Perimeter - 156 L.F.

			Cost Per Square Foot Of Living Area			% of Total
			Mat.	Inst.	Total	(roun
1	**Site Work**	Site preparation for slab; 4' deep trench excavation for foundation wall.		.61	.61	0.6%
2	**Foundation**	Continuous reinforced concrete footing 8" deep x 18" wide; dampproofed and insulated reinforced concrete foundation wall, 8" thick, 4' deep, 4" concrete slab on 4" crushed stone base and polyethylene vapor barrier, trowel finish.	3.31	4.09	7.40	7.7%
3	**Framing**	Exterior walls - 2" x 6" wood studs, 16" O.C.; 1/2" plywood sheathing; 2" x 8" rafters 16" O.C. with 1/2" plywood sheathing, 6 in 12 pitch; 2" x 8" ceiling joists 16" O.C.; 2" x 10" floor joists 16" O.C. with 5/8" plywood subfloor; 5/8" plywood subfloor on 1" x 3" wood sleepers 16" O.C.	4.17	6.74	10.91	11.3%
4	**Exterior Walls**	Horizontal beveled wood siding; building paper; 6" batt insulation; wood double hung windows; 3 solid core wood exterior doors; storms and screens.	10.46	3.64	14.10	14.6%
5	**Roofing**	30 year asphalt shingles; #15 felt building paper; aluminum gutters, downspouts and drip edge; copper flashings.	2.33	1.63	3.96	4.1%
6	**Interiors**	Walls and ceilings - 5/8" gypsum wallboard, skim coat plaster, painted with primer and 2 coats; hardwood baseboard and trim, sanded and finished; hardwood floor 70%, ceramic tile with underlayment 20%, vinyl tile with underlayment 10%; wood panel interior doors, primed and painted with 2 coats.	14.06	13.10	27.16	28.1%
7	**Specialties**	Custom grade kitchen cabinets - 20 L.F. wall and base with solid surface counter top and kitchen sink; 4 L.F. bathroom vanity; 75 gallon electric water heater, medicine cabinet.	4.32	1.01	5.33	5.5%
8	**Mechanical**	Gas fired warm air heat/air conditioning; one full bath including: bathtub, corner shower; built in lavatory and water closet; one 1/2 bath including: built in lavatory and water closet.	5.39	2.82	8.21	8.5%
9	**Electrical**	200 Amp. service; romex wiring; fluorescent and incandescent lighting fixtures, switches, receptacles.	1.12	1.60	2.72	2.8%
10	**Overhead**	Contractor's overhead and profit and design.	9.04	7.06	16.10	16.7%
	Total		54.20	42.30	**96.50**	

- **A distinct residence from designer's plans**
- **Single family — 1 full bath, 1 half bath, 1 kitchen**
- **No basement**
- **Asphalt shingles on roof**
- **Forced hot air heat/air conditioning**
- **Gypsum wallboard interior finishes**
- **Materials and workmanship are above average**

Note: The illustration shown may contain some optional components (for example: garages and/or fireplaces) whose costs are shown in the modifications, adjustments, & alternatives below or at the end of the square foot section.

Base cost per square foot of living area

Exterior Wall	Living Area										
	1500	1800	2100	2400	2800	3200	3600	4000	4500	5000	5500
Wood Siding - Wood Frame	133.30	119.90	112.00	107.30	101.15	95.30	92.05	87.00	84.30	81.90	79.45
Brick Veneer - Wood Frame	143.65	129.40	120.50	115.35	108.85	102.30	98.65	93.10	90.10	87.45	84.70
Stone Veneer - Wood Frame	149.30	134.65	125.20	119.80	113.15	106.15	102.30	96.45	93.30	90.50	87.60
Solid Masonry	154.55	139.50	129.55	123.90	117.05	109.70	105.65	99.65	96.30	93.30	90.25
Finished Basement, Add	21.50	21.50	20.35	19.80	19.35	18.65	18.20	17.70	17.30	17.05	16.80
Unfinished Basement, Add	9.10	8.60	8.00	7.75	7.50	7.15	6.90	6.65	6.45	6.35	6.15

Modifications

Add to the total cost

Upgrade Kitchen Cabinets	$ + 1108
Solid Surface Countertops (Included)	
Full Bath - including plumbing, wall and floor finishes	+ 7102
Half Bath - including plumbing, wall and floor finishes	+ 4230
Two Car Attached Garage	+ 21,916
Two Car Detached Garage	+ 25,336
Fireplace & Chimney	+ 7342

Adjustments

For multi family - add to total cost

Additional Kitchen	$ + 14,160
Additional Full Bath & Half Bath	+ 11,332
Additional Entry & Exit	+ 1640
Separate Heating & Air Conditioning	+ 6271
Separate Electric	+ 1915

For Townhouse/Rowhouse - Multiply cost per square foot by

Inner Unit	+ .87
End Unit	+ .94

Alternatives

Add to or deduct from the cost per square foot of living area

Cedar Shake Roof	+ 1.50
Clay Tile Roof	+ 1.80
Slate Roof	+ 2.70
Upgrade Ceilings to Textured Finish	+ .48
Air Conditioning, in Heating Ductwork	Base System
Heating Systems, Hot Water	+ 1.85
Heat Pump	+ 3.19
Electric Heat	– 4.56
Not Heated	– 4.16

Additional upgrades or components

Kitchen Cabinets & Countertops	Page 77
Bathroom Vanities	78
Fireplaces & Chimneys	78
Windows, Skylights & Dormers	78
Appliances	79
Breezeways & Porches	79
Finished Attic	79
Garages	80
Site Improvements	80
Wings & Ells	60

Important: See the Reference Section for Location Factors (to adjust for your city) and Estimating Form

			Cost Per Square Foot Of Living Area			% of Total
			Mat.	Inst.	Total	(roun
1	**Site Work**	Site preparation for slab; 4' deep trench excavation for foundation wall.		.53	.53	0.6%
2	**Foundation**	Continuous reinforced concrete footing 8" deep x 18" wide; dampproofed and insulated reinforced concrete foundation wall, 8" thick, 4' deep, 4" concrete slab on 4" crushed stone base and polyethylene vapor barrier, trowel finish.	2.72	3.41	6.13	6.4%
3	**Framing**	Exterior walls - 2" x 6" wood studs, 16" O.C.; 1/2" plywood sheathing; 2" x 8" rafters 16" O.C. with 1/2" plywood sheathing, 6 in 12 pitch; 2" x 8" ceiling joists 16" O.C.; 2" x 10" floor joists 16" O.C. with 5/8" plywood subfloor; 5/8" plywood subfloor on 1" x 3" wood sleepers 16" O.C.	4.52	7.03	11.55	12.1%
4	**Exterior Walls**	Horizontal beveled wood siding; building paper; 6" batt insulation; wood double hung windows; 3 solid core wood exterior doors; storms and screens.	10.81	3.78	14.59	15.3%
5	**Roofing**	30 year asphalt shingles; #15 felt building paper; aluminum gutters, downspouts and drip edge; copper flashings.	1.79	1.25	3.04	3.2%
6	**Interiors**	Walls and ceilings - 5/8" gypsum wallboard, skim coat plaster, painted with primer and 2 coats; hardwood baseboard and trim, sanded and finished; hardwood floor 70%, ceramic tile with underlayment 20%, vinyl tile with underlayment 10%; wood panel interior doors, primed and painted with 2 coats.	14.82	13.88	28.70	30.1%
7	**Specialties**	Custom grade kitchen cabinets - 20 L.F. wall and base with solid surface counter top and kitchen sink; 4 L.F. bathroom vanity; 75 gallon electric water heater, medicine cabinet.	3.79	.88	4.67	4.9%
8	**Mechanical**	Gas fired warm air heat/air conditioning; one full bath including: bathtub, corner shower; built in lavatory and water closet; one 1/2 bath including: built in lavatory and water closet.	4.89	2.70	7.59	8.0%
9	**Electrical**	200 Amp. service; romex wiring; fluorescent and incandescent lighting fixtures, switches, receptacles.	1.09	1.54	2.63	2.8%
10	**Overhead**	Contractor's overhead and profit and design.	8.87	7.00	15.87	16.7%
	Total		53.30	42.00	**95.30**	

- A distinct residence from designer's plans
- Single family — 1 full bath, 1 half bath, 1 kitchen
- No basement
- Asphalt shingles on roof
- Forced hot air heat/air conditioning
- Gypsum wallboard interior finishes
- Materials and workmanship are above average

Note: The illustration shown may contain some optional components (for example: garages and/or fireplaces) whose costs are shown in the modifications, adjustments, & alternatives below or at the end of the square foot section.

Base cost per square foot of living area

Exterior Wall	Living Area										
	1500	1800	2100	2500	3000	3500	4000	4500	5000	5500	6000
Wood Siding - Wood Frame	132.75	119.45	112.95	107.60	99.40	95.25	90.20	84.90	83.00	80.95	78.80
Brick Veneer - Wood Frame	143.45	129.40	122.25	116.45	107.45	102.85	97.15	91.30	89.15	86.85	84.40
Stone Veneer - Wood Frame	149.35	134.85	127.35	121.30	111.90	107.00	100.95	94.80	92.60	90.15	87.45
Solid Masonry	154.80	139.90	132.05	125.85	115.95	110.90	104.45	98.05	95.75	93.20	90.30
Finished Basement, Add	18.85	18.85	18.10	17.60	16.85	16.40	15.80	15.30	15.15	14.90	14.65
Unfinished Basement, Add	7.95	7.50	7.20	6.90	6.50	6.30	6.00	5.75	5.65	5.55	5.35

Modifications

Add to the total cost

Upgrade Kitchen Cabinets	$ + 1108 ✓
Solid Surface Countertops (Included)	
Full Bath - including plumbing, wall and floor finishes	+ 7102 ✓
Half Bath - including plumbing, wall and floor finishes	+ 4230 ✓
Two Car Attached Garage	+ 21,916 ✓
Two Car Detached Garage	+ 25,336
Fireplace & Chimney	+ 7342 ✓

Adjustments

For multi family - add to total cost

Additional Kitchen	$ + 14,160
Additional Full Bath & Half Bath	+ 11,332
Additional Entry & Exit	+ 1640
Separate Heating & Air Conditioning	+ 6271
Separate Electric	+ 1915

For Townhouse/Rowhouse - Multiply cost per square foot by

Inner Unit	+ .85
End Unit	+ .93

Alternatives

Add to or deduct from the cost per square foot of living area

Cedar Shake Roof	+ 1.15
Clay Tile Roof	+ 1.35
Slate Roof	+ 2.05
Upgrade Ceilings to Textured Finish	+ .48
Air Conditioning, in Heating Ductwork	Base System
Heating Systems, Hot Water	+ 1.85
Heat Pump	+ 3.19
Electric Heat	– 4.56
Not Heated	– 4.03

Additional upgrades or components

Kitchen Cabinets & Countertops	Page 77
Bathroom Vanities	78
Fireplaces & Chimneys	78
Windows, Skylights & Dormers	78
Appliances	79
Breezeways & Porches	79
Finished Attic	79
Garages	80
Site Improvements	80
Wings & Ells	60

Custom 3 Story

Living Area - 3000 S.F.
Perimeter - 135 L.F.

			Cost Per Square Foot Of Living Area			% of Total
			Mat.	Inst.	Total	(roun
1	**Site Work**	Site preparation for slab; 4' deep trench excavation for foundation wall.		.56	.56	0.6%
2	**Foundation**	Continuous reinforced concrete footing 8" deep x 18" wide; dampproofed and insulated reinforced concrete foundation wall, 8" thick, 4' deep, 4" concrete slab on 4" crushed stone base and polyethylene vapor barrier, trowel finish.	2.55	3.22	5.77	5.8%
3	**Framing**	Exterior walls - 2" x 6" wood studs, 16" O.C.; 1/2" plywood sheathing; 2" x 8" rafters 16" O.C. with 1/2" plywood sheathing, 6 in 12 pitch; 2" x 8" ceiling joists 16" O.C.; 2" x 10" floor joists 16" O.C. with 5/8" plywood subfloor; 5/8" plywood subfloor on 1" x 3" wood sleepers 16" O.C.	4.74	7.25	11.99	12.1%
4	**Exterior Walls**	Horizontal beveled wood siding; building paper; 6" batt insulation; wood double hung windows; 3 solid core wood exterior doors; storms and screens.	12.34	4.33	16.67	16.8%
5	**Roofing**	30 year asphalt shingles; #15 felt building paper; aluminum gutters, downspouts and drip edge; copper flashings.	1.56	1.09	2.65	2.7%
6	**Interiors**	Walls and ceilings - 5/8" gypsum wallboard, skim coat plaster, painted with primer and 2 coats; hardwood baseboard and trim, sanded and finished; hardwood floor 70%, ceramic tile with underlayment 20%, vinyl tile with underlayment 10%; wood panel interior doors, primed and painted with 2 coats.	15.31	14.37	29.68	29.9%
7	**Specialties**	Custon grade kitchen cabinets - 20 L.F. wall and base with solid surface counter top and kitchen sink; 4 L.F. bathroom vanity; 75 gallon electric water heater, medicine cabinet.	4.03	.94	4.97	5.0%
8	**Mechanical**	Gas fired warm air heat/air conditioning; one full bath including: bathtub, corner shower; built in lavatory and water closet; one 1/2 bath including: built in lavatory and water closet.	5.12	2.76	7.88	7.9%
9	**Electrical**	200 Amp. service; romex wiring; fluorescent and incandescent lighting fixtures, switches, receptacles.	1.10	1.57	2.67	2.7%
10	**Overhead**	Contractor's overhead and profit and design.	9.35	7.21	16.56	16.7%
	Total		56.10	43.30	**99.40**	

55

- **A distinct residence from designer's plans**
- **Single family — 1 full bath, 1 half bath, 1 kitchen**
- **No basement**
- **Asphalt shingles on roof**
- **Forced hot air heat/air conditioning**
- **Gypsum wallboard interior finishes**
- **Materials and workmanship are above average**

Note: The illustration shown may contain some optional components (for example: garages and/or fireplaces) whose costs are shown in the modifications, adjustments, & alternatives below or at the end of the square foot section.

Base cost per square foot of living area

Exterior Wall	Living Area										
	1200	1400	1600	1800	2000	2400	2800	3200	3600	4000	4400
Wood Siding - Wood Frame	128.45	120.70	115.20	110.45	105.15	97.80	91.50	87.30	84.95	82.35	80.05
Brick Veneer - Wood Frame	135.85	127.65	121.80	116.75	111.25	103.20	96.40	91.95	89.40	86.55	84.15
Stone Veneer - Wood Frame	139.95	131.45	125.45	120.15	114.50	106.20	99.15	94.50	91.85	88.85	86.35
Solid Masonry	143.80	135.00	128.85	123.35	117.55	108.95	101.65	96.80	94.10	91.05	88.45
Finished Basement, Add	27.05	27.25	26.50	25.75	25.35	24.25	23.40	22.85	22.45	22.00	21.75
Unfinished Basement, Add	11.30	10.80	10.45	10.05	9.85	9.25	8.80	8.50	8.35	8.10	7.95

Modifications

Add to the total cost

Upgrade Kitchen Cabinets	$ + 1108
Solid Surface Countertops (Included)	
Full Bath - including plumbing, wall and floor finishes	+ 7102
Half Bath - including plumbing, wall and floor finishes	+ 4230
Two Car Attached Garage	+ 21,916
Two Car Detached Garage	+ 25,336
Fireplace & Chimney	+ 5760

Adjustments

For multi family - add to total cost

Additional Kitchen	$ + 14,160
Additional Full Bath & Half Bath	+ 11,332
Additional Entry & Exit	+ 1640
Separate Heating & Air Conditioning	+ 6271
Separate Electric	+ 1915

For Townhouse/Rowhouse - Multiply cost per square foot by

Inner Unit	+ .89
End Unit	+ .95

Alternatives

Add to or deduct from the cost per square foot of living area

Cedar Shake Roof	+ 1.70
Clay Tile Roof	+ 2.05
Slate Roof	+ 3.10
Upgrade Ceilings to Textured Finish	+ .48
Air Conditioning, in Heating Ductwork	Base System
Heating Systems, Hot Water	+ 2.05
Heat Pump	+ 3.08
Electric Heat	– 2.60
Not Heated	– 4.03

Additional upgrades or components

Kitchen Cabinets & Countertops	Page 77
Bathroom Vanities	78
Fireplaces & Chimneys	78
Windows, Skylights & Dormers	78
Appliances	79
Breezeways & Porches	79
Finished Attic	79
Garages	80
Site Improvements	80
Wings & Ells	60

Important: See the Reference Section for Location Factors (to adjust for your city) and Estimating Forms

Custom Bi-Level

Living Area - 2800 S.F.
Perimeter - 156 L.F.

			Cost Per Square Foot Of Living Area			% of Total
			Mat.	Inst.	Total	(roun
1	**Site Work**	Excavation for lower level, 4' deep. Site preparation for slab.		.61	.61	0.7%
2	**Foundation**	Continuous reinforced concrete footing 8" deep x 18" wide; dampproofed and insulated reinforced concrete foundation wall, 8" thick, 4' deep, 4" concrete slab on 4" crushed stone base and polyethylene vapor barrier, trowel finish.	3.31	4.09	7.40	8.1%
3	**Framing**	Exterior walls - 2" x 6" wood studs, 16" O.C.; 1/2" plywood sheathing; 2" x 8" rafters 16" O.C. with 1/2" plywood sheathing, 6 in 12 pitch; 2" x 8" ceiling joists 16" O.C.; 2" x 10" floor joists 16" O.C. with 5/8" plywood subfloor; 5/8" plywood subfloor on 1" x 3" wood sleepers 16" O.C.	3.98	6.43	10.41	11.4%
4	**Exterior Walls**	Horizontal beveled wood siding; building paper; 6" batt insulation; wood double hung windows; 3 solid core wood exterior doors; storms and screens.	8.17	2.82	10.99	12.0%
5	**Roofing**	30 year asphalt shingles; #15 felt building paper; aluminum gutters, downspouts and drip edge; copper flashings.	2.33	1.63	3.96	4.3%
6	**Interiors**	Walls and ceilings - 5/8" gypsum wallboard, skim coat plaster, painted with primer and 2 coats; hardwood baseboard and trim, sanded and finished; hardwood floor 70%, ceramic tile with underlayment 20%, vinyl tile with underlayment 10%; wood panel interior doors, primed and painted with 2 coats.	13.87	12.74	26.61	29.1%
7	**Specialties**	Custom grade kitchen cabinets - 20 L.F. wall and base with solid surface counter top and kitchen sink; 4 L.F. bathroom vanity; 75 gallon electric water heater, medicine cabinet.	4.32	1.01	5.33	5.8%
8	**Mechanical**	Gas fired warm air heat/air conditioning; one full bath including: bathtub, corner shower, built in lavatory and water closet; one 1/2 bath including: built in lavatory and water closet.	5.39	2.82	8.21	9.0%
9	**Electrical**	200 Amp. service; romex wiring; fluorescent and incandescent lighting fixtures, switches, receptacles.	1.12	1.60	2.72	3.0%
10	**Overhead**	Contractor's overhead and profit and design.	8.51	6.75	15.26	16.7%
	Total		51.00	40.50	**91.50**	

- **A distinct residence from designer's plans**
- **Single family — 1 full bath, 1 half bath, 1 kitchen**
- **No basement**
- **Asphalt shingles on roof**
- **Forced hot air heat/air conditioning**
- **Gypsum wallboard interior finishes**
- **Materials and workmanship are above average**

Note: The illustration shown may contain some optional components (for example: garages and/or fireplaces) whose costs are shown in the modifications, adjustments, & alternatives below or at the end of the square foot section.

eDesign Basics, Inc.

Base cost per square foot of living area

Exterior Wall	Living Area										
	1200	1500	1800	2100	2400	2800	3200	3600	4000	4500	5000
Wood Siding - Wood Frame	132.40	120.30	111.05	103.45	98.30	94.60	90.20	85.55	83.60	79.25	76.85
Brick Veneer - Wood Frame	139.80	127.00	117.10	108.90	103.45	99.55	94.80	89.80	87.75	83.10	80.45
Stone Veneer - Wood Frame	143.85	130.70	120.40	111.95	106.30	102.30	97.35	92.15	90.05	85.15	82.40
Solid Masonry	147.60	134.05	123.45	114.70	108.90	104.80	99.65	94.30	92.15	87.10	84.20
Finished Basement, Add*	33.80	33.65	32.25	31.05	30.30	29.80	29.10	28.40	28.15	27.50	27.05
Unfinished Basement, Add*	13.95	13.10	12.35	11.75	11.30	11.10	10.70	10.35	10.20	9.85	9.60

*Basement under middle level only.

Modifications

Add to the total cost

Upgrade Kitchen Cabinets	$ + 1108
Solid Surface Countertops (Included)	
Full Bath - including plumbing, wall and floor finishes	+ 7102
Half Bath - including plumbing, wall and floor finishes	+ 4230
Two Car Attached Garage	+ 21,916
Two Car Detached Garage	+ 25,336
Fireplace & Chimney	+ 5760

Adjustments

For multi family - add to total cost

Additional Kitchen	$ + 14,160
Additional Full Bath & Half Bath	+ 11,332
Additional Entry & Exit	+ 1640
Separate Heating & Air Conditioning	+ 6271
Separate Electric	+ 1915

**For Townhouse/Rowhouse -
Multiply cost per square foot by**

Inner Unit	+ .87
End Unit	+ .94

Alternatives

Add to or deduct from the cost per square foot of living area

Cedar Shake Roof	+ 2.50
Clay Tile Roof	+ 2.95
Slate Roof	+ 4.50
Upgrade Ceilings to Textured Finish	+ .48
Air Conditioning, in Heating Ductwork	Base System
Heating Systems, Hot Water	+ 1.99
Heat Pump	+ 3.22
Electric Heat	− 2.31
Not Heated	− 4.03

Additional upgrades or components

Kitchen Cabinets & Countertops	Page 77
Bathroom Vanities	78
Fireplaces & Chimneys	78
Windows, Skylights & Dormers	78
Appliances	79
Breezeways & Porches	79
Finished Attic	79
Garages	80
Site Improvements	80
Wings & Ells	60

		Cost Per Square Foot Of Living Area			% of Total
		Mat.	Inst.	Total	(roun
1 Site Work	Site preparation for slab; 4' deep trench excavation for foundation wall, excavation for lower level, 4' deep.		.53	.53	0.6%
2 Foundation	Continuous reinforced concrete footing 8" deep x 18" wide; dampproofed and insulated reinforced concrete foundation wall, 8" thick, 4' deep, 4" concrete slab on 4" crushed stone base and polyethylene vapor barrier, trowel finish.	3.91	4.72	8.63	9.6%
3 Framing	Exterior walls - 2" x 6" wood studs, 16" O.C.; 1/2" plywood sheathing; 2" x 8" rafters 16" O.C. with 1/2" plywood sheathing, 6 in 12 pitch; 2" x 8" ceiling joists 16" O.C.; 2" x 10" floor joists 16" O.C. with 5/8" plywood subfloor; 5/8" plywood subfloor on 1" x 3" wood sleepers 16" O.C.	3.58	6.31	9.89	11.0%
4 Exterior Walls	Horizontal beveled wood siding; building paper; 6" batt insulation; wood double hung windows; 3 solid core wood exterior doors; storms and screens.	7.88	2.73	10.61	11.8%
5 Roofing	30 year asphalt shingles; #15 felt building paper; aluminum gutters, downspouts and drip edge; copper flashings.	3.10	2.16	5.26	5.8%
6 Interiors	Walls and ceilings - 5/8" gypsum wallboard, skim coat plaster, painted with primer and 2 coats; hardwood baseboard and trim, sanded and finished; hardwood floor 70%, ceramic tile with underlayment 20%, vinyl tile with underlayment 10%; wood panel interior doors, primed and painted with 2 coats.	13.18	12.20	25.38	28.1%
7 Specialties	Custom grade kitchen cabinets - 20 L.F. wall and base with solid surface counter top and kitchen sink; 4 L.F. bathroom vanity; 75 gallon electric water heater, medicine cabinet.	3.79	.88	4.67	5.2%
8 Mechanical	Gas fired warm air heat/air conditioning; one full bath including: bathtub, corner shower, built in lavatory and water closet; one 1/2 bath including: built in lavatory and water closet.	4.89	2.70	7.59	8.4%
9 Electrical	200 Amp. service; romex wiring; fluorescent and incandescent lighting fixtures, switches, receptacles.	1.09	1.54	2.63	2.9%
10 Overhead	Contractor's overhead and profit and design.	8.28	6.73	15.01	16.6%
Total		49.70	40.50	**90.20**	

1 Story — Base cost per square foot of living area

Exterior Wall	Living Area							
	50	100	200	300	400	500	600	700
Wood Siding - Wood Frame	210.95	164.35	144.15	122.55	115.95	111.95	109.35	110.25
Brick Veneer - Wood Frame	235.90	182.20	159.05	132.55	124.95	120.35	117.35	117.90
Stone Veneer - Wood Frame	249.65	192.00	167.20	137.95	129.80	124.90	121.65	122.05
Solid Masonry	262.40	201.15	174.80	143.05	134.35	129.20	125.75	126.00
Finished Basement, Add	80.90	69.05	62.60	51.90	49.75	48.50	47.60	47.00
Unfinished Basement, Add	59.60	40.75	32.00	24.30	22.25	21.00	20.20	19.60

1-1/2 Story — Base cost per square foot of living area

Exterior Wall	Living Area							
	100	200	300	400	500	600	700	800
Wood Siding - Wood Frame	169.35	139.35	121.15	110.40	104.85	102.25	98.90	97.85
Brick Veneer - Wood Frame	191.65	157.25	136.05	122.05	115.60	112.45	108.45	107.35
Stone Veneer - Wood Frame	203.95	167.05	144.25	128.40	121.50	118.00	113.65	112.55
Solid Masonry	215.30	176.15	151.85	134.30	126.95	123.10	118.60	117.35
Finished Basement, Add	54.05	50.10	45.80	41.05	39.80	38.95	38.10	38.00
Unfinished Basement, Add	35.35	26.65	22.50	19.05	17.80	17.00	16.30	16.05

2 Story — Base cost per square foot of living area

Exterior Wall	Living Area							
	100	200	400	600	800	1000	1200	1400
Wood Siding - Wood Frame	168.45	129.20	112.00	95.55	89.95	86.60	84.40	85.55
Brick Veneer - Wood Frame	193.45	147.10	126.90	105.50	98.90	95.00	92.35	93.25
Stone Veneer - Wood Frame	207.20	156.85	135.10	110.95	103.80	99.50	96.70	97.45
Solid Masonry	219.95	166.00	142.65	116.10	108.40	103.80	100.75	101.35
Finished Basement, Add	40.45	34.55	31.35	26.00	24.95	24.25	23.90	23.55
Unfinished Basement, Add	29.85	20.35	16.00	12.15	11.10	10.55	10.10	9.85

Base costs do not include bathroom or kitchen facilities. Use Modifications/Adjustments/Alternatives on pages 77–80 where appropriate.

1 Story

1-1/2 Story

2 Story

2-1/2 Story

Bi-Level

Tri-Level

- **Unique residence built from an architect's plan**
- **Single family — 1 full bath, 1 half bath, 1 kitchen**
- **No basement**
- **Cedar shakes on roof**
- **Forced hot air heat/air conditioning**
- **Gypsum wallboard interior finishes**
- **Many special features**
- **Extraordinary materials and workmanship**

Note: The illustration shown may contain some optional components (for example: garages and/or fireplaces) whose costs are shown in the modifications, adjustments, & alternatives below or at the end of the square foot section.

©Home Planners, Inc.

Base cost per square foot of living area

Exterior Wall	Living Area										
	1000	1200	1400	1600	1800	2000	2400	2800	3200	3600	4000
Wood Siding - Wood Frame	185.40	170.80	159.15	151.00	146.60	141.40	131.70	124.80	119.85	114.85	110.75
Brick Veneer - Wood Frame	194.65	179.10	166.70	158.10	153.45	147.80	137.55	130.25	124.85	119.50	115.15
Solid Brick	210.80	193.70	179.90	170.60	165.45	159.10	147.90	139.70	133.65	127.75	122.80
Solid Stone	208.45	191.55	178.05	168.75	163.70	157.40	146.35	138.35	132.35	126.50	121.70
Finished Basement, Add	48.80	52.45	50.30	48.85	48.00	46.90	45.30	44.05	42.95	42.00	41.25
Unfinished Basement, Add	21.40	20.05	18.90	18.25	17.80	17.20	16.40	15.80	15.20	14.70	14.30

Modifications

Add to the total cost

Upgrade Kitchen Cabinets	$ + 1462
Solid Surface Countertops (Included)	
Full Bath - including plumbing, wall and floor finishes	+ 8238
Half Bath - including plumbing, wall and floor finishes	+ 4907
Two Car Attached Garage	+ 26,381
Two Car Detached Garage	+ 30,256
Fireplace & Chimney	+ 8141

Adjustments

For multi family - add to total cost

Additional Kitchen	$ + 18,138
Additional Full Bath & Half Bath	+ 13,145
Additional Entry & Exit	+ 2342
Separate Heating & Air Conditioning	+ 6271
Separate Electric	+ 1915

For Townhouse/Rowhouse - Multiply cost per square foot by

Inner Unit	+ .90
End Unit	+ .95

Alternatives

Add to or deduct from the cost per square foot of living area

Heavyweight Asphalt Shingles	– 3.45
Clay Tile Roof	+ .65
Slate Roof	+ 2.75
Upgrade Ceilings to Textured Finish	+ .48
Air Conditioning, in Heating Ductwork	Base System
Heating Systems, Hot Water	+ 2.39
Heat Pump	+ 2.86
Electric Heat	– 2.60
Not Heated	– 5.21

Additional upgrades or components

Kitchen Cabinets & Countertops	Page 77
Bathroom Vanities	78
Fireplaces & Chimneys	78
Windows, Skylights & Dormers	78
Appliances	79
Breezeways & Porches	79
Finished Attic	79
Garages	80
Site Improvements	80
Wings & Ells	76

		Cost Per Square Foot Of Living Area			% of Total
		Mat.	**Inst.**	**Total**	(roun
1 Site Work	Site preparation for slab; 4' deep trench excavation for foundation wall.		.66	.66	0.5%
2 Foundation	Continuous reinforced concrete footing 8" deep x 18" wide; dampproofed and insulated reinforced concrete foundation wall, 12" thick, 4' deep, 4" concrete slab on 4" crushed stone base and polyethylene vapor barrier, trowel finish.	6.60	6.97	13.57	10.9%
3 Framing	Exterior walls - 2" x 6" wood studs, 16" O.C.; 5/8" plywood sheathing; 2" x 10" rafters 16" O.C. with 5/8" plywood sheathing, 6 in 12 pitch; 2" x 8" ceiling joists 16" O.C.; 5/8" plywood subfloor on 1" x 3" wood sleepers 16" O.C.	7.94	12.74	20.68	16.6%
4 Exterior Walls	Horizontal beveled wood siding; building paper; 6" batt insulation; wood double hung windows; 3 solid core wood exterior doors; storms and screens.	9.17	3.04	12.21	9.8%
5 Roofing	Red cedar shingles; #15 felt building paper; aluminum gutters, downspouts and drip edge; copper flashings.	5.45	3.80	9.25	7.4%
6 Interiors	Walls and ceilings - 5/8" gypsum wallboard, skim coat plaster, painted with primer and 2 coats; hardwood baseboard and trim, sanded and finished; hardwood floor 70%, ceramic tile with underlayment 20%, vinyl tile with underlayment 10%; wood panel interior doors, primed and painted with 2 coats.	11.91	12.93	24.84	19.9%
7 Specialties	Luxury grade kitchen cabinets - 25 L.F. wall and base with solid surface counter top and kitchen sink; 6 L.F. bathroom vanity; 75 gallon electric water heater; medicine cabinet.	5.60	1.29	6.89	5.5%
8 Mechanical	Gas fired warm air heat/air conditioning; one full bath including: bathtub, corner shower; built in lavatory and water closet; one 1/2 bath including: built in lavatory and water closet.	6.17	3.12	9.29	7.4%
9 Electrical	200 Amp. service; romex wiring; fluorescent and incandescent lighting fixtures; intercom, switches, receptacles.	1.34	1.91	3.25	2.6%
10 Overhead	Contractor's overhead and profit and architect's fees.	13.02	11.14	24.16	19.4%
	Total	67.20	57.60	**124.80**	

- **Unique residence built from an architect's plan**
- **Single family — 1 full bath, 1 half bath, 1 kitchen**
- **No basement**
- **Cedar shakes on roof**
- **Forced hot air heat/air conditioning**
- **Gypsum wallboard interior finishes**
- **Many special features**
- **Extraordinary materials and workmanship**

Note: The illustration shown may contain some optional components (for example: garages and/or fireplaces) whose costs are shown in the modifications, adjustments, & alternatives below or at the end of the square foot section.

©Larry E. Belk Designs

Base cost per square foot of living area

Exterior Wall	Living Area										
	1000	1200	1400	1600	1800	2000	2400	2800	3200	3600	4000
Wood Siding - Wood Frame	172.45	159.95	151.00	140.65	134.60	128.70	117.65	112.65	107.80	104.25	99.30
Brick Veneer - Wood Frame	183.10	169.95	160.55	149.25	142.80	136.50	124.55	119.15	113.85	110.05	104.70
Solid Brick	201.80	187.50	177.25	164.50	157.20	150.20	136.65	130.60	124.40	120.30	114.15
Solid Stone	199.05	184.95	174.75	162.20	155.10	148.15	134.85	128.90	122.85	118.80	112.75
Finished Basement, Add	34.35	37.30	36.10	34.50	33.55	32.75	31.05	30.30	29.30	28.85	28.15
Unfinished Basement, Add	15.55	14.75	14.25	13.40	12.95	12.55	11.65	11.30	10.75	10.55	10.15

Modifications

Add to the total cost

Upgrade Kitchen Cabinets	$ + 1462
Solid Surface Countertops (Included)	
Full Bath - including plumbing, wall and floor finishes	+ 8238
Half Bath - including plumbing, wall and floor finishes	+ 4907
Two Car Attached Garage	+ 26,381
Two Car Detached Garage	+ 30,256
Fireplace & Chimney	+ 8141

Adjustments

For multi family - add to total cost

Additional Kitchen	$ + 18,138
Additional Full Bath & Half Bath	+ 13,145
Additional Entry & Exit	+ 2342
Separate Heating & Air Conditioning	+ 6271
Separate Electric	+ 1915

*For Townhouse/Rowhouse -
Multiply cost per square foot by*

Inner Unit	+ .90
End Unit	+ .95

Alternatives

Add to or deduct from the cost per square foot of living area

Heavyweight Asphalt Shingles	– 2.85
Clay Tile Roof	+ .50
Slate Roof	+ 2
Upgrade Ceilings to Textured Finish	+ .48
Air Conditioning, in Heating Ductwork	Base System
Heating Systems, Hot Water	+ 2.27
Heat Pump	+ 3.17
Electric Heat	– 2.60
Not Heated	– 4.80

Additional upgrades or components

Kitchen Cabinets & Countertops	Page 77
Bathroom Vanities	78
Fireplaces & Chimneys	78
Windows, Skylights & Dormers	78
Appliances	79
Breezeways & Porches	79
Finished Attic	79
Garages	80
Site Improvements	80
Wings & Ells	76

			Cost Per Square Foot Of Living Area			% of Total
			Mat.	Inst.	Total	(roun
1	**Site Work**	Site preparation for slab; 4' deep trench excavation for foundation wall.		.66	.66	0.6%
2	**Foundation**	Continuous reinforced concrete footing 8" deep x 18" wide; dampproofed and insulated reinforced concrete foundation wall, 12" thick, 4' deep, 4" concrete slab on 4" crushed stone base and polyethylene vapor barrier, trowel finish.	4.76	5.26	10.02	8.9%
3	**Framing**	Exterior walls - 2" x 6" wood studs, 16" O.C.; 5/8" plywood sheathing; 2" x 10" rafters 16" O.C. with 5/8" plywood sheathing, 8 in 12 pitch; 2" x 8" ceiling joists 16" O.C.; 2" x 12" floor joists 16" O.C. with 5/8" plywood subfloor; 5/8" plywood subfloor on 1" x 3" wood sleepers 16" O.C.	4.73	8.28	13.01	11.5%
4	**Exterior Walls**	Horizontal beveled wood siding; building paper; 6" batt insulation; wood double hung windows; 3 solid core wood exterior doors; storms and screens.	10.17	3.42	13.59	12.1%
5	**Roofing**	Red cedar shingles; #15 felt building paper; aluminum gutters, downspouts and drip edge; copper flashings.	3.40	2.37	5.77	5.1%
6	**Interiors**	Walls and ceilings - 5/8" gypsum wallboard, skim coat plaster, painted with primer and 2 coats; hardwood baseboard and trim, sanded and finished; hardwood floor 70%, ceramic tile with underlayment 20%, vinyl tile with underlayment 10%; wood panel interior doors, primed and painted with 2 coats.	13.69	14.64	28.33	25.1%
7	**Specialties**	Luxury grade kitchen cabinets - 25 L.F. wall and base with solid surface counter top and kitchen sink; 6 L.F. bathroom vanity; 75 gallon electric water heater; medicine cabinet.	5.60	1.29	6.89	6.1%
8	**Mechanical**	Gas fired warm air heat/air conditioning; one full bath including: bathtub, corner shower; built in lavatory and water closet; one 1/2 bath including: built in lavatory and water closet.	6.17	3.12	9.29	8.2%
9	**Electrical**	200 Amp. service; romex wiring; fluorescent and incandescent lighting fixtures; intercom, switches, receptacles.	1.34	1.91	3.25	2.9%
10	**Overhead**	Contractor's overhead and profit and architect's fees.	11.99	9.85	21.84	19.4%
	Total		61.85	50.80	**112.65**	

- **Unique residence built from an architect's plan**
- **Single family — 1 full bath, 1 half bath, 1 kitchen**
- **No basement**
- **Cedar shakes on roof**
- **Forced hot air heat/air conditioning**
- **Gypsum wallboard interior finishes**
- **Many special features**
- **Extraordinary materials and workmanship**

Note: The illustration shown may contain some optional components (for example: garages and/or fireplaces) whose costs are shown in the modifications, adjustments, & alternatives below or at the end of the square foot section.

Base cost per square foot of living area

Exterior Wall	Living Area										
	1200	1400	1600	1800	2000	2400	2800	3200	3600	4000	4400
Wood Siding - Wood Frame	159.45	149.60	142.50	136.45	129.95	120.50	112.65	107.30	104.25	100.90	98.05
Brick Veneer - Wood Frame	170.85	160.25	152.65	146.00	139.15	128.80	120.20	114.40	111.05	107.30	104.25
Solid Brick	190.90	178.95	170.50	162.80	155.40	143.40	133.50	126.85	123.10	118.65	115.25
Solid Stone	187.95	176.15	167.90	160.35	153.00	141.25	131.55	125.05	121.35	116.90	113.55
Finished Basement, Add	27.65	29.95	29.10	28.15	27.60	26.30	25.15	24.45	24.10	23.50	23.15
Unfinished Basement, Add	12.45	11.85	11.50	11.00	10.75	10.00	9.50	9.15	8.95	8.60	8.40

Modifications

Add to the total cost

Upgrade Kitchen Cabinets	$ + 1462
Solid Surface Countertops (Included)	
Full Bath - including plumbing, wall and floor finishes	+ 8238
Half Bath - including plumbing, wall and floor finishes	+ 4907
Two Car Attached Garage	+ 26,381
Two Car Detached Garage	+ 30,256
Fireplace & Chimney	+ 8924

Adjustments

For multi family - add to total cost

Additional Kitchen	$ + 18,138
Additional Full Bath & Half Bath	+ 13,145
Additional Entry & Exit	+ 2342
Separate Heating & Air Conditioning	+ 6271
Separate Electric	+ 1915

For Townhouse/Rowhouse - Multiply cost per square foot by

Inner Unit	+ .86
End Unit	+ .93

Alternatives

Add to or deduct from the cost per square foot of living area

Heavyweight Asphalt Shingles	– 1.70
Clay Tile Roof	+ .35
Slate Roof	+ 1.40
Upgrade Ceilings to Textured Finish	+ .48
Air Conditioning, in Heating Ductwork	Base System
Heating Systems, Hot Water	+ 2.21
Heat Pump	+ 3.34
Electric Heat	– 2.34
Not Heated	– 4.54

Additional upgrades or components

Kitchen Cabinets & Countertops	Page 77
Bathroom Vanities	78
Fireplaces & Chimneys	78
Windows, Skylights & Dormers	78
Appliances	79
Breezeways & Porches	79
Finished Attic	79
Garages	80
Site Improvements	80
Wings & Ells	76

Luxury 2 Story

Living Area - 3200 S.F.
Perimeter - 163 L.F.

			Cost Per Square Foot Of Living Area			% of Total
			Mat.	Inst.	Total	(roun
1	**Site Work**	Site preparation for slab; 4' deep trench excavation for foundation wall.		.58	.58	0.5%
2	**Foundation**	Continuous reinforced concrete footing 8" deep x 18" wide; dampproofed and insulated reinforced concrete foundation wall, 12" thick, 4' deep, 4" concrete slab on 4" crushed stone base and polyethylene vapor barrier, trowel finish.	3.85	4.27	8.12	7.6%
3	**Framing**	Exterior walls - 2" x 6" wood studs, 16" O.C.; 5/8" plywood sheathing; 2" x 10" rafters 16" O.C. with 5/8" plywood sheathing, 6 in 12 pitch; 2" x 8" ceiling joists 16" O.C.; 2" x 12" floor joists 16" O.C. with 5/8" plywood subfloor; 5/8" plywood subfloor on 1" x 3" wood sleepers 16" O.C.	4.81	8.19	13.00	12.1%
4	**Exterior Walls**	Horizontal beveled wood siding, building paper; 6" batt insulation; wood double hung windows; 3 solid core wood exterior doors; storms and screens.	10.78	3.65	14.43	13.4%
5	**Roofing**	Red cedar shingles; #15 felt building paper; aluminum gutters, downspouts and drip edge; copper flashings.	2.72	1.90	4.62	4.3%
6	**Interiors**	Walls and ceilings - 5/8" gypsum wallboard, skim coat plaster, painted with primer and 2 coats; hardwood baseboard and trim, sanded and finished; hardwood floor 70%, ceramic tile with underlayment 20%, vinyl tile with underlayment 10%; wood panel interior doors, primed and painted with 2 coats.	13.48	14.57	28.05	26.1%
7	**Specialties**	Luxury grade kitchen cabinets - 25 L.F. wall and base with solid surface counter top and kitchen sink; 6 L.F. bathroom vanity; 75 gallon electric water heater; medicine cabinet.	4.90	1.10	6.00	5.6%
8	**Mechanical**	Gas fired warm air heat/air conditioning; one full bath including: bathtub, corner shower; built in lavatory and water closet; one 1/2 bath including: built in lavatory and water closet.	5.57	3.00	8.57	8.0%
9	**Electrical**	200 Amp. service; romex wiring; fluorescent and incandescent lighting fixtures; intercom, switches, receptacles.	1.31	1.85	3.16	2.9%
10	**Overhead**	Contractor's overhead and profit and architect's fee.	11.38	9.39	20.77	19.4%
	Total		58.80	48.50	**107.30**	

- **Unique residence built from an architect's plan**
- **Single family — 1 full bath, 1 half bath, 1 kitchen**
- **No basement**
- **Cedar shakes on roof**
- **Forced hot air heat/air conditioning**
- **Gypsum wallboard interior finishes**
- **Many special features**
- **Extraordinary materials and workmanship**

Note: The illustration shown may contain some optional components (for example: garages and/or fireplaces) whose costs are shown in the modifications, adjustments, & alternatives below or at the end of the square foot section.

©Larry W. Garnett & Associates, Inc

Base cost per square foot of living area

Exterior Wall	Living Area										
	1500	1800	2100	2500	3000	3500	4000	4500	5000	5500	6000
Wood Siding - Wood Frame	155.05	139.30	129.95	123.10	113.75	106.95	100.45	97.40	94.45	91.60	88.60
Brick Veneer - Wood Frame	166.90	150.25	139.70	132.30	122.10	114.55	107.50	104.05	100.80	97.65	94.40
Solid Brick	187.70	169.40	156.90	148.50	136.80	127.90	119.85	115.80	112.00	108.30	104.60
Solid Stone	184.65	166.60	154.25	146.10	134.65	126.00	118.05	114.05	110.30	106.70	103.15
Finished Basement, Add	22.05	23.75	22.40	21.65	20.60	19.70	19.05	18.65	18.30	17.90	17.65
Unfinished Basement, Add	10.05	9.50	8.80	8.45	7.90	7.45	7.15	6.95	6.75	6.55	6.40

Modifications

Add to the total cost

Upgrade Kitchen Cabinets	$ + 1462
Solid Surface Countertops (Included)	
Full Bath - including plumbing, wall and floor finishes	+ 8238
Half Bath - including plumbing, wall and floor finishes	+ 4907
Two Car Attached Garage	+ 26,381
Two Car Detached Garage	+ 30,256
Fireplace & Chimney	+ 9765

Adjustments

For multi family - add to total cost

Additional Kitchen	$ + 18,138
Additional Full Bath & Half Bath	+ 13,145
Additional Entry & Exit	+ 2342
Separate Heating & Air Conditioning	+ 6271
Separate Electric	+ 1915

**For Townhouse/Rowhouse -
Multiply cost per square foot by**

Inner Unit	+ .86
End Unit	+ .93

Alternatives

Add to or deduct from the cost per square foot of living area

Heavyweight Asphalt Shingles	– 1.50
Clay Tile Roof	+ .30
Slate Roof	+ 1.20
Upgrade Ceilings to Textured Finish	+ .48
Air Conditioning, in Heating Ductwork	Base System
Heating Systems, Hot Water	+ 2
Heat Pump	+ 3.44
Electric Heat	– 4.60
Not Heated	– 4.54

Additional upgrades or components

Kitchen Cabinets & Countertops	Page 77
Bathroom Vanities	78
Fireplaces & Chimneys	78
Windows, Skylights & Dormers	78
Appliances	79
Breezeways & Porches	79
Finished Attic	79
Garages	80
Site Improvements	80
Wings & Ells	76

Luxury 2-1/2 Story

Living Area - 3000 S.F.
Perimeter - 148 L.F.

			Cost Per Square Foot Of Living Area			% of Total
			Mat.	Inst.	Total	(roun
1	**Site Work**	Site preparation for slab; 4' deep trench excavation for foundation wall.		.61	.61	0.5%
2	**Foundation**	Continuous reinforced concrete footing 8" deep x 18" wide; dampproofed and insulated reinforced concrete foundation wall, 12" thick, 4' deep, 4" concrete slab on 4" crushed stone base and polyethylene vapor barrier, trowel finish.	3.38	3.88	7.26	6.4%
3	**Framing**	Exterior walls - 2" x 6" wood studs, 16" O.C.; 5/8" plywood sheathing; 2" x 10" rafters 16" O.C. with 5/8" plywood sheathing, 8 in 12 pitch; 2" x 8" ceiling joists 16" O.C.; 2" x 12" floor joists 16" O.C. with 5/8" plywood subfloor; 5/8" plywood subfloor on 1" x 3" wood sleepers 16" O.C.	5.00	8.48	13.48	11.9%
4	**Exterior Walls**	Horizontal beveled wood siding; building paper; 6" batt insulation; wood double hung windows; 3 solid core wood exterior doors; storms and screens.	12.57	4.23	16.80	14.8%
5	**Roofing**	Red cedar shingles; #15 felt building paper; aluminum gutters, downspouts and drip edge; copper flashings.	2.09	1.46	3.55	3.1%
6	**Interiors**	Walls and ceilings - 5/8" gypsum wallboard, skim coat plaster, painted with primer and 2 coats; hardwood baseboard and trim, sanded and finished; hardwood floor 70%, ceramic tile with underlayment 20%, vinyl tile with underlayment 10%; wood panel interior doors, primed and painted with 2 coats.	15.28	16.23	31.51	27.7%
7	**Specialties**	Luxury grade kitchen cabinets - 25 L.F. wall and base with solid surface counter top and kitchen sink; 6 L.F. bathroom vanity; 75 gallon electric water heater; medicine cabinet.	5.22	1.18	6.40	5.6%
8	**Mechanical**	Gas fired warm air heat/air conditioning; one full bath including: bathtub, corner shower; built in lavatory and water closet; one 1/2 bath including: built in lavatory and water closet.	5.87	3.05	8.92	7.8%
9	**Electrical**	200 Amp. service; romex wiring; fluorescent and incandescent lighting fixtures; intercom, switches, receptacles.	1.32	1.87	3.19	2.8%
10	**Overhead**	Contractor's overhead and profit and architect's fee.	12.17	9.86	22.03	19.4%
	Total		62.90	50.85	113.75	

- **Unique residence built from an architect's plan**
- **Single family — 1 full bath, 1 half bath, 1 kitchen**
- **No basement**
- **Cedar shakes on roof**
- **Forced hot air heat/air conditioning**
- **Gypsum wallboard interior finishes**
- **Many special features**
- **Extraordinary materials and workmanship**

Note: The illustration shown may contain some optional components (for example: garages and/or fireplaces) whose costs are shown in the modifications, adjustments, & alternatives below or at the end of the square foot section.

Base cost per square foot of living area

Exterior Wall	Living Area										
	1500	1800	2100	2500	3000	3500	4000	4500	5000	5500	6000
Wood Siding - Wood Frame	153.95	138.35	130.60	124.15	114.55	109.65	103.70	97.65	95.30	92.90	90.45
Brick Veneer - Wood Frame	166.25	149.75	141.25	134.35	123.75	118.35	111.65	105.00	102.40	99.75	96.90
Solid Brick	187.85	169.75	159.95	152.15	140.00	133.70	125.55	117.85	114.85	111.70	108.20
Solid Stone	184.60	166.80	157.15	149.55	137.55	131.40	123.55	115.95	113.05	110.00	106.50
Finished Basement, Add	19.35	20.80	19.95	19.35	18.40	17.85	17.10	16.50	16.25	16.00	15.60
Unfinished Basement, Add	8.85	8.30	7.90	7.60	7.15	6.85	6.55	6.15	6.10	5.95	5.75

Modifications

Add to the total cost

Upgrade Kitchen Cabinets	$ + 1462
Solid Surface Countertops (Included)	
Full Bath - including plumbing, wall and floor finishes	+ 8238
Half Bath - including plumbing, wall and floor finishes	+ 4907
Two Car Attached Garage	+ 26,381
Two Car Detached Garage	+ 30,256
Fireplace & Chimney	+ 9765

Adjustments

For multi family - add to total cost

Additional Kitchen	$ + 18,138
Additional Full Bath & Half Bath	+ 13,145
Additional Entry & Exit	+ 2342
Separate Heating & Air Conditioning	+ 6271
Separate Electric	+ 1915

For Townhouse/Rowhouse - Multiply cost per square foot by

Inner Unit	+ .84
End Unit	+ .92

Alternatives

Add to or deduct from the cost per square foot of living area

Heavyweight Asphalt Shingles	− 1.15
Clay Tile Roof	+ .20
Slate Roof	+ .90
Upgrade Ceilings to Textured Finish	+ .48
Air Conditioning, in Heating Ductwork	Base System
Heating Systems, Hot Water	+ 2
Heat Pump	+ 3.44
Electric Heat	− 4.60
Not Heated	− 4.40

Additional upgrades or components

Kitchen Cabinets & Countertops	Page 77
Bathroom Vanities	78
Fireplaces & Chimneys	78
Windows, Skylights & Dormers	78
Appliances	79
Breezeways & Porches	79
Finished Attic	79
Garages	80
Site Improvements	80
Wings & Ells	76

Important: See the Reference Section for Location Factors (to adjust for your city) and Estimating Forms

			Cost Per Square Foot Of Living Area			% of Total
			Mat.	Inst.	Total	(roun
1	**Site Work**	Site preparation for slab; 4' deep trench excavation for foundation wall.		.61	.61	0.5%
2	**Foundation**	Continuous reinforced concrete footing 8" deep x 18" wide; dampproofed and insulated reinforced concrete foundation wall, 12" thick, 4' deep, 4" concrete slab on 4" crushed stone base and polyethylene vapor barrier, trowel finish.	3.04	3.52	6.56	5.7%
3	**Framing**	Exterior walls - 2" x 6" wood studs, 16" O.C.; 5/8" plywood sheathing; 2" x 10" rafters 16" O.C. with 5/8" plywood sheathing, 6 in 12 pitch; 2" x 8" ceiling joists 16" O.C.; 2" x 12" floor joists 16" O.C. with 5/8" plywood subfloor; 5/8" plywood subfloor on 1" x 3" wood sleepers 16" O.C.	5.10	8.54	13.64	11.9%
4	**Exterior Walls**	Horizontal beveled wood siding; building paper; 6" batt insulation; wood double hung windows; 3 solid core wood exterior doors; storms and screens.	13.69	4.65	18.34	16.0%
5	**Roofing**	Red cedar shingles; #15 felt building paper; aluminum gutters, downspouts and drip edge; copper flashings.	1.82	1.27	3.09	2.7%
6	**Interiors**	Walls and ceilings - 5/8" gypsum wallboard, skim coat plaster, painted with primer and 2 coats; hardwood baseboard and trim, sanded and finished; hardwood floor 70%, ceramic tile with underlayment 20%, vinyl tile with underlayment 10%; wood panel interior doors, primed and painted with 2 coats.	15.29	16.34	31.63	27.6%
7	**Specialties**	Luxury grade kitchen cabinets - 25 L.F. wall and base with solid surface counter top and kitchen sink; 6 L.F. bathroom vanity; 75 gallon electric water heater; medicine cabinet.	5.22	1.18	6.40	5.6%
8	**Mechanical**	Gas fired warm air heat/air conditioning; one full bath including: bathtub, corner shower; built in lavatory and water closet; one 1/2 bath including: built in lavatory and water closet.	5.87	3.05	8.92	7.8%
9	**Electrical**	200 Amp. service; romex wiring; fluorescent and incandescent lighting fixtures; intercom, switches, receptacles.	1.32	1.87	3.19	2.8%
10	**Overhead**	Contractor's overhead and profit and architect's fees.	12.30	9.87	22.17	19.4%
	Total		63.65	50.90	**114.55**	

- **Unique residence built from an architect's plan**
- **Single family — 1 full bath, 1 half bath, 1 kitchen**
- **No basement**
- **Cedar shakes on roof**
- **Forced hot air heat/air conditioning**
- **Gypsum wallboard interior finishes**
- **Many special features**
- **Extraordinary materials and workmanship**

Note: The illustration shown may contain some optional components (for example: garages and/or fireplaces) whose costs are shown in the modifications, adjustments, & alternatives below or at the end of the square foot section.

Base cost per square foot of living area

Exterior Wall	Living Area										
	1200	1400	1600	1800	2000	2400	2800	3200	3600	4000	4400
Wood Siding - Wood Frame	150.85	141.60	134.85	129.20	123.05	114.15	106.85	101.85	99.05	96.05	93.40
Brick Veneer - Wood Frame	159.40	149.55	142.45	136.35	129.95	120.40	112.55	107.20	104.20	100.85	98.05
Solid Brick	174.40	163.55	155.85	148.95	142.10	131.30	122.55	116.55	113.25	109.25	106.20
Solid Stone	172.20	161.50	153.90	147.15	140.30	129.70	121.05	115.20	111.85	108.05	105.00
Finished Basement, Add	27.65	29.95	29.10	28.15	27.60	26.30	25.15	24.45	24.10	23.50	23.15
Unfinished Basement, Add	12.45	11.85	11.50	11.00	10.75	10.00	9.50	9.15	8.95	8.60	8.40

Modifications

Add to the total cost

Upgrade Kitchen Cabinets	$ + 1462
Solid Surface Countertops (Included)	
Full Bath - including plumbing, wall and floor finishes	+ 8238
Half Bath - including plumbing, wall and floor finishes	+ 4907
Two Car Attached Garage	+ 26,381
Two Car Detached Garage	+ 30,256
Fireplace & Chimney	+ 8141

Adjustments

For multi family - add to total cost

Additional Kitchen	$ + 18,138
Additional Full Bath & Half Bath	+ 13,145
Additional Entry & Exit	+ 2342
Separate Heating & Air Conditioning	+ 6271
Separate Electric	+ 1915

*For Townhouse/Rowhouse -
Multiply cost per square foot by*

Inner Unit	+ .89
End Unit	+ .94

Alternatives

Add to or deduct from the cost per square foot of living area

Heavyweight Asphalt Shingles	– 1.70
Clay Tile Roof	+ .35
Slate Roof	+ 1.40
Upgrade Ceilings to Textured Finish	+ .48
Air Conditioning, in Heating Ductwork	Base System
Heating Systems, Hot Water	+ 2.21
Heat Pump	+ 3.34
Electric Heat	– 2.34
Not Heated	– 4.54

Additional upgrades or components

Kitchen Cabinets & Countertops	Page 77
Bathroom Vanities	78
Fireplaces & Chimneys	78
Windows, Skylights & Dormers	78
Appliances	79
Breezeways & Porches	79
Finished Attic	79
Garages	80
Site Improvements	80
Wings & Ells	76

Important: See the Reference Section for Location Factors (to adjust for your city) and Estimating Form

			Cost Per Square Foot Of Living Area			% of Total
			Mat.	Inst.	Total	(roun
1	**Site Work**	Excavation for lower level, 4' deep. Site preparation for slab.		.58	.58	0.6%
2	**Foundation**	Continuous reinforced concrete footing 8" deep x 18" wide; dampproofed and insulated reinforced concrete foundation wall, 12" thick, 4' deep, 4" concrete slab on 4" crushed stone base and polyethylene vapor barrier, trowel finish.	3.85	4.27	8.12	8.0%
3	**Framing**	Exterior walls - 2" x 6" wood studs, 16" O.C.; 5/8" plywood sheathing; 2" x 10" rafters 16" O.C. with 5/8" plywood sheathing, 6 in 12 pitch; 2" x 8" ceiling joists 16" O.C.; 2" x 12" floor joists 16" O.C. with 5/8" plywood subfloor; 5/8" plywood subfloor on 1" x 3" wood sleepers 16" O.C.	4.60	7.80	12.40	12.2%
4	**Exterior Walls**	Horizontal beveled wood siding; building paper; 6" batt insulation; wood double hung windows; 3 solid core wood exterior doors; storms and screens.	8.40	2.80	11.20	11.0%
5	**Roofing**	Red cedar shingles: #15 felt building paper; aluminum gutters, downspouts and drip edge; copper flashings.	2.72	1.90	4.62	4.5%
6	**Interiors**	Walls and ceilings - 5/8" gypsum wallboard, skim coat plaster, painted with primer and 2 coats; hardwood baseboard and trim, sanded and finished; hardwood floor 70%, ceramic tile with underlayment 20%; vinyl tile with underlayment 10%; wood panel interior doors, primed and painted with 2 coats.	13.30	14.22	27.52	27.0%
7	**Specialties**	Luxury grade kitchen cabinets - 25 L.F. wall and base with solid surface counter top and kitchen sink; 6 L.F. bathroom vanity; 75 gallon electric water heater; medicine cabinet.	4.90	1.10	6.00	5.9%
8	**Mechanical**	Gas fired warm air heat/air conditioning; one full bath including: bathtub, corner shower; built in lavatory and water closet; one 1/2 bath including: built in lavatory and water closet.	5.57	3.00	8.57	8.4%
9	**Electrical**	200 Amp. service; romex wiring; fluorescent and incandescent lighting fixtures; intercom, switches, receptacles.	1.31	1.85	3.16	3.1%
10	**Overhead**	Contractor's overhead and profit and architect's fees.	10.70	8.98	19.68	19.3%
	Total		55.35	46.50	**101.85**	

- **Unique residence built from an architect's plan**
- **Single family — 1 full bath, 1 half bath, 1 kitchen**
- **No basement**
- **Cedar shakes on roof**
- **Forced hot air heat/air conditioning**
- **Gypsum wallboard interior finishes**
- **Many special features**
- **Extraordinary materials and workmanship**

Note: The illustration shown may contain some optional components (for example: garages and/or fireplaces) whose costs are shown in the modifications, adjustments, & alternatives below or at the end of the square foot section.

©Home Planners, Inc.

Base cost per square foot of living area

Exterior Wall	Living Area										
	1500	1800	2100	2400	2800	3200	3600	4000	4500	5000	5500
Wood Siding - Wood Frame	142.05	131.05	121.95	115.95	111.55	106.30	100.95	98.60	93.55	90.65	87.60
Brick Veneer - Wood Frame	149.75	138.00	128.30	121.85	117.25	111.60	105.85	103.35	97.90	94.80	91.50
Solid Brick	163.25	150.15	139.40	132.25	127.20	120.85	114.40	111.70	105.55	102.00	98.30
Solid Stone	161.25	148.30	137.75	130.75	125.70	119.50	113.10	110.45	104.45	100.90	97.30
Finished Basement, Add*	32.50	35.00	33.50	32.60	32.00	31.10	30.20	29.85	29.05	28.50	28.05
Unfinished Basement, Add*	14.25	13.35	12.65	12.20	11.85	11.35	10.95	10.75	10.30	10.05	9.80

*Basement under middle level only.

Modifications

Add to the total cost

Upgrade Kitchen Cabinets	$ + 1462
Solid Surface Countertops (Included)	
Full Bath - including plumbing, wall and floor finishes	+ 8238
Half Bath - including plumbing, wall and floor finishes	+ 4907
Two Car Attached Garage	+ 26,381
Two Car Detached Garage	+ 30,256
Fireplace & Chimney	+ 8141

Adjustments

For multi family - add to total cost

Additional Kitchen	$ + 18,138
Additional Full Bath & Half Bath	+ 13,145
Additional Entry & Exit	+ 2342
Separate Heating & Air Conditioning	+ 6271
Separate Electric	+ 1915

**For Townhouse/Rowhouse -
Multiply cost per square foot by**

Inner Unit	+ .86
End Unit	+ .93

Alternatives

Add to or deduct from the cost per square foot of living area

Heavyweight Asphalt Shingles	– 2.50
Clay Tile Roof	+ .50
Slate Roof	+ 2
Upgrade Ceilings to Textured Finish	+ .48
Air Conditioning, in Heating Ductwork	Base System
Heating Systems, Hot Water	+ 2.15
Heat Pump	+ 3.48
Electric Heat	– 2.06
Not Heated	– 4.40

Additional upgrades or components

Kitchen Cabinets & Countertops	Page 77
Bathroom Vanities	78
Fireplaces & Chimneys	78
Windows, Skylights & Dormers	78
Appliances	79
Breezeways & Porches	79
Finished Attic	79
Garages	80
Site Improvements	80
Wings & Ells	76

Important: See the Reference Section for Location Factors (to adjust for your city) and Estimating Form

			Cost Per Square Foot Of Living Area			% of Total
			Mat.	Inst.	Total	(roun
1	**Site Work**	Site preparation for slab; 4' deep trench excavation for foundation wall, excavation for lower level, 4' deep.		.51	.51	0.5%
2	**Foundation**	Continuous reinforced concrete footing 8" deep x 18" wide; dampproofed and insulated reinforced concrete foundation wall, 12" thick, 4' deep, 4" concrete slab on 4" crushed stone base and polyethylene vapor barrier, trowel finish.	4.59	4.92	9.51	9.4%
3	**Framing**	Exterior walls - 2" x 6" wood studs, 16" O.C.; 5/8" plywood sheathing; 2" x 10" rafters 16" O.C. with 5/8" plywood sheathing, 6 in 12 pitch; 2" x 8" ceiling joists 16" O.C.; 2" x 12" floor joists 16" O.C. with 5/8" plywood subfloor; 5/8" plywood subfloor on 1" x 3" wood sleepers 16" O.C.	4.48	7.83	12.31	12.2%
4	**Exterior Walls**	Horizontal beveled wood siding; building paper; 6" batt insulation; wood double hung windows; 3 solid core wood exterior doors; storms and screens.	8.05	2.68	10.73	10.6%
5	**Roofing**	Red cedar shingles; #15 felt building paper; aluminum gutters, downspouts and drip edge; copper flashings.	3.63	2.53	6.16	6.1%
6	**Interiors**	Walls and ceilings - 5/8" gypsum wallboard, skim coat plaster, painted with primer and 2 coats; hardwood baseboard and trim, sanded and finished; hardwood floor 70%, ceramic tile with underlayment 20%, vinyl tile with underlayment 10%; wood panel interior doors, primed and painted with 2 coats.	12.44	13.30	25.74	25.5%
7	**Specialties**	Luxury grade kitchen cabinets - 25 L.F. wall and base with solid surface counter top and kitchen sink; 6 L.F. bathroom vanity; 75 gallon electric water heater; medicine cabinet.	4.37	.99	5.36	5.3%
8	**Mechanical**	Gas fired warm air heat/air conditioning; one full bath including: bathtub, corner shower; built in lavatory and water closet; one 1/2 bath including: built in lavatory and water closet.	5.12	2.88	8.00	7.9%
9	**Electrical**	200 Amp. service; romex wiring; fluorescent and incandescent lighting fixtures; intercom, switches, receptacles.	1.26	1.81	3.07	3.0%
10	**Overhead**	Contractor's overhead and profit and architect's fees.	10.56	9.00	19.56	19.4%
	Total		54.50	46.45	**100.95**	

1 Story — Base cost per square foot of living area

Exterior Wall	Living Area							
	50	100	200	300	400	500	600	700
Wood Siding - Wood Frame	229.75	176.80	153.85	129.05	121.60	117.00	114.00	114.95
Brick Veneer - Wood Frame	258.50	197.30	170.95	140.45	131.85	126.60	123.15	123.75
Solid Brick	308.95	233.30	200.90	160.45	149.80	143.35	139.15	139.15
Solid Stone	301.50	228.00	196.50	157.55	147.20	140.90	136.80	136.85
Finished Basement, Add	87.35	79.10	70.90	57.25	54.60	52.90	51.85	51.05
Unfinished Basement, Add	45.65	35.00	30.50	23.15	21.65	20.75	20.15	19.75

1-1/2 Story — Base cost per square foot of living area

Exterior Wall	Living Area							
	100	200	300	400	500	600	700	800
Wood Siding - Wood Frame	183.15	149.05	128.30	115.85	109.60	106.60	102.70	101.55
Brick Veneer - Wood Frame	208.80	169.55	145.40	129.20	121.90	118.20	113.65	112.45
Solid Brick	253.80	205.55	175.45	152.60	143.45	138.60	132.95	131.60
Solid Stone	247.10	200.25	171.00	149.10	140.20	135.60	130.10	128.80
Finished Basement, Add	57.45	56.70	51.30	45.25	43.65	42.55	41.55	41.40
Unfinished Basement, Add	28.85	24.40	21.45	18.20	17.30	16.70	16.15	16.10

2 Story — Base cost per square foot of living area

Exterior Wall	Living Area							
	100	200	400	600	800	1000	1200	1400
Wood Siding - Wood Frame	180.20	135.40	115.90	96.80	90.45	86.60	84.05	85.30
Brick Veneer - Wood Frame	208.90	155.90	133.00	108.20	100.70	96.15	93.15	94.10
Solid Brick	259.35	191.90	163.00	128.20	118.65	112.95	109.15	109.50
Solid Stone	251.90	186.65	158.50	125.25	116.00	110.45	106.75	107.20
Finished Basement, Add	43.70	39.60	35.50	28.65	27.30	26.45	25.95	25.55
Unfinished Basement, Add	22.80	17.50	15.30	11.60	10.85	10.35	10.10	9.90

Base costs do not include bathroom or kitchen facilities. Use Modifications/Adjustments/Alternatives on pages 77–80 where appropriate.

Kitchen cabinets - Base units, hardwood *(Cost per Unit)*

	Economy	Average	Custom	Luxury
24" deep, 35" high,				
One top drawer,				
One door below				
12" wide	$ 213	$ 284	$ 378	$ 497
15" wide	221	295	392	516
18" wide	240	320	426	560
21" wide	251	335	446	586
24" wide	285	380	505	665
Four drawers				
12" wide	222	296	394	518
15" wide	225	300	399	525
18" wide	248	330	439	578
24" wide	278	370	492	648
Two top drawers,				
Two doors below				
27" wide	300	400	532	700
30" wide	326	435	579	761
33" wide	345	460	612	805
36" wide	360	480	638	840
42" wide	383	510	678	893
48" wide	409	545	725	954
Range or sink base				
(Cost per unit)				
Two doors below				
30" wide	278	370	492	648
33" wide	300	400	532	700
36" wide	315	420	559	735
42" wide	334	445	592	779
48" wide	349	465	618	814
Corner Base Cabinet				
(Cost per unit)				
36" wide	480	640	851	1120
Lazy Susan *(Cost per unit)*				
With revolving door	634	845	1124	1479

Kitchen cabinets - Wall cabinets, hardwood *(Cost per Unit)*

	Economy	Average	Custom	Luxury
12" deep, 2 doors				
12" high				
30" wide	$ 193	$ 257	$ 342	$ 450
36" wide	223	297	395	520
15" high				
30" wide	161	214	285	375
33" wide	212	283	376	495
36" wide	224	299	398	523
24" high				
30" wide	255	340	452	595
36" wide	278	370	492	648
42" wide	315	420	559	735
30" high, 1 door				
12" wide	180	240	319	420
15" wide	199	265	352	464
18" wide	218	290	386	508
24" wide	248	330	439	578
30" high, 2 doors				
27" wide	274	365	485	639
30" wide	281	375	499	656
36" wide	319	425	565	744
42" wide	349	465	618	814
48" wide	390	520	692	910
Corner wall, 30" high				
24" wide	225	300	399	525
30" wide	251	335	446	586
36" wide	281	375	499	656
Broom closet				
84" high, 24" deep				
18" wide	536	715	951	1251
Oven Cabinet				
84" high, 24" deep				
27" wide	788	1050	1397	1838

Kitchen countertops *(Cost per L.F.)*

	Economy	Average	Custom	Luxury
Solid Surface				
24" wide, no backsplash	92	123	164	215
with backsplash	100	133	177	233
Stock plastic laminate, 24" wide				
with backsplash	17	23	31	40
Custom plastic laminate, no splash				
7/8" thick, alum. molding	27	36	48	63
1-1/4" thick, no splash	36	48	64	84
Marble				
1/2" - 3/4" thick w/splash	48	64	86	113
Maple, laminated				
1-1/2" thick w/splash	72	95	127	167
Stainless steel				
(per S.F.)	130	173	230	303
Cutting blocks, recessed				
16" x 20" x 1" (each)	97	129	172	226

Vanity bases *(Cost per Unit)*

	Economy	Average	Custom	Luxury
2 door, 30" high, 21" deep				
24" wide	217	289	384	506
30" wide	251	335	446	586
36" wide	334	445	592	779
48" wide	398	530	705	928

Solid surface vanity tops *(Cost Each)*

	Economy	Average	Custom	Luxury
Center bowl				
22" x 25"	$ 261	$ 282	$ 305	$ 329
22" x 31"	298	322	348	376
22" x 37"	340	367	396	428
22" x 49"	420	454	490	529

Fireplaces & Chimneys *(Cost per Unit)*

	1-1/2 Story	2 Story	3 Story
Economy (prefab metal)			
Exterior chimney & 1 fireplace	$ 5266	$ 5819	$ 6382
Interior chimney & 1 fireplace	5046	5610	5869
Average (masonry)			
Exterior chimney & 1 fireplace	5233	5835	6633
Interior chimney & 1 fireplace	4902	5503	5992
For more than 1 flue, add	376	640	1073
For more than 1 fireplace, add	3710	3710	3710
Custom (masonry)			
Exterior chimney & 1 fireplace	5759	6501	7341
Interior chimney & 1 fireplace	5400	6112	6588
For more than 1 flue, add	451	782	1060
For more than 1 fireplace, add	4137	4137	4137
Luxury (masonry)			
Exterior chimney & 1 fireplace	8140	8923	9764
Interior chimney & 1 fireplace	7766	8490	8987
For more than 1 flue, add	672	1121	1566
For more than 1 fireplace, add	6416	6416	6416

Windows and Skylights *(Cost Each)*

	Economy	Average	Custom	Luxury
Fixed Picture Windows				
3'-6" x 4'-0"	$ 344	$ 458	$ 610	$ 803
4'-0" x 6'-0"	606	808	1075	1414
5'-0" x 6'-0"	677	902	1200	1579
6'-0" x 6'-0"	677	902	1200	1579
Bay/Bow Windows				
8'-0" x 5'-0"	860	1146	1525	2007
10'-0" x 5'-0"	916	1221	1625	2138
10'-0" x 6'-0"	1452	1936	2575	3388
12'-0" x 6'-0"	1889	2518	3350	4408
Palladian Windows				
3'-2" x 6'-4"		1466	1950	2566
4'-0" x 6'-0"		1710	2275	2993
5'-5" x 6'-10"		2236	2975	3914
8'-0" x 6'-0"		2650	3525	4638
Skylights				
46" x 21-1/2"	416	450	590	637
46" x 28"	453	490	625	675
57" x 44"	550	595	735	793

Dormers *(Cost/S.F. of plan area)*

	Economy	Average	Custom	Luxury
Framing and Roofing Only				
Gable dormer, 2" x 6" roof frame	$ 26	$ 29	$ 31	$ 51
2" x 8" roof frame	27	30	32	54
Shed dormer, 2" x 6" roof frame	16	18	20	33
2" x 8" roof frame	18	19	21	34
2" x 10" roof frame	19	21	22	35

Appliances (Cost per Unit)

	Economy	Average	Custom	Luxury
Range				
30" free standing, 1 oven	$ 440	$ 1345	$ 1798	$ 2250
2 oven	1575	1700	1763	1825
30" built-in, 1 oven	820	1435	1743	2050
2 oven	1900	2185	2328	2470
21" free standing				
1 oven	420	468	492	515
Counter Top Ranges				
4 burner standard	400	603	704	805
As above with griddle	1600	2713	3269	3825
Microwave Oven	228	452	564	675
Compactor				
4 to 1 compaction	665	858	954	1050
Deep Freeze				
15 to 23 C.F.	645	745	795	845
30 C.F.	990	1108	1167	1225
Dehumidifier, portable, auto.				
15 pint	170	196	209	221
30 pint	188	216	230	244
Washing Machine, automatic	540	1058	1317	1575
Water Heater				
Electric, glass lined				
30 gal.	680	828	902	975
80 gal.	1300	1638	1807	1975
Water Heater, Gas, glass lined				
30 gal.	1075	1300	1413	1525
50 gal.	1275	1575	1725	1875
Dishwasher, built-in				
2 cycles	375	503	567	630
4 or more cycles	445	550	988	1425
Dryer, automatic	625	1200	1488	1775
Garage Door Opener	500	605	658	710
Garbage Disposal	135	201	234	266
Heater, Electric, built-in				
1250 watt ceiling type	212	264	290	315
1250 watt wall type	277	301	313	325
Wall type w/blower				
1500 watt	277	319	340	360
3000 watt	490	564	601	637
Hood For Range, 2 speed				
30" wide	172	636	868	1100
42" wide	370	1298	1762	2225
Humidifier, portable				
7 gal. per day	182	210	224	237
15 gal. per day	218	251	267	283
Ice Maker, automatic				
13 lb. per day	1025	1179	1256	1333
51 lb. per day	1600	1840	1960	2080
Refrigerator, no frost				
10-12 C.F.	550	570	580	590
14-16 C.F.	585	740	818	895
18-20 C.F.	725	1038	1194	1350
21-29 C.F.	1100	2338	2957	3575
Sump Pump, 1/3 H.P.	281	398	457	515

Breezeway (Cost per S.F.)

Class	Type	Area (S.F.)			
		50	100	150	200
Economy	Open	$ 23.18	$ 19.70	$ 16.53	$ 16.26
	Enclosed	111.19	85.87	71.31	62.46
Average	Open	30.49	26.89	23.52	21.37
	Enclosed	119.08	88.74	72.58	63.89
Custom	Open	40.58	35.72	31.08	28.44
	Enclosed	166.68	124.00	101.37	89.12
Luxury	Open	42.69	37.42	33.72	32.75
	Enclosed	171.90	127.49	103.13	92.32

Porches (Cost per S.F.)

Class	Type	Area (S.F.)				
		25	50	100	200	300
Economy	Open	$ 66.45	$ 44.46	$ 34.75	$ 29.41	$ 25.09
	Enclosed	132.79	92.53	69.94	54.56	46.71
Average	Open	85.84	54.65	41.93	34.85	34.85
	Enclosed	155.77	105.54	79.83	61.81	52.37
Custom	Open	103.63	68.76	51.76	45.22	40.52
	Enclosed	206.04	140.77	107.12	83.42	71.87
Luxury	Open	113.02	73.88	54.57	49.03	43.72
	Enclosed	221.26	155.39	115.28	89.58	77.11

Finished attic (Cost per S.F.)

Class	Area (S.F.)				
	400	500	600	800	1000
Economy	$ 17.73	$ 17.14	$ 16.42	$ 16.15	$ 15.54
Average	26.66	26.08	25.44	25.12	24.42
Custom	33.03	32.29	31.56	31.08	30.44
Luxury	42.43	41.40	40.43	39.47	38.82

Alarm system (Cost per System)

	Burglar Alarm	Smoke Detector
Economy	$ 405	$ 67
Average	460	81
Custom	793	178
Luxury	1150	242

Sauna, prefabricated
(Cost per unit, including heater and controls—7' high)

Size	Cost
6' x 4'	$ 5250
6' x 5'	5850
6' x 6'	6225
6' x 9'	7625
8' x 10'	10,100
8' x 12'	11,700
10' x 12'	12,200

Garages *

(Costs include exterior wall systems comparable with the quality of the residence. Included in the cost is an allowance for one personnel door, manual overhead door(s) and electrical fixture.)

Class	Type									
	Detached			Attached			Built-in		Basement	
	One Car	Two Car	Three Car	One Car	Two Car	Three Car	One Car	Two Car	One Car	Two Car
Economy										
Wood	$14,630	$22,195	$29,761	$11,273	$19,305	$26,871	$-1477	$-2953	$1277	$1666
Masonry	19,785	28,647	37,510	14,499	23,828	32,690	-2110	-4220		
Average										
Wood	16,871	25,001	33,130	12,676	21,272	29,401	-1752	-3504	1472	2056
Masonry	20,570	29,630	38,689	14,991	24,516	33,576	-2206	-3652		
Custom										
Wood	16,887	25,336	33,785	12,844	21,916	30,365	-3574	-4365	1366	1845
Masonry	21,566	31,191	40,816	15,771	26,020	35,646	-4148	-5514		
Luxury										
Wood	19,802	30,256	40,710	15,304	26,381	36,835	-3723	-4664	2259	3216
Masonry	25,168	36,971	48,774	18,661	31,088	42,891	-4382	-5982		

*See the Introduction to this section for definitions of garage types.

Swimming pools *(Cost per S.F.)*

Residential	(includes equipment)
In-ground	$ 25.00 - 64.50
Deck equipment	1.30
Paint pool, preparation & 3 coats (epoxy)	4.75
Rubber base paint	4.03
Pool Cover	.88
Swimming Pool Heaters	
(not including wiring, external piping, base or pad)	
Gas	
155 MBH	$ 2525.00
190 MBH	3050.00
500 MBH	10,900.00
Electric	
15 KW 7200 gallon pool	2700.00
24 KW 9600 gallon pool	3125.00
54 KW 24,000 gallon pool	4850.00

Wood and coal stoves

Wood Only	
Free Standing (minimum)	$ 1825
Fireplace Insert (minimum)	1915
Coal Only	
Free Standing	$ 2164
Fireplace Insert	2369
Wood and Coal	
Free Standing	$ 4450
Fireplace Insert	4561

Sidewalks *(Cost per S.F.)*

Concrete, 3000 psi with wire mesh	4" thick	$ 3.51
	5" thick	4.27
	6" thick	4.80
Precast concrete patio blocks (natural)	2" thick	10.60
Precast concrete patio blocks (colors)	2" thick	11.20
Flagstone, bluestone	1" thick	15.15
Flagstone, bluestone	1-1/2" thick	20.15
Slate (natural, irregular)	3/4" thick	15.25
Slate (random rectangular)	1/2" thick	23.30
Seeding		
Fine grading & seeding includes lime, fertilizer & seed	per S.Y.	2.44
Lawn Sprinkler System	per S.F.	.89

Fencing *(Cost per L.F.)*

Chain Link, 4' high, galvanized	$ 16.60
Gate, 4' high (each)	157.00
Cedar Picket, 3' high, 2 rail	12.25
Gate (each)	186.00
3 Rail, 4' high	15.30
Gate (each)	197.00
Cedar Stockade, 3 Rail, 6' high	15.45
Gate (each)	197.00
Board & Battens, 2 sides 6' high, pine	21.00
6' high, cedar	29.00
No. 1 Cedar, basketweave, 6' high	16.90
Gate, 6' high (each)	225.00

Carport *(Cost per S.F.)*

Economy	$ 8.24
Average	12.26
Custom	18.03
Luxury	20.86

Assemblies Section

Table of Contents

How to Use the Assemblies Section

Illustration
Each building assembly system is accompanied by a detailed, illustrated description. Each individual component is labeled. Every element involved in the total system function is shown.

Quantities
Each material in a system is shown with the quantity required for the system unit. For example, the rafters in this system have 1.170 L.F. per S.F. of ceiling area.

Unit of Measure
In the three right-hand columns, each cost figure is adjusted to agree with the unit of measure for the entire system. In this case, COST PER SQUARE FOOT (S.F.) is the common unit of measure. NOTE: In addition, under the UNIT heading, all the elements of each system are defined in relation to the product as a selling commodity. For example, "fascia board" is defined in linear feet, instead of in board feet.

Description
Each page includes a brief outline of any special conditions to be used when pricing a system. All units of measure are defined here.

System Definition
Not only are all components broken down for each system, but alternative components can be found on the opposite page. Simply insert any chosen new element into the chart to develop a custom system.

Labor-hours
Total labor-hours for a system can be found by simply multiplying the quantity of the system required times LABOR-HOURS. The resulting figure is the total labor-hours needed to complete the system.
(QUANTITY OF SYSTEM x LABOR-HOURS = TOTAL SYSTEM LABOR-HOURS)

Materials
This column contains the MATERIAL COST of each element. These cost figures include 10% for profit.

Installation
Labor rates include both the INSTALLATION COST of the contractor and the standard contractor's O&P. On the average, the LABOR COST will be 68.8% over the above BARE LABOR COST.

Totals
This row provides the necessary system cost totals. TOTAL SYSTEM COST can be derived by multiplying the TOTAL times each system's SQUARE FOOT ESTIMATE (TOTAL x SQUARE FEET = TOTAL SYSTEM COST).

Work Sheet
Using the SELECTIVE PRICE SHEET on the page opposite each system, it is possible to create estimates with alternative items for any number of systems.

Note:
Throughout this section, the words assembly and system are used interchangeably.

Total
MATERIAL COST + INSTALLATION COST = TOTAL. Work on the table from left to right across cost columns to derive totals.

3 | FRAMING   12 | Gable End Roof Framing Systems

System Description	QUAN.	UNIT	LABOR HOURS	COST PER S.F. MAT.	COST PER S.F. INST.	COST PER S.F. TOTAL
2" X 6" RAFTERS, 16" O.C., 4/12 PITCH						
Rafters, 2" x 6", 16" O.C., 4/12 pitch	1.170	L.F.	.019	.48	.91	1.39
Ceiling joists, 2" x 4", 16" O.C.	1.000	L.F.	.013	.27	.63	.90
Ridge board, 2" x 6'	.050	L.F.	.002	.02	.08	.10
Fascia board, 2" x 6"	.100	L.F.	.005	.05	.26	.31
Rafter tie, 1" x 4", 4' O.C.	.060	L.F.	.001	.03	.06	.09
Soffit nailer (cut-gain), 2" x 4", 24" O.C.	.170	L.F.	.004	.05	.21	.26
Sheathing, exterior, plywood, CDX, 1/2" thick	1.170	S.F.	.013	.54	.66	1.20
Furring strips, 1" x 3", 16" O.C.	1.000	L.F.	.023	.38	1.12	1.50
TOTAL		S.F.	.080	1.82	3.93	5.75
2" X 8" RAFTERS, 16" O.C., 4/12 PITCH						
Rafters, 2" x 8", 16" O.C., 4/12 pitch	1.170	L.F.	.020	.71	.96	1.67
Ceiling joists, 2" x 6", 16" O.C.	1.000	L.F.	.013	.41	.63	1.04
Ridge board, 2" x 8	.050	L.F.	.002	.03	.09	.12
Fascia board, 2" x 8"	.100	L.F.	.007	.06	.35	.41
Rafter tie, 1" x 4", 4' O.C.	.060	L.F.	.001	.03	.06	.09
Soffit nailer (cut-gain), 2" x 4", 24" O.C.	.170	L.F.	.004	.05	.21	.26
Sheathing, exterior, plywood, CDX, 1/2" thick	1.170	S.F.	.013	.54	.66	1.20
Furring strips, 1" x 3", 16" O.C.	1.000	L.F.	.023	.38	1.12	1.50
TOTAL		S.F.	.083	2.21	4.08	6.29

The cost of this system is based on the square foot of plan area.
All quantities have been adjusted accordingly.

Description	QUAN.	UNIT	LABOR HOURS	COST PER S.F. MAT.	COST PER S.F. INST.	COST PER S.F. TOTAL

Division 1
Site Work

Backfill

Excavate

System Description	QUAN.	UNIT	LABOR HOURS	COST EACH		
				MAT.	INST.	TOTAL
BUILDING, 24′ X 38′, 4′ DEEP						
Cut & chip light trees to 6″ diam.	.190	Acre	9.120		646	646
Excavator, hydraulic, crawler mtd., 1 C.Y. cap. = 100 C.Y./hr.	174.000	C.Y.	3.480		341.04	341.04
Backfill, dozer, 4″ lifts, no compaction	87.000	C.Y.	.580		122.67	122.67
Rough grade, dozer, 30′ from building	87.000	C.Y.	.580		122.67	122.67
TOTAL		Ea.	13.760		1,232.38	1,232.38
BUILDING, 26′ X 46′, 4′ DEEP						
Cut & chip light trees to 6″ diam.	.210	Acre	10.080		714	714
Excavator, hydraulic, crawler mtd., 1 C.Y. cap. = 100 C.Y./hr.	201.000	C.Y.	4.020		393.96	393.96
Backfill, dozer, 4″ lifts, no compaction	100.000	C.Y.	.667		141	141
Rough grade, dozer, 30′ from building	100.000	C.Y.	.667		141	141
TOTAL		Ea.	15.434		1,389.96	1,389.96
BUILDING, 26′ X 60′, 4′ DEEP						
Cut & chip light trees to 6″ diam.	.240	Acre	11.520		816	816
Excavator, hydraulic, crawler mtd., 1 C.Y. cap. = 100 C.Y./hr.	240.000	C.Y.	4.800		470.40	470.40
Backfill, dozer, 4″ lifts, no compaction	120.000	C.Y.	.800		169.20	169.20
Rough grade, dozer, 30′ from building	120.000	C.Y.	.800		169.20	169.20
TOTAL		Ea.	17.920		1,624.80	1,624.80
BUILDING, 30′ X 66′, 4′ DEEP						
Cut & chip light trees to 6″ diam.	.260	Acre	12.480		884	884
Excavator, hydraulic, crawler mtd., 1 C.Y. cap. = 100 C.Y./hr.	268.000	C.Y.	5.360		525.28	525.28
Backfill, dozer, 4″ lifts, no compaction	134.000	C.Y.	.894		188.94	188.94
Rough grade, dozer, 30′ from building	134.000	C.Y.	.894		188.94	188.94
TOTAL		Ea.	19.628		1,787.16	1,787.16

The costs in this system are on a cost each basis.
Quantities are based on 1′-0″ clearance on each side of footing.

Description	QUAN.	UNIT	LABOR HOURS	COST EACH		
				MAT.	INST.	TOTAL

Footing Excavation Price Sheet	QUAN.	UNIT	LABOR HOURS	COST EACH		
				MAT.	INST.	TOTAL
Clear and grub, medium brush, 30' from building, 24' x 38'	.190	Acre	9.120		645	645
26' x 46'	.210	Acre	10.080		715	715
26' x 60'	.240	Acre	11.520		815	815
30' x 66'	.260	Acre	12.480		885	885
Light trees, to 6" dia. cut & chip, 24' x 38'	.190	Acre	9.120		645	645
26' x 46'	.210	Acre	10.080		715	715
26' x 60'	.240	Acre	11.520		815	815
30' x 66'	.260	Acre	12.480		885	885
Medium trees, to 10" dia. cut & chip, 24' x 38'	.190	Acre	13.029		930	930
26' x 46'	.210	Acre	14.400		1,025	1,025
26' x 60'	.240	Acre	16.457		1,175	1,175
30' x 66'	.260	Acre	17.829		1,275	1,275
Excavation, footing, 24' x 38', 2' deep	68.000	C.Y.	.906		134	134
4' deep	174.000	C.Y.	2.319		340	340
8' deep	384.000	C.Y.	5.119		750	750
26' x 46', 2' deep	79.000	C.Y.	1.053		155	155
4' deep	201.000	C.Y.	2.679		395	395
8' deep	404.000	C.Y.	5.385		790	790
26' x 60', 2' deep	94.000	C.Y.	1.253		184	184
4' deep	240.000	C.Y.	3.199		470	470
8' deep	483.000	C.Y.	6.438		945	945
30' x 66', 2' deep	105.000	C.Y.	1.400		207	207
4' deep	268.000	C.Y.	3.572		525	525
8' deep	539.000	C.Y.	7.185		1,050	1,050
Backfill, 24' x 38', 2" lifts, no compaction	34.000	C.Y.	.227		48	48
Compaction, air tamped, add	34.000	C.Y.	2.267		420	420
4" lifts, no compaction	87.000	C.Y.	.580		123	123
Compaction, air tamped, add	87.000	C.Y.	5.800		1,075	1,075
8" lifts, no compaction	192.000	C.Y.	1.281		271	271
Compaction, air tamped, add	192.000	C.Y.	12.801		2,375	2,375
26' x 46', 2" lifts, no compaction	40.000	C.Y.	.267		56.50	56.50
Compaction, air tamped, add	40.000	C.Y.	2.667		490	490
4" lifts, no compaction	100.000	C.Y.	.667		141	141
Compaction, air tamped, add	100.000	C.Y.	6.667		1,225	1,225
8" lifts, no compaction	202.000	C.Y.	1.347		285	285
Compaction, air tamped, add	202.000	C.Y.	13.467		2,500	2,500
26' x 60', 2" lifts, no compaction	47.000	C.Y.	.313		66	66
Compaction, air tamped, add	47.000	C.Y.	3.133		580	580
4" lifts, no compaction	120.000	C.Y.	.800		170	170
Compaction, air tamped, add	120.000	C.Y.	8.000		1,475	1,475
8" lifts, no compaction	242.000	C.Y.	1.614		340	340
Compaction, air tamped, add	242.000	C.Y.	16.134		2,975	2,975
30' x 66', 2" lifts, no compaction	53.000	C.Y.	.354		75	75
Compaction, air tamped, add	53.000	C.Y.	3.534		655	655
4" lifts, no compaction	134.000	C.Y.	.894		189	189
Compaction, air tamped, add	134.000	C.Y.	8.934		1,650	1,650
8" lifts, no compaction	269.000	C.Y.	1.794		380	380
Compaction, air tamped, add	269.000	C.Y.	17.934		3,300	3,300
Rough grade, 30' from building, 24' x 38'	87.000	C.Y.	.580		123	123
26' x 46'	100.000	C.Y.	.667		141	141
26' x 60'	120.000	C.Y.	.800		170	170
30' x 66'	134.000	C.Y.	.894		189	189

Backfill

Excavate

System Description	QUAN.	UNIT	LABOR HOURS	COST EACH		
				MAT.	INST.	TOTAL
BUILDING, 24′ X 38′, 8′ DEEP						
Medium clearing	.190	Acre	2.027		251.75	251.75
Excavate, track loader, 1-1/2 C.Y. bucket	550.000	C.Y.	7.860		847	847
Backfill, dozer, 8″ lifts, no compaction	180.000	C.Y.	1.201		253.80	253.80
Rough grade, dozer, 30′ from building	280.000	C.Y.	1.868		394.80	394.80
TOTAL		Ea.	12.956		1,747.35	1,747.35
BUILDING, 26′ X 46′, 8′ DEEP						
Medium clearing	.210	Acre	2.240		278.25	278.25
Excavate, track loader, 1-1/2 C.Y. bucket	672.000	C.Y.	9.603		1,034.88	1,034.88
Backfill, dozer, 8″ lifts, no compaction	220.000	C.Y.	1.467		310.20	310.20
Rough grade, dozer, 30′ from building	340.000	C.Y.	2.268		479.40	479.40
TOTAL		Ea.	15.578		2,102.73	2,102.73
BUILDING, 26′ X 60′, 8′ DEEP						
Medium clearing	.240	Acre	2.560		318	318
Excavate, track loader, 1-1/2 C.Y. bucket	829.000	C.Y.	11.846		1,276.66	1,276.66
Backfill, dozer, 8″ lifts, no compaction	270.000	C.Y.	1.801		380.70	380.70
Rough grade, dozer, 30′ from building	420.000	C.Y.	2.801		592.20	592.20
TOTAL		Ea.	19.008		2,567.56	2,567.56
BUILDING, 30′ X 66′, 8′ DEEP						
Medium clearing	.260	Acre	2.773		344.50	344.50
Excavate, track loader, 1-1/2 C.Y. bucket	990.000	C.Y.	14.147		1,524.60	1,524.60
Backfill dozer, 8″ lifts, no compaction	320.000	C.Y.	2.134		451.20	451.20
Rough grade, dozer, 30′ from building	500.000	C.Y.	3.335		705	705
TOTAL		Ea.	22.389		3,025.30	3,025.30

The costs in this system are on a cost each basis.
Quantities are based on 1′-0″ clearance beyond footing projection.

Description	QUAN.	UNIT	LABOR HOURS	COST EACH		
				MAT.	INST.	TOTAL

Foundation Excavation Price Sheet

Foundation Excavation Price Sheet	QUAN.	UNIT	LABOR HOURS	COST EACH		
				MAT.	INST.	TOTAL
Clear & grub, medium brush, 30' from building, 24' x 38'	.190	Acre	2.027		252	252
26' x 46'	.210	Acre	2.240		279	279
26' x 60'	.240	Acre	2.560		320	320
30' x 66'	.260	Acre	2.773		345	345
Light trees, to 6" dia. cut & chip, 24' x 38'	.190	Acre	9.120		645	645
26' x 46'	.210	Acre	10.080		715	715
26' x 60'	.240	Acre	11.520		815	815
30' x 66'	.260	Acre	12.480		885	885
Medium trees, to 10" dia. cut & chip, 24' x 38'	.190	Acre	13.029		930	930
26' x 46'	.210	Acre	14.400		1,025	1,025
26' x 60'	.240	Acre	16.457		1,175	1,175
30' x 66'	.260	Acre	17.829		1,275	1,275
Excavation, basement, 24' x 38', 2' deep	98.000	C.Y.	1.400		151	151
4' deep	220.000	C.Y.	3.144		340	340
8' deep	550.000	C.Y.	7.860		850	850
26' x 46', 2' deep	123.000	C.Y.	1.758		190	190
4' deep	274.000	C.Y.	3.915		420	420
8' deep	672.000	C.Y.	9.603		1,025	1,025
26' x 60', 2' deep	157.000	C.Y.	2.244		241	241
4' deep	345.000	C.Y.	4.930		530	530
8' deep	829.000	C.Y.	11.846		1,275	1,275
30' x 66', 2' deep	192.000	C.Y.	2.744		295	295
4' deep	419.000	C.Y.	5.988		645	645
8' deep	990.000	C.Y.	14.147		1,525	1,525
Backfill, 24' x 38', 2" lifts, no compaction	32.000	C.Y.	.213		45.50	45.50
Compaction, air tamped, add	32.000	C.Y.	2.133		395	395
4" lifts, no compaction	72.000	C.Y.	.480		102	102
Compaction, air tamped, add	72.000	C.Y.	4.800		890	890
8" lifts, no compaction	180.000	C.Y.	1.201		254	254
Compaction, air tamped, add	180.000	C.Y.	12.001		2,225	2,225
26' x 46', 2" lifts, no compaction	40.000	C.Y.	.267		56.50	56.50
Compaction, air tamped, add	40.000	C.Y.	2.667		490	490
4" lifts, no compaction	90.000	C.Y.	.600		127	127
Compaction, air tamped, add	90.000	C.Y.	6.000		1,100	1,100
8" lifts, no compaction	220.000	C.Y.	1.467		310	310
Compacton, air tamped, add	220.000	C.Y.	14.667		2,700	2,700
26' x 60', 2" lifts, no compaction	50.000	C.Y.	.334		70.50	70.50
Compaction, air tamped, add	50.000	C.Y.	3.334		615	615
4" lifts, no compaction	110.000	C.Y.	.734		155	155
Compaction, air tamped, add	110.000	C.Y.	7.334		1,350	1,350
8" lifts, no compaction	270.000	C.Y.	1.801		380	380
Compaction, air tamped, add	270.000	C.Y.	18.001		3,350	3,350
30' x 66', 2" lifts, no compaction	60.000	C.Y.	.400		84.50	84.50
Compaction, air tamped, add	60.000	C.Y.	4.000		740	740
4" lifts, no compaction	130.000	C.Y.	.867		184	184
Compaction, air tamped, add	130.000	C.Y.	8.667		1,600	1,600
8" lifts, no compaction	320.000	C.Y.	2.134		450	450
Compaction, air tamped, add	320.000	C.Y.	21.334		3,950	3,950
Rough grade, 30' from building, 24' x 38'	280.000	C.Y.	1.868		395	395
26' x 46'	340.000	C.Y.	2.268		480	480
26' x 60'	420.000	C.Y.	2.801		595	595
30' x 66'	500.000	C.Y.	3.335		705	705

System Description	QUAN.	UNIT	LABOR HOURS	COST PER L.F.		
				MAT.	INST.	TOTAL
2′ DEEP						
Excavation, backhoe	.296	C.Y.	.032		2.07	2.07
Alternate pricing method, 4″ deep	.111	C.Y.	.044	2.33	1.86	4.19
Utility, sewer, 6″ cast iron	1.000	L.F.	.283	20.21	13.80	34.01
Compaction in 12″ layers, hand tamp, add to above	.185	C.Y.	.044		1.57	1.57
TOTAL		L.F.	.403	22.54	19.30	41.84
4′ DEEP						
Excavation, backhoe	.889	C.Y.	.095		6.22	6.22
Alternate pricing method, 4″ deep	.111	C.Y.	.044	2.33	1.86	4.19
Utility, sewer, 6″ cast iron	1.000	L.F.	.283	20.21	13.80	34.01
Compaction in 12″ layers, hand tamp, add to above	.778	C.Y.	.183		6.61	6.61
TOTAL		L.F.	.605	22.54	28.49	51.03
6′ DEEP						
Excavation, backhoe	1.770	C.Y.	.189		12.39	12.39
Alternate pricing method, 4″ deep	.111	C.Y.	.044	2.33	1.86	4.19
Utility, sewer, 6″ cast iron	1.000	L.F.	.283	20.21	13.80	34.01
Compaction in 12″ layers, hand tamp, add to above	1.660	C.Y.	.391		14.11	14.11
TOTAL		L.F.	.907	22.54	42.16	64.70
8′ DEEP						
Excavation, backhoe	2.960	C.Y.	.316		20.72	20.72
Alternate pricing method, 4″ deep	.111	C.Y.	.044	2.33	1.86	4.19
Utility, sewer, 6″ cast iron	1.000	L.F.	.283	20.21	13.80	34.01
Compaction in 12″ layers, hand tamp, add to above	2.850	C.Y.	.671		24.23	24.23
TOTAL		L.F.	1.314	22.54	60.61	83.15

The costs in this system are based on a cost per linear foot of trench,
and based on 2′ wide at bottom of trench up to 6′ deep.

Description	QUAN.	UNIT	LABOR HOURS	COST PER L.F.		
				MAT.	INST.	TOTAL

Utility Trenching Price Sheet	QUAN.	UNIT	LABOR HOURS	COST PER UNIT		
				MAT.	INST.	TOTAL
Excavation, bottom of trench 2' wide, 2' deep	.296	C.Y.	.032		2.07	2.07
4' deep	.889	C.Y.	.095		6.20	6.20
6' deep	1.770	C.Y.	.142		9.75	9.75
8' deep	2.960	C.Y.	.105		18.90	18.90
Bedding, sand, bottom of trench 2' wide, no compaction, pipe, 2" diameter	.070	C.Y.	.028	1.47	1.18	2.65
4" diameter	.084	C.Y.	.034	1.76	1.41	3.17
6" diameter	.105	C.Y.	.042	2.21	1.77	3.98
8" diameter	.122	C.Y.	.049	2.56	2.05	4.61
Compacted, pipe, 2" diameter	.074	C.Y.	.030	1.55	1.24	2.79
4" diameter	.092	C.Y.	.037	1.93	1.55	3.48
6" diameter	.111	C.Y.	.044	2.33	1.86	4.19
8" diameter	.129	C.Y.	.052	2.71	2.17	4.88
3/4" stone, bottom of trench 2' wide, pipe, 4" diameter	.082	C.Y.	.033	1.72	1.37	3.09
6" diameter	.099	C.Y.	.040	2.08	1.66	3.74
3/8" stone, bottom of trench 2' wide, pipe, 4" diameter	.084	C.Y.	.034	1.76	1.41	3.17
6" diameter	.102	C.Y.	.041	2.14	1.71	3.85
Utilities, drainage & sewerage, corrugated plastic, 6" diameter	1.000	L.F.	.069	4	2.56	6.56
8" diameter	1.000	L.F.	.072	8.65	2.67	11.32
Bituminous fiber, 4" diameter	1.000	L.F.	.064	1.85	2.39	4.24
6" diameter	1.000	L.F.	.069	4	2.56	6.56
8" diameter	1.000	L.F.	.072	8.65	2.67	11.32
Concrete, non-reinforced, 6" diameter	1.000	L.F.	.181	6.90	8.35	15.25
8" diameter	1.000	L.F.	.214	7.55	9.90	17.45
PVC, SDR 35, 4" diameter	1.000	L.F.	.064	1.85	2.39	4.24
6" diameter	1.000	L.F.	.069	4	2.56	6.56
8" diameter	1.000	L.F.	.072	8.65	2.67	11.32
Vitrified clay, 4" diameter	1.000	L.F.	.091	1.98	3.38	5.36
6" diameter	1.000	L.F.	.120	3.32	4.47	7.79
8" diameter	1.000	L.F.	.140	4.71	6.25	10.96
Gas & service, polyethylene, 1-1/4" diameter	1.000	L.F.	.059	2.82	2.60	5.42
Steel sched.40, 1" diameter	1.000	L.F.	.107	8.55	5.90	14.45
2" diameter	1.000	L.F.	.114	13.40	6.35	19.75
Sub-drainage, PVC, perforated, 3" diameter	1.000	L.F.	.064	1.85	2.39	4.24
4" diameter	1.000	L.F.	.064	1.85	2.39	4.24
5" diameter	1.000	L.F.	.069	4	2.56	6.56
6" diameter	1.000	L.F.	.069	4	2.56	6.56
Porous wall concrete, 4" diameter	1.000	L.F.	.072	3.74	2.67	6.41
Vitrified clay, perforated, 4" diameter	1.000	L.F.	.120	3.52	5.55	9.07
6" diameter	1.000	L.F.	.152	5.85	7.05	12.90
Water service, copper, type K, 3/4"	1.000	L.F.	.083	5.10	4.70	9.80
1" diameter	1.000	L.F.	.093	6.75	5.25	12
PVC, 3/4"	1.000	L.F.	.121	1.60	6.80	8.40
1" diameter	1.000	L.F.	.134	1.85	7.55	9.40
Backfill, bottom of trench 2' wide no compact, 2' deep, pipe, 2" diameter	.226	L.F.	.053		1.92	1.92
4" diameter	.212	L.F.	.050		1.80	1.80
6" diameter	.185	L.F.	.044		1.57	1.57
4' deep, pipe, 2" diameter	.819	C.Y.	.193		6.95	6.95
4" diameter	.805	C.Y.	.189		6.85	6.85
6" diameter	.778	C.Y.	.183		6.60	6.60
6' deep, pipe, 2" diameter	1.700	C.Y.	.400		14.45	14.45
4" diameter	1.690	C.Y.	.398		14.35	14.35
6" diameter	1.660	C.Y.	.391		14.10	14.10
8' deep, pipe, 2" diameter	2.890	C.Y.	.680		24.50	24.50
4" diameter	2.870	C.Y.	.675		24.50	24.50
6" diameter	2.850	C.Y.	.671		24	24

Asphalt — Brick Edge — Gravel Fill

System Description	QUAN.	UNIT	LABOR HOURS	COST PER S.F.		
				MAT.	INST.	TOTAL
ASPHALT SIDEWALK SYSTEM, 3′ WIDE WALK						
Gravel fill, 4″ deep	1.000	S.F.	.001	.35	.05	.40
Compact fill	.012	C.Y.			.02	.02
Handgrade	1.000	S.F.	.004		.15	.15
Walking surface, bituminous paving, 2″ thick	1.000	S.F.	.007	.84	.31	1.15
Edging, brick, laid on edge	.670	L.F.	.079	2.06	3.45	5.51
TOTAL		S.F.	.091	3.25	3.98	7.23
CONCRETE SIDEWALK SYSTEM, 3′ WIDE WALK						
Gravel fill, 4″ deep	1.000	S.F.	.001	.35	.05	.40
Compact fill	.012	C.Y.			.02	.02
Handgrade	1.000	S.F.	.004		.15	.15
Walking surface, concrete, 4″ thick	1.000	S.F.	.040	1.78	1.73	3.51
Edging, brick, laid on edge	.670	L.F.	.079	2.06	3.45	5.51
TOTAL		S.F.	.124	4.19	5.40	9.59
PAVERS, BRICK SIDEWALK SYSTEM, 3′ WIDE WALK						
Sand base fill, 4″ deep	1.000	S.F.	.001	.43	.08	.51
Compact fill	.012	C.Y.			.02	.02
Handgrade	1.000	S.F.	.004		.15	.15
Walking surface, brick pavers	1.000	S.F.	.160	3.30	6.95	10.25
Edging, redwood, untreated, 1″ x 4″	.670	L.F.	.032	1.66	1.58	3.24
TOTAL		S.F.	.197	5.39	8.78	14.17

The costs in this system are based on a cost per square foot of sidewalk area. Concrete used is 3000 p.s.i.

Description	QUAN.	UNIT	LABOR HOURS	COST PER S.F.		
				MAT.	INST.	TOTAL

Sidewalk Price Sheet	QUAN.	UNIT	LABOR HOURS	COST PER S.F.		
				MAT.	INST.	TOTAL
Base, crushed stone, 3" deep	1.000	S.F.	.001	.41	.09	.50
6" deep	1.000	S.F.	.001	.83	.10	.93
9" deep	1.000	S.F.	.002	1.21	.12	1.33
12" deep	1.000	S.F.	.002	1.71	.16	1.87
Bank run gravel, 6" deep	1.000	S.F.	.001	.52	.07	.59
9" deep	1.000	S.F.	.001	.76	.10	.86
12" deep	1.000	S.F.	.001	1.05	.12	1.17
Compact base, 3" deep	.009	C.Y.	.001		.01	.01
6" deep	.019	C.Y.	.001		.03	.03
9" deep	.028	C.Y.	.001		.04	.04
Handgrade	1.000	S.F.	.004		.15	.15
Surface, brick, pavers dry joints, laid flat, running bond	1.000	S.F.	.160	3.30	6.95	10.25
Basket weave	1.000	S.F.	.168	3.84	7.35	11.19
Herringbone	1.000	S.F.	.174	3.84	7.55	11.39
Laid on edge, running bond	1.000	S.F.	.229	3.50	9.95	13.45
Mortar jts. laid flat, running bond	1.000	S.F.	.192	3.96	8.35	12.31
Basket weave	1.000	S.F.	.202	4.61	8.80	13.41
Herringbone	1.000	S.F.	.209	4.61	9.05	13.66
Laid on edge, running bond	1.000	S.F.	.274	4.20	11.95	16.15
Bituminous paving, 1-1/2" thick	1.000	S.F.	.006	.63	.23	.86
2" thick	1.000	S.F.	.007	.84	.31	1.15
2-1/2" thick	1.000	S.F.	.008	1.07	.34	1.41
Sand finish, 3/4" thick	1.000	S.F.	.001	.36	.11	.47
1" thick	1.000	S.F.	.001	.44	.13	.57
Concrete, reinforced, broom finish, 4" thick	1.000	S.F.	.040	1.78	1.73	3.51
5" thick	1.000	S.F.	.044	2.37	1.90	4.27
6" thick	1.000	S.F.	.047	2.77	2.03	4.80
Crushed stone, white marble, 3" thick	1.000	S.F.	.009	.24	.34	.58
Bluestone, 3" thick	1.000	S.F.	.009	.26	.34	.60
Flagging, bluestone, 1"	1.000	S.F.	.198	6.55	8.60	15.15
1-1/2"	1.000	S.F.	.188	11.95	8.20	20.15
Slate, natural cleft, 3/4"	1.000	S.F.	.174	7.70	7.55	15.25
Random rect., 1/2"	1.000	S.F.	.152	16.65	6.65	23.30
Granite blocks	1.000	S.F.	.174	11.05	7.55	18.60
Edging, corrugated aluminum, 4", 3' wide walk	.666	L.F.	.008	.53	.40	.93
4' wide walk	.500	L.F.	.006	.40	.30	.70
6", 3' wide walk	.666	L.F.	.010	.66	.47	1.13
4' wide walk	.500	L.F.	.007	.50	.36	.86
Redwood-cedar-cypress, 1" x 4", 3' wide walk	.666	L.F.	.021	.85	1.05	1.90
4' wide walk	.500	L.F.	.016	.64	.79	1.43
2" x 4", 3' wide walk	.666	L.F.	.032	1.66	1.58	3.24
4' wide walk	.500	L.F.	.024	1.25	1.19	2.44
Brick, dry joints, 3' wide walk	.666	L.F.	.079	2.06	3.45	5.51
4' wide walk	.500	L.F.	.059	1.54	2.58	4.12
Mortar joints, 3' wide walk	.666	L.F.	.095	2.48	4.14	6.62
4' wide walk	.500	L.F.	.071	1.85	3.09	4.94

Asphalt Topping
Asphalt Binder
Brick Edging
Excavation
Base

System Description	QUAN.	UNIT	LABOR HOURS	COST PER S.F.		
				MAT.	INST.	TOTAL
ASPHALT DRIVEWAY TO 10' WIDE						
Excavation, driveway to 10' wide, 6" deep	.019	C.Y.			.04	.04
Base, 6" crushed stone	1.000	S.F.	.001	.83	.10	.93
Handgrade base	1.000	S.F.	.004		.15	.15
2" thick base	1.000	S.F.	.002	.84	.18	1.02
1" topping	1.000	S.F.	.001	.44	.13	.57
Edging, brick pavers	.200	L.F.	.024	.62	1.03	1.65
TOTAL		S.F.	.032	2.73	1.63	4.36
CONCRETE DRIVEWAY TO 10' WIDE						
Excavation, driveway to 10' wide, 6" deep	.019	C.Y.			.04	.04
Base, 6" crushed stone	1.000	S.F.	.001	.83	.10	.93
Handgrade base	1.000	S.F.	.004		.15	.15
Surface, concrete, 4" thick	1.000	S.F.	.040	1.78	1.73	3.51
Edging, brick pavers	.200	L.F.	.024	.62	1.03	1.65
TOTAL		S.F.	.069	3.23	3.05	6.28
PAVERS, BRICK DRIVEWAY TO 10' WIDE						
Excavation, driveway to 10' wide, 6" deep	.019	C.Y.			.04	.04
Base, 6" sand	1.000	S.F.	.001	.68	.13	.81
Handgrade base	1.000	S.F.	.004		.15	.15
Surface, pavers, brick laid flat, running bond	1.000	S.F.	.160	3.30	6.95	10.25
Edging, redwood, untreated, 2" x 4"	.200	L.F.	.010	.50	.47	.97
TOTAL		S.F.	.175	4.48	7.74	12.22

Description	QUAN.	UNIT	LABOR HOURS	COST PER S.F.		
				MAT.	INST.	TOTAL

Driveway Price Sheet	QUAN.	UNIT	LABOR HOURS	COST PER S.F.		
				MAT.	INST.	TOTAL
Excavation, by machine, 10' wide, 6" deep	.019	C.Y.	.001		.04	.04
12" deep	.037	C.Y.	.001		.07	.07
18" deep	.055	C.Y.	.001		.11	.11
20' wide, 6" deep	.019	C.Y.	.001		.04	.04
12" deep	.037	C.Y.	.001		.07	.07
18" deep	.055	C.Y.	.001		.11	.11
Base, crushed stone, 10' wide, 3" deep	1.000	S.F.	.001	.42	.06	.48
6" deep	1.000	S.F.	.001	.83	.10	.93
9" deep	1.000	S.F.	.002	1.21	.12	1.33
20' wide, 3" deep	1.000	S.F.	.001	.42	.06	.48
6" deep	1.000	S.F.	.001	.83	.10	.93
9" deep	1.000	S.F.	.002	1.21	.12	1.33
Bank run gravel, 10' wide, 3" deep	1.000	S.F.	.001	.26	.04	.30
6" deep	1.000	S.F.	.001	.52	.07	.59
9" deep	1.000	S.F.	.001	.76	.10	.86
20' wide, 3" deep	1.000	S.F.	.001	.26	.04	.30
6" deep	1.000	S.F.	.001	.52	.07	.59
9" deep	1.000	S.F.	.001	.76	.10	.86
Handgrade, 10' wide	1.000	S.F.	.004		.15	.15
20' wide	1.000	S.F.	.004		.15	.15
Surface, asphalt, 10' wide, 3/4" topping, 1" base	1.000	S.F.	.002	1.01	.24	1.25
2" base	1.000	S.F.	.003	1.20	.29	1.49
1" topping, 1" base	1.000	S.F.	.002	1.09	.26	1.35
2" base	1.000	S.F.	.003	1.28	.31	1.59
20' wide, 3/4" topping, 1" base	1.000	S.F.	.002	1.01	.24	1.25
2" base	1.000	S.F.	.003	1.20	.29	1.49
1" topping, 1" base	1.000	S.F.	.002	1.09	.26	1.35
2" base	1.000	S.F.	.003	1.28	.31	1.59
Concrete, 10' wide, 4" thick	1.000	S.F.	.040	1.78	1.73	3.51
6" thick	1.000	S.F.	.047	2.77	2.03	4.80
20' wide, 4" thick	1.000	S.F.	.040	1.78	1.73	3.51
6" thick	1.000	S.F.	.047	2.77	2.03	4.80
Paver, brick 10' wide dry joints, running bond, laid flat	1.000	S.F.	.160	3.30	6.95	10.25
Laid on edge	1.000	S.F.	.229	3.50	9.95	13.45
Mortar joints, laid flat	1.000	S.F.	.192	3.96	8.35	12.31
Laid on edge	1.000	S.F.	.274	4.20	11.95	16.15
20' wide, running bond, dry jts., laid flat	1.000	S.F.	.160	3.30	6.95	10.25
Laid on edge	1.000	S.F.	.229	3.50	9.95	13.45
Mortar joints, laid flat	1.000	S.F.	.192	3.96	8.35	12.31
Laid on edge	1.000	S.F.	.274	4.20	11.95	16.15
Crushed stone, 10' wide, white marble, 3"	1.000	S.F.	.009	.24	.34	.58
Bluestone, 3"	1.000	S.F.	.009	.26	.34	.60
20' wide, white marble, 3"	1.000	S.F.	.009	.24	.34	.58
Bluestone, 3"	1.000	S.F.	.009	.26	.34	.60
Soil cement, 10' wide	1.000	S.F.	.007	.41	.88	1.29
20' wide	1.000	S.F.	.007	.41	.88	1.29
Granite blocks, 10' wide	1.000	S.F.	.174	11.05	7.55	18.60
20' wide	1.000	S.F.	.174	11.05	7.55	18.60
Asphalt block, solid 1-1/4" thick	1.000	S.F.	.119	8.60	5.15	13.75
Solid 3" thick	1.000	S.F.	.123	12.05	5.35	17.40
Edging, brick, 10' wide	.200	L.F.	.024	.62	1.03	1.65
20' wide	.100	L.F.	.012	.31	.52	.83
Redwood, untreated 2" x 4", 10' wide	.200	L.F.	.010	.50	.47	.97
20' wide	.100	L.F.	.005	.25	.24	.49
Granite, 4 1/2" x 12" straight, 10' wide	.200	L.F.	.032	1.33	1.85	3.18
20' wide	.100	L.F.	.016	.67	.93	1.60
Finishes, asphalt sealer, 10' wide	1.000	S.F.	.023	1.16	.85	2.01
20' wide	1.000	S.F.	.023	1.16	.85	2.01
Concrete, exposed aggregate 10' wide	1.000	S.F.	.013	.25	.57	.82
20' wide	1.000	S.Y.	.013	.25	.57	.82

System Description	QUAN.	UNIT	LABOR HOURS	COST EACH		
				MAT.	INST.	TOTAL
SEPTIC SYSTEM WITH 1000 S.F. LEACHING FIELD, 1000 GALLON TANK						
Tank, 1000 gallon, concrete	1.000	Ea.	3.500	825	156	981
Distribution box, concrete	1.000	Ea.	1.000	88	36	124
4″ PVC pipe	25.000	L.F.	1.600	46.25	59.75	106
Tank and field excavation	119.000	C.Y.	13.130		1,179.29	1,179.29
Crushed stone backfill	76.000	C.Y.	12.160	2,584	671.08	3,255.08
Backfill with excavated material	36.000	C.Y.	.240		50.76	50.76
Building paper	125.000	S.Y.	2.430	67.50	123.75	191.25
4″ PVC perforated pipe	145.000	L.F.	9.280	268.25	346.55	614.80
4″ pipe fittings	2.000	Ea.	1.939	22.20	98	120.20
TOTAL			45.279	3,901.20	2,721.18	6,622.38
SEPTIC SYSTEM WITH 1000 S.F. LEACHING FIELD, 1500 GALLON TANK						
Tank, 1500 gallon, concrete	1.000	Ea.	4.000	1,275	177.50	1,452.50
Distribution box, concrete	1.000	Ea.	1.000	88	36	124
4″ PVC pipe	25.000	L.F.	1.600	46.25	59.75	106
Tank and field excavation	119.000	C.Y.	13.130		1,179.29	1,179.29
Crushed stone backfill	76.000	C.Y.	12.160	2,584	671.08	3,255.08
Backfill with excavated material	36.000	C.Y.	.240		50.76	50.76
Building paper	125.000	S.Y.	2.430	67.50	123.75	191.25
4″ PVC perforated pipe	145.000	L.F.	9.280	268.25	346.55	614.80
4″ pipe fittings	2.000	Ea.	1.939	22.20	98	120.20
TOTAL			45.779	4,351.20	2,742.68	7,093.88
SEPTIC SYSTEM WITH 2 LEACHING PITS, 1000 GALLON TANK						
Tank, 1000 gallon, concrete	1.000	Ea.	3.500	825	156	981
Distribution box, concrete	1.000	Ea.	1.000	88	36	124
4″ PVC pipe	75.000	L.F.	4.800	138.75	179.25	318
Excavation for tank only	20.000	C.Y.	2.207		198.20	198.20
Crushed stone backfill	10.000	C.Y.	1.600	340	88.30	428.30
Backfill with excavated material	55.000	C.Y.	.367		77.55	77.55
Pits, 6′ diameter, including excavation and stone backfill	2.000	Ea.		2,300		2,300
TOTAL		Ea.	13.474	3,691.75	735.30	4,427.05

The costs in this system include all necessary piping and excavation.

Septic Systems Price Sheet	QUAN.	UNIT	LABOR HOURS	COST EACH		
				MAT.	INST.	TOTAL
Tank, precast concrete, 1000 gallon	1.000	Ea.	3.500	825	156	981
2000 gallon	1.000	Ea.	5.600	1,850	250	2,100
Distribution box, concrete, 5 outlets	1.000	Ea.	1.000	88	36	124
12 outlets	1.000	Ea.	2.000	490	72.50	562.50
4″ pipe, PVC, solid	25.000	L.F.	1.600	46.50	60	106.50
Tank and field excavation, 1000 S.F. field	119.000	C.Y.	6.565		1,175	1,175
2000 S.F. field	190.000	C.Y.	10.482		1,875	1,875
Tank excavation only, 1000 gallon tank	20.000	C.Y.	1.103		198	198
2000 gallon tank	32.000	C.Y.	1.765		315	315
Backfill, crushed stone 1000 S.F. field	76.000	C.Y.	12.160	2,575	675	3,250
2000 S.F. field	140.000	C.Y.	22.400	4,750	1,225	5,975
Backfill with excavated material, 1000 S.F. field	36.000	C.Y.	.240		50.50	50.50
2000 S.F. field	60.000	C.Y.	.400		84.50	84.50
6′ diameter pits	55.000	C.Y.	.367		77.50	77.50
3′ diameter pits	42.000	C.Y.	.280		59.50	59.50
Building paper, 1000 S.F. field	125.000	S.Y.	2.376	66	121	187
2000 S.F. field	250.000	S.Y.	4.860	135	248	383
4″ pipe, PVC, perforated, 1000 S.F. field	145.000	L.F.	9.280	268	345	613
2000 S.F. field	265.000	L.F.	16.960	490	635	1,125
Pipe fittings, bituminous fiber, 1000 S.F. field	2.000	Ea.	1.939	22	98	120
2000 S.F. field	4.000	Ea.	3.879	44.50	196	240.50
Leaching pit, including excavation and stone backfill, 3′ diameter	1.000	Ea.		865		865
6′ diameter	1.000	Ea.		1,150		1,150

System Description	QUAN.	UNIT	LABOR HOURS	COST PER UNIT		
				MAT.	INST.	TOTAL
Chain link fence						
Galv.9ga. wire, 1-5/8"post 10'O.C., 1-3/8"top rail, 2"corner post, 3'hi	1.000	L.F.	.130	9.45	4.84	14.29
4' high	1.000	L.F.	.141	11.35	5.25	16.60
6' high	1.000	L.F.	.209	12.85	7.80	20.65
Add for gate 3' wide 1-3/8" frame 3' high	1.000	Ea.	2.000	69	74.50	143.50
4' high	1.000	Ea.	2.400	67	89.50	156.50
6' high	1.000	Ea.	2.400	72.50	89.50	162
Add for gate 4' wide 1-3/8" frame 3' high	1.000	Ea.	2.667	70.50	99.50	170
4' high	1.000	Ea.	2.667	76	99.50	175.50
6' high	1.000	Ea.	3.000	190	112	302
Alum.9ga. wire, 1-5/8"post, 10'O.C., 1-3/8"top rail, 2"corner post,3'hi	1.000	L.F.	.130	11.20	4.84	16.04
4' high	1.000	L.F.	.141	12.75	5.25	18
6' high	1.000	L.F.	.209	16.35	7.80	24.15
Add for gate 3' wide 1-3/8" frame 3' high	1.000	Ea.	2.000	109	74.50	183.50
4' high	1.000	Ea.	2.400	149	89.50	238.50
6' high	1.000	Ea.	2.400	223	89.50	312.50
Add for gate 4' wide 1-3/8" frame 3' high	1.000	Ea.	2.400	149	89.50	238.50
4' high	1.000	Ea.	2.667	198	99.50	297.50
6' high	1.000	Ea.	3.000	310	112	422
Vinyl 9ga. wire, 1-5/8"post 10'O.C., 1-3/8"top rail, 2"corner post,3'hi	1.000	L.F.	.130	9.90	4.84	14.74
4' high	1.000	L.F.	.141	14.90	5.25	20.15
6' high	1.000	L.F.	.209	17	7.80	24.80
Add for gate 3' wide 1-3/8" frame 3' high	1.000	Ea.	2.000	106	74.50	180.50
4' high	1.000	Ea.	2.400	138	89.50	227.50
6' high	1.000	Ea.	2.400	213	89.50	302.50
Add for gate 4' wide 1-3/8" frame 3' high	1.000	Ea.	2.400	145	89.50	234.50
4' high	1.000	Ea.	2.667	192	99.50	291.50
6' high	1.000	Ea.	3.000	277	112	389
Tennis court, chain link fence, 10' high						
Galv.11ga.wire, 2"post 10'O.C., 1-3/8"top rail, 2-1/2"corner post	1.000	L.F.	.253	21.50	9.40	30.90
Add for gate 3' wide 1-3/8" frame	1.000	Ea.	2.400	266	89.50	355.50
Alum.11ga.wire, 2"post 10'O.C., 1-3/8"top rail, 2-1/2"corner post	1.000	L.F.	.253	34.50	9.40	43.90
Add for gate 3' wide 1-3/8" frame	1.000	Ea.	2.400	395	89.50	484.50
Vinyl 11ga.wire,2"post 10' O.C.,1-3/8"top rail,2-1/2"corner post	1.000	L.F.	.253	26.50	9.40	35.90
Add for gate 3' wide 1-3/8" frame	1.000	Ea.	2.400	400	89.50	489.50
Railings, commercial						
Aluminum balcony rail, 1-1/2" posts with pickets	1.000	L.F.	.164	66.50	10.75	77.25
With expanded metal panels	1.000	L.F.	.164	85.50	10.75	96.25
With porcelain enamel panel inserts	1.000	L.F.	.164	76.50	10.75	87.25
Mild steel, ornamental rounded top rail	1.000	L.F.	.164	62.50	10.75	73.25
As above, but pitch down stairs	1.000	L.F.	.183	67.50	11.95	79.45
Steel pipe, welded, 1-1/2" round, painted	1.000	L.F.	.160	25	10.50	35.50
Galvanized	1.000	L.F.	.160	35	10.50	45.50
Residential, stock units, mild steel, deluxe	1.000	L.F.	.102	14.25	6.65	20.90
Economy	1.000	L.F.	.102	10.70	6.65	17.35

System Description	QUAN.	UNIT	LABOR HOURS	COST PER UNIT		
				MAT.	INST.	TOTAL
Basketweave, 3/8"x4" boards, 2"x4" stringers on spreaders, 4"x4" posts						
No. 1 cedar, 6' high	1.000	L.F.	.150	9.70	7.20	16.90
Treated pine, 6' high	1.000	L.F.	.160	11.70	7.70	19.40
Board fence, 1"x4" boards, 2"x4" rails, 4"x4" posts						
Preservative treated, 2 rail, 3' high	1.000	L.F.	.166	7.20	8	15.20
4' high	1.000	L.F.	.178	7.90	8.55	16.45
3 rail, 5' high	1.000	L.F.	.185	8.95	8.90	17.85
6' high	1.000	L.F.	.192	10.35	9.25	19.60
Western cedar, No. 1, 2 rail, 3' high	1.000	L.F.	.166	7.85	8	15.85
3 rail, 4' high	1.000	L.F.	.178	9.40	8.55	17.95
5' high	1.000	L.F.	.185	10.85	8.90	19.75
6' high	1.000	L.F.	.192	11.85	9.25	21.10
No. 1 cedar, 2 rail, 3' high	1.000	L.F.	.166	11.90	8	19.90
4' high	1.000	L.F.	.178	13.45	8.55	22
3 rail, 5' high	1.000	L.F.	.185	15.85	8.90	24.75
6' high	1.000	L.F.	.192	17.70	9.25	26.95
Shadow box, 1"x6" boards, 2"x4" rails, 4"x4" posts						
Fir, pine or spruce, treated, 3 rail, 6' high	1.000	L.F.	.160	13.25	7.70	20.95
No. 1 cedar, 3 rail, 4' high	1.000	L.F.	.185	16.25	8.90	25.15
6' high	1.000	L.F.	.192	20	9.25	29.25
Open rail, split rails, No. 1 cedar, 2 rail, 3' high	1.000	L.F.	.150	6.60	7.20	13.80
3 rail, 4' high	1.000	L.F.	.160	8.80	7.70	16.50
No. 2 cedar, 2 rail, 3' high	1.000	L.F.	.150	5.20	7.20	12.40
3 rail, 4' high	1.000	L.F.	.160	6.20	7.70	13.90
Open rail, rustic rails, No. 1 cedar, 2 rail, 3' high	1.000	L.F.	.150	4.25	7.20	11.45
3 rail, 4' high	1.000	L.F.	.160	5.75	7.70	13.45
No. 2 cedar, 2 rail, 3' high	1.000	L.F.	.150	4.21	7.20	11.41
3 rail, 4' high	1.000	L.F.	.160	4.38	7.70	12.08
Rustic picket, molded pine pickets, 2 rail, 3' high	1.000	L.F.	.171	5.85	8.25	14.10
3 rail, 4' high	1.000	L.F.	.197	6.75	9.50	16.25
No. 1 cedar, 2 rail, 3' high	1.000	L.F.	.171	7.85	8.25	16.10
3 rail, 4' high	1.000	L.F.	.197	9.05	9.50	18.55
Picket fence, fir, pine or spruce, preserved, treated						
2 rail, 3' high	1.000	L.F.	.171	4.91	8.25	13.16
3 rail, 4' high	1.000	L.F.	.185	5.80	8.90	14.70
Western cedar, 2 rail, 3' high	1.000	L.F.	.171	6.15	8.25	14.40
3 rail, 4' high	1.000	L.F.	.185	6.30	8.90	15.20
No. 1 cedar, 2 rail, 3' high	1.000	L.F.	.171	12.30	8.25	20.55
3 rail, 4' high	1.000	L.F.	.185	14.30	8.90	23.20
Stockade, No. 1 cedar, 3-1/4" rails, 6' high	1.000	L.F.	.150	11.55	7.20	18.75
8' high	1.000	L.F.	.155	14.95	7.45	22.40
No. 2 cedar, treated rails, 6' high	1.000	L.F.	.150	11.55	7.20	18.75
Treated pine, treated rails, 6' high	1.000	L.F.	.150	11.30	7.20	18.50
Gates, No. 2 cedar, picket, 3'-6" wide 4' high	1.000	Ea.	2.667	61	129	190
No. 2 cedar, rustic round, 3' wide, 3' high	1.000	Ea.	2.667	85	129	214
No. 2 cedar, stockade screen, 3'-6" wide, 6' high	1.000	Ea.	3.000	68	144	212
General, wood, 3'-6" wide, 4' high	1.000	Ea.	2.400	64.50	115	179.50
6' high	1.000	Ea.	3.000	80.50	144	224.50

Division 2
Foundations

Dowels · Keyway · Concrete · Reinforcing

System Description	QUAN.	UNIT	LABOR HOURS	COST PER L.F.		
				MAT.	INST.	TOTAL
8″ THICK BY 18″ WIDE FOOTING						
Concrete, 3000 psi	.040	C.Y.		4.28		4.28
Place concrete, direct chute	.040	C.Y.	.016		.63	.63
Forms, footing, 4 uses	1.330	SFCA	.103	.73	4.38	5.11
Reinforcing, 1/2″ diameter bars, 2 each	1.380	Lb.	.011	.63	.58	1.21
Keyway, 2″ x 4″, beveled, 4 uses	1.000	L.F.	.015	.15	.74	.89
Dowels, 1/2″ diameter bars, 2′ long, 6′ O.C.	.166	Ea.	.006	.11	.30	.41
TOTAL		L.F.	.151	5.90	6.63	12.53
12″ THICK BY 24″ WIDE FOOTING						
Concrete, 3000 psi	.070	C.Y.		7.49		7.49
Place concrete, direct chute	.070	C.Y.	.028		1.11	1.11
Forms, footing, 4 uses	2.000	SFCA	.155	1.10	6.58	7.68
Reinforcing, 1/2″ diameter bars, 2 each	1.380	Lb.	.011	.63	.58	1.21
Keyway, 2″ x 4″, beveled, 4 uses	1.000	L.F.	.015	.15	.74	.89
Dowels, 1/2″ diameter bars, 2′ long, 6′ O.C.	.166	Ea.	.006	.11	.30	.41
TOTAL		L.F.	.215	9.48	9.31	18.79
12″ THICK BY 36″ WIDE FOOTING						
Concrete, 3000 psi	.110	C.Y.		11.77		11.77
Place concrete, direct chute	.110	C.Y.	.044		1.74	1.74
Forms, footing, 4 uses	2.000	SFCA	.155	1.10	6.58	7.68
Reinforcing, 1/2″ diameter bars, 2 each	1.380	Lb.	.011	.63	.58	1.21
Keyway, 2″ x 4″, beveled, 4 uses	1.000	L.F.	.015	.15	.74	.89
Dowels, 1/2″ diameter bars, 2′ long, 6′ O.C.	.166	Ea.	.006	.11	.30	.41
TOTAL		L.F.	.231	13.76	9.94	23.70

The footing costs in this system are on a cost per linear foot basis

Description	QUAN.	UNIT	LABOR HOURS	COST PER S.F.		
				MAT.	INST.	TOTAL

Footing Price Sheet	QUAN.	UNIT	LABOR HOURS	COST PER L.F.		
				MAT.	INST.	TOTAL
Concrete, 8″ thick by 18″ wide footing						
2000 psi concrete	.040	C.Y.		4.04		4.04
2500 psi concrete	.040	C.Y.		4.12		4.12
3000 psi concrete	.040	C.Y.		4.28		4.28
3500 psi concrete	.040	C.Y.		4.40		4.40
4000 psi concrete	.040	C.Y.		4.52		4.52
12″ thick by 24″ wide footing						
2000 psi concrete	.070	C.Y.		7.05		7.05
2500 psi concrete	.070	C.Y.		7.20		7.20
3000 psi concrete	.070	C.Y.		7.50		7.50
3500 psi concrete	.070	C.Y.		7.70		7.70
4000 psi concrete	.070	C.Y.		7.90		7.90
12″ thick by 36″ wide footing						
2000 psi concrete	.110	C.Y.		11.10		11.10
2500 psi concrete	.110	C.Y.		11.35		11.35
3000 psi concrete	.110	C.Y.		11.75		11.75
3500 psi concrete	.110	C.Y.		12.10		12.10
4000 psi concrete	.110	C.Y.		12.45		12.45
Place concrete, 8″ thick by 18″ wide footing, direct chute	.040	C.Y.	.016		.63	.63
Pumped concrete	.040	C.Y.	.017		.90	.90
Crane & bucket	.040	C.Y.	.032		1.89	1.89
12″ thick by 24″ wide footing, direct chute	.070	C.Y.	.028		1.11	1.11
Pumped concrete	.070	C.Y.	.030		1.58	1.58
Crane & bucket	.070	C.Y.	.056		3.31	3.31
12″ thick by 36″ wide footing, direct chute	.110	C.Y.	.044		1.74	1.74
Pumped concrete	.110	C.Y.	.047		2.48	2.48
Crane & bucket	.110	C.Y.	.088		5.20	5.20
Forms, 8″ thick footing, 1 use	1.330	SFCA	.140	2.26	5.95	8.21
4 uses	1.330	SFCA	.103	.73	4.38	5.11
12″ thick footing, 1 use	2.000	SFCA	.211	3.40	8.95	12.35
4 uses	2.000	SFCA	.155	1.10	6.60	7.70
Reinforcing, 3/8″ diameter bar, 1 each	.400	Lb.	.003	.18	.17	.35
2 each	.800	Lb.	.006	.37	.34	.71
3 each	1.200	Lb.	.009	.55	.50	1.05
1/2″ diameter bar, 1 each	.700	Lb.	.005	.32	.29	.61
2 each	1.380	Lb.	.011	.63	.58	1.21
3 each	2.100	Lb.	.016	.97	.88	1.85
5/8″ diameter bar, 1 each	1.040	Lb.	.008	.48	.44	.92
2 each	2.080	Lb.	.016	.96	.87	1.83
Keyway, beveled, 2″ x 4″, 1 use	1.000	L.F.	.030	.30	1.48	1.78
2 uses	1.000	L.F.	.023	.23	1.11	1.34
2″ x 6″, 1 use	1.000	L.F.	.032	.42	1.56	1.98
2 uses	1.000	L.F.	.024	.32	1.17	1.49
Dowels, 2 feet long, 6′ O.C., 3/8″ bar	.166	Ea.	.005	.06	.28	.34
1/2″ bar	.166	Ea.	.006	.11	.30	.41
5/8″ bar	.166	Ea.	.006	.17	.34	.51
3/4″ bar	.166	Ea.	.006	.17	.34	.51

System Description	QUAN.	UNIT	LABOR HOURS	COST PER S.F.		
				MAT.	INST.	TOTAL
8″ WALL, GROUTED, FULL HEIGHT						
Concrete block, 8″ x 16″ x 8″	1.000	S.F.	.094	3.19	4.18	7.37
Masonry reinforcing, every second course	.750	L.F.	.002	.14	.10	.24
Parging, plastering with portland cement plaster, 1 coat	1.000	S.F.	.014	.25	.64	.89
Dampproofing, bituminous coating, 1 coat	1.000	S.F.	.012	.22	.53	.75
Insulation, 1″ rigid polystyrene	1.000	S.F.	.010	.56	.49	1.05
Grout, solid, pumped	1.000	S.F.	.059	1.21	2.57	3.78
Anchor bolts, 1/2″ diameter, 8″ long, 4′ O.C.	.060	Ea.	.002	.05	.12	.17
Sill plate, 2″ x 4″, treated	.250	L.F.	.007	.10	.36	.46
TOTAL		S.F.	.200	5.72	8.99	14.71
12″ WALL, GROUTED, FULL HEIGHT						
Concrete block, 8″ x 16″ x 12″	1.000	S.F.	.160	4.38	6.95	11.33
Masonry reinforcing, every second course	.750	L.F.	.003	.14	.14	.28
Parging, plastering with portland cement plaster, 1 coat	1.000	S.F.	.014	.25	.64	.89
Dampproofing, bituminous coating, 1 coat	1.000	S.F.	.012	.22	.53	.75
Insulation, 1″ rigid polystyrene	1.000	S.F.	.010	.56	.49	1.05
Grout, solid, pumped	1.000	S.F.	.063	1.97	2.74	4.71
Anchor bolts, 1/2″ diameter, 8″ long, 4′ O.C.	.060	Ea.	.002	.05	.12	.17
Sill plate, 2″ x 4″, treated	.250	L.F.	.007	.10	.36	.46
TOTAL		S.F.	.271	7.67	11.97	19.64

The costs in this system are based on a square foot of wall. Do not subtract for window or door openings.

Description	QUAN.	UNIT	LABOR HOURS	COST PER S.F.		
				MAT.	INST.	TOTAL

Block Wall Systems	QUAN.	UNIT	LABOR HOURS	COST PER S.F.		
				MAT.	INST.	TOTAL
Concrete, block, 8″ x 16″ x, 6″ thick	1.000	S.F.	.089	2.87	3.91	6.78
8″ thick	1.000	S.F.	.093	3.19	4.18	7.37
10″ thick	1.000	S.F.	.095	3.90	5.10	9
12″ thick	1.000	S.F.	.122	4.38	6.95	11.33
Solid block, 8″ x 16″ x, 6″ thick	1.000	S.F.	.091	2.94	4.04	6.98
8″ thick	1.000	S.F.	.096	4.16	4.28	8.44
10″ thick	1.000	S.F.	.096	4.16	4.28	8.44
12″ thick	1.000	S.F.	.126	6	5.95	11.95
Masonry reinforcing, wire strips, to 8″ wide, every course	1.500	L.F.	.004	.27	.20	.47
Every 2nd course	.750	L.F.	.002	.14	.10	.24
Every 3rd course	.500	L.F.	.001	.09	.07	.16
Every 4th course	.400	L.F.	.001	.07	.05	.12
Wire strips to 12″ wide, every course	1.500	L.F.	.006	.29	.29	.58
Every 2nd course	.750	L.F.	.003	.14	.14	.28
Every 3rd course	.500	L.F.	.002	.10	.10	.20
Every 4th course	.400	L.F.	.002	.08	.08	.16
Parging, plastering with portland cement plaster, 1 coat	1.000	S.F.	.014	.25	.64	.89
2 coats	1.000	S.F.	.022	.39	.99	1.38
Dampproofing, bituminous, brushed on, 1 coat	1.000	S.F.	.012	.22	.53	.75
2 coats	1.000	S.F.	.016	.44	.70	1.14
Sprayed on, 1 coat	1.000	S.F.	.010	.22	.42	.64
2 coats	1.000	S.F.	.016	.43	.70	1.13
Troweled on, 1/16″ thick	1.000	S.F.	.016	.47	.70	1.17
1/8″ thick	1.000	S.F.	.020	.83	.88	1.71
1/2″ thick	1.000	S.F.	.023	2.68	1.01	3.69
Insulation, rigid, fiberglass, 1.5#/C.F., unfaced						
1-1/2″ thick R 6.2	1.000	S.F.	.008	.70	.39	1.09
2″ thick R 8.5	1.000	S.F.	.008	.76	.39	1.15
3″ thick R 13	1.000	S.F.	.010	.88	.49	1.37
Foamglass, 1-1/2″ thick R 2.64	1.000	S.F.	.010	1.54	.49	2.03
2″ thick R 5.26	1.000	S.F.	.011	3.80	.54	4.34
Perlite, 1″ thick R 2.77	1.000	S.F.	.010	.33	.49	.82
2″ thick R 5.55	1.000	S.F.	.011	.66	.54	1.20
Polystyrene, extruded, 1″ thick R 5.4	1.000	S.F.	.010	.56	.49	1.05
2″ thick R 10.8	1.000	S.F.	.011	1.54	.54	2.08
Molded 1″ thick R 3.85	1.000	S.F.	.010	.40	.49	.89
2″ thick R 7.7	1.000	S.F.	.011	1.19	.54	1.73
Grout, concrete block cores, 6″ thick	1.000	S.F.	.044	.91	1.93	2.84
8″ thick	1.000	S.F.	.059	1.21	2.57	3.78
10″ thick	1.000	S.F.	.061	1.59	2.65	4.24
12″ thick	1.000	S.F.	.063	1.97	2.74	4.71
Anchor bolts, 2′ on center, 1/2″ diameter, 8″ long	.120	Ea.	.005	.11	.23	.34
12″ long	.120	Ea.	.005	.20	.24	.44
3/4″ diameter, 8″ long	.120	Ea.	.006	.42	.29	.71
12″ long	.120	Ea.	.006	.53	.31	.84
4′ on center, 1/2″ diameter, 8″ long	.060	Ea.	.002	.05	.12	.17
12″ long	.060	Ea.	.003	.10	.12	.22
3/4″ diameter, 8″ long	.060	Ea.	.003	.21	.14	.35
12″ long	.060	Ea.	.003	.26	.15	.41
Sill plates, treated, 2″ x 4″	.250	L.F.	.007	.10	.36	.46
4″ x 4″	.250	L.F.	.007	.42	.34	.76

System Description	QUAN.	UNIT	LABOR HOURS	COST PER S.F.		
				MAT.	INST.	TOTAL
8″ THICK, POURED CONCRETE WALL						
Concrete, 8″ thick , 3000 psi	.025	C.Y.		2.68		2.68
Forms, prefabricated plywood, up to 8′ high	2.000	SFCA	.120	3.18	5.18	8.36
Reinforcing, light	.670	Lb.	.004	.31	.19	.50
Placing concrete, direct chute	.025	C.Y.	.013		.53	.53
Dampproofing, brushed on, 2 coats	1.000	S.F.	.016	.44	.70	1.14
Rigid insulation, 1″ polystyrene	1.000	S.F.	.010	.56	.49	1.05
Anchor bolts, 1/2″ diameter, 12″ long, 4′ O.C.	.060	Ea.	.003	.10	.12	.22
Sill plates, 2″ x 4″, treated	.250	L.F.	.007	.10	.36	.46
TOTAL		S.F.	.173	7.37	7.57	14.94
12″ THICK, POURED CONCRETE WALL						
Concrete, 12″ thick, 3000 psi	.040	C.Y.		4.28		4.28
Forms, prefabricated plywood, up to 8′ high	2.000	SFCA	.120	3.18	5.18	8.36
Reinforcing, light	1.000	Lb.	.005	.46	.29	.75
Placing concrete, direct chute	.040	C.Y.	.019		.76	.76
Dampproofing, brushed on, 2 coats	1.000	S.F.	.016	.44	.70	1.14
Rigid insulation, 1″ polystyrene	1.000	S.F.	.010	.56	.49	1.05
Anchor bolts, 1/2″ diameter, 12″ long, 4′ O.C.	.060	Ea.	.003	.10	.12	.22
Sill plates, 2″ x 4″ treated	.250	L.F.	.007	.10	.36	.46
TOTAL		S.F.	.180	9.12	7.90	17.02

The costs in this system are based on sq. ft. of wall. Do not subtract
for window and door openings. The costs assume a 4′ high wall.

Description	QUAN.	UNIT	LABOR HOURS	COST PER S.F.		
				MAT.	INST.	TOTAL

Concrete Wall Price Sheet	QUAN.	UNIT	LABOR HOURS	COST PER S.F.		
				MAT.	INST.	TOTAL
Formwork, prefabricated plywood, up to 8' high	2.000	SFCA	.081	3.18	5.20	8.38
Over 8' to 16' high	2.000	SFCA	.076	3.24	6.90	10.14
Job built forms, 1 use per month	2.000	SFCA	.320	4.94	11.20	16.14
4 uses per month	2.000	SFCA	.221	1.80	8.20	10
Reinforcing, 8" wall, light reinforcing	.670	Lb.	.004	.31	.19	.50
Heavy reinforcing	1.500	Lb.	.008	.69	.44	1.13
10" wall, light reinforcing	.850	Lb.	.005	.39	.25	.64
Heavy reinforcing	2.000	Lb.	.011	.92	.58	1.50
12" wall light reinforcing	1.000	Lb.	.005	.46	.29	.75
Heavy reinforcing	2.250	Lb.	.012	1.04	.65	1.69
Placing concrete, 8" wall, direct chute	.025	C.Y.	.013		.53	.53
Pumped concrete	.025	C.Y.	.016		.85	.85
Crane & bucket	.025	C.Y.	.023		1.33	1.33
10" wall, direct chute	.030	C.Y.	.016		.64	.64
Pumped concrete	.030	C.Y.	.019		1.01	1.01
Crane & bucket	.030	C.Y.	.027		1.60	1.60
12" wall, direct chute	.040	C.Y.	.019		.76	.76
Pumped concrete	.040	C.Y.	.023		1.24	1.24
Crane & bucket	.040	C.Y.	.032		1.89	1.89
Dampproofing, bituminous, brushed on, 1 coat	1.000	S.F.	.012	.22	.53	.75
2 coats	1.000	S.F.	.016	.44	.70	1.14
Sprayed on, 1 coat	1.000	S.F.	.010	.22	.42	.64
2 coats	1.000	S.F.	.016	.43	.70	1.13
Troweled on, 1/16" thick	1.000	S.F.	.016	.47	.70	1.17
1/8" thick	1.000	S.F.	.020	.83	.88	1.71
1/2" thick	1.000	S.F.	.023	2.68	1.01	3.69
Insulation rigid, fiberglass, 1.5#/C.F., unfaced						
1-1/2" thick, R 6.2	1.000	S.F.	.008	.70	.39	1.09
2" thick, R 8.3	1.000	S.F.	.008	.76	.39	1.15
3" thick, R 12.4	1.000	S.F.	.010	.88	.49	1.37
Foamglass, 1-1/2" thick R 2.64	1.000	S.F.	.010	1.54	.49	2.03
2" thick R 5.26	1.000	S.F.	.011	3.80	.54	4.34
Perlite, 1" thick R 2.77	1.000	S.F.	.010	.33	.49	.82
2" thick R 5.55	1.000	S.F.	.011	.66	.54	1.20
Polystyrene, extruded, 1" thick R 5.40	1.000	S.F.	.010	.56	.49	1.05
2" thick R 10.8	1.000	S.F.	.011	1.54	.54	2.08
Molded, 1" thick R 3.85	1.000	S.F.	.010	.40	.49	.89
2" thick R 7.70	1.000	S.F.	.011	1.19	.54	1.73
Anchor bolts, 2' on center, 1/2" diameter, 8" long	.120	Ea.	.005	.11	.23	.34
12" long	.120	Ea.	.005	.20	.24	.44
3/4" diameter, 8" long	.120	Ea.	.006	.42	.29	.71
12" long	.120	Ea.	.006	.53	.31	.84
Sill plates, treated lumber, 2" x 4"	.250	L.F.	.007	.10	.36	.46
4" x 4"	.250	L.F.	.007	.42	.34	.76

Top Plates

Sheathing

Studs

Asphalt Paper

Insulation

Vapor Barrier

Bottom Plate

System Description	QUAN.	UNIT	LABOR HOURS	COST PER S.F.		
				MAT.	INST.	TOTAL
2" X 4" STUDS, 16" O.C., WALL						
Studs, 2" x 4", 16" O.C., treated	1.000	L.F.	.015	.38	.71	1.09
Plates, double top plate, single bottom plate, treated, 2" x 4"	.750	L.F.	.011	.29	.53	.82
Sheathing, 1/2", exterior grade, CDX, treated	1.000	S.F.	.014	1.12	.70	1.82
Asphalt paper, 15# roll	1.100	S.F.	.002	.07	.12	.19
Vapor barrier, 4 mil polyethylene	1.000	S.F.	.002	.06	.11	.17
Insulation, batts, fiberglass, 3-1/2" thick, R 11	1.000	S.F.	.006	.36	.29	.65
TOTAL		S.F.	.050	2.28	2.46	4.74
2" X 6" STUDS, 16" O.C., WALL						
Studs, 2" x 6", 16" O.C., treated	1.000	L.F.	.016	.61	.78	1.39
Plates, double top plate, single bottom plate, treated, 2" x 6"	.750	L.F.	.012	.46	.59	1.05
Sheathing, 5/8" exterior grade, CDX, treated	1.000	S.F.	.015	1.71	.75	2.46
Asphalt paper, 15# roll	1.100	S.F.	.002	.07	.12	.19
Vapor barrier, 4 mil polyethylene	1.000	S.F.	.002	.06	.11	.17
Insulation, batts, fiberglass, 6" thick, R 19	1.000	S.F.	.006	.47	.29	.76
TOTAL		S.F.	.053	3.38	2.64	6.02
2" X 8" STUDS, 16" O.C., WALL						
Studs, 2" x 8", 16" O.C. treated	1.000	L.F.	.018	1.14	.87	2.01
Plates, double top plate, single bottom plate, treated, 2" x 8"	.750	L.F.	.013	.86	.65	1.51
Sheathing, 3/4" exterior grade, CDX, treated	1.000	S.F.	.016	1.87	.80	2.67
Asphalt paper, 15# roll	1.100	S.F.	.002	.07	.12	.19
Vapor barrier, 4 mil polyethylene	1.000	S.F.	.002	.06	.11	.17
Insulation, batts, fiberglass, 9" thick, R 30	1.000	S.F.	.006	.77	.29	1.06
TOTAL		S.F.	.057	4.77	2.84	7.61

The costs in this system are based on a sq. ft. of wall area. Do not subtract for window or door openings. The costs assume a 4' high wall.

Description	QUAN.	UNIT	LABOR HOURS	COST PER S.F.		
				MAT.	INST.	TOTAL

Wood Wall Foundation Price Sheet	QUAN.	UNIT	LABOR HOURS	COST PER S.F.		
				MAT.	INST.	TOTAL
Studs, treated, 2″ x 4″, 12″ O.C.	1.250	L.F.	.018	.48	.89	1.37
16″ O.C.	1.000	L.F.	.015	.38	.71	1.09
2″ x 6″, 12″ O.C.	1.250	L.F.	.020	.76	.98	1.74
16″ O.C.	1.000	L.F.	.016	.61	.78	1.39
2″ x 8″, 12″ O.C.	1.250	L.F.	.022	1.43	1.09	2.52
16″ O.C.	1.000	L.F.	.018	1.14	.87	2.01
Plates, treated double top single bottom, 2″ x 4″	.750	L.F.	.011	.29	.53	.82
2″ x 6″	.750	L.F.	.012	.46	.59	1.05
2″ x 8″	.750	L.F.	.013	.86	.65	1.51
Sheathing, treated exterior grade CDX, 1/2″ thick	1.000	S.F.	.014	1.12	.70	1.82
5/8″ thick	1.000	S.F.	.015	1.71	.75	2.46
3/4″ thick	1.000	S.F.	.016	1.87	.80	2.67
Asphalt paper, 15# roll	1.100	S.F.	.002	.07	.12	.19
Vapor barrier, polyethylene, 4 mil	1.000	S.F.	.002	.04	.11	.15
10 mil	1.000	S.F.	.002	.07	.11	.18
Insulation, rigid, fiberglass, 1.5#/C.F., unfaced	1.000	S.F.	.008	.48	.39	.87
1-1/2″ thick, R 6.2	1.000	S.F.	.008	.70	.39	1.09
2″ thick, R 8.3	1.000	S.F.	.008	.76	.39	1.15
3″ thick, R 12.4	1.000	S.F.	.010	.90	.50	1.40
Foamglass 1 1/2″ thick, R 2.64	1.000	S.F.	.010	1.54	.49	2.03
2″ thick, R 5.26	1.000	S.F.	.011	3.80	.54	4.34
Perlite 1″ thick, R 2.77	1.000	S.F.	.010	.33	.49	.82
2″ thick, R 5.55	1.000	S.F.	.011	.66	.54	1.20
Polystyrene, extruded, 1″ thick, R 5.40	1.000	S.F.	.010	.56	.49	1.05
2″ thick, R 10.8	1.000	S.F.	.011	1.54	.54	2.08
Molded 1″ thick, R 3.85	1.000	S.F.	.010	.40	.49	.89
2″ thick, R 7.7	1.000	S.F.	.011	1.19	.54	1.73
Non rigid, batts, fiberglass, paper backed, 3-1/2″ thick roll, R 11	1.000	S.F.	.005	.36	.29	.65
6″, R 19	1.000	S.F.	.006	.47	.29	.76
9″, R 30	1.000	S.F.	.006	.77	.29	1.06
12″, R 38	1.000	S.F.	.006	1.10	.29	1.39
Mineral fiber, paper backed, 3-1/2″, R 13	1.000	S.F.	.005	.42	.24	.66
6″, R 19	1.000	S.F.	.005	.53	.24	.77
10″, R 30	1.000	S.F.	.006	.80	.29	1.09

Concrete Slab — Expansion Material — Bank Run Gravel — Welded Wire Fabric — Vapor Barrier

System Description	QUAN.	UNIT	LABOR HOURS	COST PER S.F.		
				MAT.	INST.	TOTAL
4″ THICK SLAB						
Concrete, 4″ thick, 3000 psi concrete	.012	C.Y.		1.28		1.28
Place concrete, direct chute	.012	C.Y.	.005		.21	.21
Bank run gravel, 4″ deep	1.000	S.F.	.001	.39	.05	.44
Polyethylene vapor barrier, .006″ thick	1.000	S.F.	.002	.06	.11	.17
Edge forms, expansion material	.100	L.F.	.005	.03	.23	.26
Welded wire fabric, 6 x 6, 10/10 (W1.4/W1.4)	1.100	S.F.	.005	.14	.28	.42
Steel trowel finish	1.000	S.F.	.014		.61	.61
TOTAL		S.F.	.032	1.90	1.49	3.39
6″ THICK SLAB						
Concrete, 6″ thick, 3000 psi concrete	.019	C.Y.		2.03		2.03
Place concrete, direct chute	.019	C.Y.	.008		.33	.33
Bank run gravel, 4″ deep	1.000	S.F.	.001	.39	.05	.44
Polyethylene vapor barrier, .006″ thick	1.000	S.F.	.002	.06	.11	.17
Edge forms, expansion material	.100	L.F.	.005	.03	.23	.26
Welded wire fabric, 6 x 6, 10/10 (W1.4/W1.4)	1.100	S.F.	.005	.14	.28	.42
Steel trowel finish	1.000	S.F.	.014		.61	.61
TOTAL		S.F.	.035	2.65	1.61	4.26

The slab costs in this section are based on a cost per square foot of floor area.

Description	QUAN.	UNIT	LABOR HOURS	COST PER S.F.		
				MAT.	INST.	TOTAL

Floor Slab Price Sheet	QUAN.	UNIT	LABOR HOURS	COST PER S.F.		
				MAT.	INST.	TOTAL
Concrete, 4" thick slab, 2000 psi concrete	.012	C.Y.		1.21		1.21
2500 psi concrete	.012	C.Y.		1.24		1.24
3000 psi concrete	.012	C.Y.		1.28		1.28
3500 psi concrete	.012	C.Y.		1.32		1.32
4000 psi concrete	.012	C.Y.		1.36		1.36
4500 psi concrete	.012	C.Y.		1.39		1.39
5" thick slab, 2000 psi concrete	.015	C.Y.		1.52		1.52
2500 psi concrete	.015	C.Y.		1.55		1.55
3000 psi concrete	.015	C.Y.		1.61		1.61
3500 psi concrete	.015	C.Y.		1.65		1.65
4000 psi concrete	.015	C.Y.		1.70		1.70
4500 psi concrete	.015	C.Y.		1.74		1.74
6" thick slab, 2000 psi concrete	.019	C.Y.		1.92		1.92
2500 psi concrete	.019	C.Y.		1.96		1.96
3000 psi concrete	.019	C.Y.		2.03		2.03
3500 psi concrete	.019	C.Y.		2.09		2.09
4000 psi concrete	.019	C.Y.		2.15		2.15
4500 psi concrete	.019	C.Y.		2.20		2.20
Place concrete, 4" slab, direct chute	.012	C.Y.	.005		.21	.21
Pumped concrete	.012	C.Y.	.006		.31	.31
Crane & bucket	.012	C.Y.	.008		.46	.46
5" slab, direct chute	.015	C.Y.	.007		.26	.26
Pumped concrete	.015	C.Y.	.007		.39	.39
Crane & bucket	.015	C.Y.	.010		.58	.58
6" slab, direct chute	.019	C.Y.	.008		.33	.33
Pumped concrete	.019	C.Y.	.009		.50	.50
Crane & bucket	.019	C.Y.	.012		.74	.74
Gravel, bank run, 4" deep	1.000	S.F.	.001	.39	.05	.44
6" deep	1.000	S.F.	.001	.52	.07	.59
9" deep	1.000	S.F.	.001	.76	.10	.86
12" deep	1.000	S.F.	.001	1.05	.12	1.17
3/4" crushed stone, 3" deep	1.000	S.F.	.001	.42	.06	.48
6" deep	1.000	S.F.	.001	.83	.10	.93
9" deep	1.000	S.F.	.002	1.21	.12	1.33
12" deep	1.000	S.F.	.002	1.71	.16	1.87
Vapor barrier polyethylene, .004" thick	1.000	S.F.	.002	.04	.11	.15
.006" thick	1.000	S.F.	.002	.06	.11	.17
Edge forms, expansion material, 4" thick slab	.100	L.F.	.004	.02	.15	.17
6" thick slab	.100	L.F.	.005	.03	.23	.26
Welded wire fabric 6 x 6, 10/10 (W1.4/W1.4)	1.100	S.F.	.005	.14	.28	.42
6 x 6, 6/6 (W2.9/W2.9)	1.100	S.F.	.006	.29	.33	.62
4 x 4, 10/10 (W1.4/W1.4)	1.100	S.F.	.006	.22	.31	.53
Finish concrete, screed finish	1.000	S.F.	.009		.25	.25
Float finish	1.000	S.F.	.011		.25	.25
Steel trowel, for resilient floor	1.000	S.F.	.013		.79	.79
For finished floor	1.000	S.F.	.015		.61	.61

Division 3
Framing

System Description	QUAN.	UNIT	LABOR HOURS	COST PER S.F.		
				MAT.	INST.	TOTAL
2″ X 8″, 16″ O.C.						
Wood joists, 2″ x 8″, 16″ O.C.	1.000	L.F.	.015	.61	.71	1.32
Bridging, 1″ x 3″, 6′ O.C.	.080	Pr.	.005	.04	.24	.28
Box sills, 2″ x 8″	.150	L.F.	.002	.09	.11	.20
Concrete filled steel column, 4″ diameter	.125	L.F.	.002	.20	.12	.32
Girder, built up from three 2″ x 8″	.125	L.F.	.013	.23	.65	.88
Sheathing, plywood, subfloor, 5/8″ CDX	1.000	S.F.	.012	.56	.58	1.14
Furring, 1″ x 3″, 16″ O.C.	1.000	L.F.	.023	.38	1.12	1.50
TOTAL		S.F.	.072	2.11	3.53	5.64
2″ X 10″, 16″ O.C.						
Wood joists, 2″ x 10″, 16″ OC	1.000	L.F.	.018	.80	.87	1.67
Bridging, 1″ x 3″, 6′ OC	.080	Pr.	.005	.04	.24	.28
Box sills, 2″ x 10″	.150	L.F.	.003	.12	.13	.25
Concrete filled steel column, 4″ diameter	.125	L.F.	.002	.20	.12	.32
Girder, built up from three 2″ x 10″	.125	L.F.	.014	.30	.70	1
Sheathing, plywood, subfloor, 5/8″ CDX	1.000	S.F.	.012	.56	.58	1.14
Furring, 1″ x 3″,16″ OC	1.000	L.F.	.023	.38	1.12	1.50
TOTAL		S.F.	.077	2.40	3.76	6.16
2″ X 12″, 16″ O.C.						
Wood joists, 2″ x 12″, 16″ O.C.	1.000	L.F.	.018	1.17	.90	2.07
Bridging, 1″ x 3″, 6′ O.C.	.080	Pr.	.005	.04	.24	.28
Box sills, 2″ x 12″	.150	L.F.	.003	.18	.14	.32
Concrete filled steel column, 4″ diameter	.125	L.F.	.002	.20	.12	.32
Girder, built up from three 2″ x 12″	.125	L.F.	.015	.44	.74	1.18
Sheathing, plywood, subfloor, 5/8″ CDX	1.000	S.F.	.012	.56	.58	1.14
Furring, 1″ x 3″, 16″ O.C.	1.000	L.F.	.023	.38	1.12	1.50
TOTAL		S.F.	.078	2.97	3.84	6.81

Floor costs on this page are given on a cost per square foot basis.

Description	QUAN.	UNIT	LABOR HOURS	COST PER S.F.		
				MAT.	INST.	TOTAL

Floor Framing Price Sheet (Wood)

	QUAN.	UNIT	LABOR HOURS	COST PER S.F. MAT.	COST PER S.F. INST.	COST PER S.F. TOTAL
Joists, #2 or better, pine, 2" x 4", 12" O.C.	1.250	L.F.	.016	.34	.79	1.13
16" O.C.	1.000	L.F.	.013	.27	.63	.90
2" x 6", 12" O.C.	1.250	L.F.	.016	.51	.79	1.30
16" O.C.	1.000	L.F.	.013	.41	.63	1.04
2" x 8", 12" O.C.	1.250	L.F.	.018	.76	.89	1.65
16" O.C.	1.000	L.F.	.015	.61	.71	1.32
2" x 10", 12" O.C.	1.250	L.F.	.022	1	1.09	2.09
16" O.C.	1.000	L.F.	.018	.80	.87	1.67
2"x 12", 12" O.C.	1.250	L.F.	.023	1.46	1.13	2.59
16" O.C.	1.000	L.F.	.018	1.17	.90	2.07
Bridging, wood 1" x 3", joists 12" O.C.	.100	Pr.	.006	.06	.30	.36
16" O.C.	.080	Pr.	.005	.04	.24	.28
Metal, galvanized, joists 12" O.C.	.100	Pr.	.006	.17	.30	.47
16" O.C.	.080	Pr.	.005	.14	.24	.38
Compression type, joists 12" O.C.	.100	Pr.	.004	.18	.20	.38
16" O.C.	.080	Pr.	.003	.14	.16	.30
Box sills, #2 or better pine, 2" x 4"	.150	L.F.	.002	.04	.09	.13
2" x 6"	.150	L.F.	.002	.06	.09	.15
2" x 8"	.150	L.F.	.002	.09	.11	.20
2" x 10"	.150	L.F.	.003	.12	.13	.25
2" x 12"	.150	L.F.	.003	.18	.14	.32
Girders, including lally columns, 3 pieces spiked together, 2" x 8"	.125	L.F.	.015	.43	.77	1.20
2" x 10"	.125	L.F.	.016	.50	.82	1.32
2" x 12"	.125	L.F.	.017	.64	.86	1.50
Solid girders, 3" x 8"	.040	L.F.	.004	.30	.20	.50
3" x 10"	.040	L.F.	.004	.33	.21	.54
3" x 12"	.040	L.F.	.004	.36	.22	.58
4" x 8"	.040	L.F.	.004	.33	.22	.55
4" x 10"	.040	L.F.	.004	.37	.23	.60
4" x 12"	.040	L.F.	.004	.48	.24	.72
Steel girders, bolted & including fabrication, wide flange shapes						
12" deep, 14#/l.f.	.040	L.F.	.003	.88	.26	1.14
10" deep, 15#/l.f.	.040	L.F.	.003	.88	.26	1.14
8" deep, 10#/l.f.	.040	L.F.	.003	.58	.26	.84
6" deep, 9#/l.f.	.040	L.F.	.003	.52	.26	.78
5" deep, 16#/l.f.	.040	L.F.	.003	.88	.26	1.14
Sheathing, plywood exterior grade CDX, 1/2" thick	1.000	S.F.	.011	.46	.56	1.02
5/8" thick	1.000	S.F.	.012	.56	.58	1.14
3/4" thick	1.000	S.F.	.013	.64	.63	1.27
Boards, 1" x 8" laid regular	1.000	S.F.	.016	1.47	.78	2.25
Laid diagonal	1.000	S.F.	.019	1.47	.92	2.39
1" x 10" laid regular	1.000	S.F.	.015	1.62	.71	2.33
Laid diagonal	1.000	S.F.	.018	1.62	.87	2.49
Furring, 1" x 3", 12" O.C.	1.250	L.F.	.029	.48	1.40	1.88
16" O.C.	1.000	L.F.	.023	.38	1.12	1.50
24" O.C.	.750	L.F.	.017	.29	.84	1.13

113

System Description	QUAN.	UNIT	LABOR HOURS	COST PER S.F.		
				MAT.	INST.	TOTAL
9-1/2″ COMPOSITE WOOD JOISTS, 16″ O.C.						
CWJ, 9-1/2″, 16″ O.C., 15′ span	1.000	L.F.	.018	1.73	.87	2.60
Temp. strut line, 1″ x 4″, 8′ O.C.	.160	L.F.	.003	.08	.16	.24
CWJ rim joist, 9-1/2″	.150	L.F.	.003	.26	.13	.39
Concrete filled steel column, 4″ diameter	.125	L.F.	.002	.20	.12	.32
Girder, built up from three 2″ x 8″	.125	L.F.	.013	.23	.65	.88
Sheathing, plywood, subfloor, 5/8″ CDX	1.000	S.F.	.012	.56	.58	1.14
TOTAL		S.F.	.051	3.06	2.51	5.57
11-1/2″ COMPOSITE WOOD JOISTS, 16″ O.C.						
CWJ, 11-1/2″, 16″ O.C., 18′ span	1.000	L.F.	.018	1.85	.89	2.74
Temp. strut line, 1″ x 4″, 8′ O.C.	.160	L.F.	.003	.08	.16	.24
CWJ rim joist, 11-1/2″	.150	L.F.	.003	.28	.13	.41
Concrete filled steel column, 4″ diameter	.125	L.F.	.002	.20	.12	.32
Girder, built up from three 2″ x 10″	.125	L.F.	.014	.30	.70	1
Sheathing, plywood, subfloor, 5/8″ CDX	1.000	S.F.	.012	.56	.58	1.14
TOTAL		S.F.	.052	3.27	2.58	5.85
14″ COMPOSITE WOOD JOISTS, 16″ O.C.						
CWJ, 14″, 16″ O.C., 22′ span	1.000	L.F.	.020	2.58	.96	3.54
Temp. strut line, 1″ x 4″, 8′ O.C.	.160	L.F.	.003	.08	.16	.24
CWJ rim joist, 14″	.150	L.F.	.003	.39	.14	.53
Concrete filled steel column, 4″ diameter	.600	L.F.	.002	.20	.12	.32
Girder, built up from three 2″ x 12″	.600	L.F.	.015	.44	.74	1.18
Sheathing, plywood, subfloor, 5/8″ CDX	1.000	S.F.	.012	.56	.58	1.14
TOTAL		S.F.	.055	4.25	2.70	6.95

Floor costs on this page are given on a cost per square foot basis.

Description	QUAN.	UNIT	LABOR HOURS	COST PER S.F.		
				MAT.	INST.	TOTAL

Floor Framing Price Sheet (Wood)	QUAN.	UNIT	LABOR HOURS	COST PER S.F.		
				MAT.	INST.	TOTAL
Composite wood joist 9-1/2" deep, 12" O.C.	1.250	L.F.	.022	2.16	1.09	3.25
16" O.C.	1.000	L.F.	.018	1.73	.87	2.60
11-1/2" deep, 12" O.C.	1.250	L.F.	.023	2.31	1.11	3.42
16" O.C.	1.000	L.F.	.018	1.85	.89	2.74
14" deep, 12" O.C.	1.250	L.F.	.024	3.22	1.19	4.41
16" O.C.	1.000	L.F.	.020	2.58	.96	3.54
16 " deep, 12" O.C.	1.250	L.F.	.026	4.22	1.25	5.47
16" O.C.	1.000	L.F.	.021	3.38	1	4.38
CWJ rim joist, 9-1/2"	.150	L.F.	.003	.26	.13	.39
11-1/2"	.150	L.F.	.003	.28	.13	.41
14"	.150	L.F.	.003	.39	.14	.53
16"	.150	L.F.	.003	.51	.15	.66
Girders, including lally columns, 3 pieces spiked together, 2" x 8"	.125	L.F.	.015	.43	.77	1.20
2" x 10"	.125	L.F.	.016	.50	.82	1.32
2" x 12"	.125	L.F.	.017	.64	.86	1.50
Solid girders, 3" x 8"	.040	L.F.	.004	.30	.20	.50
3" x 10"	.040	L.F.	.004	.33	.21	.54
3" x 12"	.040	L.F.	.004	.36	.22	.58
4" x 8"	.040	L.F.	.004	.33	.22	.55
4" x 10"	.040	L.F.	.004	.37	.23	.60
4" x 12"	.040	L.F.	.004	.48	.24	.72
Steel girders, bolted & including fabrication, wide flange shapes						
12" deep, 14#/l.f.	.040	L.F.	.061	20	5.85	25.85
10" deep, 15#/l.f.	.040	L.F.	.067	22	6.35	28.35
8" deep, 10#/l.f.	.040	L.F.	.067	14.50	6.35	20.85
6" deep, 9#/l.f.	.040	L.F.	.067	13.05	6.35	19.40
5" deep, 16#/l.f.	.040	L.F.	.064	21.50	6.15	27.65
Sheathing, plywood exterior grade CDX, 1/2" thick	1.000	S.F.	.011	.46	.56	1.02
5/8" thick	1.000	S.F.	.012	.56	.58	1.14
3/4" thick	1.000	S.F.	.013	.64	.63	1.27
Boards, 1" x 8" laid regular	1.000	S.F.	.016	1.47	.78	2.25
Laid diagonal	1.000	S.F.	.019	1.47	.92	2.39
1" x 10" laid regular	1.000	S.F.	.015	1.62	.71	2.33
Laid diagonal	1.000	S.F.	.018	1.62	.87	2.49
Furring, 1" x 3", 12" O.C.	1.250	L.F.	.029	.48	1.40	1.88
16" O.C.	1.000	L.F.	.023	.38	1.12	1.50
24" O.C.	.750	L.F.	.017	.29	.84	1.13

- Cont. 2" x 4" Ribbon
- Plywood Sheathing
- Girder
- Wood Floor Trusses

System Description	QUAN.	UNIT	LABOR HOURS	COST PER S.F.		
				MAT.	INST.	TOTAL
12″ OPEN WEB JOISTS, 16″ O.C.						
OWJ 12″, 16″ O.C., 21′ span	1.000	L.F.	.018	3.05	.89	3.94
Continuous ribbing, 2″ x 4″	.150	L.F.	.002	.04	.09	.13
Concrete filled steel column, 4″ diameter	.125	L.F.	.002	.20	.12	.32
Girder, built up from three 2″ x 8″	.125	L.F.	.013	.23	.65	.88
Sheathing, plywood, subfloor, 5/8″ CDX	1.000	S.F.	.012	.56	.58	1.14
Furring, 1″ x 3″, 16″ O.C.	1.000	L.F.	.023	.38	1.12	1.50
TOTAL		S.F.	.070	4.46	3.45	7.91
14″ OPEN WEB WOOD JOISTS, 16″ O.C.						
OWJ 14″, 16″ O.C., 22′ span	1.000	L.F.	.020	3.28	.96	4.24
Continuous ribbing, 2″ x 4″	.150	L.F.	.002	.04	.09	.13
Concrete filled steel column, 4″ diameter	.125	L.F.	.002	.20	.12	.32
Girder, built up from three 2″ x 10″	.125	L.F.	.014	.30	.70	1
Sheathing, plywood, subfloor, 5/8″ CDX	1.000	S.F.	.012	.56	.58	1.14
Furring, 1″ x 3″,16″ O.C.	1.000	L.F.	.023	.38	1.12	1.50
TOTAL		S.F.	.073	4.76	3.57	8.33
16″ OPEN WEB WOOD JOISTS, 16″ O.C.						
OWJ 16″, 16″ O.C., 24′ span	1.000	L.F.	.021	3.25	1	4.25
Continuous ribbing, 2″ x 4″	.150	L.F.	.002	.04	.09	.13
Concrete filled steel column, 4″ diameter	.125	L.F.	.002	.20	.12	.32
Girder, built up from three 2″ x 12″	.125	L.F.	.015	.44	.74	1.18
Sheathing, plywood, subfloor, 5/8″ CDX	1.000	S.F.	.012	.56	.58	1.14
Furring, 1″ x 3″, 16″ O.C.	1.000	L.F.	.023	.38	1.12	1.50
TOTAL		S.F.	.075	4.87	3.65	8.52

Floor costs on this page are given on a cost per square foot basis.

Description	QUAN.	UNIT	LABOR HOURS	COST PER S.F.		
				MAT.	INST.	TOTAL

Floor Framing Price Sheet (Wood)	QUAN.	UNIT	LABOR HOURS	COST PER S.F.		
				MAT.	INST.	TOTAL
Open web joists, 12" deep, 12" O.C.	1.250	L.F.	.023	3.81	1.11	4.92
16" O.C.	1.000	L.F.	.018	3.05	.89	3.94
14" deep, 12" O.C.	1.250	L.F.	.024	4.09	1.19	5.28
16" O.C.	1.000	L.F.	.020	3.28	.96	4.24
16" deep, 12" O.C.	1.250	L.F.	.026	4.06	1.25	5.31
16" O.C.	1.000	L.F.	.021	3.25	1	4.25
18" deep, 12" O.C.	1.250	L.F.	.027	4.38	1.31	5.69
16" O.C.	1.000	L.F.	.022	3.50	1.05	4.55
Continuous ribbing, 2" x 4"	.150	L.F.	.002	.04	.09	.13
2" x 6"	.150	L.F.	.002	.06	.09	.15
2" x 8"	.150	L.F.	.002	.09	.11	.20
2" x 10"	.150	L.F.	.003	.12	.13	.25
2" x 12"	.150	L.F.	.003	.18	.14	.32
Girders, including lally columns, 3 pieces spiked together, 2" x 8"	.125	L.F.	.015	.43	.77	1.20
2" x 10"	.125	L.F.	.016	.50	.82	1.32
2" x 12"	.125	L.F.	.017	.64	.86	1.50
Solid girders, 3" x 8"	.040	L.F.	.004	.30	.20	.50
3" x 10"	.040	L.F.	.004	.33	.21	.54
3" x 12"	.040	L.F.	.004	.36	.22	.58
4" x 8"	.040	L.F.	.004	.33	.22	.55
4" x 10"	.040	L.F.	.004	.37	.23	.60
4" x 12"	.040	L.F.	.004	.48	.24	.72
Steel girders, bolted & including fabrication, wide flange shapes						
12" deep, 14#/l.f.	.040	L.F.	.061	20	5.85	25.85
10" deep, 15#/l.f.	.040	L.F.	.067	22	6.35	28.35
8" deep, 10#/l.f.	.040	L.F.	.067	14.50	6.35	20.85
6" deep, 9#/l.f.	.040	L.F.	.067	13.05	6.35	19.40
5" deep, 16#/l.f.	.040	L.F.	.064	21.50	6.15	27.65
Sheathing, plywood exterior grade CDX, 1/2" thick	1.000	S.F.	.011	.46	.56	1.02
5/8" thick	1.000	S.F.	.012	.56	.58	1.14
3/4" thick	1.000	S.F.	.013	.64	.63	1.27
Boards, 1" x 8" laid regular	1.000	S.F.	.016	1.47	.78	2.25
Laid diagonal	1.000	S.F.	.019	1.47	.92	2.39
1" x 10" laid regular	1.000	S.F.	.015	1.62	.71	2.33
Laid diagonal	1.000	S.F.	.018	1.62	.87	2.49
Furring, 1" x 3", 12" O.C.	1.250	L.F.	.029	.48	1.40	1.88
16" O.C.	1.000	L.F.	.023	.38	1.12	1.50
24" O.C.	.750	L.F.	.017	.29	.84	1.13

Sheathing →

Top Plates ←

Studs ←

Bottom Plate →

Corner Bracing ←

System Description	QUAN.	UNIT	LABOR HOURS	COST PER S.F.		
				MAT.	INST.	TOTAL
2" X 4", 16" O.C.						
2" x 4" studs, 16" O.C.	1.000	L.F.	.015	.27	.71	.98
Plates, 2" x 4", double top, single bottom	.375	L.F.	.005	.10	.27	.37
Corner bracing, let-in, 1" x 6"	.063	L.F.	.003	.04	.16	.20
Sheathing, 1/2" plywood, CDX	1.000	S.F.	.011	.46	.56	1.02
TOTAL		S.F.	.034	.87	1.70	2.57
2" X 4", 24" O.C.						
2" x 4" studs, 24" O.C.	.750	L.F.	.011	.20	.53	.73
Plates, 2" x 4", double top, single bottom	.375	L.F.	.005	.10	.27	.37
Corner bracing, let-in, 1" x 6"	.063	L.F.	.002	.04	.11	.15
Sheathing, 1/2" plywood, CDX	1.000	S.F.	.011	.46	.56	1.02
TOTAL		S.F.	.029	.80	1.47	2.27
2" X 6", 16" O.C.						
2" x 6" studs, 16" O.C.	1.000	L.F.	.016	.41	.78	1.19
Plates, 2" x 6", double top, single bottom	.375	L.F.	.006	.15	.29	.44
Corner bracing, let-in, 1" x 6"	.063	L.F.	.003	.04	.16	.20
Sheathing, 1/2" plywood, CDX	1.000	S.F.	.014	.46	.70	1.16
TOTAL		S.F.	.039	1.06	1.93	2.99
2" X 6", 24" O.C.						
2" x 6" studs, 24" O.C.	.750	L.F.	.012	.31	.59	.90
Plates, 2" x 6", double top, single bottom	.375	L.F.	.006	.15	.29	.44
Corner bracing, let-in, 1" x 6"	.063	L.F.	.002	.04	.11	.15
Sheathing, 1/2" plywood, CDX	1.000	S.F.	.011	.46	.56	1.02
TOTAL		S.F.	.031	.96	1.55	2.51

The wall costs on this page are given in cost per square foot of wall.
For window and door openings see below.

Description	QUAN.	UNIT	LABOR HOURS	COST PER S.F.		
				MAT.	INST.	TOTAL

Exterior Wall Framing Price Sheet	QUAN.	UNIT	LABOR HOURS	COST PER S.F.		
				MAT.	INST.	TOTAL
Studs, #2 or better, 2" x 4", 12" O.C.	1.250	L.F.	.018	.34	.89	1.23
16" O.C.	1.000	L.F.	.015	.27	.71	.98
24" O.C.	.750	L.F.	.011	.20	.53	.73
32" O.C.	.600	L.F.	.009	.16	.43	.59
2" x 6", 12" O.C.	1.250	L.F.	.020	.51	.98	1.49
16" O.C.	1.000	L.F.	.016	.41	.78	1.19
24" O.C.	.750	L.F.	.012	.31	.59	.90
32" O.C.	.600	L.F.	.010	.25	.47	.72
2" x 8", 12" O.C.	1.250	L.F.	.025	1.14	1.23	2.37
16" O.C.	1.000	L.F.	.020	.91	.98	1.89
24" O.C.	.750	L.F.	.015	.68	.74	1.42
32" O.C.	.600	L.F.	.012	.55	.59	1.14
Plates, #2 or better, double top, single bottom, 2" x 4"	.375	L.F.	.005	.10	.27	.37
2" x 6"	.375	L.F.	.006	.15	.29	.44
2" x 8"	.375	L.F.	.008	.34	.37	.71
Corner bracing, let-in 1" x 6" boards, studs, 12" O.C.	.070	L.F.	.004	.05	.18	.23
16" O.C.	.063	L.F.	.003	.04	.16	.20
24" O.C.	.063	L.F.	.002	.04	.11	.15
32" O.C.	.057	L.F.	.002	.04	.10	.14
Let-in steel ("T" shape), studs, 12" O.C.	.070	L.F.	.001	.06	.05	.11
16" O.C.	.063	L.F.	.001	.05	.04	.09
24" O.C.	.063	L.F.	.001	.05	.04	.09
32" O.C.	.057	L.F.	.001	.05	.04	.09
Sheathing, plywood CDX, 3/8" thick	1.000	S.F.	.010	.40	.51	.91
1/2" thick	1.000	S.F.	.011	.46	.56	1.02
5/8" thick	1.000	S.F.	.012	.56	.60	1.16
3/4" thick	1.000	S.F.	.013	.64	.65	1.29
Boards, 1" x 6", laid regular	1.000	S.F.	.025	1.53	1.21	2.74
Laid diagonal	1.000	S.F.	.027	1.53	1.34	2.87
1" x 8", laid regular	1.000	S.F.	.021	1.47	1.02	2.49
Laid diagonal	1.000	S.F.	.025	1.47	1.21	2.68
Wood fiber, regular, no vapor barrier, 1/2" thick	1.000	S.F.	.013	.62	.65	1.27
5/8" thick	1.000	S.F.	.013	.78	.65	1.43
Asphalt impregnated 25/32" thick	1.000	S.F.	.013	.31	.65	.96
1/2" thick	1.000	S.F.	.013	.22	.65	.87
Polystyrene, regular, 3/4" thick	1.000	S.F.	.010	.56	.49	1.05
2" thick	1.000	S.F.	.011	1.54	.54	2.08
Fiberglass, foil faced, 1" thick	1.000	S.F.	.008	1.01	.39	1.40
2" thick	1.000	S.F.	.009	1.88	.44	2.32

Window & Door Openings	QUAN.	UNIT	LABOR HOURS	COST EACH		
				MAT.	INST.	TOTAL
The following costs are to be added to the total costs of the wall for each opening. Do not subtract the area of the openings.						
Headers, 2" x 6" double, 2' long	4.000	L.F.	.178	1.64	8.70	10.34
3' long	6.000	L.F.	.267	2.46	13.10	15.56
4' long	8.000	L.F.	.356	3.28	17.45	20.73
5' long	10.000	L.F.	.444	4.10	22	26.10
2" x 8" double, 4' long	8.000	L.F.	.376	4.88	18.40	23.28
5' long	10.000	L.F.	.471	6.10	23	29.10
6' long	12.000	L.F.	.565	7.30	27.50	34.80
8' long	16.000	L.F.	.753	9.75	37	46.75
2" x 10" double, 4' long	8.000	L.F.	.400	6.40	19.60	26
6' long	12.000	L.F.	.600	9.60	29.50	39.10
8' long	16.000	L.F.	.800	12.80	39	51.80
10' long	20.000	L.F.	1.000	16	49	65
2" x 12" double, 8' long	16.000	L.F.	.853	18.70	42	60.70
12' long	24.000	L.F.	1.280	28	62.50	90.50

119

System Description	QUAN.	UNIT	LABOR HOURS	COST PER S.F.		
				MAT.	INST.	TOTAL
2″ X 6″ RAFTERS, 16″ O.C., 4/12 PITCH						
Rafters, 2″ x 6″, 16″ O.C., 4/12 pitch	1.170	L.F.	.019	.48	.91	1.39
Ceiling joists, 2″ x 4″, 16″ O.C.	1.000	L.F.	.013	.27	.63	.90
Ridge board, 2″ x 6″	.050	L.F.	.002	.02	.08	.10
Fascia board, 2″ x 6″	.100	L.F.	.005	.05	.26	.31
Rafter tie, 1″ x 4″, 4′ O.C.	.060	L.F.	.001	.03	.06	.09
Soffit nailer (outrigger), 2″ x 4″, 24″ O.C.	.170	L.F.	.004	.05	.21	.26
Sheathing, exterior, plywood, CDX, 1/2″ thick	1.170	S.F.	.013	.54	.66	1.20
Furring strips, 1″ x 3″, 16″ O.C.	1.000	L.F.	.023	.38	1.12	1.50
TOTAL		S.F.	.080	1.82	3.93	5.75
2″ X 8″ RAFTERS, 16″ O.C., 4/12 PITCH						
Rafters, 2″ x 8″, 16″ O.C., 4/12 pitch	1.170	L.F.	.020	.71	.96	1.67
Ceiling joists, 2″ x 6″, 16″ O.C.	1.000	L.F.	.013	.41	.63	1.04
Ridge board, 2″ x 8″	.050	L.F.	.002	.03	.09	.12
Fascia board, 2″ x 8″	.100	L.F.	.007	.06	.35	.41
Rafter tie, 1″ x 4″, 4′ O.C.	.060	L.F.	.001	.03	.06	.09
Soffit nailer (outrigger), 2″ x 4″, 24″ O.C.	.170	L.F.	.004	.05	.21	.26
Sheathing, exterior, plywood, CDX, 1/2″ thick	1.170	S.F.	.013	.54	.66	1.20
Furring strips, 1″ x 3″, 16″ O.C.	1.000	L.F.	.023	.38	1.12	1.50
TOTAL		S.F.	.083	2.21	4.08	6.29

The cost of this system is based on the square foot of plan area.
All quantities have been adjusted accordingly.

Description	QUAN.	UNIT	LABOR HOURS	COST PER S.F.		
				MAT.	INST.	TOTAL

Gable End Roof Framing Price Sheet

	QUAN.	UNIT	LABOR HOURS	COST PER S.F. MAT.	COST PER S.F. INST.	COST PER S.F. TOTAL
Rafters, #2 or better, 16″ O.C., 2″ x 6″, 4/12 pitch	1.170	L.F.	.019	.48	.91	1.39
8/12 pitch	1.330	L.F.	.027	.55	1.30	1.85
2″ x 8″, 4/12 pitch	1.170	L.F.	.020	.71	.96	1.67
8/12 pitch	1.330	L.F.	.028	.81	1.38	2.19
2″ x 10″, 4/12 pitch	1.170	L.F.	.030	.94	1.45	2.39
8/12 pitch	1.330	L.F.	.043	1.06	2.10	3.16
24″ O.C., 2″ x 6″, 4/12 pitch	.940	L.F.	.015	.39	.73	1.12
8/12 pitch	1.060	L.F.	.021	.43	1.04	1.47
2″ x 8″, 4/12 pitch	.940	L.F.	.016	.57	.77	1.34
8/12 pitch	1.060	L.F.	.023	.65	1.10	1.75
2″ x 10″, 4/12 pitch	.940	L.F.	.024	.75	1.17	1.92
8/12 pitch	1.060	L.F.	.034	.85	1.67	2.52
Ceiling joist, #2 or better, 2″ x 4″, 16″ O.C.	1.000	L.F.	.013	.27	.63	.90
24″ O.C.	.750	L.F.	.010	.20	.47	.67
2″ x 6″, 16″ O.C.	1.000	L.F.	.013	.41	.63	1.04
24″ O.C.	.750	L.F.	.010	.31	.47	.78
2″ x 8″, 16″ O.C.	1.000	L.F.	.015	.61	.71	1.32
24″ O.C.	.750	L.F.	.011	.46	.53	.99
2″ x 10″, 16″ O.C.	1.000	L.F.	.018	.80	.87	1.67
24″ O.C.	.750	L.F.	.013	.60	.65	1.25
Ridge board, #2 or better, 1″ x 6″	.050	L.F.	.001	.04	.07	.11
1″ x 8″	.050	L.F.	.001	.05	.07	.12
1″ x 10″	.050	L.F.	.002	.06	.08	.14
2″ x 6″	.050	L.F.	.002	.02	.08	.10
2″ x 8″	.050	L.F.	.002	.03	.09	.12
2″ x 10″	.050	L.F.	.002	.04	.10	.14
Fascia board, #2 or better, 1″ x 6″	.100	L.F.	.004	.03	.19	.22
1″ x 8″	.100	L.F.	.005	.04	.22	.26
1″ x 10″	.100	L.F.	.005	.04	.25	.29
2″ x 6″	.100	L.F.	.006	.05	.28	.33
2″ x 8″	.100	L.F.	.007	.06	.35	.41
2″ x 10″	.100	L.F.	.004	.16	.17	.33
Rafter tie, #2 or better, 4′ O.C., 1″ x 4″	.060	L.F.	.001	.03	.06	.09
1″ x 6″	.060	L.F.	.001	.03	.06	.09
2″ x 4″	.060	L.F.	.002	.04	.08	.12
2″ x 6″	.060	L.F.	.002	.05	.10	.15
Soffit nailer (outrigger), 2″ x 4″, 16″ O.C.	.220	L.F.	.006	.06	.28	.34
24″ O.C.	.170	L.F.	.004	.05	.21	.26
2″ x 6″, 16″ O.C.	.220	L.F.	.006	.07	.32	.39
24″ O.C.	.170	L.F.	.005	.05	.25	.30
Sheathing, plywood CDX, 4/12 pitch, 3/8″ thick.	1.170	S.F.	.012	.47	.60	1.07
1/2″ thick	1.170	S.F.	.013	.54	.66	1.20
5/8″ thick	1.170	S.F.	.014	.66	.70	1.36
8/12 pitch, 3/8″	1.330	S.F.	.014	.53	.68	1.21
1/2″ thick	1.330	S.F.	.015	.61	.74	1.35
5/8″ thick	1.330	S.F.	.016	.74	.80	1.54
Boards, 4/12 pitch roof, 1″ x 6″	1.170	S.F.	.026	1.79	1.26	3.05
1″ x 8″	1.170	S.F.	.021	1.72	1.05	2.77
8/12 pitch roof, 1″ x 6″	1.330	S.F.	.029	2.03	1.44	3.47
1″ x 8″	1.330	S.F.	.024	1.96	1.20	3.16
Furring, 1″ x 3″, 12″ O.C.	1.200	L.F.	.027	.46	1.34	1.80
16″ O.C.	1.000	L.F.	.023	.38	1.12	1.50
24″ O.C.	.800	L.F.	.018	.30	.90	1.20

Sheathing → | Trusses
Fascia Board | Furring

System Description	QUAN.	UNIT	LABOR HOURS	COST PER S.F.		
				MAT.	INST.	TOTAL
TRUSS, 16" O.C., 4/12 PITCH, 1' OVERHANG, 26' SPAN						
Truss, 40# loading, 16" O.C., 4/12 pitch, 26' span	.030	Ea.	.021	2.64	1.31	3.95
Fascia board, 2" x 6"	.100	L.F.	.005	.05	.26	.31
Sheathing, exterior, plywood, CDX, 1/2" thick	1.170	S.F.	.013	.54	.66	1.20
Furring, 1" x 3", 16" O.C.	1.000	L.F.	.023	.38	1.12	1.50
TOTAL		S.F.	.062	3.61	3.35	6.96
TRUSS, 16" O.C., 8/12 PITCH, 1' OVERHANG, 26' SPAN						
Truss, 40# loading, 16" O.C., 8/12 pitch, 26' span	.030	Ea.	.023	3.33	1.44	4.77
Fascia board, 2" x 6"	.100	L.F.	.005	.05	.26	.31
Sheathing, exterior, plywood, CDX, 1/2" thick	1.330	S.F.	.015	.61	.74	1.35
Furring, 1" x 3", 16" O.C.	1.000	L.F.	.023	.38	1.12	1.50
TOTAL		S.F.	.066	4.37	3.56	7.93
TRUSS, 24" O.C., 4/12 PITCH, 1' OVERHANG, 26' SPAN						
Truss, 40# loading, 24" O.C., 4/12 pitch, 26' span	.020	Ea.	.014	1.76	.87	2.63
Fascia board, 2" x 6"	.100	L.F.	.005	.05	.26	.31
Sheathing, exterior, plywood, CDX, 1/2" thick	1.170	S.F.	.013	.54	.66	1.20
Furring, 1" x 3", 16" O.C.	1.000	L.F.	.023	.38	1.12	1.50
TOTAL		S.F.	.055	2.73	2.91	5.64
TRUSS, 24" O.C., 8/12 PITCH, 1' OVERHANG, 26' SPAN						
Truss, 40# loading, 24" O.C., 8/12 pitch, 26' span	.020	Ea.	.015	2.22	.96	3.18
Fascia board, 2" x 6"	.100	L.F.	.005	.05	.26	.31
Sheathing, exterior, plywood, CDX, 1/2" thick	1.330	S.F.	.015	.61	.74	1.35
Furring, 1" x 3", 16" O.C.	1.000	L.F.	.023	.38	1.12	1.50
TOTAL		S.F.	.058	3.26	3.08	6.34

The cost of this system is based on the square foot of plan area.
A one foot overhang is included.

Description	QUAN.	UNIT	LABOR HOURS	COST PER S.F.		
				MAT.	INST.	TOTAL

Truss Roof Framing Price Sheet	QUAN.	UNIT	LABOR HOURS	COST PER S.F.		
				MAT.	INST.	TOTAL
Truss, 40# loading, including 1' overhang, 4/12 pitch, 24' span, 16" O.C.	.033	Ea.	.022	2.92	1.37	4.29
24" O.C.	.022	Ea.	.015	1.95	.91	2.86
26' span, 16" O.C.	.030	Ea.	.021	2.64	1.31	3.95
24" O.C.	.020	Ea.	.014	1.76	.87	2.63
28' span, 16" O.C.	.027	Ea.	.020	2.61	1.27	3.88
24" O.C.	.019	Ea.	.014	1.83	.90	2.73
32' span, 16" O.C.	.024	Ea.	.019	2.88	1.20	4.08
24" O.C.	.016	Ea.	.013	1.92	.80	2.72
36' span, 16" O.C.	.022	Ea.	.019	3.59	1.20	4.79
24" O.C.	.015	Ea.	.013	2.45	.82	3.27
8/12 pitch, 24' span, 16" O.C.	.033	Ea.	.024	3.53	1.49	5.02
24" O.C.	.022	Ea.	.016	2.35	.99	3.34
26' span, 16" O.C.	.030	Ea.	.023	3.33	1.44	4.77
24" O.C.	.020	Ea.	.015	2.22	.96	3.18
28' span, 16" O.C.	.027	Ea.	.022	3.32	1.37	4.69
24" O.C.	.019	Ea.	.016	2.34	.96	3.30
32' span, 16" O.C.	.024	Ea.	.021	3.53	1.33	4.86
24" O.C.	.016	Ea.	.014	2.35	.88	3.23
36' span, 16" O.C.	.022	Ea.	.021	4.03	1.34	5.37
24" O.C.	.015	Ea.	.015	2.75	.91	3.66
Fascia board, #2 or better, 1" x 6"	.100	L.F.	.004	.03	.19	.22
1" x 8"	.100	L.F.	.005	.04	.22	.26
1" x 10"	.100	L.F.	.005	.04	.25	.29
2" x 6"	.100	L.F.	.006	.05	.28	.33
2" x 8"	.100	L.F.	.007	.06	.35	.41
2" x 10"	.100	L.F.	.009	.08	.44	.52
Sheathing, plywood CDX, 4/12 pitch, 3/8" thick	1.170	S.F.	.012	.47	.60	1.07
1/2" thick	1.170	S.F.	.013	.54	.66	1.20
5/8" thick	1.170	S.F.	.014	.66	.70	1.36
8/12 pitch, 3/8" thick	1.330	S.F.	.014	.53	.68	1.21
1/2" thick	1.330	S.F.	.015	.61	.74	1.35
5/8" thick	1.330	S.F.	.016	.74	.80	1.54
Boards, 4/12 pitch, 1" x 6"	1.170	S.F.	.026	1.79	1.26	3.05
1" x 8"	1.170	S.F.	.021	1.72	1.05	2.77
8/12 pitch, 1" x 6"	1.330	S.F.	.029	2.03	1.44	3.47
1" x 8"	1.330	S.F.	.024	1.96	1.20	3.16
Furring, 1" x 3", 12" O.C.	1.200	L.F.	.027	.46	1.34	1.80
16" O.C.	1.000	L.F.	.023	.38	1.12	1.50
24" O.C.	.800	L.F.	.018	.30	.90	1.20

System Description	QUAN.	UNIT	LABOR HOURS	COST PER S.F.		
				MAT.	INST.	TOTAL
2″ X 6″, 16″ O.C., 4/12 PITCH						
Hip rafters, 2″ x 8″, 4/12 pitch	.160	L.F.	.004	.10	.17	.27
Jack rafters, 2″ x 6″, 16″ O.C., 4/12 pitch	1.430	L.F.	.038	.59	1.87	2.46
Ceiling joists, 2″ x 6″, 16″ O.C.	1.000	L.F.	.013	.41	.63	1.04
Fascia board, 2″ x 8″	.220	L.F.	.016	.13	.77	.90
Soffit nailer (outrigger), 2″ x 4″, 24″ O.C.	.220	L.F.	.006	.06	.28	.34
Sheathing, 1/2″ exterior plywood, CDX	1.570	S.F.	.018	.72	.88	1.60
Furring strips, 1″ x 3″, 16″ O.C.	1.000	L.F.	.023	.38	1.12	1.50
TOTAL		S.F.	.118	2.39	5.72	8.11
2″ X 8″, 16″ O.C., 4/12 PITCH						
Hip rafters, 2″ x 10″, 4/12 pitch	.160	L.F.	.004	.13	.22	.35
Jack rafters, 2″ x 8″, 16″ O.C., 4/12 pitch	1.430	L.F.	.047	.87	2.29	3.16
Ceiling joists, 2″ x 6″, 16″ O.C.	1.000	L.F.	.013	.41	.63	1.04
Fascia board, 2″ x 8″	.220	L.F.	.012	.10	.59	.69
Soffit nailer (outrigger), 2″ x 4″, 24″ O.C.	.220	L.F.	.006	.06	.28	.34
Sheathing, 1/2″ exterior plywood, CDX	1.570	S.F.	.018	.72	.88	1.60
Furring strips, 1″ x 3″, 16″ O.C.	1.000	L.F.	.023	.38	1.12	1.50
TOTAL		S.F.	.123	2.67	6.01	8.68

The cost of this system is based on S.F. of plan area. Measurement is area under the hip roof only. See gable roof system for added costs.

Description	QUAN.	UNIT	LABOR HOURS	COST PER S.F.		
				MAT.	INST.	TOTAL

Hip Roof Framing Price Sheet	QUAN.	UNIT	LABOR HOURS	COST PER S.F.		
				MAT.	INST.	TOTAL
Hip rafters, #2 or better, 2" x 6", 4/12 pitch	.160	L.F.	.003	.07	.16	.23
8/12 pitch	.210	L.F.	.006	.09	.28	.37
2" x 8", 4/12 pitch	.160	L.F.	.004	.10	.17	.27
8/12 pitch	.210	L.F.	.006	.13	.30	.43
2" x 10", 4/12 pitch	.160	L.F.	.004	.13	.22	.35
8/12 pitch roof	.210	L.F.	.008	.17	.37	.54
Jack rafters, #2 or better, 16" O.C., 2" x 6", 4/12 pitch	1.430	L.F.	.038	.59	1.87	2.46
8/12 pitch	1.800	L.F.	.061	.74	2.97	3.71
2" x 8", 4/12 pitch	1.430	L.F.	.047	.87	2.29	3.16
8/12 pitch	1.800	L.F.	.075	1.10	3.65	4.75
2" x 10", 4/12 pitch	1.430	L.F.	.051	1.14	2.49	3.63
8/12 pitch	1.800	L.F.	.082	1.44	4.03	5.47
24" O.C., 2" x 6", 4/12 pitch	1.150	L.F.	.031	.47	1.51	1.98
8/12 pitch	1.440	L.F.	.048	.59	2.38	2.97
2" x 8", 4/12 pitch	1.150	L.F.	.038	.70	1.84	2.54
8/12 pitch	1.440	L.F.	.060	.88	2.92	3.80
2" x 10", 4/12 pitch	1.150	L.F.	.041	.92	2	2.92
8/12 pitch	1.440	L.F.	.066	1.15	3.23	4.38
Ceiling joists, #2 or better, 2" x 4", 16" O.C.	1.000	L.F.	.013	.27	.63	.90
24" O.C.	.750	L.F.	.010	.20	.47	.67
2" x 6", 16" O.C.	1.000	L.F.	.013	.41	.63	1.04
24" O.C.	.750	L.F.	.010	.31	.47	.78
2" x 8", 16" O.C.	1.000	L.F.	.015	.61	.71	1.32
24" O.C.	.750	L.F.	.011	.46	.53	.99
2" x 10", 16" O.C.	1.000	L.F.	.018	.80	.87	1.67
24" O.C.	.750	L.F.	.013	.60	.65	1.25
Fascia board, #2 or better, 1" x 6"	.220	L.F.	.009	.07	.42	.49
1" x 8"	.220	L.F.	.010	.09	.49	.58
1" x 10"	.220	L.F.	.011	.10	.55	.65
2" x 6"	.220	L.F.	.013	.11	.61	.72
2" x 8"	.220	L.F.	.016	.13	.77	.90
2" x 10"	.220	L.F.	.020	.18	.96	1.14
Soffit nailer (outrigger), 2" x 4", 16" O.C.	.280	L.F.	.007	.08	.35	.43
24" O.C.	.220	L.F.	.006	.06	.28	.34
2" x 8", 16" O.C.	.280	L.F.	.007	.13	.33	.46
24" O.C.	.220	L.F.	.005	.10	.27	.37
Sheathing, plywood CDX, 4/12 pitch, 3/8" thick	1.570	S.F.	.016	.63	.80	1.43
1/2" thick	1.570	S.F.	.018	.72	.88	1.60
5/8" thick	1.570	S.F.	.019	.88	.94	1.82
8/12 pitch, 3/8" thick	1.900	S.F.	.020	.76	.97	1.73
1/2" thick	1.900	S.F.	.022	.87	1.06	1.93
5/8" thick	1.900	S.F.	.023	1.06	1.14	2.20
Boards, 4/12 pitch, 1" x 6" boards	1.450	S.F.	.032	2.22	1.57	3.79
1" x 8" boards	1.450	S.F.	.027	2.13	1.31	3.44
8/12 pitch, 1" x 6" boards	1.750	S.F.	.039	2.68	1.89	4.57
1" x 8" boards	1.750	S.F.	.032	2.57	1.58	4.15
Furring, 1" x 3", 12" O.C.	1.200	L.F.	.027	.46	1.34	1.80
16" O.C.	1.000	L.F.	.023	.38	1.12	1.50
24" O.C.	.800	L.F.	.018	.30	.90	1.20

Sheathing — Ridge Board — Ceiling Joists — Rafters — Furring — Studs — Fascia Board

System Description	QUAN.	UNIT	LABOR HOURS	COST PER S.F.		
				MAT.	INST.	TOTAL
2″ X 6″ RAFTERS, 16″ O.C.						
Roof rafters, 2″ x 6″, 16″ O.C.	1.430	L.F.	.029	.59	1.40	1.99
Ceiling joists, 2″ x 6″, 16″ O.C.	.710	L.F.	.009	.29	.45	.74
Stud wall, 2″ x 4″, 16″ O.C., including plates	.790	L.F.	.012	.21	.61	.82
Furring strips, 1″ x 3″, 16″ O.C.	.710	L.F.	.016	.27	.80	1.07
Ridge board, 2″ x 8″	.050	L.F.	.002	.03	.09	.12
Fascia board, 2″ x 6″	.100	L.F.	.006	.05	.28	.33
Sheathing, exterior grade plywood, 1/2″ thick	1.450	S.F.	.017	.67	.81	1.48
TOTAL		S.F.	.091	2.11	4.44	6.55
2″ X 8″ RAFTERS, 16″ O.C.						
Roof rafters, 2″ x 8″, 16″ O.C.	1.430	L.F.	.031	.87	1.49	2.36
Ceiling joists, 2″ x 6″, 16″ O.C.	.710	L.F.	.009	.29	.45	.74
Stud wall, 2″ x 4″, 16″ O.C., including plates	.790	L.F.	.012	.21	.61	.82
Furring strips, 1″ x 3″, 16″ O.C.	.710	L.F.	.016	.27	.80	1.07
Ridge board, 2″ x 8″	.050	L.F.	.002	.03	.09	.12
Fascia board, 2″ x 8″	.100	L.F.	.007	.06	.35	.41
Sheathing, exterior grade plywood, 1/2″ thick	1.450	S.F.	.017	.67	.81	1.48
TOTAL		S.F.	.094	2.40	4.60	7

The cost of this system is based on the square foot of plan area on the first floor.

Description	QUAN.	UNIT	LABOR HOURS	COST PER S.F.		
				MAT.	INST.	TOTAL

Gambrel Roof Framing Price Sheet

	QUAN.	UNIT	LABOR HOURS	COST PER S.F.		
				MAT.	INST.	TOTAL
Roof rafters, #2 or better, 2" x 6", 16" O.C.	1.430	L.F.	.029	.59	1.40	1.99
24" O.C.	1.140	L.F.	.023	.47	1.12	1.59
2" x 8", 16" O.C.	1.430	L.F.	.031	.87	1.49	2.36
24" O.C.	1.140	L.F.	.024	.70	1.19	1.89
2" x 10", 16" O.C.	1.430	L.F.	.046	1.14	2.26	3.40
24" O.C.	1.140	L.F.	.037	.91	1.80	2.71
Ceiling joist, #2 or better, 2" x 4", 16" O.C.	.710	L.F.	.009	.19	.45	.64
24" O.C.	.570	L.F.	.007	.15	.36	.51
2" x 6", 16" O.C.	.710	L.F.	.009	.29	.45	.74
24" O.C.	.570	L.F.	.007	.23	.36	.59
2" x 8", 16" O.C.	.710	L.F.	.010	.43	.50	.93
24" O.C.	.570	L.F.	.008	.35	.40	.75
Stud wall, #2 or better, 2" x 4", 16" O.C.	.790	L.F.	.012	.21	.61	.82
24" O.C.	.630	L.F.	.010	.17	.49	.66
2" x 6", 16" O.C.	.790	L.F.	.014	.32	.70	1.02
24" O.C.	.630	L.F.	.011	.26	.55	.81
Furring, 1" x 3", 16" O.C.	.710	L.F.	.016	.27	.80	1.07
24" O.C.	.590	L.F.	.013	.22	.66	.88
Ridge board, #2 or better, 1" x 6"	.050	L.F.	.001	.04	.07	.11
1" x 8"	.050	L.F.	.001	.05	.07	.12
1" x 10"	.050	L.F.	.002	.06	.08	.14
2" x 6"	.050	L.F.	.002	.02	.08	.10
2" x 8"	.050	L.F.	.002	.03	.09	.12
2" x 10"	.050	L.F.	.002	.04	.10	.14
Fascia board, #2 or better, 1" x 6"	.100	L.F.	.004	.03	.19	.22
1" x 8"	.100	L.F.	.005	.04	.22	.26
1" x 10"	.100	L.F.	.005	.04	.25	.29
2" x 6"	.100	L.F.	.006	.05	.28	.33
2" x 8"	.100	L.F.	.007	.06	.35	.41
2" x 10"	.100	L.F.	.009	.08	.44	.52
Sheathing, plywood, exterior grade CDX, 3/8" thick	1.450	S.F.	.015	.58	.74	1.32
1/2" thick	1.450	S.F.	.017	.67	.81	1.48
5/8" thick	1.450	S.F.	.018	.81	.87	1.68
3/4" thick	1.450	S.F.	.019	.93	.94	1.87
Boards, 1" x 6", laid regular	1.450	S.F.	.032	2.22	1.57	3.79
Laid diagonal	1.450	S.F.	.036	2.22	1.75	3.97
1" x 8", laid regular	1.450	S.F.	.027	2.13	1.31	3.44
Laid diagonal	1.450	S.F.	.032	2.13	1.57	3.70

System Description	QUAN.	UNIT	LABOR HOURS	COST PER S.F.		
				MAT.	INST.	TOTAL
2″ X 6″ RAFTERS, 16″ O.C.						
Roof rafters, 2″ x 6″, 16″ O.C.	1.210	L.F.	.033	.50	1.61	2.11
Rafter plates, 2″ x 6″, double top, single bottom	.364	L.F.	.010	.15	.48	.63
Ceiling joists, 2″ x 4″, 16″ O.C.	.920	L.F.	.012	.25	.58	.83
Hip rafter, 2″ x 6″	.070	L.F.	.002	.03	.11	.14
Jack rafter, 2″ x 6″, 16″ O.C.	1.000	L.F.	.039	.41	1.91	2.32
Ridge board, 2″ x 6″	.018	L.F.	.001	.01	.03	.04
Sheathing, exterior grade plywood, 1/2″ thick	2.210	S.F.	.025	1.02	1.24	2.26
Furring strips, 1″ x 3″, 16″ O.C.	.920	L.F.	.021	.35	1.03	1.38
TOTAL		S.F.	.143	2.72	6.99	9.71
2″ X 8″ RAFTERS, 16″ O.C.						
Roof rafters, 2″ x 8″, 16″ O.C.	1.210	L.F.	.036	.74	1.75	2.49
Rafter plates, 2″ x 8″, double top, single bottom	.364	L.F.	.011	.22	.53	.75
Ceiling joists, 2″ x 6″, 16″ O.C.	.920	L.F.	.012	.38	.58	.96
Hip rafter, 2″ x 8″	.070	L.F.	.002	.04	.12	.16
Jack rafter, 2″ x 8″, 16″ O.C.	1.000	L.F.	.048	.61	2.34	2.95
Ridge board, 2″ x 8″	.018	L.F.	.001	.01	.03	.04
Sheathing, exterior grade plywood, 1/2″ thick	2.210	S.F.	.025	1.02	1.24	2.26
Furring strips, 1″ x 3″, 16″ O.C.	.920	L.F.	.021	.35	1.03	1.38
TOTAL		S.F.	.156	3.37	7.62	10.99

The cost of this system is based on the square foot of plan area.

Description	QUAN.	UNIT	LABOR HOURS	COST PER S.F.		
				MAT.	INST.	TOTAL

Mansard Roof Framing Price Sheet	QUAN.	UNIT	LABOR HOURS	COST PER S.F.		
				MAT.	INST.	TOTAL
Roof rafters, #2 or better, 2" x 6", 16" O.C.	1.210	L.F.	.033	.50	1.61	2.11
24" O.C.	.970	L.F.	.026	.40	1.29	1.69
2" x 8", 16" O.C.	1.210	L.F.	.036	.74	1.75	2.49
24" O.C.	.970	L.F.	.029	.59	1.41	2
2" x 10", 16" O.C.	1.210	L.F.	.046	.97	2.23	3.20
24" O.C.	.970	L.F.	.037	.78	1.78	2.56
Rafter plates, #2 or better double top single bottom, 2" x 6"	.364	L.F.	.010	.15	.48	.63
2" x 8"	.364	L.F.	.011	.22	.53	.75
2" x 10"	.364	L.F.	.014	.29	.67	.96
Ceiling joist, #2 or better, 2" x 4", 16" O.C.	.920	L.F.	.012	.25	.58	.83
24" O.C.	.740	L.F.	.009	.20	.47	.67
2" x 6", 16" O.C.	.920	L.F.	.012	.38	.58	.96
24" O.C.	.740	L.F.	.009	.30	.47	.77
2" x 8", 16" O.C.	.920	L.F.	.013	.56	.65	1.21
24" O.C.	.740	L.F.	.011	.45	.53	.98
Hip rafter, #2 or better, 2" x 6"	.070	L.F.	.002	.03	.11	.14
2" x 8"	.070	L.F.	.002	.04	.12	.16
2" x 10"	.070	L.F.	.003	.06	.14	.20
Jack rafter, #2 or better, 2" x 6", 16" O.C.	1.000	L.F.	.039	.41	1.91	2.32
24" O.C.	.800	L.F.	.031	.33	1.53	1.86
2" x 8", 16" O.C.	1.000	L.F.	.048	.61	2.34	2.95
24" O.C.	.800	L.F.	.038	.49	1.87	2.36
Ridge board, #2 or better, 1" x 6"	.018	L.F.	.001	.01	.02	.03
1" x 8"	.018	L.F.	.001	.02	.03	.05
1" x 10"	.018	L.F.	.001	.02	.03	.05
2" x 6"	.018	L.F.	.001	.01	.03	.04
2" x 8"	.018	L.F.	.001	.01	.03	.04
2" x 10"	.018	L.F.	.001	.01	.04	.05
Sheathing, plywood exterior grade CDX, 3/8" thick	2.210	S.F.	.023	.88	1.13	2.01
1/2" thick	2.210	S.F.	.025	1.02	1.24	2.26
5/8" thick	2.210	S.F.	.027	1.24	1.33	2.57
3/4" thick	2.210	S.F.	.029	1.41	1.44	2.85
Boards, 1" x 6", laid regular	2.210	S.F.	.049	3.38	2.39	5.77
Laid diagonal	2.210	S.F.	.054	3.38	2.67	6.05
1" x 8", laid regular	2.210	S.F.	.040	3.25	1.99	5.24
Laid diagonal	2.210	S.F.	.049	3.25	2.39	5.64
Furring, 1" x 3", 12" O.C.	1.150	L.F.	.026	.44	1.29	1.73
24" O.C.	.740	L.F.	.017	.28	.83	1.11

Sheathing · Fascia · Fascia · Rafters

System Description	QUAN.	UNIT	LABOR HOURS	COST PER S.F.		
				MAT.	INST.	TOTAL
2″ X 6″, 16″ O.C., 4/12 PITCH						
Rafters, 2″ x 6″, 16″ O.C., 4/12 pitch	1.170	L.F.	.019	.48	.91	1.39
Fascia, 2″ x 6″	.100	L.F.	.006	.05	.28	.33
Bridging, 1″ x 3″, 6′ O.C.	.080	Pr.	.005	.04	.24	.28
Sheathing, exterior grade plywood, 1/2″ thick	1.230	S.F.	.014	.57	.69	1.26
TOTAL		S.F.	.044	1.14	2.12	3.26
2″ X 6″, 24″ O.C., 4/12 PITCH						
Rafters, 2″ x 6″, 24″ O.C., 4/12 pitch	.940	L.F.	.015	.39	.73	1.12
Fascia, 2″ x 6″	.100	L.F.	.006	.05	.28	.33
Bridging, 1″ x 3″, 6′ O.C.	.060	Pr.	.004	.03	.18	.21
Sheathing, exterior grade plywood, 1/2″ thick	1.230	S.F.	.014	.57	.69	1.26
TOTAL		S.F.	.039	1.04	1.88	2.92
2″ X 8″, 16″ O.C., 4/12 PITCH						
Rafters, 2″ x 8″, 16″ O.C., 4/12 pitch	1.170	L.F.	.020	.71	.96	1.67
Fascia, 2″ x 8″	.100	L.F.	.007	.06	.35	.41
Bridging, 1″ x 3″, 6′ O.C.	.080	Pr.	.005	.04	.24	.28
Sheathing, exterior grade plywood, 1/2″ thick	1.230	S.F.	.014	.57	.69	1.26
TOTAL		S.F.	.046	1.38	2.24	3.62
2″ X 8″, 24″ O.C., 4/12 PITCH						
Rafters, 2″ x 8″, 24″ O.C., 4/12 pitch	.940	L.F.	.016	.57	.77	1.34
Fascia, 2″ x 8″	.100	L.F.	.007	.06	.35	.41
Bridging, 1″ x 3″, 6′ O.C.	.060	Pr.	.004	.03	.18	.21
Sheathing, exterior grade plywood, 1/2″ thick	1.230	S.F.	.014	.57	.69	1.26
TOTAL		S.F.	.041	1.23	1.99	3.22

The cost of this system is based on the square foot of plan area.
A 1′ overhang is assumed. No ceiling joists or furring are included.

Description	QUAN.	UNIT	LABOR HOURS	COST PER S.F.		
				MAT.	INST.	TOTAL

Shed/Flat Roof Framing Price Sheet	QUAN.	UNIT	LABOR HOURS	COST PER S.F. MAT.	COST PER S.F. INST.	COST PER S.F. TOTAL
Rafters, #2 or better, 16" O.C., 2" x 4", 0 - 4/12 pitch	1.170	L.F.	.014	.36	.68	1.04
5/12 - 8/12 pitch	1.330	L.F.	.020	.41	.98	1.39
2" x 6", 0 - 4/12 pitch	1.170	L.F.	.019	.48	.91	1.39
5/12 - 8/12 pitch	1.330	L.F.	.027	.55	1.30	1.85
2" x 8", 0 - 4/12 pitch	1.170	L.F.	.020	.71	.96	1.67
5/12 - 8/12 pitch	1.330	L.F.	.028	.81	1.38	2.19
2" x 10", 0 - 4/12 pitch	1.170	L.F.	.030	.94	1.45	2.39
5/12 - 8/12 pitch	1.330	L.F.	.043	1.06	2.10	3.16
24" O.C., 2" x 4", 0 - 4/12 pitch	.940	L.F.	.011	.29	.55	.84
5/12 - 8/12 pitch	1.060	L.F.	.021	.43	1.04	1.47
2" x 6", 0 - 4/12 pitch	.940	L.F.	.015	.39	.73	1.12
5/12 - 8/12 pitch	1.060	L.F.	.021	.43	1.04	1.47
2" x 8", 0 - 4/12 pitch	.940	L.F.	.016	.57	.77	1.34
5/12 - 8/12 pitch	1.060	L.F.	.023	.65	1.10	1.75
2" x 10", 0 - 4/12 pitch	.940	L.F.	.024	.75	1.17	1.92
5/12 - 8/12 pitch	1.060	L.F.	.034	.85	1.67	2.52
Fascia, #2 or better,, 1" x 4"	.100	L.F.	.003	.02	.14	.16
1" x 6"	.100	L.F.	.004	.03	.19	.22
1" x 8"	.100	L.F.	.005	.04	.22	.26
1" x 10"	.100	L.F.	.005	.04	.25	.29
2" x 4"	.100	L.F.	.005	.04	.24	.28
2" x 6"	.100	L.F.	.006	.05	.28	.33
2" x 8"	.100	L.F.	.007	.06	.35	.41
2" x 10"	.100	L.F.	.009	.08	.44	.52
Bridging, wood 6' O.C., 1" x 3", rafters, 16" O.C.	.080	Pr.	.005	.04	.24	.28
24" O.C.	.060	Pr.	.004	.03	.18	.21
Metal, galvanized, rafters, 16" O.C.	.080	Pr.	.005	.14	.24	.38
24" O.C.	.060	Pr.	.003	.11	.17	.28
Compression type, rafters, 16" O.C.	.080	Pr.	.003	.14	.16	.30
24" O.C.	.060	Pr.	.002	.11	.12	.23
Sheathing, plywood, exterior grade, 3/8" thick, flat 0 - 4/12 pitch	1.230	S.F.	.013	.49	.63	1.12
5/12 - 8/12 pitch	1.330	S.F.	.014	.53	.68	1.21
1/2" thick, flat 0 - 4/12 pitch	1.230	S.F.	.014	.57	.69	1.26
5/12 - 8/12 pitch	1.330	S.F.	.015	.61	.74	1.35
5/8" thick, flat 0 - 4/12 pitch	1.230	S.F.	.015	.69	.74	1.43
5/12 - 8/12 pitch	1.330	S.F.	.016	.74	.80	1.54
3/4" thick, flat 0 - 4/12 pitch	1.230	S.F.	.016	.79	.80	1.59
5/12 - 8/12 pitch	1.330	S.F.	.018	.85	.86	1.71
Boards, 1" x 6", laid regular, flat 0 - 4/12 pitch	1.230	S.F.	.027	1.88	1.33	3.21
5/12 - 8/12 pitch	1.330	S.F.	.041	2.03	2.01	4.04
Laid diagonal, flat 0 - 4/12 pitch	1.230	S.F.	.030	1.88	1.49	3.37
5/12 - 8/12 pitch	1.330	S.F.	.044	2.03	2.17	4.20
1" x 8", laid regular, flat 0 - 4/12 pitch	1.230	S.F.	.022	1.81	1.11	2.92
5/12 - 8/12 pitch	1.330	S.F.	.034	1.96	1.64	3.60
Laid diagonal, flat 0 - 4/12 pitch	1.230	S.F.	.027	1.81	1.33	3.14
5/12 - 8/12 pitch	1.330	S.F.	.044	2.03	2.17	4.20

System Description	QUAN.	UNIT	LABOR HOURS	COST PER S.F.		
				MAT.	INST.	TOTAL
2″ X 6″, 16″ O.C.						
Dormer rafter, 2″ x 6″, 16″ O.C.	1.330	L.F.	.036	.55	1.77	2.32
Ridge board, 2″ x 6″	.280	L.F.	.009	.11	.44	.55
Trimmer rafters, 2″ x 6″	.880	L.F.	.014	.36	.69	1.05
Wall studs & plates, 2″ x 4″, 16″ O.C.	3.160	L.F.	.056	.85	2.75	3.60
Fascia, 2″ x 6″	.220	L.F.	.012	.10	.59	.69
Valley rafter, 2″ x 6″, 16″ O.C.	.280	L.F.	.009	.11	.43	.54
Cripple rafter, 2″ x 6″, 16″ O.C.	.560	L.F.	.022	.23	1.07	1.30
Headers, 2″ x 6″, doubled	.670	L.F.	.030	.27	1.46	1.73
Ceiling joist, 2″ x 4″, 16″ O.C.	1.000	L.F.	.013	.27	.63	.90
Sheathing, exterior grade plywood, 1/2″ thick	3.610	S.F.	.041	1.66	2.02	3.68
TOTAL		S.F.	.242	4.51	11.85	16.36
2″ X 8″, 16″ O.C.						
Dormer rafter, 2″ x 8″, 16″ O.C.	1.330	L.F.	.039	.81	1.93	2.74
Ridge board, 2″ x 8″	.280	L.F.	.010	.17	.49	.66
Trimmer rafter, 2″ x 8″	.880	L.F.	.015	.54	.72	1.26
Wall studs & plates, 2″ x 4″, 16″ O.C.	3.160	L.F.	.056	.85	2.75	3.60
Fascia, 2″ x 8″	.220	L.F.	.016	.13	.77	.90
Valley rafter, 2″ x 8″, 16″ O.C.	.280	L.F.	.010	.17	.47	.64
Cripple rafter, 2″ x 8″, 16″ O.C.	.560	L.F.	.027	.34	1.31	1.65
Headers, 2″ x 8″, doubled	.670	L.F.	.032	.41	1.54	1.95
Ceiling joist, 2″ x 4″, 16″ O.C.	1.000	L.F.	.013	.27	.63	.90
Sheathing,, exterior grade plywood, 1/2″ thick	3.610	S.F.	.041	1.66	2.02	3.68
TOTAL		S.F.	.259	5.35	12.63	17.98

The cost in this system is based on the square foot of plan area.
The measurement being the plan area of the dormer only.

Description	QUAN.	UNIT	LABOR HOURS	COST PER S.F.		
				MAT.	INST.	TOTAL

Reed Construction Data
The leader in construction information and BIM solutions

Reed Construction Data, Inc. is a leading provider of construction information and building information modeling (BIM) solutions. The company's portfolio of information products and services is designed specifically to help construction industry professionals advance their business with timely and accurate project, product, and cost data. Reed Construction Data is a division of Reed Business Information, a member of the Reed Elsevier PLC group of companies.

Cost Information

RSMeans, the undisputed market leader in construction costs, provides current cost and estimating information through its innovative MeansCostworks.com® web-based solution. In addition, RSMeans publishes annual cost books, estimating software, and a rich library of reference books. RSMeans also conducts a series of professional seminars and provides construction cost consulting for owners, manufacturers, designers, and contractors to sharpen personal skills and maximize the effective use of cost estimating and management tools.

Project Data

Reed Construction Data assembles one of the largest databases of public and private project data for use by contractors, distributors, and building product manufacturers in the U.S. and Canadian markets. In addition, Reed Construction Data is the North American construction community's premier resource for project leads and bid documents. Reed Bulletin and Reed CONNECT™ provide project leads and project data through all stages of construction for many of the country's largest public sector, commercial, industrial, and multi-family residential projects.

Research and Analytics

Reed Construction Data's forecasting tools cover most aspects of the construction business in the U.S. and Canada. With a vast network of resources, Reed Construction Data is uniquely qualified to give you the information you need to keep your business profitable.

SmartBIM Solutions

Reed Construction Data has emerged as the leader in the field of building information modeling (BIM) with products and services that have helped to advance the evolution of BIM. Through an in-depth SmartBIM Object Creation Program, BPMs can rely on Reed to create high-quality, real world objects embedded with superior cost data (RSMeans). In addition, Reed has made it easy for architects to manage these manufacturer-specific objects as well as generic objects in Revit with the SmartBIM Library.

SmartBuilding Index

The leading industry source for product research, product documentation, BIM objects, design ideas, and source locations. Search, select, and specify available building products with our online directories of manufacturer profiles, MANU-SPEC, SPEC-DATA, guide specs, manufacturer catalogs, building codes, historical project data, and BIM objects.

SmartBuilding Studio

A vibrant online resource library which brings together a comprehensive catalog of commercial interior finishes and products under a single standard for high-definition imagery, product data, and searchable attributes.

Associated Construction Publications (ACP)

Reed Construction Data's regional construction magazines cover the nation through a network of 14 regional magazines. Serving the construction market for more than 100 years, our magazines are a trusted source of news and information in the local and national construction communities.

For more information, please visit our website at www.reedconstructiondata.com

The leader in construction information and BIM solutions.

Gable Dormer Framing Price Sheet	QUAN.	UNIT	LABOR HOURS	COST PER S.F.		
				MAT.	INST.	TOTAL
Dormer rafters, #2 or better, 2" x 4", 16" O.C.	1.330	L.F.	.029	.44	1.42	1.86
24" O.C.	1.060	L.F.	.023	.35	1.13	1.48
2" x 6", 16" O.C.	1.330	L.F.	.036	.55	1.77	2.32
24" O.C.	1.060	L.F.	.029	.43	1.41	1.84
2" x 8", 16" O.C.	1.330	L.F.	.039	.81	1.93	2.74
24" O.C.	1.060	L.F.	.031	.65	1.54	2.19
Ridge board, #2 or better, 1" x 4"	.280	L.F.	.006	.16	.29	.45
1" x 6"	.280	L.F.	.007	.20	.37	.57
1" x 8"	.280	L.F.	.008	.26	.40	.66
2" x 4"	.280	L.F.	.007	.09	.35	.44
2" x 6"	.280	L.F.	.009	.11	.44	.55
2" x 8"	.280	L.F.	.010	.17	.49	.66
Trimmer rafters, #2 or better, 2" x 4"	.880	L.F.	.011	.29	.55	.84
2" x 6"	.880	L.F.	.014	.36	.69	1.05
2" x 8"	.880	L.F.	.015	.54	.72	1.26
2" x 10"	.880	L.F.	.022	.70	1.09	1.79
Wall studs & plates, #2 or better, 2" x 4" studs, 16" O.C.	3.160	L.F.	.056	.85	2.75	3.60
24" O.C.	2.800	L.F.	.050	.76	2.44	3.20
2" x 6" studs, 16" O.C.	3.160	L.F.	.063	1.30	3.10	4.40
24" O.C.	2.800	L.F.	.056	1.15	2.74	3.89
Fascia, #2 or better, 1" x 4"	.220	L.F.	.006	.05	.31	.36
1" x 6"	.220	L.F.	.008	.07	.38	.45
1" x 8"	.220	L.F.	.009	.08	.45	.53
2" x 4"	.220	L.F.	.011	.09	.52	.61
2" x 6"	.220	L.F.	.014	.12	.66	.78
2" x 8"	.220	L.F.	.016	.13	.77	.90
Valley rafter, #2 or better, 2" x 4"	.280	L.F.	.007	.09	.34	.43
2" x 6"	.280	L.F.	.009	.11	.43	.54
2" x 8"	.280	L.F.	.010	.17	.47	.64
2" x 10"	.280	L.F.	.012	.22	.58	.80
Cripple rafter, #2 or better, 2" x 4", 16" O.C.	.560	L.F.	.018	.18	.86	1.04
24" O.C.	.450	L.F.	.014	.15	.69	.84
2" x 6", 16" O.C.	.560	L.F.	.022	.23	1.07	1.30
24" O.C.	.450	L.F.	.018	.18	.86	1.04
2" x 8", 16" O.C.	.560	L.F.	.027	.34	1.31	1.65
24" O.C.	.450	L.F.	.021	.27	1.05	1.32
Headers, #2 or better double header, 2" x 4"	.670	L.F.	.024	.22	1.18	1.40
2" x 6"	.670	L.F.	.030	.27	1.46	1.73
2" x 8"	.670	L.F.	.032	.41	1.54	1.95
2" x 10"	.670	L.F.	.034	.54	1.64	2.18
Ceiling joist, #2 or better, 2" x 4", 16" O.C.	1.000	L.F.	.013	.27	.63	.90
24" O.C.	.800	L.F.	.010	.22	.50	.72
2" x 6", 16" O.C.	1.000	L.F.	.013	.41	.63	1.04
24" O.C.	.800	L.F.	.010	.33	.50	.83
Sheathing, plywood exterior grade, 3/8" thick	3.610	S.F.	.038	1.44	1.84	3.28
1/2" thick	3.610	S.F.	.041	1.66	2.02	3.68
5/8" thick	3.610	S.F.	.044	2.02	2.17	4.19
3/4" thick	3.610	S.F.	.048	2.31	2.35	4.66
Boards, 1" x 6", laid regular	3.610	S.F.	.089	5.50	4.37	9.87
Laid diagonal	3.610	S.F.	.099	5.50	4.84	10.34
1" x 8", laid regular	3.610	S.F.	.076	5.30	3.68	8.98
Laid diagonal	3.610	S.F.	.089	5.30	4.37	9.67

Sheathing
Ceiling Joists
Fascia Board
Studs & Plates
Rafters
Trimmer Rafters

System Description	QUAN.	UNIT	LABOR HOURS	COST PER S.F.		
				MAT.	INST.	TOTAL
2" X 6" RAFTERS, 16" O.C.						
Dormer rafter, 2" x 6", 16" O.C.	1.080	L.F.	.029	.44	1.44	1.88
Trimmer rafter, 2" x 6"	.400	L.F.	.006	.16	.31	.47
Studs & plates, 2" x 4", 16" O.C.	2.750	L.F.	.049	.74	2.39	3.13
Fascia, 2" x 6"	.250	L.F.	.014	.12	.66	.78
Ceiling joist, 2" x 4", 16" O.C.	1.000	L.F.	.013	.27	.63	.90
Sheathing, exterior grade plywood, CDX, 1/2" thick	2.940	S.F.	.034	1.35	1.65	3
TOTAL		S.F.	.145	3.08	7.08	10.16
2" X 8" RAFTERS, 16" O.C.						
Dormer rafter, 2" x 8", 16" O.C.	1.080	L.F.	.032	.66	1.57	2.23
Trimmer rafter, 2" x 8"	.400	L.F.	.007	.24	.33	.57
Studs & plates, 2" x 4", 16" O.C.	2.750	L.F.	.049	.74	2.39	3.13
Fascia, 2" x 8"	.250	L.F.	.018	.15	.87	1.02
Ceiling joist, 2" x 6", 16" O.C.	1.000	L.F.	.013	.41	.63	1.04
Sheathing, exterior grade plywood, CDX, 1/2" thick	2.940	S.F.	.034	1.35	1.65	3
TOTAL		S.F.	.153	3.55	7.44	10.99
2" X 10" RAFTERS, 16" O.C.						
Dormer rafter, 2" x 10", 16" O.C.	1.080	L.F.	.041	.86	1.99	2.85
Trimmer rafter, 2" x 10"	.400	L.F.	.010	.32	.50	.82
Studs & plates, 2" x 4", 16" O.C.	2.750	L.F.	.049	.74	2.39	3.13
Fascia, 2" x 10"	.250	L.F.	.022	.20	1.09	1.29
Ceiling joist, 2" x 6", 16" O.C.	1.000	L.F.	.013	.41	.63	1.04
Sheathing, exterior grade plywood, CDX, 1/2" thick	2.940	S.F.	.034	1.35	1.65	3
TOTAL		S.F.	.169	3.88	8.25	12.13

The cost in this system is based on the square foot of plan area.
The measurement is the plan area of the dormer only.

Description	QUAN.	UNIT	LABOR HOURS	COST PER S.F.		
				MAT.	INST.	TOTAL

Shed Dormer Framing Price Sheet	QUAN.	UNIT	LABOR HOURS	COST PER S.F.		
				MAT.	INST.	TOTAL
Dormer rafters, #2 or better, 2" x 4", 16" O.C.	1.080	L.F.	.023	.35	1.15	1.50
24" O.C.	.860	L.F.	.019	.28	.92	1.20
2" x 6", 16" O.C.	1.080	L.F.	.029	.44	1.44	1.88
24" O.C.	.860	L.F.	.023	.35	1.14	1.49
2" x 8", 16" O.C.	1.080	L.F.	.032	.66	1.57	2.23
24" O.C.	.860	L.F.	.025	.52	1.25	1.77
2" x 10", 16" O.C.	1.080	L.F.	.041	.86	1.99	2.85
24" O.C.	.860	L.F.	.032	.69	1.58	2.27
Trimmer rafter, #2 or better, 2" x 4"	.400	L.F.	.005	.13	.25	.38
2" x 6"	.400	L.F.	.006	.16	.31	.47
2" x 8"	.400	L.F.	.007	.24	.33	.57
2" x 10"	.400	L.F.	.010	.32	.50	.82
Studs & plates, #2 or better, 2" x 4", 16" O.C.	2.750	L.F.	.049	.74	2.39	3.13
24" O.C.	2.200	L.F.	.039	.59	1.91	2.50
2" x 6", 16" O.C.	2.750	L.F.	.055	1.13	2.70	3.83
24" O.C.	2.200	L.F.	.044	.90	2.16	3.06
Fascia, #2 or better, 1" x 4"	.250	L.F.	.006	.05	.31	.36
1" x 6"	.250	L.F.	.008	.07	.38	.45
1" x 8"	.250	L.F.	.009	.08	.45	.53
2" x 4"	.250	L.F.	.011	.09	.52	.61
2" x 6"	.250	L.F.	.014	.12	.66	.78
2" x 8"	.250	L.F.	.018	.15	.87	1.02
Ceiling joist, #2 or better, 2" x 4", 16" O.C.	1.000	L.F.	.013	.27	.63	.90
24" O.C.	.800	L.F.	.010	.22	.50	.72
2" x 6", 16" O.C.	1.000	L.F.	.013	.41	.63	1.04
24" O.C.	.800	L.F.	.010	.33	.50	.83
2" x 8", 16" O.C.	1.000	L.F.	.015	.61	.71	1.32
24" O.C.	.800	L.F.	.012	.49	.57	1.06
Sheathing, plywood exterior grade, 3/8" thick	2.940	S.F.	.031	1.18	1.50	2.68
1/2" thick	2.940	S.F.	.034	1.35	1.65	3
5/8" thick	2.940	S.F.	.036	1.65	1.76	3.41
3/4" thick	2.940	S.F.	.039	1.88	1.91	3.79
Boards, 1" x 6", laid regular	2.940	S.F.	.072	4.50	3.56	8.06
Laid diagonal	2.940	S.F.	.080	4.50	3.94	8.44
1" x 8", laid regular	2.940	S.F.	.062	4.32	3	7.32
Laid diagonal	2.940	S.F.	.072	4.32	3.56	7.88

Window Openings	QUAN.	UNIT	LABOR HOURS	COST EACH		
				MAT.	INST.	TOTAL
The following are to be added to the total cost of the dormers for window openings. Do not subtract window area from the stud wall quantities.						
Headers, 2" x 6" doubled, 2' long	4.000	L.F.	.178	1.64	8.70	10.34
3' long	6.000	L.F.	.267	2.46	13.10	15.56
4' long	8.000	L.F.	.356	3.28	17.45	20.73
5' long	10.000	L.F.	.444	4.10	22	26.10
2" x 8" doubled, 4' long	8.000	L.F.	.376	4.88	18.40	23.28
5' long	10.000	L.F.	.471	6.10	23	29.10
6' long	12.000	L.F.	.565	7.30	27.50	34.80
8' long	16.000	L.F.	.753	9.75	37	46.75
2" x 10" doubled, 4' long	8.000	L.F.	.400	6.40	19.60	26
6' long	12.000	L.F.	.600	9.60	29.50	39.10
8' long	16.000	L.F.	.800	12.80	39	51.80
10' long	20.000	L.F.	1.000	16	49	65

Bracing — Top Plates
Studs — Bottom Plate

System Description	QUAN.	UNIT	LABOR HOURS	COST PER S.F.		
				MAT.	INST.	TOTAL
2" X 4", 16" O.C.						
2" x 4" studs, #2 or better, 16" O.C.	1.000	L.F.	.015	.27	.71	.98
Plates, double top, single bottom	.375	L.F.	.005	.10	.27	.37
Cross bracing, let-in, 1" x 6"	.080	L.F.	.004	.06	.21	.27
TOTAL		S.F.	.024	.43	1.19	1.62
2" X 4", 24" O.C.						
2" x 4" studs, #2 or better, 24" O.C.	.800	L.F.	.012	.22	.57	.79
Plates, double top, single bottom	.375	L.F.	.005	.10	.27	.37
Cross bracing, let-in, 1" x 6"	.080	L.F.	.003	.06	.14	.20
TOTAL		S.F.	.020	.38	.98	1.36
2" X 6", 16" O.C.						
2" x 6" studs, #2 or better, 16" O.C.	1.000	L.F.	.016	.41	.78	1.19
Plates, double top, single bottom	.375	L.F.	.006	.15	.29	.44
Cross bracing, let-in, 1" x 6"	.080	L.F.	.004	.06	.21	.27
TOTAL		S.F.	.026	.62	1.28	1.90
2" X 6", 24" O.C.						
2" x 6" studs, #2 or better, 24" O.C.	.800	L.F.	.013	.33	.62	.95
Plates, double top, single bottom	.375	L.F.	.006	.15	.29	.44
Cross bracing, let-in, 1" x 6"	.080	L.F.	.003	.06	.14	.20
TOTAL		S.F.	.022	.54	1.05	1.59

The costs in this system are based on a square foot of wall area. Do not subtract for door or window openings.

Description	QUAN.	UNIT	LABOR HOURS	COST PER S.F.		
				MAT.	INST.	TOTAL

Partition Framing Price Sheet	QUAN.	UNIT	LABOR HOURS	COST PER S.F.		
				MAT.	INST.	TOTAL
Wood studs, #2 or better, 2" x 4", 12" O.C.	1.250	L.F.	.018	.34	.89	1.23
16" O.C.	1.000	L.F.	.015	.27	.71	.98
24" O.C.	.800	L.F.	.012	.22	.57	.79
32" O.C.	.650	L.F.	.009	.18	.46	.64
2" x 6", 12" O.C.	1.250	L.F.	.020	.51	.98	1.49
16" O.C.	1.000	L.F.	.016	.41	.78	1.19
24" O.C.	.800	L.F.	.013	.33	.62	.95
32" O.C.	.650	L.F.	.010	.27	.51	.78
Plates, #2 or better double top single bottom, 2" x 4"	.375	L.F.	.005	.10	.27	.37
2" x 6"	.375	L.F.	.006	.15	.29	.44
2" x 8"	.375	L.F.	.005	.23	.27	.50
Cross bracing, let-in, 1" x 6" boards studs, 12" O.C.	.080	L.F.	.005	.07	.26	.33
16" O.C.	.080	L.F.	.004	.06	.21	.27
24" O.C.	.080	L.F.	.003	.06	.14	.20
32" O.C.	.080	L.F.	.002	.04	.11	.15
Let-in steel (T shaped) studs, 12" O.C.	.080	L.F.	.001	.08	.07	.15
16" O.C.	.080	L.F.	.001	.07	.05	.12
24" O.C.	.080	L.F.	.001	.07	.05	.12
32" O.C.	.080	L.F.	.001	.05	.04	.09
Steel straps studs, 12" O.C.	.080	L.F.	.001	.09	.06	.15
16" O.C.	.080	L.F.	.001	.09	.05	.14
24" O.C.	.080	L.F.	.001	.09	.05	.14
32" O.C.	.080	L.F.	.001	.08	.05	.13
Metal studs, load bearing 24" O.C., 20 ga. galv., 2-1/2" wide	1.000	S.F.	.015	.62	.73	1.35
3-5/8" wide	1.000	S.F.	.015	.74	.75	1.49
4" wide	1.000	S.F.	.016	.78	.76	1.54
6" wide	1.000	S.F.	.016	.98	.78	1.76
16 ga., 2-1/2" wide	1.000	S.F.	.017	.72	.84	1.56
3-5/8" wide	1.000	S.F.	.017	.86	.85	1.71
4" wide	1.000	S.F.	.018	.91	.87	1.78
6" wide	1.000	S.F.	.018	1.14	.89	2.03
Non-load bearing 24" O.C., 25 ga. galv., 1-5/8" wide	1.000	S.F.	.011	.19	.52	.71
2-1/2" wide	1.000	S.F.	.011	.23	.52	.75
3-5/8" wide	1.000	S.F.	.011	.26	.53	.79
4" wide	1.000	S.F.	.011	.27	.53	.80
6" wide	1.000	S.F.	.011	.40	.54	.94
20 ga., 2-1/2" wide	1.000	S.F.	.013	.30	.65	.95
3-5/8" wide	1.000	S.F.	.014	.33	.66	.99
4" wide	1.000	S.F.	.014	.39	.66	1.05
6" wide	1.000	S.F.	.014	.46	.68	1.14

Window & Door Openings	QUAN.	UNIT	LABOR HOURS	COST EACH		
				MAT.	INST.	TOTAL
The following costs are to be added to the total costs of the walls.						
Do not subtract openings from total wall area.						
Headers, 2" x 6" double, 2' long	4.000	L.F.	.178	1.64	8.70	10.34
3' long	6.000	L.F.	.267	2.46	13.10	15.56
4' long	8.000	L.F.	.356	3.28	17.45	20.73
5' long	10.000	L.F.	.444	4.10	22	26.10
2" x 8" double, 4' long	8.000	L.F.	.376	4.88	18.40	23.28
5' long	10.000	L.F.	.471	6.10	23	29.10
6' long	12.000	L.F.	.565	7.30	27.50	34.80
8' long	16.000	L.F.	.753	9.75	37	46.75
2" x 10" double, 4' long	8.000	L.F.	.400	6.40	19.60	26
6' long	12.000	L.F.	.600	9.60	29.50	39.10
8' long	16.000	L.F.	.800	12.80	39	51.80
10' long	20.000	L.F.	1.000	16	49	65
2" x 12" double, 8' long	16.000	L.F.	.853	18.70	42	60.70
12' long	24.000	L.F.	1.280	28	62.50	90.50

Division 4
Exterior Walls

System Description	QUAN.	UNIT	LABOR HOURS	COST PER S.F.		
				MAT.	INST.	TOTAL
6″ THICK CONCRETE BLOCK WALL						
6″ thick concrete block, 6″ x 8″ x 16″	1.000	S.F.	.100	2.29	4.44	6.73
Masonry reinforcing, truss strips every other course	.625	L.F.	.002	.11	.08	.19
Furring, 1″ x 3″, 16″ O.C.	1.000	L.F.	.016	.38	.79	1.17
Masonry insulation, poured vermiculite	1.000	S.F.	.013	.64	.65	1.29
Stucco, 2 coats	1.000	S.F.	.069	.21	3.08	3.29
Masonry paint, 2 coats	1.000	S.F.	.016	.19	.67	.86
TOTAL		S.F.	.216	3.82	9.71	13.53
8″ THICK CONCRETE BLOCK WALL						
8″ thick concrete block, 8″ x 8″ x 16″	1.000	S.F.	.107	2.60	4.74	7.34
Masonry reinforcing, truss strips every other course	.625	L.F.	.002	.11	.08	.19
Furring, 1″ x 3″, 16″ O.C.	1.000	L.F.	.016	.38	.79	1.17
Masonry insulation, poured vermiculite	1.000	S.F.	.018	.85	.86	1.71
Stucco, 2 coats	1.000	S.F.	.069	.21	3.08	3.29
Masonry paint, 2 coats	1.000	S.F.	.016	.19	.67	.86
TOTAL		S.F.	.228	4.34	10.22	14.56
12″ THICK CONCRETE BLOCK WALL						
12″ thick concrete block, 12″ x 8″ x 16″	1.000	S.F.	.141	3.76	6.15	9.91
Masonry reinforcing, truss strips every other course	.625	L.F.	.003	.12	.12	.24
Furring, 1″ x 3″, 16″ O.C.	1.000	L.F.	.016	.38	.79	1.17
Masonry insulation, poured vermiculite	1.000	S.F.	.026	1.25	1.27	2.52
Stucco, 2 coats	1.000	S.F.	.069	.21	3.08	3.29
Masonry paint, 2 coats	1.000	S.F.	.016	.19	.67	.86
TOTAL		S.F.	.271	5.91	12.08	17.99

Costs for this system are based on a square foot of wall area. Do not subtract for window openings.

Description	QUAN.	UNIT	LABOR HOURS	COST PER S.F.		
				MAT.	INST.	TOTAL

Masonry Block Price Sheet	QUAN.	UNIT	LABOR HOURS	COST PER S.F.		
				MAT.	INST.	TOTAL
Block concrete, 8" x 16" regular, 4" thick	1.000	S.F.	.093	1.61	4.13	5.74
6" thick	1.000	S.F.	.100	2.29	4.44	6.73
8" thick	1.000	S.F.	.107	2.60	4.74	7.34
10" thick	1.000	S.F.	.111	3.30	4.94	8.24
12" thick	1.000	S.F.	.141	3.76	6.15	9.91
Solid block, 4" thick	1.000	S.F.	.096	2	4.28	6.28
6" thick	1.000	S.F.	.104	2.36	4.62	6.98
8" thick	1.000	S.F.	.111	3.57	4.94	8.51
10" thick	1.000	S.F.	.133	4.82	5.75	10.57
12" thick	1.000	S.F.	.148	5.35	6.40	11.75
Lightweight, 4" thick	1.000	S.F.	.093	1.61	4.13	5.74
6" thick	1.000	S.F.	.100	2.29	4.44	6.73
8" thick	1.000	S.F.	.107	2.60	4.74	7.34
10" thick	1.000	S.F.	.111	3.30	4.94	8.24
12" thick	1.000	S.F.	.141	3.76	6.15	9.91
Split rib profile, 4" thick	1.000	S.F.	.116	3.48	5.15	8.63
6" thick	1.000	S.F.	.123	4	5.45	9.45
8" thick	1.000	S.F.	.131	4.58	5.95	10.53
10" thick	1.000	S.F.	.157	4.91	6.85	11.76
12" thick	1.000	S.F.	.175	5.45	7.60	13.05
Masonry reinforcing, wire truss strips, every course, 8" block	1.375	L.F.	.004	.25	.18	.43
12" block	1.375	L.F.	.006	.26	.26	.52
Every other course, 8" block	.625	L.F.	.002	.11	.08	.19
12" block	.625	L.F.	.003	.12	.12	.24
Furring, wood, 1" x 3", 12" O.C.	1.250	L.F.	.020	.48	.99	1.47
16" O.C.	1.000	L.F.	.016	.38	.79	1.17
24" O.C.	.800	L.F.	.013	.30	.63	.93
32" O.C.	.640	L.F.	.010	.24	.51	.75
Steel, 3/4" channels, 12" O.C.	1.250	L.F.	.034	.34	1.42	1.76
16" O.C.	1.000	L.F.	.030	.31	1.26	1.57
24" O.C.	.800	L.F.	.023	.20	.95	1.15
32" O.C.	.640	L.F.	.018	.16	.76	.92
Masonry insulation, vermiculite or perlite poured 4" thick	1.000	S.F.	.009	.41	.42	.83
6" thick	1.000	S.F.	.013	.64	.65	1.29
8" thick	1.000	S.F.	.018	.85	.86	1.71
10" thick	1.000	S.F.	.021	1.03	1.04	2.07
12" thick	1.000	S.F.	.026	1.25	1.27	2.52
Block inserts polystyrene, 6" thick	1.000	S.F.		1.99		1.99
8" thick	1.000	S.F.		1.99		1.99
10" thick	1.000	S.F.		2.34		2.34
12" thick	1.000	S.F.		2.46		2.46
Stucco, 1 coat	1.000	S.F.	.057	.18	2.53	2.71
2 coats	1.000	S.F.	.069	.21	3.08	3.29
3 coats	1.000	S.F.	.081	.25	3.62	3.87
Painting, 1 coat	1.000	S.F.	.011	.13	.47	.60
2 coats	1.000	S.F.	.016	.19	.67	.86
Primer & 1 coat	1.000	S.F.	.013	.21	.55	.76
2 coats	1.000	S.F.	.018	.28	.76	1.04
Lath, metal lath expanded 2.5 lb/S.Y., painted	1.000	S.F.	.010	.50	.44	.94
Galvanized	1.000	S.F.	.012	.55	.48	1.03

Brick

Building Paper

Wall Ties

System Description	QUAN.	UNIT	LABOR HOURS	COST PER S.F.		
				MAT.	INST.	TOTAL
SELECT COMMON BRICK						
Brick, select common, running bond	1.000	S.F.	.174	3.97	7.75	11.72
Wall ties, 7/8" x 7", 22 gauge	1.000	Ea.	.008	.11	.37	.48
Building paper, spunbonded polypropylene	1.100	S.F.	.002	.15	.11	.26
Trim, pine, painted	.125	L.F.	.004	.06	.20	.26
TOTAL		S.F.	.188	4.29	8.43	12.72
RED FACED COMMON BRICK						
Brick, common, red faced, running bond	1.000	S.F.	.182	5.15	8.10	13.25
Wall ties, 7/8" x 7", 22 gauge	1.000	Ea.	.008	.11	.37	.48
Building paper, spundbonded polypropylene	1.100	S.F.	.002	.15	.11	.26
Trim, pine, painted	.125	L.F.	.004	.06	.20	.26
TOTAL		S.F.	.196	5.47	8.78	14.25
BUFF OR GREY FACE BRICK						
Brick, buff or grey	1.000	S.F.	.182	5.45	8.10	13.55
Wall ties, 7/8" x 7", 22 gauge	1.000	Ea.	.008	.11	.37	.48
Building paper, spundbonded polypropylene	1.100	S.F.	.002	.15	.11	.26
Trim, pine, painted	.125	L.F.	.004	.06	.20	.26
TOTAL		S.F.	.196	5.77	8.78	14.55
STONE WORK, ROUGH STONE, AVERAGE						
Field stone veneer	1.000	S.F.	.223	7.34	9.92	17.26
Wall ties, 7/8" x 7", 22 gauge	1.000	Ea.	.008	.11	.37	.48
Building paper, spundbonded polypropylene	1.000	S.F.	.002	.15	.11	.26
Trim, pine, painted	.125	L.F.	.004	.06	.20	.26
TOTAL		S.F.	.237	7.66	10.60	18.26

The costs in this system are based on a square foot of wall area. Do not subtract area for window & door openings.

Description	QUAN.	UNIT	LABOR HOURS	COST PER S.F.		
				MAT.	INST.	TOTAL

Brick/Stone Veneer Price Sheet	QUAN.	UNIT	LABOR HOURS	COST PER S.F.		
				MAT.	INST.	TOTAL
Brick						
Select common, running bond	1.000	S.F.	.174	3.97	7.75	11.72
Red faced, running bond	1.000	S.F.	.182	5.15	8.10	13.25
Buff or grey faced, running bond	1.000	S.F.	.182	5.45	8.10	13.55
Header every 6th course	1.000	S.F.	.216	6	9.60	15.60
English bond	1.000	S.F.	.286	7.65	12.70	20.35
Flemish bond	1.000	S.F.	.195	5.40	8.65	14.05
Common bond	1.000	S.F.	.267	6.80	11.85	18.65
Stack bond	1.000	S.F.	.182	5.45	8.10	13.55
Jumbo, running bond	1.000	S.F.	.092	5.35	4.09	9.44
Norman, running bond	1.000	S.F.	.125	6.25	5.55	11.80
Norwegian, running bond	1.000	S.F.	.107	4.56	4.74	9.30
Economy, running bond	1.000	S.F.	.129	4.61	5.75	10.36
Engineer, running bond	1.000	S.F.	.154	3.79	6.85	10.64
Roman, running bond	1.000	S.F.	.160	6.35	7.10	13.45
Utility, running bond	1.000	S.F.	.089	4.96	3.95	8.91
Glazed, running bond	1.000	S.F.	.190	13.15	8.45	21.60
Stone work, rough stone, average	1.000	S.F.	.179	7.35	9.90	17.25
Maximum	1.000	S.F.	.267	10.95	14.80	25.75
Wall ties, galvanized, corrugated 7/8" x 7", 22 gauge	1.000	Ea.	.008	.11	.37	.48
16 gauge	1.000	Ea.	.008	.26	.37	.63
Cavity wall, every 3rd course 6" long Z type, 1/4" diameter	1.330	L.F.	.010	.55	.47	1.02
3/16" diameter	1.330	L.F.	.010	.29	.47	.76
8" long, Z type, 1/4" diameter	1.330	L.F.	.010	.64	.47	1.11
3/16" diameter	1.330	L.F.	.010	.33	.47	.80
Building paper, aluminum and kraft laminated foil, 1 side	1.000	S.F.	.002	.10	.11	.21
2 sides	1.000	S.F.	.002	.10	.11	.21
#15 asphalt paper	1.100	S.F.	.002	.07	.12	.19
Polyethylene, .002" thick	1.000	S.F.	.002	.01	.11	.12
.004" thick	1.000	S.F.	.002	.04	.11	.15
.006" thick	1.000	S.F.	.002	.06	.11	.17
.010" thick	1.000	S.F.	.002	.07	.11	.18
Trim, 1" x 4", cedar	.125	L.F.	.005	.16	.25	.41
Fir	.125	L.F.	.005	.11	.25	.36
Redwood	.125	L.F.	.005	.16	.25	.41
White pine	.125	L.F.	.005	.11	.25	.36

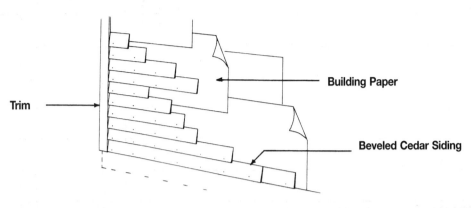

Trim

Building Paper

Beveled Cedar Siding

System Description	QUAN.	UNIT	LABOR HOURS	COST PER S.F.		
				MAT.	INST.	TOTAL
1/2" X 6" BEVELED CEDAR SIDING, "A" GRADE						
1/2" x 6" beveled cedar siding	1.000	S.F.	.027	5.20	1.33	6.53
Building wrap, spundbonded polypropylene	1.100	S.F.	.002	.15	.11	.26
Trim, cedar	.125	L.F.	.005	.16	.25	.41
Paint, primer & 2 coats	1.000	S.F.	.017	.18	.72	.90
TOTAL		S.F.	.051	5.69	2.41	8.10
1/2" X 8" BEVELED CEDAR SIDING, "A" GRADE						
1/2" x 8" beveled cedar siding	1.000	S.F.	.024	6.10	1.19	7.29
Building wrap, spundbonded polypropylene	1.100	S.F.	.002	.15	.11	.26
Trim, cedar	.125	L.F.	.005	.16	.25	.41
Paint, primer & 2 coats	1.000	S.F.	.017	.18	.72	.90
TOTAL		S.F.	.048	6.59	2.27	8.86
1" X 4" TONGUE & GROOVE, REDWOOD, VERTICAL GRAIN						
Redwood, clear, vertical grain, 1" x 10"	1.000	S.F.	.020	5.32	.95	6.27
Building wrap, spunbonded polypropylene	1.100	S.F.	.002	.15	.11	.26
Trim, redwood	.125	L.F.	.005	.16	.25	.41
Sealer, 1 coat, stain, 1 coat	1.000	S.F.	.013	.12	.56	.68
TOTAL		S.F.	.040	5.75	1.87	7.62
1" X 6" TONGUE & GROOVE, REDWOOD, VERTICAL GRAIN						
Redwood, clear, vertical grain, 1" x 10"	1.000	S.F.	.020	5.47	.98	6.45
Building wrap, spunbonded polypropylene	1.100	S.F.	.002	.15	.11	.26
Trim, redwood	.125	L.F.	.005	.16	.25	.41
Sealer, 1 coat, stain, 1 coat	1.000	S.F.	.013	.12	.56	.68
TOTAL		S.F.	.040	5.90	1.90	7.80

The costs in this system are based on a square foot of wall area.
Do not subtract area for door or window openings.

Description	QUAN.	UNIT	LABOR HOURS	COST PER S.F.		
				MAT.	INST.	TOTAL

Wood Siding Price Sheet	QUAN.	UNIT	LABOR HOURS	COST PER S.F.		
				MAT.	INST.	TOTAL
Siding, beveled cedar, "A" grade, 1/2" x 6"	1.000	S.F.	.028	5.20	1.33	6.53
1/2" x 8"	1.000	S.F.	.023	6.10	1.19	7.29
"B" grade, 1/2" x 6"	1.000	S.F.	.032	5.80	1.48	7.28
1/2" x 8"	1.000	S.F.	.029	6.80	1.32	8.12
Clear grade, 1/2" x 6"	1.000	S.F.	.028	6.50	1.66	8.16
1/2" x 8"	1.000	S.F.	.023	7.65	1.49	9.14
Redwood, clear vertical grain, 1/2" x 6"	1.000	S.F.	.036	3.41	1.33	4.74
1/2" x 8"	1.000	S.F.	.032	3.56	1.19	4.75
Clear all heart vertical grain, 1/2" x 6"	1.000	S.F.	.028	3.79	1.48	5.27
1/2" x 8"	1.000	S.F.	.023	3.96	1.32	5.28
Siding board & batten, cedar, "B" grade, 1" x 10"	1.000	S.F.	.031	4.33	.93	5.26
1" x 12"	1.000	S.F.	.031	4.33	.93	5.26
Redwood, clear vertical grain, 1" x 6"	1.000	S.F.	.043	3.41	1.33	4.74
1" x 8"	1.000	S.F.	.018	3.56	1.19	4.75
White pine, #2 & better, 1" x 10"	1.000	S.F.	.029	2.42	1.19	3.61
1" x 12"	1.000	S.F.	.029	2.42	1.19	3.61
Siding vertical, tongue & groove, cedar "B" grade, 1" x 4"	1.000	S.F.	.033	2.72	.95	3.67
1" x 6"	1.000	S.F.	.024	2.79	.98	3.77
1" x 8"	1.000	S.F.	.024	2.87	1.01	3.88
1" x 10"	1.000	S.F.	.021	2.96	1.04	4
"A" grade, 1" x 4"	1.000	S.F.	.033	2.49	.87	3.36
1" x 6"	1.000	S.F.	.024	2.55	.90	3.45
1" x 8"	1.000	S.F.	.024	2.62	.92	3.54
1" x 10"	1.000	S.F.	.021	2.69	.95	3.64
Clear vertical grain, 1" x 4"	1.000	S.F.	.033	2.29	.81	3.10
1" x 6"	1.000	S.F.	.024	2.35	.83	3.18
1" x 8"	1.000	S.F.	.024	2.41	.85	3.26
1" x 10"	1.000	S.F.	.021	2.47	.87	3.34
Redwood, clear vertical grain, 1" x 4"	1.000	S.F.	.033	5.30	.95	6.25
1" x 6"	1.000	S.F.	.024	5.45	.98	6.43
1" x 8"	1.000	S.F.	.024	5.65	1.01	6.66
1" x 10"	1.000	S.F.	.021	5.80	1.04	6.84
Clear all heart vertical grain, 1" x 4"	1.000	S.F.	.033	4.87	.87	5.74
1" x 6"	1.000	S.F.	.024	5	.90	5.90
1" x 8"	1.000	S.F.	.024	5.15	.92	6.07
1" x 10"	1.000	S.F.	.021	5.25	.95	6.20
White pine, 1" x 10"	1.000	S.F.	.024	1.82	1.04	2.86
Siding plywood, texture 1-11 cedar, 3/8" thick	1.000	S.F.	.024	1.32	1.16	2.48
5/8" thick	1.000	S.F.	.024	2.67	1.16	3.83
Redwood, 3/8" thick	1.000	S.F.	.024	1.32	1.16	2.48
5/8" thick	1.000	S.F.	.024	2.11	1.16	3.27
Fir, 3/8" thick	1.000	S.F.	.024	.84	1.16	2
5/8" thick	1.000	S.F.	.024	1.51	1.16	2.67
Southern yellow pine, 3/8" thick	1.000	S.F.	.024	.84	1.16	2
5/8" thick	1.000	S.F.	.024	1.31	1.16	2.47
Paper, #15 asphalt felt	1.100	S.F.	.002	.07	.12	.19
Trim, cedar	.125	L.F.	.005	.16	.25	.41
Fir	.125	L.F.	.005	.11	.25	.36
Redwood	.125	L.F.	.005	.16	.25	.41
White pine	.125	L.F.	.005	.11	.25	.36
Painting, primer, & 1 coat	1.000	S.F.	.013	.12	.56	.68
2 coats	1.000	S.F.	.017	.18	.72	.90
Stain, sealer, & 1 coat	1.000	S.F.	.017	.13	.73	.86
2 coats	1.000	S.F.	.019	.21	.79	1

Trim → | ← Building Paper

→ White Cedar Shingles

System Description	QUAN.	UNIT	LABOR HOURS	COST PER S.F.		
				MAT.	INST.	TOTAL
WHITE CEDAR SHINGLES, 5″ EXPOSURE						
White cedar shingles, 16″ long, grade "A", 5″ exposure	1.000	S.F.	.033	1.91	1.63	3.54
Building wrap, spunbonded polypropylene	1.100	S.F.	.002	.15	.11	.26
Trim, cedar	.125	S.F.	.005	.16	.25	.41
Paint, primer & 1 coat	1.000	S.F.	.017	.13	.73	.86
TOTAL		S.F.	.057	2.35	2.72	5.07
RESQUARED & REBUTTED PERFECTIONS, 5-1/2″ EXPOSURE						
Resquared & rebutted perfections, 5-1/2″ exposure	1.000	S.F.	.027	2.59	1.31	3.90
Building wrap, spunbonded polypropylene	1.100	S.F.	.002	.15	.11	.26
Trim, cedar	.125	S.F.	.005	.16	.25	.41
Stain, sealer & 1 coat	1.000	S.F.	.017	.13	.73	.86
TOTAL		S.F.	.051	3.03	2.40	5.43
HAND-SPLIT SHAKES, 8-1/2″ EXPOSURE						
Hand-split red cedar shakes, 18″ long, 8-1/2″ exposure	1.000	S.F.	.040	1.61	1.96	3.57
Building wrap, spunbonded polypropylene	1.100	S.F.	.002	.15	.11	.26
Trim, cedar	.125	S.F.	.005	.16	.25	.41
Stain, sealer & 1 coat	1.000	S.F.	.017	.13	.73	.86
TOTAL		S.F.	.064	2.05	3.05	5.10

The costs in this system are based on a square foot of wall area.
Do not subtract area for door or window openings.

Description	QUAN.	UNIT	LABOR HOURS	COST PER S.F.		
				MAT.	INST.	TOTAL

Shingle Siding Price Sheet	QUAN.	UNIT	LABOR HOURS	COST PER S.F.		
				MAT.	INST.	TOTAL
Shingles wood, white cedar 16" long, "A" grade, 5" exposure	1.000	S.F.	.033	1.91	1.63	3.54
7" exposure	1.000	S.F.	.030	1.72	1.47	3.19
8-1/2" exposure	1.000	S.F.	.032	1.10	1.57	2.67
10" exposure	1.000	S.F.	.028	.96	1.37	2.33
"B" grade, 5" exposure	1.000	S.F.	.040	1.65	1.96	3.61
7" exposure	1.000	S.F.	.028	1.16	1.37	2.53
8-1/2" exposure	1.000	S.F.	.024	.99	1.18	2.17
10" exposure	1.000	S.F.	.020	.83	.98	1.81
Fire retardant, "A" grade, 5" exposure	1.000	S.F.	.033	2.52	1.63	4.15
7" exposure	1.000	S.F.	.028	1.58	1.37	2.95
8-1/2" exposure	1.000	S.F.	.032	1.93	1.57	3.50
10" exposure	1.000	S.F.	.025	1.50	1.22	2.72
Fire retardant, 5" exposure	1.000	S.F.	.029	3.53	1.42	4.95
7" exposure	1.000	S.F.	.036	2.75	1.74	4.49
8-1/2" exposure	1.000	S.F.	.032	2.47	1.57	4.04
10" exposure	1.000	S.F.	.025	1.92	1.22	3.14
Resquared & rebutted, 5-1/2" exposure	1.000	S.F.	.027	2.59	1.31	3.90
7" exposure	1.000	S.F.	.024	2.33	1.18	3.51
8-1/2" exposure	1.000	S.F.	.021	2.07	1.05	3.12
10" exposure	1.000	S.F.	.019	1.81	.92	2.73
Fire retardant, 5" exposure	1.000	S.F.	.027	3.20	1.31	4.51
7" exposure	1.000	S.F.	.024	2.87	1.18	4.05
8-1/2" exposure	1.000	S.F.	.021	2.55	1.05	3.60
10" exposure	1.000	S.F.	.023	1.75	1.12	2.87
Hand-split, red cedar, 24" long, 7" exposure	1.000	S.F.	.045	2.55	2.20	4.75
8-1/2" exposure	1.000	S.F.	.038	2.18	1.88	4.06
10" exposure	1.000	S.F.	.032	1.82	1.57	3.39
12" exposure	1.000	S.F.	.026	1.46	1.26	2.72
Fire retardant, 7" exposure	1.000	S.F.	.045	3.40	2.20	5.60
8-1/2" exposure	1.000	S.F.	.038	2.91	1.88	4.79
10" exposure	1.000	S.F.	.032	2.43	1.57	4
12" exposure	1.000	S.F.	.026	1.94	1.26	3.20
18" long, 5" exposure	1.000	S.F.	.068	2.74	3.33	6.07
7" exposure	1.000	S.F.	.048	1.93	2.35	4.28
8-1/2" exposure	1.000	S.F.	.040	1.61	1.96	3.57
10" exposure	1.000	S.F.	.036	1.45	1.76	3.21
Fire retardant, 5" exposure	1.000	S.F.	.068	3.77	3.33	7.10
7" exposure	1.000	S.F.	.048	2.66	2.35	5.01
8-1/2" exposure	1.000	S.F.	.040	2.22	1.96	4.18
10" exposure	1.000	S.F.	.036	1.99	1.76	3.75
Paper, #15 asphalt felt	1.100	S.F.	.002	.06	.11	.17
Trim, cedar	.125	S.F.	.005	.16	.25	.41
Fir	.125	S.F.	.005	.11	.25	.36
Redwood	.125	S.F.	.005	.16	.25	.41
White pine	.125	S.F.	.005	.11	.25	.36
Painting, primer, & 1 coat	1.000	S.F.	.013	.12	.56	.68
2 coats	1.000	S.F.	.017	.18	.72	.90
Staining, sealer, & 1 coat	1.000	S.F.	.017	.13	.73	.86
2 coats	1.000	S.F.	.019	.21	.79	1

Aluminum Trim

Building Paper

Alum. Horizontal Siding

Backer Insulation Board

System Description	QUAN.	UNIT	LABOR HOURS	COST PER S.F.		
				MAT.	INST.	TOTAL
ALUMINUM CLAPBOARD SIDING, 8″ WIDE, WHITE						
Aluminum horizontal siding, 8″ clapboard	1.000	S.F.	.031	1.90	1.52	3.42
Backer, insulation board	1.000	S.F.	.008	.70	.39	1.09
Trim, aluminum	.600	L.F.	.016	.92	.77	1.69
Building wrap, spunbonded polypropylene	1.100	S.F.	.002	.15	.11	.26
TOTAL		S.F.	.057	3.67	2.79	6.46
ALUMINUM VERTICAL BOARD & BATTEN, WHITE						
Aluminum vertical board & batten	1.000	S.F.	.027	2.16	1.33	3.49
Backer insulation board	1.000	S.F.	.008	.70	.39	1.09
Trim, aluminum	.600	L.F.	.016	.92	.77	1.69
Building wrap, spunbonded polypropylene	1.100	S.F.	.002	.15	.11	.26
TOTAL		S.F.	.053	3.93	2.60	6.53
VINYL CLAPBOARD SIDING, 8″ WIDE, WHITE						
Vinyl siding, clabboard profile, smooth texture, .042 thick, single 8	1.000	S.F.	.032	1.06	1.58	2.64
Backer, insulation board	1.000	S.F.	.008	.70	.39	1.09
Vinyl siding, access., outside corner, woodgrain, 4″ face, 3/4″ pocket	1.000	L.F.	.023	1.93	1.12	3.05
Building wrap, spunbonded polypropylene	1.100	S.F.	.002	.15	.11	.26
TOTAL		S.F.	.065	3.84	3.20	7.04
VINYL VERTICAL BOARD & BATTEN, WHITE						
Vinyl siding, vertical pattern, .046 thick, double 5	1.000	S.F.	.029	1.34	1.42	2.76
Backer, insulation board	1.000	S.F.	.008	.70	.39	1.09
Vinyl siding, access., outside corner, woodgrain, 4″ face, 3/4″ pocket	.600	L.F.	.014	1.16	.67	1.83
Building wrap, spunbonded polypropylene	1.100	S.F.	.002	.15	.11	.26
TOTAL		S.F.	.053	3.35	2.59	5.94

The costs in this system are on a square foot of wall basis.
Subtract openings from wall area.

Description	QUAN.	UNIT	LABOR HOURS	COST PER S.F.		
				MAT.	INST.	TOTAL

Metal & Plastic Siding Price Sheet	QUAN.	UNIT	LABOR HOURS	COST PER S.F.		
				MAT.	INST.	TOTAL
Siding, aluminum, .024" thick, smooth, 8" wide, white	1.000	S.F.	.031	1.90	1.52	3.42
Color	1.000	S.F.	.031	2.03	1.52	3.55
Double 4" pattern, 8" wide, white	1.000	S.F.	.031	2.24	1.52	3.76
Color	1.000	S.F.	.031	2.37	1.52	3.89
Double 5" pattern, 10" wide, white	1.000	S.F.	.029	2.31	1.42	3.73
Color	1.000	S.F.	.029	2.44	1.42	3.86
Embossed, single, 8" wide, white	1.000	S.F.	.031	1.90	1.52	3.42
Color	1.000	S.F.	.031	2.03	1.52	3.55
Double 4" pattern, 8" wide, white	1.000	S.F.	.031	2.37	1.52	3.89
Color	1.000	S.F.	.031	2.50	1.52	4.02
Double 5" pattern, 10" wide, white	1.000	S.F.	.029	2.34	1.42	3.76
Color	1.000	S.F.	.029	2.47	1.42	3.89
Alum siding with insulation board, smooth, 8" wide, white	1.000	S.F.	.031	2.08	1.52	3.60
Color	1.000	S.F.	.031	2.21	1.52	3.73
Double 4" pattern, 8" wide, white	1.000	S.F.	.031	2.06	1.52	3.58
Color	1.000	S.F.	.031	2.19	1.52	3.71
Double 5" pattern, 10" wide, white	1.000	S.F.	.029	2.06	1.42	3.48
Color	1.000	S.F.	.029	2.19	1.42	3.61
Embossed, single, 8" wide, white	1.000	S.F.	.031	2.40	1.52	3.92
Color	1.000	S.F.	.031	2.53	1.52	4.05
Double 4" pattern, 8" wide, white	1.000	S.F.	.031	2.43	1.52	3.95
Color	1.000	S.F.	.031	2.56	1.52	4.08
Double 5" pattern, 10" wide, white	1.000	S.F.	.029	2.43	1.42	3.85
Color	1.000	S.F.	.029	2.56	1.42	3.98
Aluminum, shake finish, 10" wide, white	1.000	S.F.	.029	2.59	1.42	4.01
Color	1.000	S.F.	.029	2.72	1.42	4.14
Aluminum, vertical, 12" wide, white	1.000	S.F.	.027	2.16	1.33	3.49
Color	1.000	S.F.	.027	2.29	1.33	3.62
Vinyl siding, 8" wide, smooth, white	1.000	S.F.	.032	1.06	1.58	2.64
Color	1.000	S.F.	.032	1.24	1.58	2.82
10" wide, Dutch lap, smooth, white	1.000	S.F.	.029	1.01	1.42	2.43
Color	1.000	S.F.	.029	1.19	1.42	2.61
Double 4" pattern, 8" wide, white	1.000	S.F.	.032	.83	1.58	2.41
Color	1.000	S.F.	.032	1.01	1.58	2.59
Double 5" pattern, 10" wide, white	1.000	S.F.	.029	.83	1.42	2.25
Color	1.000	S.F.	.029	1.01	1.42	2.43
Embossed, single, 8" wide, white	1.000	S.F.	.032	1.06	1.58	2.64
Color	1.000	S.F.	.032	1.24	1.58	2.82
10" wide, white	1.000	S.F.	.029	1.27	1.42	2.69
Color	1.000	S.F.	.029	1.45	1.42	2.87
Double 4" pattern, 8" wide, white	1.000	S.F.	.032	1.01	1.58	2.59
Color	1.000	S.F.	.032	1.19	1.58	2.77
Double 5" pattern, 10" wide, white	1.000	S.F.	.029	1.01	1.42	2.43
Color	1.000	S.F.	.029	1.19	1.42	2.61
Vinyl, shake finish, 10" wide, white	1.000	S.F.	.029	2.41	1.96	4.37
Color	1.000	S.F.	.029	2.59	1.96	4.55
Vinyl, vertical, double 5" pattern, 10" wide, white	1.000	S.F.	.029	1.34	1.42	2.76
Color	1.000	S.F.	.029	1.52	1.42	2.94
Backer board, installed in siding panels 8" or 10" wide	1.000	S.F.	.008	.70	.39	1.09
4' x 8' sheets, polystyrene, 3/4" thick	1.000	S.F.	.010	.56	.49	1.05
4' x 8' fiberboard, plain	1.000	S.F.	.008	.70	.39	1.09
Trim, aluminum, white	.600	L.F.	.016	.92	.77	1.69
Color	.600	L.F.	.016	.99	.77	1.76
Vinyl, white	.600	L.F.	.014	1.16	.67	1.83
Color	.600	L.F.	.014	1.37	.67	2.04
Paper, #15 asphalt felt	1.100	S.F.	.002	.07	.12	.19
Kraft paper, plain	1.100	S.F.	.002	.11	.12	.23
Foil backed	1.100	S.F.	.002	.11	.12	.23

Description	QUAN.	UNIT	LABOR HOURS	COST PER S.F.		
				MAT.	INST.	TOTAL
Poured insulation, cellulose fiber, R3.8 per inch (1" thick)	1.000	S.F.	.003	.05	.16	.21
Fiberglass , R4.0 per inch (1" thick)	1.000	S.F.	.003	.04	.16	.20
Mineral wool, R3.0 per inch (1" thick)	1.000	S.F.	.003	.04	.16	.20
Polystyrene, R4.0 per inch (1" thick)	1.000	S.F.	.003	.28	.16	.44
Vermiculite, R2.7 per inch (1" thick)	1.000	S.F.	.003	.16	.16	.32
Perlite, R2.7 per inch (1" thick)	1.000	S.F.	.003	.16	.16	.32
Reflective insulation, aluminum foil reinforced with scrim	1.000	S.F.	.004	.16	.21	.37
Reinforced with woven polyolefin	1.000	S.F.	.004	.19	.21	.40
With single bubble air space, R8.8	1.000	S.F.	.005	.28	.26	.54
With double bubble air space, R9.8	1.000	S.F.	.005	.29	.26	.55
Rigid insulation, fiberglass, unfaced,						
1-1/2" thick, R6.2	1.000	S.F.	.008	.70	.39	1.09
2" thick, R8.3	1.000	S.F.	.008	.76	.39	1.15
2-1/2" thick, R10.3	1.000	S.F.	.010	.88	.49	1.37
3" thick, R12.4	1.000	S.F.	.010	.88	.49	1.37
Foil faced, 1" thick, R4.3	1.000	S.F.	.008	1.01	.39	1.40
1-1/2" thick, R6.2	1.000	S.F.	.008	1.50	.39	1.89
2" thick, R8.7	1.000	S.F.	.009	1.88	.44	2.32
2-1/2" thick, R10.9	1.000	S.F.	.010	2.22	.49	2.71
3" thick, R13.0	1.000	S.F.	.010	2.41	.49	2.90
Foam glass, 1-1/2" thick R2.64	1.000	S.F.	.010	1.54	.49	2.03
2" thick R5.26	1.000	S.F.	.011	3.80	.54	4.34
Perlite, 1" thick R2.77	1.000	S.F.	.010	.33	.49	.82
2" thick R5.55	1.000	S.F.	.011	.66	.54	1.20
Polystyrene, extruded, blue, 2.2#/C.F., 3/4" thick R4	1.000	S.F.	.010	.56	.49	1.05
1-1/2" thick R8.1	1.000	S.F.	.011	1.14	.54	1.68
2" thick R10.8	1.000	S.F.	.011	1.54	.54	2.08
Molded bead board, white, 1" thick R3.85	1.000	S.F.	.010	.40	.49	.89
1-1/2" thick, R5.6	1.000	S.F.	.011	.79	.54	1.33
2" thick, R7.7	1.000	S.F.	.011	1.19	.54	1.73
Non-rigid insulation, batts						
Fiberglass, kraft faced, 3-1/2" thick, R13, 11" wide	1.000	S.F.	.005	.36	.29	.65
15" wide	1.000	S.F.	.005	.36	.29	.65
23" wide	1.000	S.F.	.005	.36	.29	.65
6" thick, R19, 11" wide	1.000	S.F.	.006	.47	.29	.76
15" wide	1.000	S.F.	.006	.47	.29	.76
23" wide	1.000	S.F.	.006	.47	.29	.76
9" thick, R30, 15" wide	1.000	S.F.	.006	.77	.29	1.06
23" wide	1.000	S.F.	.006	.77	.29	1.06
12" thick, R38, 15" wide	1.000	S.F.	.006	1.10	.29	1.39
23" wide	1.000	S.F.	.006	1.10	.29	1.39
Fiberglass, foil faced, 3-1/2" thick, R13, 15" wide	1.000	S.F.	.005	.59	.29	.88
23" wide	1.000	S.F.	.005	.59	.29	.88
6" thick, R19, 15" thick	1.000	S.F.	.005	.85	.24	1.09
23" wide	1.000	S.F.	.005	.85	.24	1.09
9" thick, R30, 15" wide	1.000	S.F.	.006	.98	.29	1.27
23" wide	1.000	S.F.	.006	.98	.29	1.27

Insulation Systems	QUAN.	UNIT	LABOR HOURS	COST PER S.F.		
				MAT.	INST.	TOTAL
Non-rigid insulation batts						
Fiberglass unfaced, 3-1/2" thick, R13, 15" wide	1.000	S.F.	.005	.33	.24	.57
23" wide	1.000	S.F.	.005	.33	.24	.57
6" thick, R19, 15" wide	1.000	S.F.	.006	.50	.29	.79
23" wide	1.000	S.F.	.006	.50	.29	.79
9" thick, R19, 15" wide	1.000	S.F.	.007	.70	.34	1.04
23" wide	1.000	S.F.	.007	.70	.34	1.04
12" thick, R38, 15" wide	1.000	S.F.	.007	.89	.34	1.23
23" wide	1.000	S.F.	.007	.89	.34	1.23
Mineral fiber batts, 3" thick, R11	1.000	S.F.	.005	.42	.24	.66
3-1/2" thick, R13	1.000	S.F.	.005	.42	.24	.66
6" thick, R19	1.000	S.F.	.005	.53	.24	.77
6-1/2" thick, R22	1.000	S.F.	.005	.53	.24	.77
10" thick, R30	1.000	S.F.	.006	.80	.29	1.09

Drip Cap — Snap-in Grille

Caulking

Interior Trim —

Window

System Description	QUAN.	UNIT	LABOR HOURS	COST EACH		
				MAT.	INST.	TOTAL
BUILDER'S QUALITY WOOD WINDOW 2' X 3', DOUBLE HUNG						
Window, primed, builder's quality, 2' x 3', insulating glass	1.000	Ea.	.800	229	39	268
Trim, interior casing	11.000	L.F.	.367	16.06	17.93	33.99
Paint, interior & exterior, primer & 2 coats	2.000	Face	1.778	2.14	75	77.14
Caulking	10.000	L.F.	.278	1.70	13.40	15.10
Snap-in grille	1.000	Set	.333	53	16.30	69.30
Drip cap, metal	2.000	L.F.	.040	.84	1.96	2.80
TOTAL		Ea.	3.596	302.74	163.59	466.33
PLASTIC CLAD WOOD WINDOW 3' X 4', DOUBLE HUNG						
Window, plastic clad, premium, 3' x 4', insulating glass	1.000	Ea.	.889	405	43.50	448.50
Trim, interior casing	15.000	L.F.	.500	21.90	24.45	46.35
Paint, interior, primer & 2 coats	1.000	Face	.889	1.07	37.50	38.57
Caulking	14.000	L.F.	.389	2.38	18.76	21.14
Snap-in grille	1.000	Set	.333	53	16.30	69.30
TOTAL		Ea.	3.000	483.35	140.51	623.86
METAL CLAD WOOD WINDOW, 3' X 5', DOUBLE HUNG						
Window, metal clad, deluxe, 3' x 5', insulating glass	1.000	Ea.	1.000	400	49	449
Trim, interior casing	17.000	L.F.	.567	24.82	27.71	52.53
Paint, interior, primer & 2 coats	1.000	Face	.889	1.07	37.50	38.57
Caulking	16.000	L.F.	.444	2.72	21.44	24.16
Snap-in grille	1.000	Set	.235	141	11.50	152.50
Drip cap, metal	3.000	L.F.	.060	1.26	2.94	4.20
TOTAL		Ea.	3.195	570.87	150.09	720.96

The cost of this system is on a cost per each window basis.

Description	QUAN.	UNIT	LABOR HOURS	COST EACH		
				MAT.	INST.	TOTAL

Double Hung Window Price Sheet	QUAN.	UNIT	LABOR HOURS	COST EACH		
				MAT.	INST.	TOTAL
Windows, double-hung, builder's quality, 2' x 3', single glass	1.000	Ea.	.800	202	39	241
Insulating glass	1.000	Ea.	.800	229	39	268
3' x 4', single glass	1.000	Ea.	.889	283	43.50	326.50
Insulating glass	1.000	Ea.	.889	305	43.50	348.50
4' x 4'-6", single glass	1.000	Ea.	1.000	345	49	394
Insulating glass	1.000	Ea.	1.000	375	49	424
Plastic clad premium insulating glass, 2'-6" x 3'	1.000	Ea.	.800	248	39	287
3' x 3'-6"	1.000	Ea.	.800	287	39	326
3' x 4'	1.000	Ea.	.889	405	43.50	448.50
3' x 4'-6"	1.000	Ea.	.889	370	43.50	413.50
3' x 5'	1.000	Ea.	1.000	345	49	394
3'-6" x 6'	1.000	Ea.	1.000	405	49	454
Metal clad deluxe insulating glass, 2'-6" x 3'	1.000	Ea.	.800	292	39	331
3' x 3'-6"	1.000	Ea.	.800	335	39	374
3' x 4'	1.000	Ea.	.889	350	43.50	393.50
3' x 4'-6"	1.000	Ea.	.889	370	43.50	413.50
3' x 5'	1.000	Ea.	1.000	400	49	449
3'-6" x 6'	1.000	Ea.	1.000	480	49	529
Trim, interior casing, window 2' x 3'	11.000	L.F.	.367	16.05	17.95	34
2'-6" x 3'	12.000	L.F.	.400	17.50	19.55	37.05
3' x 3'-6"	14.000	L.F.	.467	20.50	23	43.50
3' x 4'	15.000	L.F.	.500	22	24.50	46.50
3' x 4'-6"	16.000	L.F.	.533	23.50	26	49.50
3' x 5'	17.000	L.F.	.567	25	27.50	52.50
3'-6" x 6'	20.000	L.F.	.667	29	32.50	61.50
4' x 4'-6"	18.000	L.F.	.600	26.50	29.50	56
Paint or stain, interior or exterior, 2' x 3' window, 1 coat	1.000	Face	.444	.35	18.65	19
2 coats	1.000	Face	.727	.70	30.50	31.20
Primer & 1 coat	1.000	Face	.727	.73	30.50	31.23
Primer & 2 coats	1.000	Face	.889	1.07	37.50	38.57
3' x 4' window, 1 coat	1.000	Face	.667	1.18	28	29.18
2 coats	1.000	Face	.667	1.75	28	29.75
Primer & 1 coat	1.000	Face	.727	1.09	30.50	31.59
Primer & 2 coats	1.000	Face	.889	1.07	37.50	38.57
4' x 4'-6" window, 1 coat	1.000	Face	.667	1.18	28	29.18
2 coats	1.000	Face	.667	1.75	28	29.75
Primer & 1 coat	1.000	Face	.727	1.09	30.50	31.59
Primer & 2 coats	1.000	Face	.889	1.07	37.50	38.57
Caulking, window, 2' x 3'	10.000	L.F.	.323	1.70	13.40	15.10
2'-6" x 3'	11.000	L.F.	.355	1.87	14.75	16.62
3' x 3'-6"	13.000	L.F.	.419	2.21	17.40	19.61
3' x 4'	14.000	L.F.	.452	2.38	18.75	21.13
3' x 4'-6"	15.000	L.F.	.484	2.55	20	22.55
3' x 5'	16.000	L.F.	.516	2.72	21.50	24.22
3'-6" x 6'	19.000	L.F.	.613	3.23	25.50	28.73
4' x 4'-6"	17.000	L.F.	.548	2.89	23	25.89
Grilles, glass size to, 16" x 24" per sash	1.000	Set	.333	53	16.30	69.30
32" x 32" per sash	1.000	Set	.235	141	11.50	152.50
Drip cap, aluminum, 2' long	2.000	L.F.	.040	.84	1.96	2.80
3' long	3.000	L.F.	.060	1.26	2.94	4.20
4' long	4.000	L.F.	.080	1.68	3.92	5.60
Wood, 2' long	2.000	L.F.	.067	2.92	3.26	6.18
3' long	3.000	L.F.	.100	4.38	4.89	9.27
4' long	4.000	L.F.	.133	5.85	6.50	12.35

Drip Cap

Snap-in Grille

Interior Trim

Caulking

Window

System Description	QUAN.	UNIT	LABOR HOURS	COST EACH		
				MAT.	INST.	TOTAL
BUILDER'S QUALITY WINDOW, WOOD, 2' BY 3', CASEMENT						
Window, primed, builder's quality, 2' x 3', insulating glass	1.000	Ea.	.800	248	39	287
Trim, interior casing	11.000	L.F.	.367	16.06	17.93	33.99
Paint, interior & exterior, primer & 2 coats	2.000	Face	1.778	2.14	75	77.14
Caulking	10.000	L.F.	.278	1.70	13.40	15.10
Snap-in grille	1.000	Ea.	.267	31.50	13.05	44.55
Drip cap, metal	2.000	L.F.	.040	.84	1.96	2.80
TOTAL		Ea.	3.530	300.24	160.34	460.58
PLASTIC CLAD WOOD WINDOW, 2' X 4', CASEMENT						
Window, plastic clad, premium, 2' x 4', insulating glass	1.000	Ea.	.889	340	43.50	383.50
Trim, interior casing	13.000	L.F.	.433	18.98	21.19	40.17
Paint, interior, primer & 2 coats	1.000	Ea.	.889	1.07	37.50	38.57
Caulking	12.000	L.F.	.333	2.04	16.08	18.12
Snap-in grille	1.000	Ea.	.267	31.50	13.05	44.55
TOTAL		Ea.	2.811	393.59	131.32	524.91
METAL CLAD WOOD WINDOW, 2' X 5', CASEMENT						
Window, metal clad, deluxe, 2' x 5', insulating glass	1.000	Ea.	1.000	350	49	399
Trim, interior casing	15.000	L.F.	.500	21.90	24.45	46.35
Paint, interior, primer & 2 coats	1.000	Ea.	.889	1.07	37.50	38.57
Caulking	14.000	L.F.	.389	2.38	18.76	21.14
Snap-in grille	1.000	Ea.	.250	44	12.25	56.25
Drip cap, metal	12.000	L.F.	.040	.84	1.96	2.80
TOTAL		Ea.	3.068	420.19	143.92	564.11

The cost of this system is on a cost per each window basis.

Description	QUAN.	UNIT	LABOR HOURS	COST EACH		
				MAT.	INST.	TOTAL

Casement Window Price Sheet	QUAN.	UNIT	LABOR HOURS	COST EACH		
				MAT.	INST.	TOTAL
Window, casement, builders quality, 2' x 3', single glass	1.000	Ea.	.800	305	39	344
Insulating glass	1.000	Ea.	.800	248	39	287
2' x 4'-6", single glass	1.000	Ea.	.727	940	35.50	975.50
Insulating glass	1.000	Ea.	.727	515	35.50	550.50
2' x 6', single glass	1.000	Ea.	.889	390	49	439
Insulating glass	1.000	Ea.	.889	1,200	43.50	1,243.50
Plastic clad premium insulating glass, 2' x 3'	1.000	Ea.	.800	277	39	316
2' x 4'	1.000	Ea.	.889	430	43.50	473.50
2' x 5'	1.000	Ea.	1.000	580	49	629
2' x 6'	1.000	Ea.	1.000	390	49	439
Metal clad deluxe insulating glass, 2' x 3'	1.000	Ea.	.800	299	39	338
2' x 4'	1.000	Ea.	.889	299	43.50	342.50
2' x 5'	1.000	Ea.	1.000	340	49	389
2' x 6'	1.000	Ea.	1.000	390	49	439
Trim, interior casing, window 2' x 3'	11.000	L.F.	.367	16.05	17.95	34
2' x 4'	13.000	L.F.	.433	19	21	40
2' x 4'-6"	14.000	L.F.	.467	20.50	23	43.50
2' x 5'	15.000	L.F.	.500	22	24.50	46.50
2' x 6'	17.000	L.F.	.567	25	27.50	52.50
Paint or stain, interior or exterior, 2' x 3' window, 1 coat	1.000	Face	.444	.35	18.65	19
2 coats	1.000	Face	.727	.70	30.50	31.20
Primer & 1 coat	1.000	Face	.727	.73	30.50	31.23
Primer & 2 coats	1.000	Face	.889	1.07	37.50	38.57
2' x 4' window, 1 coat	1.000	Face	.444	.35	18.65	19
2 coats	1.000	Face	.727	.70	30.50	31.20
Primer & 1 coat	1.000	Face	.727	.73	30.50	31.23
Primer & 2 coats	1.000	Face	.889	1.07	37.50	38.57
2' x 6' window, 1 coat	1.000	Face	.667	1.18	28	29.18
2 coats	1.000	Face	.667	1.75	28	29.75
Primer & 1 coat	1.000	Face	.727	1.09	30.50	31.59
Primer & 2 coats	1.000	Face	.889	1.07	37.50	38.57
Caulking, window, 2' x 3'	10.000	L.F.	.323	1.70	13.40	15.10
2' x 4'	12.000	L.F.	.387	2.04	16.10	18.14
2' x 4'-6"	13.000	L.F.	.419	2.21	17.40	19.61
2' x 5'	14.000	L.F.	.452	2.38	18.75	21.13
2' x 6'	16.000	L.F.	.516	2.72	21.50	24.22
Grilles, glass size, to 20" x 36"	1.000	Ea.	.267	31.50	13.05	44.55
To 20" x 56"	1.000	Ea.	.250	44	12.25	56.25
Drip cap, metal, 2' long	2.000	L.F.	.040	.84	1.96	2.80
Wood, 2' long	2.000	L.F.	.067	2.92	3.26	6.18

Drip Cap —
Interior Trim —
Snap-in Grille —
Caulking —
Window —

System Description	QUAN.	UNIT	LABOR HOURS	COST EACH		
				MAT.	INST.	TOTAL
BUILDER'S QUALITY WINDOW, WOOD, 34" X 22", AWNING						
Window, builder quality, 34" x 22", insulating glass	1.000	Ea.	.800	282	39	321
Trim, interior casing	10.500	L.F.	.350	15.33	17.12	32.45
Paint, interior & exterior, primer & 2 coats	2.000	Face	1.778	2.14	75	77.14
Caulking	9.500	L.F.	.264	1.62	12.73	14.35
Snap-in grille	1.000	Ea.	.267	26.50	13.05	39.55
Drip cap, metal	3.000	L.F.	.060	1.26	2.94	4.20
TOTAL		Ea.	3.519	328.85	159.84	488.69
PLASTIC CLAD WOOD WINDOW, 40" X 28", AWNING						
Window, plastic clad, premium, 40" x 28", insulating glass	1.000	Ea.	.889	370	43.50	413.50
Trim interior casing	13.500	L.F.	.450	19.71	22.01	41.72
Paint, interior, primer & 2 coats	1.000	Face	.889	1.07	37.50	38.57
Caulking	12.500	L.F.	.347	2.13	16.75	18.88
Snap-in grille	1.000	Ea.	.267	26.50	13.05	39.55
TOTAL		Ea.	2.842	419.41	132.81	552.22
METAL CLAD WOOD WINDOW, 48" X 36", AWNING						
Window, metal clad, deluxe, 48" x 36", insulating glass	1.000	Ea.	1.000	405	49	454
Trim, interior casing	15.000	L.F.	.500	21.90	24.45	46.35
Paint, interior, primer & 2 coats	1.000	Face	.889	1.07	37.50	38.57
Caulking	14.000	L.F.	.389	2.38	18.76	21.14
Snap-in grille	1.000	Ea.	.250	39.50	12.25	51.75
Drip cap, metal	4.000	L.F.	.080	1.68	3.92	5.60
TOTAL		Ea.	3.108	471.53	145.88	617.41

The cost of this system is on a cost per each window basis.

Description	QUAN.	UNIT	LABOR HOURS	COST EACH		
				MAT.	INST.	TOTAL

Awning Window Price Sheet	QUAN.	UNIT	LABOR HOURS	COST EACH		
				MAT.	INST.	TOTAL
Windows, awning, builder's quality, 34" x 22", insulated glass	1.000	Ea.	.800	278	39	317
Low E glass	1.000	Ea.	.800	282	39	321
40" x 28", insulated glass	1.000	Ea.	.889	340	43.50	383.50
Low E glass	1.000	Ea.	.889	365	43.50	408.50
48" x 36", insulated glass	1.000	Ea.	1.000	495	49	544
Low E glass	1.000	Ea.	1.000	520	49	569
Plastic clad premium insulating glass, 34" x 22"	1.000	Ea.	.800	285	39	324
40" x 22"	1.000	Ea.	.800	310	39	349
36" x 28"	1.000	Ea.	.889	330	43.50	373.50
36" x 36"	1.000	Ea.	.889	370	43.50	413.50
48" x 28"	1.000	Ea.	1.000	400	49	449
60" x 36"	1.000	Ea.	1.000	555	49	604
Metal clad deluxe insulating glass, 34" x 22"	1.000	Ea.	.800	266	39	305
40" x 22"	1.000	Ea.	.800	315	39	354
36" x 25"	1.000	Ea.	.889	296	43.50	339.50
40" x 30"	1.000	Ea.	.889	370	43.50	413.50
48" x 28"	1.000	Ea.	1.000	380	49	429
60" x 36"	1.000	Ea.	1.000	405	49	454
Trim, interior casing window, 34" x 22"	10.500	L.F.	.350	15.35	17.10	32.45
40" x 22"	11.500	L.F.	.383	16.80	18.75	35.55
36" x 28"	12.500	L.F.	.417	18.25	20.50	38.75
40" x 28"	13.500	L.F.	.450	19.70	22	41.70
48" x 28"	14.500	L.F.	.483	21	23.50	44.50
48" x 36"	15.000	L.F.	.500	22	24.50	46.50
Paint or stain, interior or exterior, 34" x 22", 1 coat	1.000	Face	.444	.35	18.65	19
2 coats	1.000	Face	.727	.70	30.50	31.20
Primer & 1 coat	1.000	Face	.727	.73	30.50	31.23
Primer & 2 coats	1.000	Face	.889	1.07	37.50	38.57
36" x 28", 1 coat	1.000	Face	.444	.35	18.65	19
2 coats	1.000	Face	.727	.70	30.50	31.20
Primer & 1 coat	1.000	Face	.727	.73	30.50	31.23
Primer & 2 coats	1.000	Face	.889	1.07	37.50	38.57
48" x 36", 1 coat	1.000	Face	.667	1.18	28	29.18
2 coats	1.000	Face	.667	1.75	28	29.75
Primer & 1 coat	1.000	Face	.727	1.09	30.50	31.59
Primer & 2 coats	1.000	Face	.889	1.07	37.50	38.57
Caulking, window, 34" x 22"	9.500	L.F.	.306	1.62	12.75	14.37
40" x 22"	10.500	L.F.	.339	1.79	14.05	15.84
36" x 28"	11.500	L.F.	.371	1.96	15.40	17.36
40" x 28"	12.500	L.F.	.403	2.13	16.75	18.88
48" x 28"	13.500	L.F.	.436	2.30	18.10	20.40
48" x 36"	14.000	L.F.	.452	2.38	18.75	21.13
Grilles, glass size, to 28" by 16"	1.000	Ea.	.267	26.50	13.05	39.55
To 44" by 24"	1.000	Ea.	.250	39.50	12.25	51.75
Drip cap, aluminum, 3' long	3.000	L.F.	.060	1.26	2.94	4.20
3'-6" long	3.500	L.F.	.070	1.47	3.43	4.90
4' long	4.000	L.F.	.080	1.68	3.92	5.60
Wood, 3' long	3.000	L.F.	.100	4.38	4.89	9.27
3'-6" long	3.500	L.F.	.117	5.10	5.70	10.80
4' long	4.000	L.F.	.133	5.85	6.50	12.35

157

Drip Cap

Snap-in Grille

Caulking

Interior Trim

Window

System Description	QUAN.	UNIT	LABOR HOURS	COST EACH		
				MAT.	INST.	TOTAL
BUILDER'S QUALITY WOOD WINDOW, 3' X 2', SLIDING						
Window, primed, builder's quality, 3' x 3', insul. glass	1.000	Ea.	.800	320	39	359
Trim, interior casing	11.000	L.F.	.367	16.06	17.93	33.99
Paint, interior & exterior, primer & 2 coats	2.000	Face	1.778	2.14	75	77.14
Caulking	10.000	L.F.	.278	1.70	13.40	15.10
Snap-in grille	1.000	Set	.333	29	16.30	45.30
Drip cap, metal	3.000	L.F.	.060	1.26	2.94	4.20
TOTAL		Ea.	3.616	370.16	164.57	534.73
PLASTIC CLAD WOOD WINDOW, 4' X 3'-6", SLIDING						
Window, plastic clad, premium, 4' x 3'-6", insulating glass	1.000	Ea.	.889	735	43.50	778.50
Trim, interior casing	16.000	L.F.	.533	23.36	26.08	49.44
Paint, interior, primer & 2 coats	1.000	Face	.889	1.07	37.50	38.57
Caulking	17.000	L.F.	.472	2.89	22.78	25.67
Snap-in grille	1.000	Set	.333	29	16.30	45.30
TOTAL		Ea.	3.116	791.32	146.16	937.48
METAL CLAD WOOD WINDOW, 6' X 5', SLIDING						
Window, metal clad, deluxe, 6' x 5', insulating glass	1.000	Ea.	1.000	775	49	824
Trim, interior casing	23.000	L.F.	.767	33.58	37.49	71.07
Paint, interior, primer & 2 coats	1.000	Face	.889	1.07	37.50	38.57
Caulking	22.000	L.F.	.611	3.74	29.48	33.22
Snap-in grille	1.000	Set	.364	43	17.80	60.80
Drip cap, metal	6.000	L.F.	.120	2.52	5.88	8.40
TOTAL		Ea.	3.751	858.91	177.15	1,036.06

The cost of this system is on a cost per each window basis.

Description	QUAN.	UNIT	LABOR HOURS	COST EACH		
				MAT.	INST.	TOTAL

Sliding Window Price Sheet	QUAN.	UNIT	LABOR HOURS	COST EACH		
				MAT.	INST.	TOTAL
Windows, sliding, builder's quality, 3' x 3', single glass	1.000	Ea.	.800	299	39	338
Insulating glass	1.000	Ea.	.800	320	39	359
4' x 3'-6", single glass	1.000	Ea.	.889	360	43.50	403.50
Insulating glass	1.000	Ea.	.889	385	43.50	428.50
6' x 5', single glass	1.000	Ea.	1.000	510	49	559
Insulating glass	1.000	Ea.	1.000	550	49	599
Plastic clad premium insulating glass, 3' x 3'	1.000	Ea.	.800	630	39	669
4' x 3'-6"	1.000	Ea.	.889	735	43.50	778.50
5' x 4'	1.000	Ea.	.889	945	43.50	988.50
6' x 5'	1.000	Ea.	1.000	1,200	49	1,249
Metal clad deluxe insulating glass, 3' x 3'	1.000	Ea.	.800	360	39	399
4' x 3'-6"	1.000	Ea.	.889	440	43.50	483.50
5' x 4'	1.000	Ea.	.889	525	43.50	568.50
6' x 5'	1.000	Ea.	1.000	775	49	824
Trim, interior casing, window 3' x 2'	11.000	L.F.	.367	16.05	17.95	34
3' x 3'	13.000	L.F.	.433	19	21	40
4' x 3'-6"	16.000	L.F.	.533	23.50	26	49.50
5' x 4'	19.000	L.F.	.633	27.50	31	58.50
6' x 5'	23.000	L.F.	.767	33.50	37.50	71
Paint or stain, interior or exterior, 3' x 2' window, 1 coat	1.000	Face	.444	.35	18.65	19
2 coats	1.000	Face	.727	.70	30.50	31.20
Primer & 1 coat	1.000	Face	.727	.73	30.50	31.23
Primer & 2 coats	1.000	Face	.889	1.07	37.50	38.57
4' x 3'-6" window, 1 coat	1.000	Face	.667	1.18	28	29.18
2 coats	1.000	Face	.667	1.75	28	29.75
Primer & 1 coat	1.000	Face	.727	1.09	30.50	31.59
Primer & 2 coats	1.000	Face	.889	1.07	37.50	38.57
6' x 5' window, 1 coat	1.000	Face	.889	1.99	37.50	39.49
2 coats	1.000	Face	1.333	3.63	56	59.63
Primer & 1 coat	1.000	Face	1.333	3.88	56	59.88
Primer & 2 coats	1.000	Face	1.600	5.70	67	72.70
Caulking, window, 3' x 2'	10.000	L.F.	.323	1.70	13.40	15.10
3' x 3'	12.000	L.F.	.387	2.04	16.10	18.14
4' x 3'-6"	15.000	L.F.	.484	2.55	20	22.55
5' x 4'	18.000	L.F.	.581	3.06	24	27.06
6' x 5'	22.000	L.F.	.710	3.74	29.50	33.24
Grilles, glass size, to 14" x 36"	1.000	Set	.333	29	16.30	45.30
To 36" x 36"	1.000	Set	.364	43	17.80	60.80
Drip cap, aluminum, 3' long	3.000	L.F.	.060	1.26	2.94	4.20
4' long	4.000	L.F.	.080	1.68	3.92	5.60
5' long	5.000	L.F.	.100	2.10	4.90	7
6' long	6.000	L.F.	.120	2.52	5.90	8.42
Wood, 3' long	3.000	L.F.	.100	4.38	4.89	9.27
4' long	4.000	L.F.	.133	5.85	6.50	12.35
5' long	5.000	L.F.	.167	7.30	8.15	15.45
6' long	6.000	L.F.	.200	8.75	9.80	18.55

Drip Cap

Caulking

Snap-in Grille

Window

System Description	QUAN.	UNIT	LABOR HOURS	COST EACH		
				MAT.	INST.	TOTAL
AWNING TYPE BOW WINDOW, BUILDER'S QUALITY, 8′ X 5′						
Window, primed, builder's quality, 8′ x 5′, insulating glass	1.000	Ea.	1.600	1,450	78.50	1,528.50
Trim, interior casing	27.000	L.F.	.900	39.42	44.01	83.43
Paint, interior & exterior, primer & 1 coat	2.000	Face	3.200	11.40	134	145.40
Drip cap, vinyl	1.000	Ea.	.533	110	26	136
Caulking	26.000	L.F.	.722	4.42	34.84	39.26
Snap-in grilles	1.000	Set	1.067	126	52.20	178.20
TOTAL		Ea.	8.022	1,741.24	369.55	2,110.79
CASEMENT TYPE BOW WINDOW, PLASTIC CLAD, 10′ X 6′						
Window, plastic clad, premium, 10′ x 6′, insulating glass	1.000	Ea.	2.286	2,775	112	2,887
Trim, interior casing	33.000	L.F.	1.100	48.18	53.79	101.97
Paint, interior, primer & 1 coat	1.000	Face	1.778	2.14	75	77.14
Drip cap, vinyl	1.000	Ea.	.615	121	30	151
Caulking	32.000	L.F.	.889	5.44	42.88	48.32
Snap-in grilles	1.000	Set	1.333	157.50	65.25	222.75
TOTAL		Ea.	8.001	3,109.26	378.92	3,488.18
DOUBLE HUNG TYPE, METAL CLAD, 9′ X 5′						
Window, metal clad, deluxe, 9′ x 5′, insulating glass	1.000	Ea.	2.667	1,550	131	1,681
Trim, interior casing	29.000	L.F.	.967	42.34	47.27	89.61
Paint, interior, primer & 1 coat	1.000	Face	1.778	2.14	75	77.14
Drip cap, vinyl	1.000	Set	.615	121	30	151
Caulking	28.000	L.F.	.778	4.76	37.52	42.28
Snap-in grilles	1.000	Set	1.067	126	52.20	178.20
TOTAL		Ea.	7.872	1,846.24	372.99	2,219.23

The cost of this system is on a cost per each window basis.

Description	QUAN.	UNIT	LABOR HOURS	COST EACH		
				MAT.	INST.	TOTAL

Bow/Bay Window Price Sheet	QUAN.	UNIT	LABOR HOURS	COST EACH		
				MAT.	INST.	TOTAL
Windows, bow awning type, builder's quality, 8' x 5', insulating glass	1.000	Ea.	1.600	1,650	78.50	1,728.50
Low E glass	1.000	Ea.	1.600	1,450	78.50	1,528.50
12' x 6', insulating glass	1.000	Ea.	2.667	1,500	131	1,631
Low E glass	1.000	Ea.	2.667	1,600	131	1,731
Plastic clad premium insulating glass, 6' x 4'	1.000	Ea.	1.600	1,125	78.50	1,203.50
9' x 4'	1.000	Ea.	2.000	1,500	98	1,598
10' x 5'	1.000	Ea.	2.286	2,475	112	2,587
12' x 6'	1.000	Ea.	2.667	3,225	131	3,356
Metal clad deluxe insulating glass, 6' x 4'	1.000	Ea.	1.600	1,000	78.50	1,078.50
9' x 4'	1.000	Ea.	2.000	1,375	98	1,473
10' x 5'	1.000	Ea.	2.286	1,900	112	2,012
12' x 6'	1.000	Ea.	2.667	2,650	131	2,781
Bow casement type, builder's quality, 8' x 5', single glass	1.000	Ea.	1.600	2,025	78.50	2,103.50
Insulating glass	1.000	Ea.	1.600	2,450	78.50	2,528.50
12' x 6', single glass	1.000	Ea.	2.667	2,525	131	2,656
Insulating glass	1.000	Ea.	2.667	2,600	131	2,731
Plastic clad premium insulating glass, 8' x 5'	1.000	Ea.	1.600	1,925	78.50	2,003.50
10' x 5'	1.000	Ea.	2.000	2,500	98	2,598
10' x 6'	1.000	Ea.	2.286	2,775	112	2,887
12' x 6'	1.000	Ea.	2.667	3,525	131	3,656
Metal clad deluxe insulating glass, 8' x 5'	1.000	Ea.	1.600	1,775	78.50	1,853.50
10' x 5'	1.000	Ea.	2.000	1,925	98	2,023
10' x 6'	1.000	Ea.	2.286	2,275	112	2,387
12' x 6'	1.000	Ea.	2.667	3,150	131	3,281
Bow, double hung type, builder's quality, 8' x 4', single glass	1.000	Ea.	1.600	1,425	78.50	1,503.50
Insulating glass	1.000	Ea.	1.600	1,525	78.50	1,603.50
9' x 5', single glass	1.000	Ea.	2.667	1,525	131	1,656
Insulating glass	1.000	Ea.	2.667	1,625	131	1,756
Plastic clad premium insulating glass, 7' x 4'	1.000	Ea.	1.600	1,475	78.50	1,553.50
8' x 4'	1.000	Ea.	2.000	1,500	98	1,598
8' x 5'	1.000	Ea.	2.286	1,575	112	1,687
9' x 5'	1.000	Ea.	2.667	1,625	131	1,756
Metal clad deluxe insulating glass, 7' x 4'	1.000	Ea.	1.600	1,350	78.50	1,428.50
8' x 4'	1.000	Ea.	2.000	1,400	98	1,498
8' x 5'	1.000	Ea.	2.286	1,450	112	1,562
9' x 5'	1.000	Ea.	2.667	1,550	131	1,681
Trim, interior casing, window 7' x 4'	1.000	Ea.	.767	33.50	37.50	71
8' x 5'	1.000	Ea.	.900	39.50	44	83.50
10' x 6'	1.000	Ea.	1.100	48	54	102
12' x 6'	1.000	Ea.	1.233	54	60.50	114.50
Paint or stain, interior, or exterior, 7' x 4' window, 1 coat	1.000	Face	.889	1.99	37.50	39.49
Primer & 1 coat	1.000	Face	1.333	3.88	56	59.88
8' x 5' window, 1 coat	1.000	Face	.889	1.99	37.50	39.49
Primer & 1 coat	1.000	Face	1.333	3.88	56	59.88
10' x 6' window, 1 coat	1.000	Face	1.333	2.36	56	58.36
Primer & 1 coat	1.000	Face	1.778	2.14	75	77.14
12' x 6' window, 1 coat	1.000	Face	1.778	3.98	75	78.98
Primer & 1 coat	1.000	Face	2.667	7.75	112	119.75
Drip cap, vinyl moulded window, 7' long	1.000	Ea.	.533	96.50	23	119.50
8' long	1.000	Ea.	.533	110	26	136
Caulking, window, 7' x 4'	1.000	Ea.	.710	3.74	29.50	33.24
8' x 5'	1.000	Ea.	.839	4.42	35	39.42
10' x 6'	1.000	Ea.	1.032	5.45	43	48.45
12' x 6'	1.000	Ea.	1.161	6.10	48	54.10
Grilles, window, 7' x 4'	1.000	Set	.800	94.50	39	133.50
8' x 5'	1.000	Set	1.067	126	52	178
10' x 6'	1.000	Set	1.333	158	65.50	223.50
12' x 6'	1.000	Set	1.600	189	78.50	267.50

Drip Cap — Interior Trim — Caulking — Snap-in Grille — Window

System Description	QUAN.	UNIT	LABOR HOURS	COST EACH		
				MAT.	INST.	TOTAL
BUILDER'S QUALITY PICTURE WINDOW, 4' X 4'						
Window, primed, builder's quality, 3'-0" x 4', insulating glass	1.000	Ea.	1.333	450	65.50	515.50
Trim, interior casing	17.000	L.F.	.567	24.82	27.71	52.53
Paint, interior & exterior, primer & 2 coats	2.000	Face	1.778	2.14	75	77.14
Caulking	16.000	L.F.	.444	2.72	21.44	24.16
Snap-in grille	1.000	Ea.	.267	125	13.05	138.05
Drip cap, metal	4.000	L.F.	.080	1.68	3.92	5.60
TOTAL		Ea.	4.469	606.36	206.62	812.98
PLASTIC CLAD WOOD WINDOW, 4'-6" X 6'-6"						
Window, plastic clad, prem., 4'-6" x 6'-6", insul. glass	1.000	Ea.	1.455	1,000	71	1,071
Trim, interior casing	23.000	L.F.	.767	33.58	37.49	71.07
Paint, interior, primer & 2 coats	1.000	Face	.889	1.07	37.50	38.57
Caulking	22.000	L.F.	.611	3.74	29.48	33.22
Snap-in grille	1.000	Ea.	.267	125	13.05	138.05
TOTAL		Ea.	3.989	1,163.39	188.52	1,351.91
METAL CLAD WOOD WINDOW, 6'-6" X 6'-6"						
Window, metal clad, deluxe, 6'-0" x 6'-0", insulating glass	1.000	Ea.	1.600	750	78.50	828.50
Trim interior casing	27.000	L.F.	.900	39.42	44.01	83.43
Paint, interior, primer & 2 coats	1.000	Face	1.600	5.70	67	72.70
Caulking	26.000	L.F.	.722	4.42	34.84	39.26
Snap-in grille	1.000	Ea.	.267	125	13.05	138.05
Drip cap, metal	6.500	L.F.	.130	2.73	6.37	9.10
TOTAL		Ea.	5.219	927.27	243.77	1,171.04

The cost of this system is on a cost per each window basis.

Description	QUAN.	UNIT	LABOR HOURS	COST EACH		
				MAT.	INST.	TOTAL

Fixed Window Price Sheet	QUAN.	UNIT	LABOR HOURS	COST EACH		
				MAT.	INST.	TOTAL
Window-picture, builder's quality, 4' x 4', single glass	1.000	Ea.	1.333	380	65.50	445.50
Insulating glass	1.000	Ea.	1.333	450	65.50	515.50
4' x 4'-6", single glass	1.000	Ea.	1.455	540	71	611
Insulating glass	1.000	Ea.	1.455	570	71	641
5' x 4', single glass	1.000	Ea.	1.455	625	71	696
Insulating glass	1.000	Ea.	1.455	650	71	721
6' x 4'-6", single glass	1.000	Ea.	1.600	675	78.50	753.50
Insulating glass	1.000	Ea.	1.600	685	78.50	763.50
Plastic clad premium insulating glass, 4' x 4'	1.000	Ea.	1.333	545	65.50	610.50
4'-6" x 6'-6"	1.000	Ea.	1.455	1,000	71	1,071
5'-6" x 6'-6"	1.000	Ea.	1.600	1,125	78.50	1,203.50
6'-6" x 6'-6"	1.000	Ea.	1.600	1,125	78.50	1,203.50
Metal clad deluxe insulating glass, 4' x 4'	1.000	Ea.	1.333	405	65.50	470.50
4'-6" x 6'-6"	1.000	Ea.	1.455	590	71	661
5'-6" x 6'-6"	1.000	Ea.	1.600	655	78.50	733.50
6'-6" x 6'-6"	1.000	Ea.	1.600	750	78.50	828.50
Trim, interior casing, window 4' x 4'	17.000	L.F.	.567	25	27.50	52.50
4'-6" x 4'-6"	19.000	L.F.	.633	27.50	31	58.50
5'-0" x 4'-0"	19.000	L.F.	.633	27.50	31	58.50
4'-6" x 6'-6"	23.000	L.F.	.767	33.50	37.50	71
5'-6" x 6'-6"	25.000	L.F.	.833	36.50	41	77.50
6'-6" x 6'-6"	27.000	L.F.	.900	39.50	44	83.50
Paint or stain, interior or exterior, 4' x 4' window, 1 coat	1.000	Face	.667	1.18	28	29.18
2 coats	1.000	Face	.667	1.75	28	29.75
Primer & 1 coat	1.000	Face	.727	1.09	30.50	31.59
Primer & 2 coats	1.000	Face	.889	1.07	37.50	38.57
4'-6" x 6'-6" window, 1 coat	1.000	Face	.667	1.18	28	29.18
2 coats	1.000	Face	.667	1.75	28	29.75
Primer & 1 coat	1.000	Face	.727	1.09	30.50	31.59
Primer & 2 coats	1.000	Face	.889	1.07	37.50	38.57
6'-6" x 6'-6" window, 1 coat	1.000	Face	.889	1.99	37.50	39.49
2 coats	1.000	Face	1.333	3.63	56	59.63
Primer & 1 coat	1.000	Face	1.333	3.88	56	59.88
Primer & 2 coats	1.000	Face	1.600	5.70	67	72.70
Caulking, window, 4' x 4'	1.000	Ea.	.516	2.72	21.50	24.22
4'-6" x 4'-6"	1.000	Ea.	.581	3.06	24	27.06
5'-0" x 4'-0"	1.000	Ea.	.581	3.06	24	27.06
4'-6" x 6'-6"	1.000	Ea.	.710	3.74	29.50	33.24
5'-6" x 6'-6"	1.000	Ea.	.774	4.08	32	36.08
6'-6" x 6'-6"	1.000	Ea.	.839	4.42	35	39.42
Grilles, glass size, to 48" x 48"	1.000	Ea.	.267	125	13.05	138.05
To 60" x 68"	1.000	Ea.	.286	176	14	190
Drip cap, aluminum, 4' long	4.000	L.F.	.080	1.68	3.92	5.60
4'-6" long	4.500	L.F.	.090	1.89	4.41	6.30
5' long	5.000	L.F.	.100	2.10	4.90	7
6' long	6.000	L.F.	.120	2.52	5.90	8.42
Wood, 4' long	4.000	L.F.	.133	5.85	6.50	12.35
4'-6" long	4.500	L.F.	.150	6.55	7.35	13.90
5' long	5.000	L.F.	.167	7.30	8.15	15.45
6' long	6.000	L.F.	.200	8.75	9.80	18.55

System Description	QUAN.	UNIT	LABOR HOURS	COST EACH		
				MAT.	INST.	TOTAL
COLONIAL, 6 PANEL, 3′ X 6′-8″, WOOD						
Door, 3′ x 6′-8″ x 1-3/4″ thick, pine, 6 panel colonial	1.000	Ea.	1.067	475	52	527
Frame, 5-13/16″ deep, incl. exterior casing & drip cap	17.000	L.F.	.725	212.50	35.53	248.03
Interior casing, 2-1/2″ wide	18.000	L.F.	.600	26.28	29.34	55.62
Sill, 8/4 x 8″ deep	3.000	L.F.	.480	56.40	23.55	79.95
Butt hinges, brass, 4-1/2″ x 4-1/2″	1.500	Pr.		26.55		26.55
Lockset	1.000	Ea.	.571	44	28	72
Weatherstripping, metal, spring type, bronze	1.000	Set	1.053	24	51.50	75.50
Paint, interior & exterior, primer & 2 coats	2.000	Face	1.778	11.30	75	86.30
TOTAL		Ea.	6.274	876.03	294.92	1,170.95
SOLID CORE BIRCH, FLUSH, 3′ X 6′-8″						
Door, 3′ x 6′-8″, 1-3/4″ thick, birch, flush solid core	1.000	Ea.	1.067	125	52	177
Frame, 5-13/16″ deep, incl. exterior casing & drip cap	17.000	L.F.	.725	212.50	35.53	248.03
Interior casing, 2-1/2″ wide	18.000	L.F.	.600	26.28	29.34	55.62
Sill, 8/4 x 8″ deep	3.000	L.F.	.480	56.40	23.55	79.95
Butt hinges, brass, 4-1/2″ x 4-1/2″	1.500	Pr.		26.55		26.55
Lockset	1.000	Ea.	.571	44	28	72
Weatherstripping, metal, spring type, bronze	1.000	Set	1.053	24	51.50	75.50
Paint, Interior & exterior, primer & 2 coats	2.000	Face	1.778	10.60	75	85.60
TOTAL		Ea.	6.274	525.33	294.92	820.25

These systems are on a cost per each door basis.

Description	QUAN.	UNIT	LABOR HOURS	COST EACH		
				MAT.	INST.	TOTAL

Entrance Door Price Sheet	QUAN.	UNIT	LABOR HOURS	COST EACH		
				MAT.	INST.	TOTAL
Door exterior wood 1-3/4" thick, pine, dutch door, 2'-8" x 6'-8" minimum	1.000	Ea.	1.333	745	65.50	810.50
Maximum	1.000	Ea.	1.600	910	78.50	988.50
3'-0" x 6'-8", minimum	1.000	Ea.	1.333	755	65.50	820.50
Maximum	1.000	Ea.	1.600	990	78.50	1,068.50
Colonial, 6 panel, 2'-8" x 6'-8"	1.000	Ea.	1.000	505	49	554
3'-0" x 6'-8"	1.000	Ea.	1.067	475	52	527
8 panel, 2'-6" x 6'-8"	1.000	Ea.	1.000	630	49	679
3'-0" x 6'-8"	1.000	Ea.	1.067	610	52	662
Flush, birch, solid core, 2'-8" x 6'-8"	1.000	Ea.	1.000	114	49	163
3'-0" x 6'-8"	1.000	Ea.	1.067	125	52	177
Porch door, 2'-8" x 6'-8"	1.000	Ea.	1.000	615	49	664
3'-0" x 6'-8"	1.000	Ea.	1.067	645	52	697
Hand carved mahogany, 2'-8" x 6'-8"	1.000	Ea.	1.067	715	52	767
3'-0" x 6'-8"	1.000	Ea.	1.067	735	52	787
Rosewood, 2'-8" x 6'-8"	1.000	Ea.	1.067	890	52	942
3'-0" x 6-8"	1.000	Ea.	1.067	915	52	967
Door, metal clad wood 1-3/8" thick raised panel, 2'-8" x 6'-8"	1.000	Ea.	1.067	320	46	366
3'-0" x 6'-8"	1.000	Ea.	1.067	299	52	351
Deluxe metal door, 3'-0" x 6'-8"	1.000	Ea.	1.231	299	52	351
3'-0" x 6'-8"	1.000	Ea.	1.231	299	52	351
Frame, pine, including exterior trim & drip cap, 5/4, x 4-9/16" deep	17.000	L.F.	.725	104	35.50	139.50
5-13/16" deep	17.000	L.F.	.725	213	35.50	248.50
6-9/16" deep	17.000	L.F.	.725	159	35.50	194.50
Safety glass lites, add	1.000	Ea.		82		82
Interior casing, 2'-8" x 6'-8" door	18.000	L.F.	.600	26.50	29.50	56
3'-0" x 6'-8" door	19.000	L.F.	.633	27.50	31	58.50
Sill, oak, 8/4 x 8" deep	3.000	L.F.	.480	56.50	23.50	80
8/4 x 10" deep	3.000	L.F.	.533	70.50	26	96.50
Butt hinges, steel plated, 4-1/2" x 4-1/2", plain	1.500	Pr.		26.50		26.50
Ball bearing	1.500	Pr.		52.50		52.50
Bronze, 4-1/2" x 4-1/2", plain	1.500	Pr.		37.50		37.50
Ball bearing	1.500	Pr.		55.50		55.50
Lockset, minimum	1.000	Ea.	.571	44	28	72
Maximum	1.000	Ea.	1.000	176	49	225
Weatherstripping, metal, interlocking, zinc	1.000	Set	2.667	17.25	131	148.25
Bronze	1.000	Set	2.667	27.50	131	158.50
Spring type, bronze	1.000	Set	1.053	24	51.50	75.50
Rubber, minimum	1.000	Set	1.053	5.90	51.50	57.40
Maximum	1.000	Set	1.143	6.45	56	62.45
Felt minimum	1.000	Set	.571	2.74	28	30.74
Maximum	1.000	Set	.615	3.14	30	33.14
Paint or stain, flush door, interior or exterior, 1 coat	2.000	Face	.941	3.76	39.50	43.26
2 coats	2.000	Face	1.455	7.50	61	68.50
Primer & 1 coat	2.000	Face	1.455	7.05	61	68.05
Primer & 2 coats	2.000	Face	1.778	10.60	75	85.60
Paneled door, interior & exterior, 1 coat	2.000	Face	1.143	4.02	48	52.02
2 coats	2.000	Face	2.000	8.05	84	92.05
Primer & 1 coat	2.000	Face	1.455	7.50	61	68.50
Primer & 2 coats	2.000	Face	1.778	11.30	75	86.30

Drip Cap

Frame & Exterior Casing

Door

Interior Casing

Sill

System Description	QUAN.	UNIT	LABOR HOURS	COST EACH		
				MAT.	INST.	TOTAL
WOOD SLIDING DOOR, 8' WIDE, PREMIUM						
Wood, 5/8" thick tempered insul. glass, 8' wide, premium	1.000	Ea.	5.333	1,950	261	2,211
Interior casing	22.000	L.F.	.733	32.12	35.86	67.98
Exterior casing	22.000	L.F.	.733	32.12	35.86	67.98
Sill, oak, 8/4 x 8" deep	8.000	L.F.	1.280	150.40	62.80	213.20
Drip cap	8.000	L.F.	.160	3.36	7.84	11.20
Paint, interior & exterior, primer & 2 coats	2.000	Face	2.816	15.84	117.92	133.76
TOTAL		Ea.	11.055	2,183.84	521.28	2,705.12
ALUMINUM SLIDING DOOR, 8' WIDE, PREMIUM						
Aluminum, 5/8" tempered insul. glass, 8' wide, premium	1.000	Ea.	5.333	1,775	261	2,036
Interior casing	22.000	L.F.	.733	32.12	35.86	67.98
Exterior casing	22.000	L.F.	.733	32.12	35.86	67.98
Sill, oak, 8/4 x 8" deep	8.000	L.F.	1.280	150.40	62.80	213.20
Drip cap	8.000	L.F.	.160	3.36	7.84	11.20
Paint, interior & exterior, primer & 2 coats	2.000	Face	2.816	15.84	117.92	133.76
TOTAL		Ea.	11.055	2,008.84	521.28	2,530.12

The cost of this system is on a cost per each door basis.

Description	QUAN.	UNIT	LABOR HOURS	COST EACH		
				MAT.	INST.	TOTAL

Sliding Door Price Sheet	QUAN.	UNIT	LABOR HOURS	COST PER UNIT		
				MAT.	INST.	TOTAL
Sliding door, wood, 5/8" thick, tempered insul. glass, 6' wide, premium	1.000	Ea.	4.000	1,525	196	1,721
Economy	1.000	Ea.	4.000	1,225	196	1,421
8'wide, wood premium	1.000	Ea.	5.333	1,950	261	2,211
Economy	1.000	Ea.	5.333	1,625	261	1,886
12' wide, wood premium	1.000	Ea.	6.400	3,225	315	3,540
Economy	1.000	Ea.	6.400	2,650	315	2,965
Aluminum, 5/8" thick, tempered insul. glass, 6'wide, premium	1.000	Ea.	4.000	1,725	196	1,921
Economy	1.000	Ea.	4.000	960	196	1,156
8'wide, premium	1.000	Ea.	5.333	1,775	261	2,036
Economy	1.000	Ea.	5.333	1,525	261	1,786
12' wide, premium	1.000	Ea.	6.400	3,250	315	3,565
Economy	1.000	Ea.	6.400	1,650	315	1,965
Interior casing, 6' wide door	20.000	L.F.	.667	29	32.50	61.50
8' wide door	22.000	L.F.	.733	32	36	68
12' wide door	26.000	L.F.	.867	38	42.50	80.50
Exterior casing, 6' wide door	20.000	L.F.	.667	29	32.50	61.50
8' wide door	22.000	L.F.	.733	32	36	68
12' wide door	26.000	L.F.	.867	38	42.50	80.50
Sill, oak, 8/4 x 8" deep, 6' wide door	6.000	L.F.	.960	113	47	160
8' wide door	8.000	L.F.	1.280	150	63	213
12' wide door	12.000	L.F.	1.920	226	94	320
8/4 x 10" deep, 6' wide door	6.000	L.F.	1.067	141	52	193
8' wide door	8.000	L.F.	1.422	188	69.50	257.50
12' wide door	12.000	L.F.	2.133	282	104	386
Drip cap, 6' wide door	6.000	L.F.	.120	2.52	5.90	8.42
8' wide door	8.000	L.F.	.160	3.36	7.85	11.21
12' wide door	12.000	L.F.	.240	5.05	11.75	16.80
Paint or stain, interior & exterior, 6' wide door, 1 coat	2.000	Face	1.600	4.80	67	71.80
2 coats	2.000	Face	1.600	4.80	67	71.80
Primer & 1 coat	2.000	Face	1.778	10.40	74.50	84.90
Primer & 2 coats	2.000	Face	2.560	14.40	107	121.40
8' wide door, 1 coat	2.000	Face	1.760	5.30	74	79.30
2 coats	2.000	Face	1.760	5.30	74	79.30
Primer & 1 coat	2.000	Face	1.955	11.45	82	93.45
Primer & 2 coats	2.000	Face	2.816	15.85	118	133.85
12' wide door, 1 coat	2.000	Face	2.080	6.25	87.50	93.75
2 coats	2.000	Face	2.080	6.25	87.50	93.75
Primer & 1 coat	2.000	Face	2.311	13.50	96.50	110
Primer & 2 coats	2.000	Face	3.328	18.70	139	157.70
Aluminum door, trim only, interior & exterior, 6' door, 1 coat	2.000	Face	.800	2.40	33.50	35.90
2 coats	2.000	Face	.800	2.40	33.50	35.90
Primer & 1 coat	2.000	Face	.889	5.20	37	42.20
Primer & 2 coats	2.000	Face	1.280	7.20	53.50	60.70
8' wide door, 1 coat	2.000	Face	.880	2.64	37	39.64
2 coats	2.000	Face	.880	2.64	37	39.64
Primer & 1 coat	2.000	Face	.978	5.70	41	46.70
Primer & 2 coats	2.000	Face	1.408	7.90	59	66.90
12' wide door, 1 coat	2.000	Face	1.040	3.12	43.50	46.62
2 coats	2.000	Face	1.040	3.12	43.50	46.62
Primer & 1 coat	2.000	Face	1.155	6.75	48.50	55.25
Primer & 2 coats	2.000	Face	1.664	9.35	69.50	78.85

Exterior Trim

Door

Jamb

Drip Cap

Weatherstripping

System Description	QUAN.	UNIT	LABOR HOURS	COST EACH		
				MAT.	INST.	TOTAL
OVERHEAD, SECTIONAL GARAGE DOOR, 9' X 7'						
Wood, overhead sectional door, std., incl. hardware, 9' x 7'	1.000	Ea.	2.000	790	98	888
Jamb & header blocking, 2" x 6"	25.000	L.F.	.901	10.25	44	54.25
Exterior trim	25.000	L.F.	.833	36.50	40.75	77.25
Paint, interior & exterior, primer & 2 coats	2.000	Face	3.556	22.60	150	172.60
Weatherstripping, molding type	1.000	Set	.767	33.58	37.49	71.07
Drip cap	9.000	L.F.	.180	3.78	8.82	12.60
TOTAL		Ea.	8.237	896.71	379.06	1,275.77
OVERHEAD, SECTIONAL GARAGE DOOR, 16' X 7'						
Wood, overhead sectional, std., incl. hardware, 16' x 7'	1.000	Ea.	2.667	1,575	131	1,706
Jamb & header blocking, 2" x 6"	30.000	L.F.	1.081	12.30	52.80	65.10
Exterior trim	30.000	L.F.	1.000	43.80	48.90	92.70
Paint, interior & exterior, primer & 2 coats	2.000	Face	5.333	33.90	225	258.90
Weatherstripping, molding type	1.000	Set	1.000	43.80	48.90	92.70
Drip cap	16.000	L.F.	.320	6.72	15.68	22.40
TOTAL		Ea.	11.401	1,715.52	522.28	2,237.80
OVERHEAD, SWING-UP TYPE, GARAGE DOOR, 16' X 7'						
Wood, overhead, swing-up, std., incl. hardware, 16' x 7'	1.000	Ea.	2.667	800	131	931
Jamb & header blocking, 2" x 6"	30.000	L.F.	1.081	12.30	52.80	65.10
Exterior trim	30.000	L.F.	1.000	43.80	48.90	92.70
Paint, interior & exterior, primer & 2 coats	2.000	Face	5.333	33.90	225	258.90
Weatherstripping, molding type	1.000	Set	1.000	43.80	48.90	92.70
Drip cap	16.000	L.F.	.320	6.72	15.68	22.40
TOTAL		Ea.	11.401	940.52	522.28	1,462.80

This system is on a cost per each door basis.

Description	QUAN.	UNIT	LABOR HOURS	COST EACH		
				MAT.	INST.	TOTAL

Resi Garage Door Price Sheet	QUAN.	UNIT	LABOR HOURS	COST EACH		
				MAT.	INST.	TOTAL
Overhead, sectional, including hardware, fiberglass, 9' x 7', standard	1.000	Ea.	3.030	805	148	953
Deluxe	1.000	Ea.	3.030	1,025	148	1,173
16' x 7', standard	1.000	Ea.	2.667	1,700	131	1,831
Deluxe	1.000	Ea.	2.667	2,175	131	2,306
Hardboard, 9' x 7', standard	1.000	Ea.	2.000	605	98	703
Deluxe	1.000	Ea.	2.000	855	98	953
16' x 7', standard	1.000	Ea.	2.667	1,250	131	1,381
Deluxe	1.000	Ea.	2.667	1,475	131	1,606
Metal, 9' x 7', standard	1.000	Ea.	3.030	640	148	788
Deluxe	1.000	Ea.	2.000	940	98	1,038
16' x 7', standard	1.000	Ea.	5.333	800	261	1,061
Deluxe	1.000	Ea.	2.667	1,500	131	1,631
Wood, 9' x 7', standard	1.000	Ea.	2.000	790	98	888
Deluxe	1.000	Ea.	2.000	2,250	98	2,348
16' x 7', standard	1.000	Ea.	2.667	1,575	131	1,706
Deluxe	1.000	Ea.	2.667	3,275	131	3,406
Overhead swing-up type including hardware, fiberglass, 9' x 7', standard	1.000	Ea.	2.000	1,075	98	1,173
Deluxe	1.000	Ea.	2.000	870	98	968
16' x 7', standard	1.000	Ea.	2.667	1,350	131	1,481
Deluxe	1.000	Ea.	2.667	1,075	131	1,206
Hardboard, 9' x 7', standard	1.000	Ea.	2.000	380	98	478
Deluxe	1.000	Ea.	2.000	505	98	603
16' x 7', standard	1.000	Ea.	2.667	530	131	661
Deluxe	1.000	Ea.	2.667	785	131	916
Metal, 9' x 7', standard	1.000	Ea.	2.000	420	98	518
Deluxe	1.000	Ea.	2.000	915	98	1,013
16' x 7', standard	1.000	Ea.	2.667	660	131	791
Deluxe	1.000	Ea.	2.667	1,050	131	1,181
Wood, 9' x 7', standard	1.000	Ea.	2.000	495	98	593
Deluxe	1.000	Ea.	2.000	1,025	98	1,123
16' x 7', standard	1.000	Ea.	2.667	800	131	931
Deluxe	1.000	Ea.	2.667	1,125	131	1,256
Jamb & header blocking, 2" x 6", 9' x 7' door	25.000	L.F.	.901	10.25	44	54.25
16' x 7' door	30.000	L.F.	1.081	12.30	53	65.30
2" x 8", 9' x 7' door	25.000	L.F.	1.000	15.25	49	64.25
16' x 7' door	30.000	L.F.	1.200	18.30	59	77.30
Exterior trim, 9' x 7' door	25.000	L.F.	.833	36.50	41	77.50
16' x 7' door	30.000	L.F.	1.000	44	49	93
Paint or stain, interior & exterior, 9' x 7' door, 1 coat	1.000	Face	2.286	8.05	96	104.05
2 coats	1.000	Face	4.000	16.10	168	184.10
Primer & 1 coat	1.000	Face	2.909	15.05	122	137.05
Primer & 2 coats	1.000	Face	3.556	22.50	150	172.50
16' x 7' door, 1 coat	1.000	Face	3.429	12.05	144	156.05
2 coats	1.000	Face	6.000	24	252	276
Primer & 1 coat	1.000	Face	4.364	22.50	183	205.50
Primer & 2 coats	1.000	Face	5.333	34	225	259
Weatherstripping, molding type, 9' x 7' door	1.000	Set	.767	33.50	37.50	71
16' x 7' door	1.000	Set	1.000	44	49	93
Drip cap, 9' door	9.000	L.F.	.180	3.78	8.80	12.58
16' door	16.000	L.F.	.320	6.70	15.70	22.40
Garage door opener, economy	1.000	Ea.	1.000	450	49	499
Deluxe, including remote control	1.000	Ea.	1.000	660	49	709

Drywall → | ← Finish Drywall

Corner Bead → | ← Window

Sill

System Description	QUAN.	UNIT	LABOR HOURS	COST EACH		
				MAT.	INST.	TOTAL
SINGLE HUNG, 2' X 3' OPENING						
Window, 2' x 3' opening, enameled, insulating glass	1.000	Ea.	1.600	264	95.50	359.50
Blocking, 1" x 3" furring strip nailers	10.000	L.F.	.146	3.80	7.10	10.90
Drywall, 1/2" thick, standard	5.000	S.F.	.040	1.30	1.95	3.25
Corner bead, 1" x 1", galvanized steel	8.000	L.F.	.160	1.28	7.84	9.12
Finish drywall, tape and finish corners inside and outside	16.000	L.F.	.269	1.60	13.12	14.72
Sill, slate	2.000	L.F.	.400	25.30	17.40	42.70
TOTAL		Ea.	2.615	297.28	142.91	440.19
SLIDING, 3' X 2' OPENING						
Window, 3' x 2' opening, enameled, insulating glass	1.000	Ea.	1.600	246	95.50	341.50
Blocking, 1" x 3" furring strip nailers	10.000	L.F.	.146	3.80	7.10	10.90
Drywall, 1/2" thick, standard	5.000	S.F.	.040	1.30	1.95	3.25
Corner bead, 1" x 1", galvanized steel	7.000	L.F.	.140	1.12	6.86	7.98
Finish drywall, tape and finish corners inside and outside	14.000	L.F.	.236	1.40	11.48	12.88
Sill, slate	3.000	L.F.	.600	37.95	26.10	64.05
TOTAL		Ea.	2.762	291.57	148.99	440.56
AWNING, 3'-1" X 3'-2"						
Window, 3'-1" x 3'-2" opening, enameled, insul. glass	1.000	Ea.	1.600	320	95.50	415.50
Blocking, 1" x 3" furring strip, nailers	12.500	L.F.	.182	4.75	8.88	13.63
Drywall, 1/2" thick, standard	4.500	S.F.	.036	1.17	1.76	2.93
Corner bead, 1" x 1", galvanized steel	9.250	L.F.	.185	1.48	9.07	10.55
Finish drywall, tape and finish corners, inside and outside	18.500	L.F.	.312	1.85	15.17	17.02
Sill, slate	3.250	L.F.	.650	41.11	28.28	69.39
TOTAL		Ea.	2.965	370.36	158.66	529.02

Description	QUAN.	UNIT	LABOR HOURS	COST PER S.F.		
				MAT.	INST.	TOTAL

Aluminum Window Price Sheet	QUAN.	UNIT	LABOR HOURS	COST EACH		
				MAT.	INST.	TOTAL
Window, aluminum, awning, 3'-1" x 3'-2", standard glass	1.000	Ea.	1.600	370	95.50	465.50
Insulating glass	1.000	Ea.	1.600	320	95.50	415.50
4'-5" x 5'-3", standard glass	1.000	Ea.	2.000	420	119	539
Insulating glass	1.000	Ea.	2.000	445	119	564
Casement, 3'-1" x 3'-2", standard glass	1.000	Ea.	1.600	390	95.50	485.50
Insulating glass	1.000	Ea.	1.600	505	95.50	600.50
Single hung, 2' x 3', standard glass	1.000	Ea.	1.600	218	95.50	313.50
Insulating glass	1.000	Ea.	1.600	264	95.50	359.50
2'-8" x 6'-8", standard glass	1.000	Ea.	2.000	385	119	504
Insulating glass	1.000	Ea.	2.000	495	119	614
3'-4" x 5'-0", standard glass	1.000	Ea.	1.778	315	106	421
Insulating glass	1.000	Ea.	1.778	350	106	456
Sliding, 3' x 2', standard glass	1.000	Ea.	1.600	230	95.50	325.50
Insulating glass	1.000	Ea.	1.600	246	95.50	341.50
5' x 3', standard glass	1.000	Ea.	1.778	350	106	456
Insulating glass	1.000	Ea.	1.778	410	106	516
8' x 4', standard glass	1.000	Ea.	2.667	370	159	529
Insulating glass	1.000	Ea.	2.667	595	159	754
Blocking, 1" x 3" furring, opening 3' x 2'	10.000	L.F.	.146	3.80	7.10	10.90
3' x 3'	12.500	L.F.	.182	4.75	8.90	13.65
3' x 5'	16.000	L.F.	.233	6.10	11.35	17.45
4' x 4'	16.000	L.F.	.233	6.10	11.35	17.45
4' x 5'	18.000	L.F.	.262	6.85	12.80	19.65
4' x 6'	20.000	L.F.	.291	7.60	14.20	21.80
4' x 8'	24.000	L.F.	.349	9.10	17.05	26.15
6'-8" x 2'-8"	19.000	L.F.	.276	7.20	13.50	20.70
Drywall, 1/2" thick, standard, opening 3' x 2'	5.000	S.F.	.040	1.30	1.95	3.25
3' x 3'	6.000	S.F.	.048	1.56	2.34	3.90
3' x 5'	8.000	S.F.	.064	2.08	3.12	5.20
4' x 4'	8.000	S.F.	.064	2.08	3.12	5.20
4' x 5'	9.000	S.F.	.072	2.34	3.51	5.85
4' x 6'	10.000	S.F.	.080	2.60	3.90	6.50
4' x 8'	12.000	S.F.	.096	3.12	4.68	7.80
6'-8" x 2'	9.500	S.F.	.076	2.47	3.71	6.18
Corner bead, 1" x 1", galvanized steel, opening 3' x 2'	7.000	L.F.	.140	1.12	6.85	7.97
3' x 3'	9.000	L.F.	.180	1.44	8.80	10.24
3' x 5'	11.000	L.F.	.220	1.76	10.80	12.56
4' x 4'	12.000	L.F.	.240	1.92	11.75	13.67
4' x 5'	13.000	L.F.	.260	2.08	12.75	14.83
4' x 6'	14.000	L.F.	.280	2.24	13.70	15.94
4' x 8'	16.000	L.F.	.320	2.56	15.70	18.26
6'-8" x 2'	15.000	L.F.	.300	2.40	14.70	17.10
Tape and finish corners, inside and outside, opening 3' x 2'	14.000	L.F.	.204	1.40	11.50	12.90
3' x 3'	18.000	L.F.	.262	1.80	14.75	16.55
3' x 5'	22.000	L.F.	.320	2.20	18.05	20.25
4' x 4'	24.000	L.F.	.349	2.40	19.70	22.10
4' x 5'	26.000	L.F.	.378	2.60	21.50	24.10
4' x 6'	28.000	L.F.	.407	2.80	23	25.80
4' x 8'	32.000	L.F.	.466	3.20	26	29.20
6'-8" x 2'	30.000	L.F.	.437	3	24.50	27.50
Sill, slate, 2' long	2.000	L.F.	.400	25.50	17.40	42.90
3' long	3.000	L.F.	.600	38	26	64
4' long	4.000	L.F.	.800	50.50	35	85.50
Wood, 1-5/8" x 6-1/4", 2' long	2.000	L.F.	.128	14.90	6.25	21.15
3' long	3.000	L.F.	.192	22.50	9.40	31.90
4' long	4.000	L.F.	.256	30	12.50	42.50

Aluminum Window → ← Aluminum Door

System Description	QUAN.	UNIT	LABOR HOURS	COST EACH		
				MAT.	INST.	TOTAL
Storm door, aluminum, combination, storm & screen, anodized, 2'-6" x 6'-8"	1.000	Ea.	1.067	189	52	241
2'-8" x 6'-8"	1.000	Ea.	1.143	171	56	227
3'-0" x 6'-8"	1.000	Ea.	1.143	171	56	227
Mill finish, 2'-6" x 6'-8"	1.000	Ea.	1.067	248	52	300
2'-8" x 6'-8"	1.000	Ea.	1.143	248	56	304
3'-0" x 6'-8"	1.000	Ea.	1.143	271	56	327
Painted, 2'-6" x 6'-8"	1.000	Ea.	1.067	310	52	362
2'-8" x 6'-8"	1.000	Ea.	1.143	305	56	361
3'-0" x 6'-8"	1.000	Ea.	1.143	320	56	376
Wood, combination, storm & screen, crossbuck, 2'-6" x 6'-9"	1.000	Ea.	1.455	360	71	431
2'-8" x 6'-9"	1.000	Ea.	1.600	315	78.50	393.50
3'-0" x 6'-9"	1.000	Ea.	1.778	325	87	412
Full lite, 2'-6" x 6'-9"	1.000	Ea.	1.455	325	71	396
2'-8" x 6'-9"	1.000	Ea.	1.600	325	78.50	403.50
3'-0" x 6'-9"	1.000	Ea.	1.778	330	87	417
Windows, aluminum, combination storm & screen, basement, 1'-10" x 1'-0"	1.000	Ea.	.533	38.50	26	64.50
2'-9" x 1'-6"	1.000	Ea.	.533	42	26	68
3'-4" x 2'-0"	1.000	Ea.	.533	48.50	26	74.50
Double hung, anodized, 2'-0" x 3'-5"	1.000	Ea.	.533	99	26	125
2'-6" x 5'-0"	1.000	Ea.	.571	121	28	149
4'-0" x 6'-0"	1.000	Ea.	.640	249	31.50	280.50
Painted, 2'-0" x 3'-5"	1.000	Ea.	.533	110	26	136
2'-6" x 5'-0"	1.000	Ea.	.571	176	28	204
4'-0" x 6'-0"	1.000	Ea.	.640	300	31.50	331.50
Fixed window, anodized, 4'-6" x 4'-6"	1.000	Ea.	.640	132	31.50	163.50
5'-8" x 4'-6"	1.000	Ea.	.800	158	39	197
Painted, 4'-6" x 4'-6"	1.000	Ea.	.640	139	31.50	170.50
5'-8" x 4'-6"	1.000	Ea.	.800	158	39	197

Aluminum Louvered →

← Raised Panel

Wood Louvered

System Description	QUAN.	UNIT	LABOR HOURS	COST PER PAIR		
				MAT.	INST.	TOTAL
Shutters, exterior blinds, aluminum, louvered, 1'-4" wide, 3"-0" long	1.000	Set	.800	66.50	39	105.50
4'-0" long	1.000	Set	.800	79.50	39	118.50
5'-4" long	1.000	Set	.800	105	39	144
6'-8" long	1.000	Set	.889	134	43.50	177.50
Wood, louvered, 1'-2" wide, 3'-3" long	1.000	Set	.800	116	39	155
4'-7" long	1.000	Set	.800	156	39	195
5'-3" long	1.000	Set	.800	177	39	216
1'-6" wide, 3'-3" long	1.000	Set	.800	123	39	162
4'-7" long	1.000	Set	.800	173	39	212
Polystyrene, louvered, 1'-2" wide, 3'-3" long	1.000	Set	.800	30.50	39	69.50
4'-7" long	1.000	Set	.800	37.50	39	76.50
5'-3" long	1.000	Set	.800	43	39	82
6'-8" long	1.000	Set	.889	51	43.50	94.50
Vinyl, louvered, 1'-2" wide, 4'-7" long	1.000	Set	.720	34	35	69
1'-4" x 6'-8" long	1.000	Set	.889	52.50	43.50	96

Division 5
Roofing

Ridge Shingles

Shingles

Building Paper

Rake Board

Drip Edge

Gutter

Soffit & Fascia

Downspouts

System Description	QUAN.	UNIT	LABOR HOURS	COST PER S.F.		
				MAT.	INST.	TOTAL
ASPHALT, ROOF SHINGLES, CLASS A						
Shingles, inorganic class A, 210-235 lb./sq., 4/12 pitch	1.160	S.F.	.017	.97	.77	1.74
Drip edge, metal, 5″ wide	.150	L.F.	.003	.08	.15	.23
Building paper, #15 felt	1.300	S.F.	.002	.08	.08	.16
Ridge shingles, asphalt	.042	L.F.	.001	.09	.04	.13
Soffit & fascia, white painted aluminum, 1′ overhang	.083	L.F.	.012	.28	.59	.87
Rake trim, 1″ x 6″	.040	L.F.	.002	.05	.08	.13
Rake trim, prime and paint	.040	L.F.	.002	.01	.07	.08
Gutter, seamless, aluminum painted	.083	L.F.	.006	.22	.30	.52
Downspouts, aluminum painted	.035	L.F.	.002	.07	.08	.15
TOTAL		S.F.	.047	1.85	2.16	4.01
WOOD, CEDAR SHINGLES NO. 1 PERFECTIONS, 18″ LONG						
Shingles, wood, cedar, No. 1 perfections, 4/12 pitch	1.160	S.F.	.035	3.50	1.70	5.20
Drip edge, metal, 5″ wide	.150	L.F.	.003	.08	.15	.23
Building paper, #15 felt	1.300	S.F.	.002	.08	.08	.16
Ridge shingles, cedar	.042	L.F.	.001	.17	.06	.23
Soffit & fascia, white painted aluminum, 1′ overhang	.083	L.F.	.012	.28	.59	.87
Rake trim, 1″ x 6″	.040	L.F.	.002	.05	.08	.13
Rake trim, prime and paint	.040	L.F.	.002	.01	.07	.08
Gutter, seamless, aluminum, painted	.083	L.F.	.006	.22	.30	.52
Downspouts, aluminum, painted	.035	L.F.	.002	.07	.08	.15
TOTAL		S.F.	.065	4.46	3.11	7.57

The prices in these systems are based on a square foot of plan area.
All quantities have been adjusted accordingly.

Description	QUAN.	UNIT	LABOR HOURS	COST PER S.F.		
				MAT.	INST.	TOTAL

Gable End Roofing Price Sheet	QUAN.	UNIT	LABOR HOURS	COST PER S.F.		
				MAT.	INST.	TOTAL
Shingles, asphalt, inorganic, class A, 210-235 lb./sq., 4/12 pitch	1.160	S.F.	.017	.97	.77	1.74
8/12 pitch	1.330	S.F.	.019	1.05	.83	1.88
Laminated, multi-layered, 240-260 lb./sq., 4/12 pitch	1.160	S.F.	.021	1.15	.94	2.09
8/12 pitch	1.330	S.F.	.023	1.24	1.02	2.26
Premium laminated, multi-layered, 260-300 lb./sq., 4/12 pitch	1.160	S.F.	.027	1.32	1.21	2.53
8/12 pitch	1.330	S.F.	.030	1.43	1.31	2.74
Clay tile, Spanish tile, red, 4/12 pitch	1.160	S.F.	.053	4.26	2.36	6.62
8/12 pitch	1.330	S.F.	.058	4.62	2.56	7.18
Mission tile, red, 4/12 pitch	1.160	S.F.	.083	9.80	3.72	13.52
8/12 pitch	1.330	S.F.	.090	10.60	4.03	14.63
French tile, red, 4/12 pitch	1.160	S.F.	.071	8.90	3.14	12.04
8/12 pitch	1.330	S.F.	.077	9.60	3.41	13.01
Slate, Buckingham, Virginia, black, 4/12 pitch	1.160	S.F.	.055	6.30	2.42	8.72
8/12 pitch	1.330	S.F.	.059	6.85	2.63	9.48
Vermont, black or grey, 4/12 pitch	1.160	S.F.	.055	6.05	2.42	8.47
8/12 pitch	1.330	S.F.	.059	6.55	2.63	9.18
Wood, No. 1 red cedar, 5X, 16" long, 5" exposure, 4/12 pitch	1.160	S.F.	.038	4.08	1.88	5.96
8/12 pitch	1.330	S.F.	.042	4.42	2.04	6.46
Fire retardant, 4/12 pitch	1.160	S.F.	.038	4.81	1.88	6.69
8/12 pitch	1.330	S.F.	.042	5.20	2.04	7.24
18" long, No.1 perfections, 5" exposure, 4/12 pitch	1.160	S.F.	.035	3.50	1.70	5.20
8/12 pitch	1.330	S.F.	.038	3.80	1.85	5.65
Fire retardant, 4/12 pitch	1.160	S.F.	.035	4.23	1.70	5.93
8/12 pitch	1.330	S.F.	.038	4.59	1.85	6.44
Resquared & rebutted, 18" long, 6" exposure, 4/12 pitch	1.160	S.F.	.032	3.11	1.57	4.68
8/12 pitch	1.330	S.F.	.035	3.37	1.70	5.07
Fire retardant, 4/12 pitch	1.160	S.F.	.032	3.84	1.57	5.41
8/12 pitch	1.330	S.F.	.035	4.16	1.70	5.86
Wood shakes hand split, 24" long, 10" exposure, 4/12 pitch	1.160	S.F.	.038	2.18	1.88	4.06
8/12 pitch	1.330	S.F.	.042	2.37	2.04	4.41
Fire retardant, 4/12 pitch	1.160	S.F.	.038	2.91	1.88	4.79
8/12 pitch	1.330	S.F.	.042	3.16	2.04	5.20
18" long, 8" exposure, 4/12 pitch	1.160	S.F.	.048	1.93	2.35	4.28
8/12 pitch	1.330	S.F.	.052	2.09	2.55	4.64
Fire retardant, 4/12 pitch	1.160	S.F.	.048	2.66	2.35	5.01
8/12 pitch	1.330	S.F.	.052	2.88	2.55	5.43
Drip edge, metal, 5" wide	.150	L.F.	.003	.08	.15	.23
8" wide	.150	L.F.	.003	.11	.15	.26
Building paper, #15 asphalt felt	1.300	S.F.	.002	.08	.08	.16
Ridge shingles, asphalt	.042	L.F.	.001	.09	.04	.13
Clay	.042	L.F.	.002	.50	.07	.57
Slate	.042	L.F.	.002	.43	.07	.50
Wood, shingles	.042	L.F.	.001	.17	.06	.23
Shakes	.042	L.F.	.001	.17	.06	.23
Soffit & fascia, aluminum, vented, 1' overhang	.083	L.F.	.012	.28	.59	.87
2' overhang	.083	L.F.	.013	.46	.65	1.11
Vinyl, vented, 1' overhang	.083	L.F.	.011	.31	.54	.85
2' overhang	.083	L.F.	.012	.42	.65	1.07
Wood, board fascia, plywood soffit, 1' overhang	.083	L.F.	.004	.02	.15	.17
2' overhang	.083	L.F.	.006	.03	.23	.26
Rake trim, painted, 1" x 6"	.040	L.F.	.004	.06	.15	.21
1" x 8"	.040	L.F.	.004	.10	.16	.26
Gutter, 5" box, aluminum, seamless, painted	.083	L.F.	.006	.22	.30	.52
Vinyl	.083	L.F.	.006	.13	.30	.43
Downspout, 2" x 3", aluminum, one story house	.035	L.F.	.001	.06	.08	.14
Two story house	.060	L.F.	.003	.11	.14	.25
Vinyl, one story house	.035	L.F.	.002	.07	.08	.15
Two story house	.060	L.F.	.003	.11	.14	.25

System Description	QUAN.	UNIT	LABOR HOURS	COST PER S.F.		
				MAT.	INST.	TOTAL
ASPHALT, ROOF SHINGLES, CLASS A						
Shingles, inorganic, class A, 210-235 lb./sq. 4/12 pitch	1.570	S.F.	.023	1.29	1.02	2.31
Drip edge, metal, 5" wide	.122	L.F.	.002	.06	.12	.18
Building paper, #15 asphalt felt	1.800	S.F.	.002	.12	.11	.23
Ridge shingles, asphalt	.075	L.F.	.002	.16	.08	.24
Soffit & fascia, white painted aluminum, 1' overhang	.120	L.F.	.017	.40	.85	1.25
Gutter, seamless, aluminum, painted	.120	L.F.	.008	.32	.43	.75
Downspouts, aluminum, painted	.035	L.F.	.002	.07	.08	.15
TOTAL		S.F.	.056	2.42	2.69	5.11
WOOD, CEDAR SHINGLES, NO. 1 PERFECTIONS, 18" LONG						
Shingles, red cedar, No. 1 perfections, 5" exp., 4/12 pitch	1.570	S.F.	.047	4.67	2.27	6.94
Drip edge, metal, 5" wide	.122	L.F.	.002	.06	.12	.18
Building paper, #15 asphalt felt	1.800	S.F.	.002	.12	.11	.23
Ridge shingles, wood, cedar	.075	L.F.	.002	.30	.11	.41
Soffit & fascia, white painted aluminum, 1' overhang	.120	L.F.	.017	.40	.85	1.25
Gutter, seamless, aluminum, painted	.120	L.F.	.008	.32	.43	.75
Downspouts, aluminum, painted	.035	L.F.	.002	.07	.08	.15
TOTAL		S.F.	.080	5.94	3.97	9.91

The prices in these systems are based on a square foot of plan area.
All quantities have been adjusted accordingly.

Description	QUAN.	UNIT	LABOR HOURS	COST PER S.F.		
				MAT.	INST.	TOTAL

Hip Roof - Roofing Price Sheet	QUAN.	UNIT	LABOR HOURS	COST PER S.F.		
				MAT.	INST.	TOTAL
Shingles, asphalt, inorganic, class A, 210-235 lb./sq., 4/12 pitch	1.570	S.F.	.023	1.29	1.02	2.31
8/12 pitch	1.850	S.F.	.028	1.53	1.22	2.75
Laminated, multi-layered, 240-260 lb./sq., 4/12 pitch	1.570	S.F.	.028	1.53	1.26	2.79
8/12 pitch	1.850	S.F.	.034	1.81	1.49	3.30
Prem. laminated, multi-layered, 260-300 lb./sq., 4/12 pitch	1.570	S.F.	.037	1.76	1.62	3.38
8/12 pitch	1.850	S.F.	.043	2.09	1.92	4.01
Clay tile, Spanish tile, red, 4/12 pitch	1.570	S.F.	.071	5.70	3.15	8.85
8/12 pitch	1.850	S.F.	.084	6.75	3.74	10.49
Mission tile, red, 4/12 pitch	1.570	S.F.	.111	13.05	4.96	18.01
8/12 pitch	1.850	S.F.	.132	15.50	5.90	21.40
French tile, red, 4/12 pitch	1.570	S.F.	.095	11.85	4.19	16.04
8/12 pitch	1.850	S.F.	.113	14.05	4.98	19.03
Slate, Buckingham, Virginia, black, 4/12 pitch	1.570	S.F.	.073	8.40	3.23	11.63
8/12 pitch	1.850	S.F.	.087	10	3.84	13.84
Vermont, black or grey, 4/12 pitch	1.570	S.F.	.073	8.10	3.23	11.33
8/12 pitch	1.850	S.F.	.087	9.60	3.84	13.44
Wood, red cedar, No.1 5X, 16" long, 5" exposure, 4/12 pitch	1.570	S.F.	.051	5.45	2.51	7.96
8/12 pitch	1.850	S.F.	.061	6.45	2.98	9.43
Fire retardant, 4/12 pitch	1.570	S.F.	.051	6.40	2.51	8.91
8/12 pitch	1.850	S.F.	.061	7.60	2.98	10.58
18" long, No.1 perfections, 5" exposure, 4/12 pitch	1.570	S.F.	.047	4.67	2.27	6.94
8/12 pitch	1.850	S.F.	.055	5.55	2.70	8.25
Fire retardant, 4/12 pitch	1.570	S.F.	.047	5.65	2.27	7.92
8/12 pitch	1.850	S.F.	.055	6.70	2.70	9.40
Resquared & rebutted, 18" long, 6" exposure, 4/12 pitch	1.570	S.F.	.043	4.14	2.10	6.24
8/12 pitch	1.850	S.F.	.051	4.92	2.49	7.41
Fire retardant, 4/12 pitch	1.570	S.F.	.043	5.10	2.10	7.20
8/12 pitch	1.850	S.F.	.051	6.05	2.49	8.54
Wood shakes hand split, 24" long, 10" exposure, 4/12 pitch	1.570	S.F.	.051	2.91	2.51	5.42
8/12 pitch	1.850	S.F.	.061	3.46	2.98	6.44
Fire retardant, 4/12 pitch	1.570	S.F.	.051	3.88	2.51	6.39
8/12 pitch	1.850	S.F.	.061	4.61	2.98	7.59
18" long, 8" exposure, 4/12 pitch	1.570	S.F.	.064	2.58	3.14	5.72
8/12 pitch	1.850	S.F.	.076	3.06	3.72	6.78
Fire retardant, 4/12 pitch	1.570	S.F.	.064	3.55	3.14	6.69
8/12 pitch	1.850	S.F.	.076	4.21	3.72	7.93
Drip edge, metal, 5" wide	.122	L.F.	.002	.06	.12	.18
8" wide	.122	L.F.	.002	.09	.12	.21
Building paper, #15 asphalt felt	1.800	S.F.	.002	.12	.11	.23
Ridge shingles, asphalt	.075	L.F.	.002	.16	.08	.24
Clay	.075	L.F.	.003	.89	.13	1.02
Slate	.075	L.F.	.003	.77	.13	.90
Wood, shingles	.075	L.F.	.002	.30	.11	.41
Shakes	.075	L.F.	.002	.30	.11	.41
Soffit & fascia, aluminum, vented, 1' overhang	.120	L.F.	.017	.40	.85	1.25
2' overhang	.120	L.F.	.019	.66	.94	1.60
Vinyl, vented, 1' overhang	.120	L.F.	.016	.44	.79	1.23
2' overhang	.120	L.F.	.017	.61	.94	1.55
Wood, board fascia, plywood soffit, 1' overhang	.120	L.F.	.004	.02	.15	.17
2' overhang	.120	L.F.	.006	.03	.23	.26
Gutter, 5" box, aluminum, seamless, painted	.120	L.F.	.008	.32	.43	.75
Vinyl	.120	L.F.	.009	.18	.43	.61
Downspout, 2" x 3", aluminum, one story house	.035	L.F.	.002	.07	.08	.15
Two story house	.060	L.F.	.003	.11	.14	.25
Vinyl, one story house	.035	L.F.	.001	.06	.08	.14
Two story house	.060	L.F.	.003	.11	.14	.25

System Description	QUAN.	UNIT	LABOR HOURS	COST PER S.F.		
				MAT.	INST.	TOTAL
ASPHALT, ROOF SHINGLES, CLASS A						
Shingles, asphalt, inorganic, class A, 210-235 lb./sq.	1.450	S.F.	.022	1.21	.96	2.17
Drip edge, metal, 5" wide	.146	L.F.	.003	.08	.14	.22
Building paper, #15 asphalt felt	1.500	S.F.	.002	.10	.09	.19
Ridge shingles, asphalt	.042	L.F.	.001	.09	.04	.13
Soffit & fascia, painted aluminum, 1' overhang	.083	L.F.	.012	.28	.59	.87
Rake trim, 1" x 6"	.063	L.F.	.003	.07	.12	.19
Rake trim, prime and paint	.063	L.F.	.003	.02	.12	.14
Gutter, seamless, alumunum, painted	.083	L.F.	.006	.22	.30	.52
Downspouts, aluminum, painted	.042	L.F.	.002	.08	.10	.18
TOTAL		S.F.	.054	2.15	2.46	4.61
WOOD, CEDAR SHINGLES, NO. 1 PERFECTIONS, 18" LONG						
Shingles, wood, red cedar, No. 1 perfections, 5" exposure	1.450	S.F.	.044	4.38	2.13	6.51
Drip edge, metal, 5" wide	.146	L.F.	.003	.08	.14	.22
Building paper, #15 asphalt felt	1.500	S.F.	.002	.10	.09	.19
Ridge shingles, wood	.042	L.F.	.001	.17	.06	.23
Soffit & fascia, white painted aluminum, 1' overhang	.083	L.F.	.012	.28	.59	.87
Rake trim, 1" x 6"	.063	L.F.	.003	.07	.12	.19
Rake trim, prime and paint	.063	L.F.	.001	.01	.05	.06
Gutter, seamless, aluminum, painted	.083	L.F.	.006	.22	.30	.52
Downspouts, aluminum, painted	.042	L.F.	.002	.08	.10	.18
TOTAL		S.F.	.074	5.39	3.58	8.97

The prices in this system are based on a square foot of plan area.
All quantities have been adjusted accordingly.

Description	QUAN.	UNIT	LABOR HOURS	COST PER S.F.		
				MAT.	INST.	TOTAL

Gambrel Roofing Price Sheet	QUAN.	UNIT	LABOR HOURS	COST PER S.F.		
				MAT.	INST.	TOTAL
Shingles, asphalt, standard, inorganic, class A, 210-235 lb./sq.	1.450	S.F.	.022	1.21	.96	2.17
Laminated, multi-layered, 240-260 lb./sq.	1.450	S.F.	.027	1.43	1.18	2.61
Premium laminated, multi-layered, 260-300 lb./sq.	1.450	S.F.	.034	1.65	1.52	3.17
Slate, Buckingham, Virginia, black	1.450	S.F.	.069	7.90	3.03	10.93
Vermont, black or grey	1.450	S.F.	.069	7.60	3.03	10.63
Wood, red cedar, No.1 5X, 16" long, 5" exposure, plain	1.450	S.F.	.048	5.10	2.36	7.46
Fire retardant	1.450	S.F.	.048	6	2.36	8.36
18" long, No.1 perfections, 6" exposure, plain	1.450	S.F.	.044	4.38	2.13	6.51
Fire retardant	1.450	S.F.	.044	5.30	2.13	7.43
Resquared & rebutted, 18" long, 6" exposure, plain	1.450	S.F.	.040	3.89	1.97	5.86
Fire retardant	1.450	S.F.	.040	4.80	1.97	6.77
Shakes, hand split, 24" long, 10" exposure, plain	1.450	S.F.	.048	2.73	2.36	5.09
Fire retardant	1.450	S.F.	.048	3.64	2.36	6
18" long, 8" exposure, plain	1.450	S.F.	.060	2.42	2.94	5.36
Fire retardant	1.450	S.F.	.060	3.33	2.94	6.27
Drip edge, metal, 5" wide	.146	L.F.	.003	.08	.14	.22
8" wide	.146	L.F.	.003	.11	.14	.25
Building paper, #15 asphalt felt	1.500	S.F.	.002	.10	.09	.19
Ridge shingles, asphalt	.042	L.F.	.001	.09	.04	.13
Slate	.042	L.F.	.002	.43	.07	.50
Wood, shingles	.042	L.F.	.001	.17	.06	.23
Shakes	.042	L.F.	.001	.17	.06	.23
Soffit & fascia, aluminum, vented, 1' overhang	.083	L.F.	.012	.28	.59	.87
2' overhang	.083	L.F.	.013	.46	.65	1.11
Vinyl vented, 1' overhang	.083	L.F.	.011	.31	.54	.85
2' overhang	.083	L.F.	.012	.42	.65	1.07
Wood board fascia, plywood soffit, 1' overhang	.083	L.F.	.004	.02	.15	.17
2' overhang	.083	L.F.	.006	.03	.23	.26
Rake trim, painted, 1" x 6"	.063	L.F.	.006	.09	.24	.33
1" x 8"	.063	L.F.	.007	.12	.31	.43
Gutter, 5" box, aluminum, seamless, painted	.083	L.F.	.006	.22	.30	.52
Vinyl	.083	L.F.	.006	.13	.30	.43
Downspout 2" x 3", aluminum, one story house	.042	L.F.	.002	.07	.09	.16
Two story house	.070	L.F.	.003	.12	.16	.28
Vinyl, one story house	.042	L.F.	.002	.07	.09	.16
Two story house	.070	L.F.	.003	.12	.16	.28

System Description	QUAN.	UNIT	LABOR HOURS	COST PER S.F.		
				MAT.	INST.	TOTAL
ASPHALT, ROOF SHINGLES, CLASS A						
Shingles, standard inorganic class A 210-235 lb./sq.	2.210	S.F.	.032	1.77	1.41	3.18
Drip edge, metal, 5″ wide	.122	L.F.	.002	.06	.12	.18
Building paper, #15 asphalt felt	2.300	S.F.	.003	.15	.14	.29
Ridge shingles, asphalt	.090	L.F.	.002	.19	.10	.29
Soffit & fascia, white painted aluminum, 1′ overhang	.122	L.F.	.018	.41	.87	1.28
Gutter, seamless, aluminum, painted	.122	L.F.	.008	.33	.44	.77
Downspouts, aluminum, painted	.042	L.F.	.002	.08	.10	.18
TOTAL		S.F.	.067	2.99	3.18	6.17
WOOD, CEDAR SHINGLES, NO. 1 PERFECTIONS, 18″ LONG						
Shingles, wood, red cedar, No. 1 perfections, 5″ exposure	2.210	S.F.	.064	6.42	3.12	9.54
Drip edge, metal, 5″ wide	.122	L.F.	.002	.06	.12	.18
Building paper, #15 asphalt felt	2.300	S.F.	.003	.15	.14	.29
Ridge shingles, wood	.090	L.F.	.003	.36	.13	.49
Soffit & fascia, white painted aluminum, 1′ overhang	.122	L.F.	.018	.41	.87	1.28
Gutter, seamless, aluminum, painted	.122	L.F.	.008	.33	.44	.77
Downspouts, aluminum, painted	.042	L.F.	.002	.08	.10	.18
TOTAL		S.F.	.100	7.81	4.92	12.73

The prices in these systems are based on a square foot of plan area.
All quantities have been adjusted accordingly.

Description	QUAN.	UNIT	LABOR HOURS	COST PER S.F.		
				MAT.	INST.	TOTAL

Mansard Roofing Price Sheet	QUAN.	UNIT	LABOR HOURS	COST PER S.F.		
				MAT.	INST.	TOTAL
Shingles, asphalt, standard, inorganic, class A, 210-235 lb./sq.	2.210	S.F.	.032	1.77	1.41	3.18
Laminated, multi-layered, 240-260 lb./sq.	2.210	S.F.	.039	2.10	1.73	3.83
Premium laminated, multi-layered, 260-300 lb./sq.	2.210	S.F.	.050	2.42	2.22	4.64
Slate Buckingham, Virginia, black	2.210	S.F.	.101	11.55	4.44	15.99
Vermont, black or grey	2.210	S.F.	.101	11.10	4.44	15.54
Wood, red cedar, No.1 5X, 16" long, 5" exposure, plain	2.210	S.F.	.070	7.50	3.45	10.95
Fire retardant	2.210	S.F.	.070	8.80	3.45	12.25
18" long, No.1 perfections 6" exposure, plain	2.210	S.F.	.064	6.40	3.12	9.52
Fire retardant	2.210	S.F.	.064	7.75	3.12	10.87
Fire retardant	2.210	S.F.	.059	7.05	2.88	9.93
Shakes, hand split, 24" long 10" exposure, plain	2.210	S.F.	.070	4	3.45	7.45
Fire retardant	2.210	S.F.	.070	5.35	3.45	8.80
18" long, 8" exposure, plain	2.210	S.F.	.088	3.54	4.31	7.85
Fire retardant	2.210	S.F.	.088	4.87	4.31	9.18
Drip edge, metal, 5" wide	.122	S.F.	.002	.06	.12	.18
8" wide	.122	S.F.	.002	.09	.12	.21
Building paper, #15 asphalt felt	2.300	S.F.	.003	.15	.14	.29
Ridge shingles, asphalt	.090	L.F.	.002	.19	.10	.29
Slate	.090	L.F.	.004	.92	.16	1.08
Wood, shingles	.090	L.F.	.003	.36	.13	.49
Shakes	.090	L.F.	.003	.36	.13	.49
Soffit & fascia, aluminum vented, 1' overhang	.122	L.F.	.018	.41	.87	1.28
2' overhang	.122	L.F.	.020	.67	.96	1.63
Vinyl vented, 1' overhang	.122	L.F.	.016	.45	.80	1.25
2' overhang	.122	L.F.	.018	.62	.96	1.58
Wood board fascia, plywood soffit, 1' overhang	.122	L.F.	.013	.30	.59	.89
2' overhang	.122	L.F.	.019	.40	.90	1.30
Gutter, 5" box, aluminum, seamless, painted	.122	L.F.	.008	.33	.44	.77
Vinyl	.122	L.F.	.009	.19	.43	.62
Downspout 2" x 3", aluminum, one story house	.042	L.F.	.002	.07	.09	.16
Two story house	.070	L.F.	.003	.12	.16	.28
Vinyl, one story house	.042	L.F.	.002	.07	.09	.16
Two story house	.070	L.F.	.003	.12	.16	.28

System Description	QUAN.	UNIT	LABOR HOURS	COST PER S.F.		
				MAT.	INST.	TOTAL
ASPHALT, ROOF SHINGLES, CLASS A						
Shingles, inorganic class A 210-235 lb./sq. 4/12 pitch	1.230	S.F.	.019	1.05	.83	1.88
Drip edge, metal, 5″ wide	.100	L.F.	.002	.05	.10	.15
Building paper, #15 asphalt felt	1.300	S.F.	.002	.08	.08	.16
Soffit & fascia, white painted aluminum, 1′ overhang	.080	L.F.	.012	.27	.57	.84
Rake trim, 1″ x 6″	.043	L.F.	.002	.05	.08	.13
Rake trim, prime and paint	.043	L.F.	.002	.01	.08	.09
Gutter, seamless, aluminum, painted	.040	L.F.	.003	.11	.14	.25
Downspouts, painted aluminum	.020	L.F.	.001	.04	.05	.09
TOTAL		S.F.	.043	1.66	1.93	3.59
WOOD, CEDAR SHINGLES, NO. 1 PERFECTIONS, 18″ LONG						
Shingles, red cedar, No. 1 perfections, 5″ exp., 4/12 pitch	1.230	S.F.	.035	3.50	1.70	5.20
Drip edge, metal, 5″ wide	.100	L.F.	.002	.05	.10	.15
Building paper, #15 asphalt felt	1.300	S.F.	.002	.08	.08	.16
Soffit & fascia, white painted aluminum, 1′ overhang	.080	L.F.	.012	.27	.57	.84
Rake trim, 1″ x 6″	.043	L.F.	.002	.05	.08	.13
Rake trim, prime and paint	.043	L.F.	.001	.01	.04	.05
Gutter, seamless, aluminum, painted	.040	L.F.	.003	.11	.14	.25
Downspouts, painted aluminum	.020	L.F.	.001	.04	.05	.09
TOTAL		S.F.	.058	4.11	2.76	6.87

The prices in these systems are based on a square foot of plan area.
All quantities have been adjusted accordingly.

Description	QUAN.	UNIT	LABOR HOURS	COST PER S.F.		
				MAT.	INST.	TOTAL

Shed Roofing Price Sheet	QUAN.	UNIT	LABOR HOURS	COST PER S.F.		
				MAT.	INST.	TOTAL
Shingles, asphalt, inorganic, class A, 210-235 lb./sq., 4/12 pitch	1.230	S.F.	.017	.97	.77	1.74
8/12 pitch	1.330	S.F.	.019	1.05	.83	1.88
Laminated, multi-layered, 240-260 lb./sq. 4/12 pitch	1.230	S.F.	.021	1.15	.94	2.09
8/12 pitch	1.330	S.F.	.023	1.24	1.02	2.26
Premium laminated, multi-layered, 260-300 lb./sq. 4/12 pitch	1.230	S.F.	.027	1.32	1.21	2.53
8/12 pitch	1.330	S.F.	.030	1.43	1.31	2.74
Clay tile, Spanish tile, red, 4/12 pitch	1.230	S.F.	.053	4.26	2.36	6.62
8/12 pitch	1.330	S.F.	.058	4.62	2.56	7.18
Mission tile, red, 4/12 pitch	1.230	S.F.	.083	9.80	3.72	13.52
8/12 pitch	1.330	S.F.	.090	10.60	4.03	14.63
French tile, red, 4/12 pitch	1.230	S.F.	.071	8.90	3.14	12.04
8/12 pitch	1.330	S.F.	.077	9.60	3.41	13.01
Slate, Buckingham, Virginia, black, 4/12 pitch	1.230	S.F.	.055	6.30	2.42	8.72
8/12 pitch	1.330	S.F.	.059	6.85	2.63	9.48
Vermont, black or grey, 4/12 pitch	1.230	S.F.	.055	6.05	2.42	8.47
8/12 pitch	1.330	S.F.	.059	6.55	2.63	9.18
Wood, red cedar, No.1 5X, 16" long, 5" exposure, 4/12 pitch	1.230	S.F.	.038	4.08	1.88	5.96
8/12 pitch	1.330	S.F.	.042	4.42	2.04	6.46
Fire retardant, 4/12 pitch	1.230	S.F.	.038	4.81	1.88	6.69
8/12 pitch	1.330	S.F.	.042	5.20	2.04	7.24
18" long, 6" exposure, 4/12 pitch	1.230	S.F.	.035	3.50	1.70	5.20
8/12 pitch	1.330	S.F.	.038	3.80	1.85	5.65
Fire retardant, 4/12 pitch	1.230	S.F.	.035	4.23	1.70	5.93
8/12 pitch	1.330	S.F.	.038	4.59	1.85	6.44
Resquared & rebutted, 18" long, 6" exposure, 4/12 pitch	1.230	S.F.	.032	3.11	1.57	4.68
8/12 pitch	1.330	S.F.	.035	3.37	1.70	5.07
Fire retardant, 4/12 pitch	1.230	S.F.	.032	3.84	1.57	5.41
8/12 pitch	1.330	S.F.	.035	4.16	1.70	5.86
Wood shakes, hand split, 24" long, 10" exposure, 4/12 pitch	1.230	S.F.	.038	2.18	1.88	4.06
8/12 pitch	1.330	S.F.	.042	2.37	2.04	4.41
Fire retardant, 4/12 pitch	1.230	S.F.	.038	2.91	1.88	4.79
8/12 pitch	1.330	S.F.	.042	3.16	2.04	5.20
18" long, 8" exposure, 4/12 pitch	1.230	S.F.	.048	1.93	2.35	4.28
8/12 pitch	1.330	S.F.	.052	2.09	2.55	4.64
Fire retardant, 4/12 pitch	1.230	S.F.	.048	2.66	2.35	5.01
8/12 pitch	1.330	S.F.	.052	2.88	2.55	5.43
Drip edge, metal, 5" wide	.100	L.F.	.002	.05	.10	.15
8" wide	.100	L.F.	.002	.08	.10	.18
Building paper, #15 asphalt felt	1.300	S.F.	.002	.08	.08	.16
Soffit & fascia, aluminum vented, 1' overhang	.080	L.F.	.012	.27	.57	.84
2' overhang	.080	L.F.	.013	.44	.63	1.07
Vinyl vented, 1' overhang	.080	L.F.	.011	.30	.52	.82
2' overhang	.080	L.F.	.012	.40	.63	1.03
Wood board fascia, plywood soffit, 1' overhang	.080	L.F.	.010	.21	.44	.65
2' overhang	.080	L.F.	.014	.28	.66	.94
Rake, trim, painted, 1" x 6"	.043	L.F.	.004	.06	.16	.22
1" x 8"	.043	L.F.	.004	.06	.16	.22
Gutter, 5" box, aluminum, seamless, painted	.040	L.F.	.003	.11	.14	.25
Vinyl	.040	L.F.	.003	.06	.14	.20
Downspout 2" x 3", aluminum, one story house	.020	L.F.	.001	.04	.05	.09
Two story house	.020	L.F.	.001	.06	.07	.13
Vinyl, one story house	.020	L.F.	.001	.04	.05	.09
Two story house	.020	L.F.	.001	.06	.07	.13

System Description	QUAN.	UNIT	LABOR HOURS	COST PER S.F.		
				MAT.	INST.	TOTAL
ASPHALT, ROOF SHINGLES, CLASS A						
Shingles, standard inorganic class A 210-235 lb./sq	1.400	S.F.	.020	1.13	.90	2.03
Drip edge, metal, 5" wide	.220	L.F.	.004	.12	.22	.34
Building paper, #15 asphalt felt	1.500	S.F.	.002	.10	.09	.19
Ridge shingles, asphalt	.280	L.F.	.007	.59	.30	.89
Soffit & fascia, aluminum, vented	.220	L.F.	.032	.74	1.56	2.30
Flashing, aluminum, mill finish, .013" thick	1.500	S.F.	.083	1.11	3.65	4.76
TOTAL		S.F.	.148	3.79	6.72	10.51
WOOD, CEDAR, NO. 1 PERFECTIONS						
Shingles, red cedar, No.1 perfections, 18" long, 5" exp.	1.400	S.F.	.041	4.09	1.99	6.08
Drip edge, metal, 5" wide	.220	L.F.	.004	.12	.22	.34
Building paper, #15 asphalt felt	1.500	S.F.	.002	.10	.09	.19
Ridge shingles, wood	.280	L.F.	.008	1.11	.39	1.50
Soffit & fascia, aluminum, vented	.220	L.F.	.032	.74	1.56	2.30
Flashing, aluminum, mill finish, .013" thick	1.500	S.F.	.083	1.11	3.65	4.76
TOTAL		S.F.	.170	7.27	7.90	15.17
SLATE, BUCKINGHAM, BLACK						
Shingles, Buckingham, Virginia, black	1.400	S.F.	.064	7.35	2.83	10.18
Drip edge, metal, 5" wide	.220	L.F.	.004	.12	.22	.34
Building paper, #15 asphalt felt	1.500	S.F.	.002	.10	.09	.19
Ridge shingles, slate	.280	L.F.	.011	2.86	.50	3.36
Soffit & fascia, aluminum, vented	.220	L.F.	.032	.74	1.56	2.30
Flashing, copper, 16 oz.	1.500	S.F.	.104	12.45	4.59	17.04
TOTAL		S.F.	.217	23.62	9.79	33.41

The prices in these systems are based on a square foot of plan area under the dormer roof.

Description	QUAN.	UNIT	LABOR HOURS	COST PER S.F.		
				MAT.	INST.	TOTAL

Gable Dormer Roofing Price Sheet

	QUAN.	UNIT	LABOR HOURS	COST PER S.F.		
				MAT.	INST.	TOTAL
Shingles, asphalt, standard, inorganic, class A, 210-235 lb./sq.	1.400	S.F.	.020	1.13	.90	2.03
Laminated, multi-layered, 240-260 lb./sq.	1.400	S.F.	.025	1.34	1.10	2.44
Premium laminated, multi-layered, 260-300 lb./sq.	1.400	S.F.	.032	1.54	1.41	2.95
Clay tile, Spanish tile, red	1.400	S.F.	.062	4.97	2.76	7.73
Mission tile, red	1.400	S.F.	.097	11.40	4.34	15.74
French tile, red	1.400	S.F.	.083	10.35	3.67	14.02
Slate Buckingham, Virginia, black	1.400	S.F.	.064	7.35	2.83	10.18
Vermont, black or grey	1.400	S.F.	.064	7.05	2.83	9.88
Wood, red cedar, No.1 5X, 16" long, 5" exposure	1.400	S.F.	.045	4.76	2.20	6.96
Fire retardant	1.400	S.F.	.045	5.60	2.20	7.80
18" long, No.1 perfections, 5" exposure	1.400	S.F.	.041	4.09	1.99	6.08
Fire retardant	1.400	S.F.	.041	4.94	1.99	6.93
Resquared & rebutted, 18" long, 5" exposure	1.400	S.F.	.037	3.63	1.83	5.46
Fire retardant	1.400	S.F.	.037	4.48	1.83	6.31
Shakes hand split, 24" long, 10" exposure	1.400	S.F.	.045	2.55	2.20	4.75
Fire retardant	1.400	S.F.	.045	3.40	2.20	5.60
18" long, 8" exposure	1.400	S.F.	.056	2.25	2.74	4.99
Fire retardant	1.400	S.F.	.056	3.10	2.74	5.84
Drip edge, metal, 5" wide	.220	L.F.	.004	.12	.22	.34
8" wide	.220	L.F.	.004	.17	.22	.39
Building paper, #15 asphalt felt	1.500	S.F.	.002	.10	.09	.19
Ridge shingles, asphalt	.280	L.F.	.007	.59	.30	.89
Clay	.280	L.F.	.011	3.30	.50	3.80
Slate	.280	L.F.	.011	2.86	.50	3.36
Wood	.280	L.F.	.008	1.11	.39	1.50
Soffit & fascia, aluminum, vented	.220	L.F.	.032	.74	1.56	2.30
Vinyl, vented	.220	L.F.	.029	.81	1.44	2.25
Wood, board fascia, plywood soffit	.220	L.F.	.026	.58	1.20	1.78
Flashing, aluminum, .013" thick	1.500	S.F.	.083	1.11	3.65	4.76
.032" thick	1.500	S.F.	.083	2.45	3.65	6.10
.040" thick	1.500	S.F.	.083	3.65	3.65	7.30
.050" thick	1.500	S.F.	.083	4.16	3.65	7.81
Copper, 16 oz.	1.500	S.F.	.104	12.45	4.59	17.04
20 oz.	1.500	S.F.	.109	14.95	4.80	19.75
24 oz.	1.500	S.F.	.114	18.70	5.05	23.75
32 oz.	1.500	S.F.	.120	23.50	5.30	28.80

System Description	QUAN.	UNIT	LABOR HOURS	COST PER S.F.		
				MAT.	INST.	TOTAL
ASPHALT, ROOF SHINGLES, CLASS A						
Shingles, standard inorganic class A 210-235 lb./sq.	1.100	S.F.	.016	.89	.70	1.59
Drip edge, aluminum, 5″ wide	.250	L.F.	.005	.11	.25	.36
Building paper, #15 asphalt felt	1.200	S.F.	.002	.08	.07	.15
Soffit & fascia, aluminum, vented, 1′ overhang	.250	L.F.	.036	.84	1.78	2.62
Flashing, aluminum, mill finish, 0.013″ thick	.800	L.F.	.044	.59	1.94	2.53
TOTAL		S.F.	.103	2.51	4.74	7.25
WOOD, CEDAR, NO. 1 PERFECTIONS, 18″ LONG						
Shingles, wood, red cedar, #1 perfections, 5″ exposure	1.100	S.F.	.032	3.21	1.56	4.77
Drip edge, aluminum, 5″ wide	.250	L.F.	.005	.11	.25	.36
Building paper, #15 asphalt felt	1.200	S.F.	.002	.08	.07	.15
Soffit & fascia, aluminum, vented, 1′ overhang	.250	L.F.	.036	.84	1.78	2.62
Flashing, aluminum, mill finish, 0.013″ thick	.800	L.F.	.044	.59	1.94	2.53
TOTAL		S.F.	.119	4.83	5.60	10.43
SLATE, BUCKINGHAM, BLACK						
Shingles, slate, Buckingham, black	1.100	S.F.	.050	5.78	2.22	8
Drip edge, aluminum, 5″ wide	.250	L.F.	.005	.11	.25	.36
Building paper, #15 asphalt felt	1.200	S.F.	.002	.08	.07	.15
Soffit & fascia, aluminum, vented, 1′ overhang	.250	L.F.	.036	.84	1.78	2.62
Flashing, copper, 16 oz.	.800	L.F.	.056	6.64	2.45	9.09
TOTAL		S.F.	.149	13.45	6.77	20.22

The prices in this system are based on a square foot of plan area under
the dormer roof.

Description	QUAN.	UNIT	LABOR HOURS	COST PER S.F.		
				MAT.	INST.	TOTAL

Shed Dormer Roofing Price Sheet

	QUAN.	UNIT	LABOR HOURS	COST PER S.F.		
				MAT.	INST.	TOTAL
Shingles, asphalt, standard, inorganic, class A, 210-235 lb./sq.	1.100	S.F.	.016	.89	.70	1.59
Laminated, multi-layered, 240-260 lb./sq.	1.100	S.F.	.020	1.05	.86	1.91
Premium laminated, multi-layered, 260-300 lb./sq.	1.100	S.F.	.025	1.21	1.11	2.32
Clay tile, Spanish tile, red	1.100	S.F.	.049	3.91	2.17	6.08
Mission tile, red	1.100	S.F.	.077	8.95	3.41	12.36
French tile, red	1.100	S.F.	.065	8.15	2.88	11.03
Slate Buckingham, Virginia, black	1.100	S.F.	.050	5.80	2.22	8.02
Vermont, black or grey	1.100	S.F.	.050	5.55	2.22	7.77
Wood, red cedar, No. 1 5X, 16" long, 5" exposure	1.100	S.F.	.035	3.74	1.73	5.47
Fire retardant	1.100	S.F.	.035	4.41	1.73	6.14
18" long, No.1 perfections, 5" exposure	1.100	S.F.	.032	3.21	1.56	4.77
Fire retardant	1.100	S.F.	.032	3.88	1.56	5.44
Resquared & rebutted, 18" long, 5" exposure	1.100	S.F.	.029	2.85	1.44	4.29
Fire retardant	1.100	S.F.	.029	3.52	1.44	4.96
Shakes hand split, 24" long, 10" exposure	1.100	S.F.	.035	2	1.73	3.73
Fire retardant	1.100	S.F.	.035	2.67	1.73	4.40
18" long, 8" exposure	1.100	S.F.	.044	1.77	2.16	3.93
Fire retardant	1.100	S.F.	.044	2.44	2.16	4.60
Drip edge, metal, 5" wide	.250	L.F.	.005	.11	.25	.36
8" wide	.250	L.F.	.005	.19	.25	.44
Building paper, #15 asphalt felt	1.200	S.F.	.002	.08	.07	.15
Soffit & fascia, aluminum, vented	.250	L.F.	.036	.84	1.78	2.62
Vinyl, vented	.250	L.F.	.033	.93	1.64	2.57
Wood, board fascia, plywood soffit	.250	L.F.	.030	.65	1.38	2.03
Flashing, aluminum, .013" thick	.800	L.F.	.044	.59	1.94	2.53
.032" thick	.800	L.F.	.044	1.30	1.94	3.24
.040" thick	.800	L.F.	.044	1.94	1.94	3.88
.050" thick	.800	L.F.	.044	2.22	1.94	4.16
Copper, 16 oz.	.800	L.F.	.056	6.65	2.45	9.10
20 oz.	.800	L.F.	.058	7.95	2.56	10.51
24 oz.	.800	L.F.	.061	9.95	2.69	12.64
32 oz.	.800	L.F.	.064	12.40	2.82	15.22

System Description	QUAN.	UNIT	LABOR HOURS	COST EACH		
				MAT.	INST.	TOTAL
SKYLIGHT, FIXED, 32″ X 32″						
Skylight, fixed bubble, insulating, 32″ x 32″	1.000	Ea.	1.422	192	64	256
Trimmer rafters, 2″ x 6″	28.000	L.F.	.448	11.48	21.84	33.32
Headers, 2″ x 6″	6.000	L.F.	.267	2.46	13.08	15.54
Curb, 2″ x 4″	12.000	L.F.	.154	3.24	7.56	10.80
Flashing, aluminum, .013″ thick	13.500	S.F.	.745	9.99	32.81	42.80
Trim, stock pine, 11/16″ x 2-1/2″	12.000	L.F.	.400	17.52	19.56	37.08
Trim primer coat, oil base, brushwork	12.000	L.F.	.148	.48	6.24	6.72
Trim paint, 1 coat, brushwork	12.000	L.F.	.148	.72	6.24	6.96
TOTAL		Ea.	3.732	237.89	171.33	409.22
SKYLIGHT, FIXED, 48″ X 48″						
Skylight, fixed bubble, insulating, 48″ x 48″	1.000	Ea.	1.296	416	58.24	474.24
Trimmer rafters, 2″ x 6″	28.000	L.F.	.448	11.48	21.84	33.32
Headers, 2″ x 6″	8.000	L.F.	.356	3.28	17.44	20.72
Curb, 2″ x 4″	16.000	L.F.	.205	4.32	10.08	14.40
Flashing, aluminum, .013″ thick	16.000	S.F.	.883	11.84	38.88	50.72
Trim, stock pine, 11/16″ x 2-1/2″	16.000	L.F.	.533	23.36	26.08	49.44
Trim primer coat, oil base, brushwork	16.000	L.F.	.197	.64	8.32	8.96
Trim paint, 1 coat, brushwork	16.000	L.F.	.197	.96	8.32	9.28
TOTAL		Ea.	4.115	471.88	189.20	661.08
SKYWINDOW, OPERATING, 24″ X 48″						
Skywindow, operating, thermopane glass, 24″ x 48″	1.000	Ea.	3.200	620	144	764
Trimmer rafters, 2″ x 6″	28.000	L.F.	.448	11.48	21.84	33.32
Headers, 2″ x 6″	8.000	L.F.	.267	2.46	13.08	15.54
Curb, 2″ x 4″	14.000	L.F.	.179	3.78	8.82	12.60
Flashing, aluminum, .013″ thick	14.000	S.F.	.772	10.36	34.02	44.38
Trim, stock pine, 11/16″ x 2-1/2″	14.000	L.F.	.467	20.44	22.82	43.26
Trim primer coat, oil base, brushwork	14.000	L.F.	.172	.56	7.28	7.84
Trim paint, 1 coat, brushwork	14.000	L.F.	.172	.84	7.28	8.12
TOTAL		Ea.	5.677	669.92	259.14	929.06

The prices in these systems are on a cost each basis.

Description	QUAN.	UNIT	LABOR HOURS	COST EACH		
				MAT.	INST.	TOTAL

Skylight/Skywindow Price Sheet	QUAN.	UNIT	LABOR HOURS	COST EACH		
				MAT.	INST.	TOTAL
Skylight, fixed bubble insulating, 24" x 24"	1.000	Ea.	.800	108	36	144
32" x 32"	1.000	Ea.	1.422	192	64	256
32" x 48"	1.000	Ea.	.864	277	39	316
48" x 48"	1.000	Ea.	1.296	415	58	473
Ventilating bubble insulating, 36" x 36"	1.000	Ea.	2.667	505	120	625
52" x 52"	1.000	Ea.	2.667	705	120	825
28" x 52"	1.000	Ea.	3.200	515	144	659
36" x 52"	1.000	Ea.	3.200	570	144	714
Skywindow, operating, thermopane glass, 24" x 48"	1.000	Ea.	3.200	620	144	764
32" x 48"	1.000	Ea.	3.556	645	160	805
Trimmer rafters, 2" x 6"	28.000	L.F.	.448	11.50	22	33.50
2" x 8"	28.000	L.F.	.472	17.10	23	40.10
2" x 10"	28.000	L.F.	.711	22.50	34.50	57
Headers, 24" window, 2" x 6"	4.000	L.F.	.178	1.64	8.70	10.34
2" x 8"	4.000	L.F.	.188	2.44	9.20	11.64
2" x 10"	4.000	L.F.	.200	3.20	9.80	13
32" window, 2" x 6"	6.000	L.F.	.267	2.46	13.10	15.56
2" x 8"	6.000	L.F.	.282	3.66	13.80	17.46
2" x 10"	6.000	L.F.	.300	4.80	14.70	19.50
48" window, 2" x 6"	8.000	L.F.	.356	3.28	17.45	20.73
2" x 8"	8.000	L.F.	.376	4.88	18.40	23.28
2" x 10"	8.000	L.F.	.400	6.40	19.60	26
Curb, 2" x 4", skylight, 24" x 24"	8.000	L.F.	.102	2.16	5.05	7.21
32" x 32"	12.000	L.F.	.154	3.24	7.55	10.79
32" x 48"	14.000	L.F.	.179	3.78	8.80	12.58
48" x 48"	16.000	L.F.	.205	4.32	10.10	14.42
Flashing, aluminum .013" thick, skylight, 24" x 24"	9.000	S.F.	.497	6.65	22	28.65
32" x 32"	13.500	S.F.	.745	10	33	43
32" x 48"	14.000	S.F.	.772	10.35	34	44.35
48" x 48"	16.000	S.F.	.883	11.85	39	50.85
Copper 16 oz., skylight, 24" x 24"	9.000	S.F.	.626	74.50	27.50	102
32" x 32"	13.500	S.F.	.939	112	41.50	153.50
32" x 48"	14.000	S.F.	.974	116	43	159
48" x 48"	16.000	S.F.	1.113	133	49	182
Trim, interior casing painted, 24" x 24"	8.000	L.F.	.347	12.55	16.40	28.95
32" x 32"	12.000	L.F.	.520	18.85	24.50	43.35
32" x 48"	14.000	L.F.	.607	22	28.50	50.50
48" x 48"	16.000	L.F.	.693	25	33	58

191

Flashing
4" x 4" Cant
6" x 2-1/4" Wood Blocking
Gravel
Asphalt
Felt
Insulation Board

System Description	QUAN.	UNIT	LABOR HOURS	COST PER S.F.		
				MAT.	INST.	TOTAL
ASPHALT, ORGANIC, 4-PLY, INSULATED DECK						
Membrane, asphalt, 4-plies #15 felt, gravel surfacing	1.000	S.F.	.025	1.33	1.29	2.62
Insulation board, 2-layers of 1-1/16" glass fiber	2.000	S.F.	.016	2.04	.70	2.74
Wood blocking, 2" x 6"	.040	L.F.	.004	.05	.21	.26
Treated 4" x 4" cant strip	.040	L.F.	.001	.07	.05	.12
Flashing, aluminum, 0.040" thick	.050	S.F.	.003	.12	.12	.24
TOTAL		S.F.	.049	3.61	2.37	5.98
ASPHALT, INORGANIC, 3-PLY, INSULATED DECK						
Membrane, asphalt, 3-plies type IV glass felt, gravel surfacing	1.000	S.F.	.028	1.21	1.42	2.63
Insulation board, 2-layers of 1-1/16" glass fiber	2.000	S.F.	.016	2.04	.70	2.74
Wood blocking, 2" x 6"	.040	L.F.	.004	.05	.21	.26
Treated 4" x 4" cant strip	.040	L.F.	.001	.07	.05	.12
Flashing, aluminum, 0.040" thick	.050	S.F.	.003	.12	.12	.24
TOTAL		S.F.	.052	3.49	2.50	5.99
COAL TAR, ORGANIC, 4-PLY, INSULATED DECK						
Membrane, coal tar, 4-plies #15 felt, gravel surfacing	1.000	S.F.	.027	2.01	1.35	3.36
Insulation board, 2-layers of 1-1/16" glass fiber	2.000	S.F.	.016	2.04	.70	2.74
Wood blocking, 2" x 6"	.040	L.F.	.004	.05	.21	.26
Treated 4" x 4" cant strip	.040	L.F.	.001	.07	.05	.12
Flashing, aluminum, 0.040" thick	.050	S.F.	.003	.12	.12	.24
TOTAL		S.F.	.051	4.29	2.43	6.72
COAL TAR, INORGANIC, 3-PLY, INSULATED DECK						
Membrane, coal tar, 3-plies type IV glass felt, gravel surfacing	1.000	S.F.	.029	1.65	1.50	3.15
Insulation board, 2-layers of 1-1/16" glass fiber	2.000	S.F.	.016	2.04	.70	2.74
Wood blocking, 2" x 6"	.040	L.F.	.004	.05	.21	.26
Treated 4" x 4" cant strip	.040	L.F.	.001	.07	.05	.12
Flashing, aluminum, 0.040" thick	.050	S.F.	.003	.12	.12	.24
TOTAL		S.F.	.053	3.93	2.58	6.51

Built-Up Roofing Price Sheet	QUAN.	UNIT	LABOR HOURS	COST PER S.F.		
				MAT.	INST.	TOTAL
Membrane, asphalt, 4-plies #15 organic felt, gravel surfacing	1.000	S.F.	.025	1.33	1.29	2.62
Asphalt base sheet & 3-plies #15 asphalt felt	1.000	S.F.	.025	1.03	1.29	2.32
3-plies type IV glass fiber felt	1.000	S.F.	.028	1.21	1.42	2.63
4-plies type IV glass fiber felt	1.000	S.F.	.028	1.48	1.42	2.90
Coal tar, 4-plies #15 organic felt, gravel surfacing	1.000	S.F.	.027			
4-plies tarred felt	1.000	S.F.	.027	2.01	1.35	3.36
3-plies type IV glass fiber felt	1.000	S.F.	.029	1.65	1.50	3.15
4-plies type IV glass fiber felt	1.000	S.F.	.027	2.26	1.35	3.61
Roll, asphalt, 1-ply #15 organic felt, 2-plies mineral surfaced	1.000	S.F.	.021	.70	1.05	1.75
3-plies type IV glass fiber, 1-ply mineral surfaced	1.000	S.F.	.022	1.14	1.14	2.28
Insulation boards, glass fiber, 1-1/16" thick	1.000	S.F.	.008	1.02	.35	1.37
2-1/16" thick	1.000	S.F.	.010	1.49	.44	1.93
2-7/16" thick	1.000	S.F.	.010	1.71	.44	2.15
Expanded perlite, 1" thick	1.000	S.F.	.010	.51	.44	.95
1-1/2" thick	1.000	S.F.	.010	.53	.44	.97
2" thick	1.000	S.F.	.011	.88	.50	1.38
Fiberboard, 1" thick	1.000	S.F.	.010	.46	.44	.90
1-1/2" thick	1.000	S.F.	.010	.70	.44	1.14
2" thick	1.000	S.F.	.010	.94	.44	1.38
Extruded polystyrene, 15 PSI compressive strength, 2" thick R10	1.000	S.F.	.006	.68	.28	.96
3" thick R15	1.000	S.F.	.008	1.40	.35	1.75
4" thick R20	1.000	S.F.	.008	1.80	.35	2.15
Tapered for drainage	1.000	S.F.	.005	.58	.23	.81
40 PSI compressive strength, 1" thick R5	1.000	S.F.	.005	.56	.23	.79
2" thick R10	1.000	S.F.	.006	1.06	.28	1.34
3" thick R15	1.000	S.F.	.008	1.54	.35	1.89
4" thick R20	1.000	S.F.	.008	2.07	.35	2.42
Fiberboard high density, 1/2" thick R1.3	1.000	S.F.	.008	.24	.35	.59
1" thick R2.5	1.000	S.F.	.010	.48	.44	.92
1 1/2" thick R3.8	1.000	S.F.	.010	.73	.44	1.17
Polyisocyanurate, 1 1/2" thick	1.000	S.F.	.006	.68	.28	.96
2" thick	1.000	S.F.	.007	.95	.32	1.27
3 1/2" thick	1.000	S.F.	.008	2.15	.35	2.50
Tapered for drainage	1.000	S.F.	.006	2.15	.25	2.40
Expanded polystyrene, 1" thick	1.000	S.F.	.005	.40	.23	.63
2" thick R10	1.000	S.F.	.006	.79	.28	1.07
3" thick	1.000	S.F.	.006	1.19	.28	1.47
Wood blocking, treated, 6" x 2" & 4" x 4" cant	.040	L.F.	.002	.11	.12	.23
6" x 4-1/2" & 4" x 4" cant	.040	L.F.	.005	.15	.26	.41
6" x 5" & 4" x 4" cant	.040	L.F.	.007	.17	.33	.50
Flashing, aluminum, 0.019" thick	.050	S.F.	.003	.06	.12	.18
0.032" thick	.050	S.F.	.003	.08	.12	.20
0.040" thick	.050	S.F.	.003	.12	.12	.24
Copper sheets, 16 oz., under 500 lbs.	.050	S.F.	.003	.42	.15	.57
Over 500 lbs.	.050	S.F.	.003	.37	.11	.48
20 oz., under 500 lbs.	.050	S.F.	.004	.50	.16	.66
Over 500 lbs.	.050	S.F.	.003	.45	.12	.57
Stainless steel, 32 gauge	.050	S.F.	.003	.21	.11	.32
28 gauge	.050	S.F.	.003	.26	.11	.37
26 gauge	.050	S.F.	.003	.31	.11	.42
24 gauge	.050	S.F.	.003	.41	.11	.52

Division 6
Interiors

System Description	QUAN.	UNIT	LABOR HOURS	COST PER S.F.		
				MAT.	INST.	TOTAL
1/2″ DRYWALL, TAPED & FINISHED						
Gypsum wallboard, 1/2″ thick, standard	1.000	S.F.	.008	.26	.39	.65
Finish, taped & finished joints	1.000	S.F.	.008	.05	.39	.44
Corners, taped & finished, 32 L.F. per 12′ x 12′ room	.083	L.F.	.002	.01	.07	.08
Painting, primer & 2 coats	1.000	S.F.	.011	.17	.44	.61
Paint trim, to 6″ wide, primer + 1 coat enamel	.125	L.F.	.001	.01	.05	.06
Trim, baseboard	.125	L.F.	.005	.34	.25	.59
TOTAL		S.F.	.035	.84	1.59	2.43
THINCOAT, SKIM-COAT, ON 1/2″ BACKER DRYWALL						
Gypsum wallboard, 1/2″ thick, thincoat backer	1.000	S.F.	.008	.26	.39	.65
Thincoat plaster	1.000	S.F.	.011	.09	.50	.59
Corners, taped & finished, 32 L.F. per 12′ x 12′ room	.083	L.F.	.002	.01	.07	.08
Painting, primer & 2 coats	1.000	S.F.	.011	.17	.44	.61
Paint trim, to 6″ wide, primer + 1 coat enamel	.125	L.F.	.001	.01	.05	.06
Trim, baseboard	.125	L.F.	.005	.34	.25	.59
TOTAL		S.F.	.038	.88	1.70	2.58
5/8″ DRYWALL, TAPED & FINISHED						
Gypsum wallboard, 5/8″ thick, standard	1.000	S.F.	.008	.31	.39	.70
Finish, taped & finished joints	1.000	S.F.	.008	.05	.39	.44
Corners, taped & finished, 32 L.F. per 12′ x 12′ room	.083	L.F.	.002	.01	.07	.08
Painting, primer & 2 coats	1.000	S.F.	.011	.17	.44	.61
Trim, baseboard	.125	L.F.	.005	.34	.25	.59
Paint trim, to 6″ wide, primer + 1 coat enamel	.125	L.F.	.001	.01	.05	.06
TOTAL		S.F.	.035	.89	1.59	2.48

The costs in this system are based on a square foot of wall.
Do not deduct for openings.

Description	QUAN.	UNIT	LABOR HOURS	COST PER S.F.		
				MAT.	INST.	TOTAL

Drywall & Thincoat Wall Price Sheet	QUAN.	UNIT	LABOR HOURS	COST PER S.F.		
				MAT.	INST.	TOTAL
Gypsum wallboard, 1/2" thick, standard	1.000	S.F.	.008	.26	.39	.65
Fire resistant	1.000	S.F.	.008	.31	.39	.70
Water resistant	1.000	S.F.	.008	.39	.39	.78
5/8" thick, standard	1.000	S.F.	.008	.31	.39	.70
Fire resistant	1.000	S.F.	.008	.30	.39	.69
Water resistant	1.000	S.F.	.008	.47	.39	.86
Gypsum wallboard backer for thincoat system, 1/2" thick	1.000	S.F.	.008	.26	.39	.65
5/8" thick	1.000	S.F.	.008	.31	.39	.70
Gypsum wallboard, taped & finished	1.000	S.F.	.008	.05	.39	.44
Texture spray	1.000	S.F.	.010	.06	.42	.48
Thincoat plaster, including tape	1.000	S.F.	.011	.09	.50	.59
Gypsum wallboard corners, taped & finished, 32 L.F. per 4' x 4' room	.250	L.F.	.004	.03	.21	.24
6' x 6' room	.110	L.F.	.002	.01	.09	.10
10' x 10' room	.100	L.F.	.001	.01	.08	.09
12' x 12' room	.083	L.F.	.001	.01	.07	.08
16' x 16' room	.063	L.F.	.001	.01	.05	.06
Thincoat system, 32 L.F. per 4' x 4' room	.250	L.F.	.003	.02	.13	.15
6' x 6' room	.110	L.F.	.001	.01	.05	.06
10' x 10' room	.100	L.F.	.001	.01	.05	.06
12' x 12' room	.083	L.F.	.001	.01	.04	.05
16' x 16' room	.063	L.F.	.001	.01	.03	.04
Painting, primer, & 1 coat	1.000	S.F.	.008	.11	.34	.45
& 2 coats	1.000	S.F.	.011	.17	.44	.61
Wallpaper, $7/double roll	1.000	S.F.	.013	.41	.53	.94
$17/double roll	1.000	S.F.	.015	.78	.63	1.41
$40/double roll	1.000	S.F.	.018	2.72	.78	3.50
Wallcovering, medium weight vinyl		S.F.	.017	.90	.70	1.60
Tile, ceramic adhesive thin set, 4 1/4" x 4 1/4" tiles	1.000	S.F.	.084	2.58	3.33	5.91
6" x 6" tiles	1.000	S.F.	.080	3.35	3.16	6.51
Pregrouted sheets	1.000	S.F.	.067	5.20	2.64	7.84
Trim, painted or stained, baseboard	.125	L.F.	.006	.35	.30	.65
Base shoe	.125	L.F.	.005	.17	.25	.42
Chair rail	.125	L.F.	.005	.21	.23	.44
Cornice molding	.125	L.F.	.004	.15	.20	.35
Cove base, vinyl	.125	L.F.	.003	.11	.14	.25
Paneling, not including furring or trim						
Plywood, prefinished, 1/4" thick, 4' x 8' sheets, vert. grooves						
Birch faced, minimum	1.000	S.F.	.032	.98	1.57	2.55
Average	1.000	S.F.	.038	1.49	1.87	3.36
Maximum	1.000	S.F.	.046	2.17	2.24	4.41
Mahogany, African	1.000	S.F.	.040	2.76	1.96	4.72
Philippine (lauan)	1.000	S.F.	.032	1.19	1.57	2.76
Oak or cherry, minimum	1.000	S.F.	.032	2.31	1.57	3.88
Maximum	1.000	S.F.	.040	3.54	1.96	5.50
Rosewood	1.000	S.F.	.050	5.05	2.45	7.50
Teak	1.000	S.F.	.040	3.54	1.96	5.50
Chestnut	1.000	S.F.	.043	5.25	2.09	7.34
Pecan	1.000	S.F.	.040	2.27	1.96	4.23
Walnut, minimum	1.000	S.F.	.032	3.03	1.57	4.60
Maximum	1.000	S.F.	.040	5.75	1.96	7.71

System Description	QUAN.	UNIT	LABOR HOURS	COST PER S.F.		
				MAT.	INST.	TOTAL
1/2″ SHEETROCK, TAPED & FINISHED						
Gypsum wallboard, 1/2″ thick, standard	1.000	S.F.	.008	.26	.39	.65
Finish, taped & finished	1.000	S.F.	.008	.05	.39	.44
Corners, taped & finished, 12′ x 12′ room	.333	L.F.	.006	.03	.27	.30
Paint, primer & 2 coats	1.000	S.F.	.011	.17	.44	.61
TOTAL		S.F.	.033	.51	1.49	2
THINCOAT, SKIM COAT ON 1/2″ GYPSUM WALLBOARD						
Gypsum wallboard, 1/2″ thick, thincoat backer	1.000	S.F.	.008	.26	.39	.65
Thincoat plaster	1.000	S.F.	.011	.09	.50	.59
Corners, taped & finished, 12′ x 12′ room	.333	L.F.	.006	.03	.27	.30
Paint, primer & 2 coats	1.000	S.F.	.011	.17	.44	.61
TOTAL		S.F.	.036	.55	1.60	2.15
WATER-RESISTANT GYPSUM WALLBOARD, 1/2″ THICK, TAPED & FINISHED						
Gypsum wallboard, 1/2″ thick, water-resistant	1.000	S.F.	.008	.39	.39	.78
Finish, taped & finished	1.000	S.F.	.008	.05	.39	.44
Corners, taped & finished, 12′ x 12′ room	.333	L.F.	.006	.03	.27	.30
Paint, primer & 2 coats	1.000	S.F.	.011	.17	.44	.61
TOTAL		S.F.	.033	.64	1.49	2.13
5/8″ GYPSUM WALLBOARD, TAPED & FINISHED						
Gypsum wallboard, 5/8″ thick, standard	1.000	S.F.	.008	.31	.39	.70
Finish, taped & finished	1.000	S.F.	.008	.05	.39	.44
Corners, taped & finished, 12′ x 12′ room	.333	L.F.	.006	.03	.27	.30
Paint, primer & 2 coats	1.000	S.F.	.011	.17	.44	.61
TOTAL		S.F.	.033	.56	1.49	2.05

The costs in this system are based on a square foot of ceiling.

Description	QUAN.	UNIT	LABOR HOURS	COST PER S.F.		
				MAT.	INST.	TOTAL

Drywall & Thincoat Ceilings	QUAN.	UNIT	LABOR HOURS	COST PER S.F.		
				MAT.	INST.	TOTAL
Gypsum wallboard ceilings, 1/2" thick, standard	1.000	S.F.	.008	.26	.39	.65
Fire resistant	1.000	S.F.	.008	.31	.39	.70
Water resistant	1.000	S.F.	.008	.39	.39	.78
5/8" thick, standard	1.000	S.F.	.008	.31	.39	.70
Fire resistant	1.000	S.F.	.008	.30	.39	.69
Water resistant	1.000	S.F.	.008	.47	.39	.86
Gypsum wallboard backer for thincoat ceiling system, 1/2" thick	1.000	S.F.	.016	.57	.78	1.35
5/8" thick	1.000	S.F.	.016	.62	.78	1.40
Gypsum wallboard ceilings, taped & finished	1.000	S.F.	.008	.05	.39	.44
Texture spray	1.000	S.F.	.010	.06	.42	.48
Thincoat plaster	1.000	S.F.	.011	.09	.50	.59
Corners taped & finished, 4' x 4' room	1.000	L.F.	.015	.10	.82	.92
6' x 6' room	.667	L.F.	.010	.07	.55	.62
10' x 10' room	.400	L.F.	.006	.04	.33	.37
12' x 12' room	.333	L.F.	.005	.03	.27	.30
16' x 16' room	.250	L.F.	.003	.02	.15	.17
Thincoat system, 4' x 4' room	1.000	L.F.	.011	.09	.50	.59
6' x 6' room	.667	L.F.	.007	.06	.34	.40
10' x 10' room	.400	L.F.	.004	.04	.20	.24
12' x 12' room	.333	L.F.	.004	.03	.16	.19
16' x 16' room	.250	L.F.	.002	.02	.10	.12
Painting, primer & 1 coat	1.000	S.F.	.008	.11	.34	.45
& 2 coats	1.000	S.F.	.011	.17	.44	.61
Wallpaper, double roll, solid pattern, avg. workmanship	1.000	S.F.	.013	.41	.53	.94
Basic pattern, avg. workmanship	1.000	S.F.	.015	.78	.63	1.41
Basic pattern, quality workmanship	1.000	S.F.	.018	2.72	.78	3.50
Tile, ceramic adhesive thin set, 4 1/4" x 4 1/4" tiles	1.000	S.F.	.084	2.58	3.33	5.91
6" x 6" tiles	1.000	S.F.	.080	3.35	3.16	6.51
Pregrouted sheets	1.000	S.F.	.067	5.20	2.64	7.84

System Description	QUAN.	UNIT	LABOR HOURS	COST PER S.F.		
				MAT.	INST.	TOTAL
PLASTER ON GYPSUM LATH						
Plaster, gypsum or perlite, 2 coats	1.000	S.F.	.053	.46	2.39	2.85
Lath, 3/8" gypsum	1.000	S.F.	.010	.62	.44	1.06
Corners, expanded metal, 32 L.F. per 12' x 12' room	.083	L.F.	.002	.01	.08	.09
Painting, primer & 2 coats	1.000	S.F.	.011	.17	.44	.61
Paint trim, to 6" wide, primer + 1 coat enamel	.125	L.F.	.001	.01	.05	.06
Trim, baseboard	.125	L.F.	.005	.34	.25	.59
TOTAL		S.F.	.082	1.61	3.65	5.26
PLASTER ON METAL LATH						
Plaster, gypsum or perlite, 2 coats	1.000	S.F.	.053	.46	2.39	2.85
Lath, 2.5 Lb. diamond, metal	1.000	S.F.	.010	.50	.44	.94
Corners, expanded metal, 32 L.F. per 12' x 12' room	.083	L.F.	.002	.01	.08	.09
Painting, primer & 2 coats	1.000	S.F.	.011	.17	.44	.61
Paint trim, to 6" wide, primer + 1 coat enamel	.125	L.F.	.001	.01	.05	.06
Trim, baseboard	.125	L.F.	.005	.34	.25	.59
TOTAL		S.F.	.082	1.49	3.65	5.14
STUCCO ON METAL LATH						
Stucco, 2 coats	1.000	S.F.	.041	.26	1.83	2.09
Lath, 2.5 Lb. diamond, metal	1.000	S.F.	.010	.50	.44	.94
Corners, expanded metal, 32 L.F. per 12' x 12' room	.083	L.F.	.002	.01	.08	.09
Painting, primer & 2 coats	1.000	S.F.	.011	.17	.44	.61
Paint trim, to 6" wide, primer + 1 coat enamel	.125	L.F.	.001	.01	.05	.06
Trim, baseboard	.125	L.F.	.005	.34	.25	.59
TOTAL		S.F.	.070	1.29	3.09	4.38

The costs in these systems are based on a per square foot of wall area.
Do not deduct for openings.

Description	QUAN.	UNIT	LABOR HOURS	COST PER S.F.		
				MAT.	INST.	TOTAL

Plaster & Stucco Wall Price Sheet	QUAN.	UNIT	LABOR HOURS	COST PER S.F.		
				MAT.	INST.	TOTAL
Plaster, gypsum or perlite, 2 coats	1.000	S.F.	.053	.46	2.39	2.85
3 coats	1.000	S.F.	.065	.66	2.89	3.55
Lath, gypsum, standard, 3/8" thick	1.000	S.F.	.010	.62	.44	1.06
Fire resistant, 3/8" thick	1.000	S.F.	.013	.30	.53	.83
1/2" thick	1.000	S.F.	.014	.30	.57	.87
Metal, diamond, 2.5 Lb.	1.000	S.F.	.010	.50	.44	.94
3.4 Lb.	1.000	S.F.	.012	.52	.49	1.01
Rib, 2.75 Lb.	1.000	S.F.	.012	.41	.49	.90
3.4 Lb.	1.000	S.F.	.013	.63	.53	1.16
Corners, expanded metal, 32 L.F. per 4' x 4' room	.250	L.F.	.005	.04	.25	.29
6' x 6' room	.110	L.F.	.002	.02	.11	.13
10' x 10' room	.100	L.F.	.002	.02	.10	.12
12' x 12' room	.083	L.F.	.002	.01	.08	.09
16' x 16' room	.063	L.F.	.001	.01	.06	.07
Painting, primer & 1 coats	1.000	S.F.	.008	.11	.34	.45
Primer & 2 coats	1.000	S.F.	.011	.17	.44	.61
Wallpaper, low price double roll	1.000	S.F.	.013	.41	.53	.94
Medium price double roll	1.000	S.F.	.015	.78	.63	1.41
High price double roll	1.000	S.F.	.018	2.72	.78	3.50
Tile, ceramic thin set, 4-1/4" x 4-1/4" tiles	1.000	S.F.	.084	2.58	3.33	5.91
6" x 6" tiles	1.000	S.F.	.080	3.35	3.16	6.51
Pregrouted sheets	1.000	S.F.	.067	5.20	2.64	7.84
Trim, painted or stained, baseboard	.125	L.F.	.006	.35	.30	.65
Base shoe	.125	L.F.	.005	.17	.25	.42
Chair rail	.125	L.F.	.005	.21	.23	.44
Cornice molding	.125	L.F.	.004	.15	.20	.35
Cove base, vinyl	.125	L.F.	.003	.11	.14	.25
Paneling not including furring or trim						
Plywood, prefinished, 1/4" thick, 4' x 8' sheets, vert. grooves						
Birch faced, minimum	1.000	S.F.	.032	.98	1.57	2.55
Average	1.000	S.F.	.038	1.49	1.87	3.36
Maximum	1.000	S.F.	.046	2.17	2.24	4.41
Mahogany, African	1.000	S.F.	.040	2.76	1.96	4.72
Philippine (lauan)	1.000	S.F.	.032	1.19	1.57	2.76
Oak or cherry, minimum	1.000	S.F.	.032	2.31	1.57	3.88
Maximum	1.000	S.F.	.040	3.54	1.96	5.50
Rosewood	1.000	S.F.	.050	5.05	2.45	7.50
Teak	1.000	S.F.	.040	3.54	1.96	5.50
Chestnut	1.000	S.F.	.043	5.25	2.09	7.34
Pecan	1.000	S.F.	.040	2.27	1.96	4.23
Walnut, minimum	1.000	S.F.	.032	3.03	1.57	4.60
Maximum	1.000	S.F.	.040	5.75	1.96	7.71

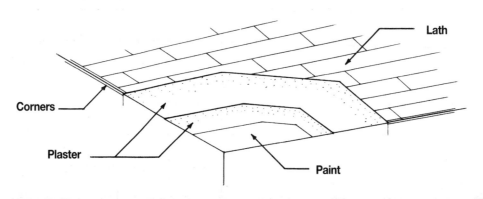

System Description	QUAN.	UNIT	LABOR HOURS	COST PER S.F.		
				MAT.	INST.	TOTAL
PLASTER ON GYPSUM LATH						
Plaster, gypsum or perlite, 2 coats	1.000	S.F.	.061	.46	2.72	3.18
Gypsum lath, plain or perforated, nailed, 3/8" thick	1.000	S.F.	.010	.62	.44	1.06
Gypsum lath, ceiling installation adder	1.000	S.F.	.004		.17	.17
Corners, expanded metal, 12' x 12' room	.330	L.F.	.007	.05	.32	.37
Painting, primer & 2 coats	1.000	S.F.	.011	.17	.44	.61
TOTAL		S.F.	.093	1.30	4.09	5.39
PLASTER ON METAL LATH						
Plaster, gypsum or perlite, 2 coats	1.000	S.F.	.061	.46	2.72	3.18
Lath, 2.5 Lb. diamond, metal	1.000	S.F.	.012	.50	.49	.99
Corners, expanded metal, 12' x 12' room	.330	L.F.	.007	.05	.32	.37
Painting, primer & 2 coats	1.000	S.F.	.011	.17	.44	.61
TOTAL		S.F.	.091	1.18	3.97	5.15
STUCCO ON GYPSUM LATH						
Stucco, 2 coats	1.000	S.F.	.041	.26	1.83	2.09
Gypsum lath, plain or perforated, nailed, 3/8" thick	1.000	S.F.	.010	.62	.44	1.06
Gypsum lath, ceiling installation adder	1.000	S.F.	.004		.17	.17
Corners, expanded metal, 12' x 12' room	.330	L.F.	.007	.05	.32	.37
Painting, primer & 2 coats	1.000	S.F.	.011	.17	.44	.61
TOTAL		S.F.	.073	1.10	3.20	4.30
STUCCO ON METAL LATH						
Stucco, 2 coats	1.000	S.F.	.041	.26	1.83	2.09
Lath, 2.5 Lb. diamond, metal	1.000	S.F.	.012	.50	.49	.99
Corners, expanded metal, 12' x 12' room	.330	L.F.	.007	.05	.32	.37
Painting, primer & 2 coats	1.000	S.F.	.011	.17	.44	.61
TOTAL		S.F.	.071	.98	3.08	4.06

The costs in these systems are based on a square foot of ceiling area.

Description	QUAN.	UNIT	LABOR HOURS	COST PER S.F.		
				MAT.	INST.	TOTAL

Plaster & Stucco Ceiling Price Sheet	QUAN.	UNIT	LABOR HOURS	COST PER S.F.		
				MAT.	INST.	TOTAL
Plaster, gypsum or perlite, 2 coats	1.000	S.F.	.061	.46	2.72	3.18
3 coats	1.000	S.F.	.065	.66	2.89	3.55
Lath, gypsum, standard, 3/8" thick	1.000	S.F.	.014	.62	.61	1.23
1/2" thick	1.000	S.F.	.015	.61	.63	1.24
Fire resistant, 3/8" thick	1.000	S.F.	.017	.30	.70	1
1/2" thick	1.000	S.F.	.018	.30	.74	1.04
Metal, diamond, 2.5 Lb.	1.000	S.F.	.012	.50	.49	.99
3.4 Lb.	1.000	S.F.	.015	.52	.62	1.14
Rib, 2.75 Lb.	1.000	S.F.	.012	.41	.49	.90
3.4 Lb.	1.000	S.F.	.013	.63	.53	1.16
Corners expanded metal, 4' x 4' room	1.000	L.F.	.020	.16	.98	1.14
6' x 6' room	.667	L.F.	.013	.11	.66	.77
10' x 10' room	.400	L.F.	.008	.06	.39	.45
12' x 12' room	.333	L.F.	.007	.05	.32	.37
16' x 16' room	.250	L.F.	.004	.03	.18	.21
Painting, primer & 1 coat	1.000	S.F.	.008	.11	.34	.45
Primer & 2 coats	1.000	S.F.	.011	.17	.44	.61

System Description	QUAN.	UNIT	LABOR HOURS	COST PER S.F.		
				MAT.	INST.	TOTAL
2' X 2' GRID, FILM FACED FIBERGLASS, 5/8" THICK						
Suspension system, 2' x 2' grid, T bar	1.000	S.F.	.012	.93	.60	1.53
Ceiling board, film faced fiberglass, 5/8" thick	1.000	S.F.	.013	.77	.63	1.40
Carrier channels, 1-1/2" x 3/4"	1.000	S.F.	.017	.12	.83	.95
Hangers, #12 wire	1.000	S.F.	.002	.09	.08	.17
TOTAL		S.F.	.044	1.91	2.14	4.05
2' X 4' GRID, FILM FACED FIBERGLASS, 5/8" THICK						
Suspension system, 2' x 4' grid, T bar	1.000	S.F.	.010	.75	.49	1.24
Ceiling board, film faced fiberglass, 5/8" thick	1.000	S.F.	.013	.77	.63	1.40
Carrier channels, 1-1/2" x 3/4"	1.000	S.F.	.017	.12	.83	.95
Hangers, #12 wire	1.000	S.F.	.002	.09	.08	.17
TOTAL		S.F.	.042	1.73	2.03	3.76
2' X 2' GRID, MINERAL FIBER, REVEAL EDGE, 1" THICK						
Suspension system, 2' x 2' grid, T bar	1.000	S.F.	.012	.93	.60	1.53
Ceiling board, mineral fiber, reveal edge, 1" thick	1.000	S.F.	.013	1.69	.65	2.34
Carrier channels, 1-1/2" x 3/4"	1.000	S.F.	.017	.12	.83	.95
Hangers, #12 wire	1.000	S.F.	.002	.09	.08	.17
TOTAL		S.F.	.044	2.83	2.16	4.99
2' X 4' GRID, MINERAL FIBER, REVEAL EDGE, 1" THICK						
Suspension system, 2' x 4' grid, T bar	1.000	S.F.	.010	.75	.49	1.24
Ceiling board, mineral fiber, reveal edge, 1" thick	1.000	S.F.	.013	1.69	.65	2.34
Carrier channels, 1-1/2" x 3/4"	1.000	S.F.	.017	.12	.83	.95
Hangers, #12 wire	1.000	S.F.	.002	.09	.08	.17
TOTAL		S.F.	.042	2.65	2.05	4.70

Description	QUAN.	UNIT	LABOR HOURS	COST PER S.F.		
				MAT.	INST.	TOTAL

Suspended Ceiling Price Sheet	QUAN.	UNIT	LABOR HOURS	COST PER S.F.		
				MAT.	INST.	TOTAL
Suspension systems, T bar, 2' x 2' grid	1.000	S.F.	.012	.93	.60	1.53
2' x 4' grid	1.000	S.F.	.010	.75	.49	1.24
Concealed Z bar, 12" module	1.000	S.F.	.015	.76	.75	1.51
Ceiling boards, fiberglass, film faced, 2' x 2' or 2' x 4', 5/8" thick	1.000	S.F.	.013	.77	.63	1.40
3/4" thick	1.000	S.F.	.013	1.77	.65	2.42
3" thick thermal R11	1.000	S.F.	.018	1.68	.87	2.55
Glass cloth faced, 3/4" thick	1.000	S.F.	.016	3.16	.78	3.94
1" thick	1.000	S.F.	.016	2.40	.81	3.21
1-1/2" thick, nubby face	1.000	S.F.	.017	2.93	.82	3.75
Mineral fiber boards, 5/8" thick, aluminum face 2' x 2'	1.000	S.F.	.013	2	.65	2.65
2' x 4'	1.000	S.F.	.012	1.62	.60	2.22
Standard faced, 2' x 2' or 2' x 4'	1.000	S.F.	.012	.86	.58	1.44
Plastic coated face, 2' x 2' or 2' x 4'	1.000	S.F.	.020	1.35	.98	2.33
Fire rated, 2 hour rating, 5/8" thick	1.000	S.F.	.012	1.29	.58	1.87
Tegular edge, 2' x 2' or 2' x 4', 5/8" thick, fine textured	1.000	S.F.	.013	1.60	.83	2.43
Rough textured	1.000	S.F.	.015	2.09	.83	2.92
3/4" thick, fine textured	1.000	S.F.	.016	2.29	.87	3.16
Rough textured	1.000	S.F.	.018	2.59	.87	3.46
Luminous panels, prismatic, acrylic	1.000	S.F.	.020	2.44	.98	3.42
Polystyrene	1.000	S.F.	.020	1.25	.98	2.23
Flat or ribbed, acrylic	1.000	S.F.	.020	4.25	.98	5.23
Polystyrene	1.000	S.F.	.020	2.92	.98	3.90
Drop pan, white, acrylic	1.000	S.F.	.020	6.25	.98	7.23
Polystyrene	1.000	S.F.	.020	5.20	.98	6.18
Carrier channels, 4'-0" on center, 3/4" x 1-1/2"	1.000	S.F.	.017	.12	.83	.95
1-1/2" x 3-1/2"	1.000	S.F.	.017	.30	.83	1.13
Hangers, #12 wire	1.000	S.F.	.002	.09	.08	.17

Door — Trim

Lockset

Frame

System Description	QUAN.	UNIT	LABOR HOURS	COST EACH		
				MAT.	INST.	TOTAL
LAUAN, FLUSH DOOR, HOLLOW CORE						
Door, flush, lauan, hollow core, 2'-8" wide x 6'-8" high	1.000	Ea.	.889	39.50	43.50	83
Frame, pine, 4-5/8" jamb	17.000	L.F.	.725	121.55	35.53	157.08
Trim, stock pine, 11/16" x 2-1/2"	34.000	L.F.	1.133	49.64	55.42	105.06
Paint trim, to 6" wide, primer + 1 coat enamel	34.000	L.F.	.340	3.74	14.28	18.02
Butt hinges, chrome, 3-1/2" x 3-1/2"	1.500	Pr.		42.75		42.75
Lockset, passage	1.000	Ea.	.500	24	24.50	48.50
Prime door & frame, oil, brushwork	2.000	Face	1.600	6.38	67	73.38
Paint door and frame, oil, 2 coats	2.000	Face	2.667	11.30	112	123.30
TOTAL		Ea.	7.854	298.86	352.23	651.09
BIRCH, FLUSH DOOR, HOLLOW CORE						
Door, flush, birch, hollow core, 2'-8" wide x 6'-8" high	1.000	Ea.	.889	54.50	43.50	98
Frame, pine, 4-5/8" jamb	17.000	L.F.	.725	121.55	35.53	157.08
Trim, stock pine, 11/16" x 2-1/2"	34.000	L.F.	1.133	49.64	55.42	105.06
Butt hinges, chrome, 3-1/2" x 3-1/2"	1.500	Pr.		42.75		42.75
Lockset, passage	1.000	Ea.	.500	24	24.50	48.50
Prime door & frame, oil, brushwork	2.000	Face	1.600	6.38	67	73.38
Paint door and frame, oil, 2 coats	2.000	Face	2.667	11.30	112	123.30
TOTAL		Ea.	7.514	310.12	337.95	648.07
RAISED PANEL, SOLID, PINE DOOR						
Door, pine, raised panel, 2'-8" wide x 6'-8" high	1.000	Ea.	.889	177	43.50	220.50
Frame, pine, 4-5/8" jamb	17.000	L.F.	.725	121.55	35.53	157.08
Trim, stock pine, 11/16" x 2-1/2"	34.000	L.F.	1.133	49.64	55.42	105.06
Butt hinges, bronze, 3-1/2" x 3-1/2"	1.500	Pr.		52.50		52.50
Lockset, passage	1.000	Ea.	.500	24	24.50	48.50
Prime door & frame, oil, brushwork	2.000		1.600	6.38	67	73.38
Paint door and frame, oil, 2 coats	2.000		2.667	11.30	112	123.30
TOTAL		Ea.	7.514	442.37	337.95	780.32

The costs in these systems are based on a cost per each door.

Description	QUAN.	UNIT	LABOR HOURS	COST EACH		
				MAT.	INST.	TOTAL

Interior Door Price Sheet	QUAN.	UNIT	LABOR HOURS	COST EACH MAT.	INST.	TOTAL
Door, hollow core, lauan 1-3/8″ thick, 6′-8″ high x 1′-6″ wide	1.000	Ea.	.889	34	43.50	77.50
2′-0″ wide	1.000	Ea.	.889	34	43.50	77.50
2′-6″ wide	1.000	Ea.	.889	38	43.50	81.50
2′-8″ wide	1.000	Ea.	.889	39.50	43.50	83
3′-0″ wide	1.000	Ea.	.941	40.50	46	86.50
Birch 1-3/8″ thick, 6′-8″ high x 1′-6″ wide	1.000	Ea.	.889	42	43.50	85.50
2′-0″ wide	1.000	Ea.	.889	45	43.50	88.50
2′-6″ wide	1.000	Ea.	.889	53.50	43.50	97
2′-8″ wide	1.000	Ea.	.889	54.50	43.50	98
3′-0″ wide	1.000	Ea.	.941	56	46	102
Louvered pine 1-3/8″ thick, 6′-8″ high x 1′-6″ wide	1.000	Ea.	.842	111	41	152
2′-0″ wide	1.000	Ea.	.889	140	43.50	183.50
2′-6″ wide	1.000	Ea.	.889	153	43.50	196.50
2′-8″ wide	1.000	Ea.	.889	161	43.50	204.50
3′-0″ wide	1.000	Ea.	.941	183	46	229
Paneled pine 1-3/8″ thick, 6′-8″ high x 1′-6″ wide	1.000	Ea.	.842	122	41	163
2′-0″ wide	1.000	Ea.	.889	143	43.50	186.50
2′-6″ wide	1.000	Ea.	.889	173	43.50	216.50
2′-8″ wide	1.000	Ea.	.889	177	43.50	220.50
3′-0″ wide	1.000	Ea.	.941	183	46	229
Frame, pine, 1′-6″ thru 2′-0″ wide door, 3-5/8″ deep	16.000	L.F.	.683	97.50	33.50	131
4-5/8″ deep	16.000	L.F.	.683	114	33.50	147.50
5-5/8″ deep	16.000	L.F.	.683	75.50	33.50	109
2′-6″ thru 3′0″ wide door, 3-5/8″ deep	17.000	L.F.	.725	104	35.50	139.50
4-5/8″ deep	17.000	L.F.	.725	122	35.50	157.50
5-5/8″ deep	17.000	L.F.	.725	80	35.50	115.50
Trim, casing, painted, both sides, 1′-6″ thru 2′-6″ wide door	32.000	L.F.	1.855	50	85.50	135.50
2′-6″ thru 3′-0″ wide door	34.000	L.F.	1.971	53	91	144
Butt hinges 3-1/2″ x 3-1/2″, steel plated, chrome	1.500	Pr.		43		43
Bronze	1.500	Pr.		52.50		52.50
Locksets, passage, minimum	1.000	Ea.	.500	24	24.50	48.50
Maximum	1.000	Ea.	.575	27.50	28	55.50
Privacy, miniumum	1.000	Ea.	.625	30	30.50	60.50
Maximum	1.000	Ea.	.675	32.50	33	65.50
Paint 2 sides, primer & 2 cts., flush door, 1′-6″ to 2′-0″ wide	2.000	Face	5.547	24	233	257
2′-6″ thru 3′-0″ wide	2.000	Face	6.933	30	291	321
Louvered door, 1′-6″ thru 2′-0″ wide	2.000	Face	6.400	23.50	269	292.50
2′-6″ thru 3′-0″ wide	2.000	Face	8.000	29.50	335	364.50
Paneled door, 1′-6″ thru 2′-0″ wide	2.000	Face	6.400	23.50	269	292.50
2′-6″ thru 3′-0″ wide	2.000	Face	8.000	29.50	335	364.50

Trim

Door

Frame

System Description	QUAN.	UNIT	LABOR HOURS	COST EACH		
				MAT.	INST.	TOTAL
BI-PASSING, FLUSH, LAUAN, HOLLOW CORE, 4'-0" X 6'-8"						
Door, flush, lauan, hollow core, 4'-0" x 6'-8" opening	1.000	Ea.	1.333	185	65.50	250.50
Frame, pine, 4-5/8" jamb	18.000	L.F.	.768	128.70	37.62	166.32
Trim, stock pine, 11/16" x 2-1/2"	36.000	L.F.	1.200	52.56	58.68	111.24
Prime door & frame, oil, brushwork	2.000	Face	1.600	6.38	67	73.38
Paint door and frame, oil, 2 coats	2.000	Face	2.667	11.30	112	123.30
TOTAL		Ea.	7.568	383.94	340.80	724.74
BI-PASSING, FLUSH, BIRCH, HOLLOW CORE, 6'-0" X 6'-8"						
Door, flush, birch, hollow core, 6'-0" x 6'-8" opening	1.000	Ea.	1.600	279	78.50	357.50
Frame, pine, 4-5/8" jamb	19.000	L.F.	.811	135.85	39.71	175.56
Trim, stock pine, 11/16" x 2-1/2"	38.000	L.F.	1.267	55.48	61.94	117.42
Prime door & frame, oil, brushwork	2.000	Face	2.000	7.98	83.75	91.73
Paint door and frame, oil, 2 coats	2.000	Face	3.333	14.13	140	154.13
TOTAL		Ea.	9.011	492.44	403.90	896.34
BI-FOLD, PINE, PANELED, 3'-0" X 6'-8"						
Door, pine, paneled, 3'-0" x 6'-8" opening	1.000	Ea.	1.231	217	60.50	277.50
Frame, pine, 4-5/8" jamb	17.000	L.F.	.725	121.55	35.53	157.08
Trim, stock pine, 11/16" x 2-1/2"	34.000	L.F.	1.133	49.64	55.42	105.06
Prime door & frame, oil, brushwork	2.000	Face	1.600	6.38	67	73.38
Paint door and frame, oil, 2 coats	2.000	Face	2.667	11.30	112	123.30
TOTAL		Ea.	7.356	405.87	330.45	736.32
BI-FOLD, PINE, LOUVERED, 6'-0" X 6'-8"						
Door, pine, louvered, 6'-0" x 6'-8" opening	1.000	Ea.	1.600	305	78.50	383.50
Frame, pine, 4-5/8" jamb	19.000	L.F.	.811	135.85	39.71	175.56
Trim, stock pine, 11/16" x 2-1/2"	38.000	L.F.	1.267	55.48	61.94	117.42
Prime door & frame, oil, brushwork	2.500	Face	2.000	7.98	83.75	91.73
Paint door and frame, oil, 2 coats	2.500	Face	3.333	14.13	140	154.13
TOTAL		Ea.	9.011	518.44	403.90	922.34

The costs in this system are based on a cost per each door.

Description	QUAN.	UNIT	LABOR HOURS	COST EACH		
				MAT.	INST.	TOTAL

Closet Door Price Sheet	QUAN.	UNIT	LABOR HOURS	COST EACH		
				MAT.	INST.	TOTAL
Doors, bi-passing, pine, louvered, 4'-0" x 6'-8" opening	1.000	Ea.	1.333	440	65.50	505.50
6'-0" x 6'-8" opening	1.000	Ea.	1.600	570	78.50	648.50
Paneled, 4'-0" x 6'-8" opening	1.000	Ea.	1.333	550	65.50	615.50
6'-0" x 6'-8" opening	1.000	Ea.	1.600	655	78.50	733.50
Flush, birch, hollow core, 4'-0" x 6'-8" opening	1.000	Ea.	1.333	239	65.50	304.50
6'-0" x 6'-8" opening	1.000	Ea.	1.600	279	78.50	357.50
Flush, lauan, hollow core, 4'-0" x 6'-8" opening	1.000	Ea.	1.333	185	65.50	250.50
6'-0" x 6'-8" opening	1.000	Ea.	1.600	218	78.50	296.50
Bi-fold, pine, louvered, 3'-0" x 6'-8" opening	1.000	Ea.	1.231	217	60.50	277.50
6'-0" x 6'-8" opening	1.000	Ea.	1.600	305	78.50	383.50
Paneled, 3'-0" x 6'-8" opening	1.000	Ea.	1.231	217	60.50	277.50
6'-0" x 6'-8" opening	1.000	Ea.	1.600	305	78.50	383.50
Flush, birch, hollow core, 3'-0" x 6'-8" opening	1.000	Ea.	1.231	60	60.50	120.50
6'-0" x 6'-8" opening	1.000	Ea.	1.600	139	78.50	217.50
Flush, lauan, hollow core, 3'-0" x 6'8" opening	1.000	Ea.	1.231	300	60.50	360.50
6'-0" x 6'-8" opening	1.000	Ea.	1.600	440	78.50	518.50
Frame pine, 3'-0" door, 3-5/8" deep	17.000	L.F.	.725	104	35.50	139.50
4-5/8" deep	17.000	L.F.	.725	122	35.50	157.50
5-5/8" deep	17.000	L.F.	.725	80	35.50	115.50
4'-0" door, 3-5/8" deep	18.000	L.F.	.768	110	37.50	147.50
4-5/8" deep	18.000	L.F.	.768	129	37.50	166.50
5-5/8" deep	18.000	L.F.	.768	85	37.50	122.50
6'-0" door, 3-5/8" deep	19.000	L.F.	.811	116	39.50	155.50
4-5/8" deep	19.000	L.F.	.811	136	39.50	175.50
5-5/8" deep	19.000	L.F.	.811	89.50	39.50	129
Trim both sides, painted 3'-0" x 6'-8" door	34.000	L.F.	1.971	53	91	144
4'-0" x 6'-8" door	36.000	L.F.	2.086	56	96	152
6'-0" x 6'-8" door	38.000	L.F.	2.203	59.50	101	160.50
Paint 2 sides, primer & 2 cts., flush door & frame, 3' x 6'-8" opng	2.000	Face	2.914	13.25	134	147.25
4'-0" x 6'-8" opening	2.000	Face	3.886	17.70	1/9	196.70
6'-0" x 6'-8" opening	2.000	Face	4.857	22	224	246
Paneled door & frame, 3'-0" x 6'-8" opening	2.000	Face	6.000	22.50	252	274.50
4'-0" x 6'-8" opening	2.000	Face	8.000	29.50	335	364.50
6'-0" x 6'-8" opening	2.000	Face	10.000	37	420	457
Louvered door & frame, 3'-0" x 6'-8" opening	2.000	Face	6.000	22.50	252	274.50
4'-0" x 6'-8" opening	2.000	Face	8.000	29.50	335	364.50
6'-0" x 6'-8" opening	2.000	Face	10.000	37	420	457

209

System Description	QUAN.	UNIT	LABOR HOURS	COST PER S.F.		
				MAT.	INST.	TOTAL
Carpet, direct glue-down, nylon, level loop, 26 oz.	1.000	S.F.	.018	3.27	.79	4.06
32 oz.	1.000	S.F.	.018	4.06	.79	4.85
40 oz.	1.000	S.F.	.018	6.05	.79	6.84
Nylon, plush, 20 oz.	1.000	S.F.	.018	2.11	.79	2.90
24 oz.	1.000	S.F.	.018	2.11	.79	2.90
30 oz.	1.000	S.F.	.018	3.12	.79	3.91
42 oz.	1.000	S.F.	.022	4.64	.95	5.59
48 oz.	1.000	S.F.	.022	5.45	.95	6.40
54 oz.	1.000	S.F.	.022	5.95	.95	6.90
Olefin, 15 oz.	1.000	S.F.	.018	1.10	.79	1.89
22 oz.	1.000	S.F.	.018	1.33	.79	2.12
Tile, foam backed, needle punch	1.000	S.F.	.014	4.32	.62	4.94
Tufted loop or shag	1.000	S.F.	.014	2.86	.62	3.48
Wool, 36 oz., level loop	1.000	S.F.	.018	14.20	.79	14.99
32 oz., patterned	1.000	S.F.	.020	14.05	.88	14.93
48 oz., patterned	1.000	S.F.	.020	14.40	.88	15.28
Padding, sponge rubber cushion, minimum	1.000	S.F.	.006	.49	.26	.75
Maximum	1.000	S.F.	.006	1.22	.26	1.48
Felt, 32 oz. to 56 oz., minimum	1.000	S.F.	.006	.51	.26	.77
Maximum	1.000	S.F.	.006	.86	.26	1.12
Bonded urethane, 3/8" thick, minimum	1.000	S.F.	.006	.56	.26	.82
Maximum	1.000	S.F.	.006	.95	.26	1.21
Prime urethane, 1/4" thick, minimum	1.000	S.F.	.006	.32	.26	.58
Maximum	1.000	S.F.	.006	.59	.26	.85
Stairs, for stairs, add to above carpet prices	1.000	Riser	.267		11.75	11.75
Underlayment plywood, 3/8" thick	1.000	S.F.	.011	.85	.52	1.37
1/2" thick	1.000	S.F.	.011	.88	.54	1.42
5/8" thick	1.000	S.F.	.011	1.29	.56	1.85
3/4" thick	1.000	S.F.	.012	1.35	.60	1.95
Particle board, 3/8" thick	1.000	S.F.	.011	.40	.52	.92
1/2" thick	1.000	S.F.	.011	.43	.54	.97
5/8" thick	1.000	S.F.	.011	.55	.56	1.11
3/4" thick	1.000	S.F.	.012	.72	.60	1.32
Hardboard, 4' x 4', 0.215" thick	1.000	S.F.	.011	.63	.52	1.15

System Description	QUAN.	UNIT	LABOR HOURS	COST PER S.F.		
				MAT.	INST.	TOTAL
Resilient flooring, asphalt tile on concrete, 1/8" thick						
Color group B	1.000	S.F.	.020	1.31	.88	2.19
Color group C & D	1.000	S.F.	.020	1.43	.88	2.31
Asphalt tile on wood subfloor, 1/8" thick						
Color group B	1.000	S.F.	.020	1.53	.88	2.41
Color group C & D	1.000	S.F.	.020	1.65	.88	2.53
Vinyl composition tile, 12" x 12", 1/16" thick	1.000	S.F.	.016	1.01	.71	1.72
Embossed	1.000	S.F.	.016	2.39	.71	3.10
Marbleized	1.000	S.F.	.016	2.39	.71	3.10
Plain	1.000	S.F.	.016	3.07	.71	3.78
.080" thick, embossed	1.000	S.F.	.016	1.52	.71	2.23
Marbleized	1.000	S.F.	.016	2.74	.71	3.45
Plain	1.000	S.F.	.016	2.54	.71	3.25
1/8" thick, marbleized	1.000	S.F.	.016	1.80	.71	2.51
Plain	1.000	S.F.	.016	1.98	.71	2.69
Vinyl tile, 12" x 12", .050" thick, minimum	1.000	S.F.	.016	3.30	.71	4.01
Maximum	1.000	S.F.	.016	6.60	.71	7.31
1/8" thick, minimum	1.000	S.F.	.016	4.79	.71	5.50
Maximum	1.000	S.F.	.016	5.45	.71	6.16
1/8" thick, solid colors	1.000	S.F.	.016	6.20	.71	6.91
Florentine pattern	1.000	S.F.	.016	6.60	.71	7.31
Marbleized or travertine pattern	1.000	S.F.	.016	13.95	.71	14.66
Vinyl sheet goods, backed, .070" thick, minimum	1.000	S.F.	.032	3.85	1.41	5.26
Maximum	1.000	S.F.	.040	3.97	1.76	5.73
.093" thick, minimum	1.000	S.F.	.035	3.96	1.53	5.49
Maximum	1.000	S.F.	.040	5.60	1.76	7.36
.125" thick, minimum	1.000	S.F.	.035	4.51	1.53	6.04
Maximum	1.000	S.F.	.040	6.70	1.76	8.46
Wood, oak, finished in place, 25/32" x 2-1/2" clear	1.000	S.F.	.074	3.50	3.28	6.78
Select	1.000	S.F.	.074	4.09	3.28	7.37
No. 1 common	1.000	S.F.	.074	5.05	3.28	8.33
Prefinished, oak, 2-1/2" wide	1.000	S.F.	.047	5.25	2.30	7.55
3-1/4" wide	1.000	S.F.	.043	6.75	2.12	8.87
Ranch plank, oak, random width	1.000	S.F.	.055	7.40	2.70	10.10
Parquet, 5/16" thick, finished in place, oak, minimum	1.000	S.F.	.077	5.70	3.43	9.13
Maximum	1.000	S.F.	.107	6.30	4.90	11.20
Teak, minimum	1.000	S.F.	.077	6.10	3.43	9.53
Maximum	1.000	S.F.	.107	10.05	4.90	14.95
Sleepers, treated, 16" O.C., 1" x 2"	1.000	S.F.	.007	.36	.33	.69
1" x 3"	1.000	S.F.	.008	.58	.39	.97
2" x 4"	1.000	S.F.	.011	.38	.52	.90
2" x 6"	1.000	S.F.	.012	.61	.60	1.21
Subfloor, plywood, 1/2" thick	1.000	S.F.	.011	.46	.52	.98
5/8" thick	1.000	S.F.	.012	.56	.58	1.14
3/4" thick	1.000	S.F.	.013	.64	.63	1.27
Ceramic tile, color group 2, 1" x 1"	1.000	S.F.	.087	5.20	3.46	8.66
2" x 2" or 2" x 1"	1.000	S.F.	.084	5.50	3.33	8.83
Color group 1, 8" x 8"		S.F.	.064	3.94	2.53	6.47
12" x 12"		S.F.	.049	4.92	1.95	6.87
16" x 16"		S.F.	.029	6.75	1.15	7.90

System Description	QUAN.	UNIT	LABOR HOURS	COST EACH		
				MAT.	INST.	TOTAL
7 RISERS, OAK TREADS, BOX STAIRS						
Treads, oak, 1-1/4" x 10" wide, 3' long	6.000	Ea.	2.667	495	132	627
Risers, 3/4" thick, beech	7.000	Ea.	2.625	145.95	128.10	274.05
30" primed pine balusters	12.000	Ea.	1.000	37.68	48.96	86.64
Newels, 3" wide	2.000	Ea.	2.286	92	112	204
Handrails, oak laminated	7.000	L.F.	.933	266	45.85	311.85
Stringers, 2" x 10", 3 each	21.000	L.F.	.306	5.67	14.91	20.58
TOTAL		Ea.	9.817	1,042.30	481.82	1,524.12
14 RISERS, OAK TREADS, BOX STAIRS						
Treads, oak, 1-1/4" x 10" wide, 3' long	13.000	Ea.	5.778	1,072.50	286	1,358.50
Risers, 3/4" thick, beech	14.000	Ea.	5.250	291.90	256.20	548.10
30" primed pine balusters	26.000	Ea.	2.167	81.64	106.08	187.72
Newels, 3" wide	2.000	Ea.	2.286	92	112	204
Handrails, oak, laminated	14.000	L.F.	1.867	532	91.70	623.70
Stringers, 2" x 10", 3 each	42.000	L.F.	5.169	33.60	252	285.60
TOTAL		Ea.	22.517	2,103.64	1,103.98	3,207.62
14 RISERS, PINE TREADS, BOX STAIRS						
Treads, pine, 9-1/2" x 3/4" thick	13.000	Ea.	5.778	188.50	286	474.50
Risers, 3/4" thick, pine	14.000	Ea.	5.091	143.22	249.90	393.12
30" primed pine balusters	26.000	Ea.	2.167	81.64	106.08	187.72
Newels, 3" wide	2.000	Ea.	2.286	92	112	204
Handrails, oak, laminated	14.000	L.F.	1.867	532	91.70	623.70
Stringers, 2" x 10", 3 each	42.000	L.F.	5.169	33.60	252	285.60
TOTAL		Ea.	22.358	1,070.96	1,097.68	2,168.64

Description	QUAN.	UNIT	LABOR HOURS	COST EACH		
				MAT.	INST.	TOTAL

Stairway Price Sheet	QUAN.	UNIT	LABOR HOURS	COST EACH		
				MAT.	INST.	TOTAL
Treads, oak, 1-1/16" x 9-1/2", 3' long, 7 riser stair	6.000	Ea.	2.667	495	132	627
14 riser stair	13.000	Ea.	5.778	1,075	286	1,361
1-1/16" x 11-1/2", 3' long, 7 riser stair	6.000	Ea.	2.667	535	132	667
14 riser stair	13.000	Ea.	5.778	1,150	286	1,436
Pine, 3/4" x 9-1/2", 3' long, 7 riser stair	6.000	Ea.	2.667	87	132	219
14 riser stair	13.000	Ea.	5.778	189	286	475
3/4" x 11-1/4", 3' long, 7 riser stair	6.000	Ea.	2.667	132	132	264
14 riser stair	13.000	Ea.	5.778	286	286	572
Risers, oak, 3/4" x 7-1/2" high, 7 riser stair	7.000	Ea.	2.625	125	128	253
14 riser stair	14.000	Ea.	5.250	250	256	506
Beech, 3/4" x 7-1/2" high, 7 riser stair	7.000	Ea.	2.625	146	128	274
14 riser stair	14.000	Ea.	5.250	292	256	548
Baluster, turned, 30" high, primed pine, 7 riser stair	12.000	Ea.	3.429	37.50	49	86.50
14 riser stair	26.000	Ea.	7.428	81.50	106	187.50
30" birch, 7 riser stair	12.000	Ea.	3.429	34.50	44.50	79
14 riser stair	26.000	Ea.	7.428	74	96.50	170.50
42" pine, 7 riser stair	12.000	Ea.	3.556	58.50	49	107.50
14 riser stair	26.000	Ea.	7.704	126	106	232
42" birch, 7 riser stair	12.000	Ea.	3.556	58.50	49	107.50
14 riser stair	26.000	Ea.	7.704	126	106	232
Newels, 3-1/4" wide, starting, 7 riser stair	2.000	Ea.	2.286	92	112	204
14 riser stair	2.000	Ea.	2.286	92	112	204
Landing, 7 riser stair	2.000	Ea.	3.200	250	157	407
14 riser stair	2.000	Ea.	3.200	250	157	407
Handrails, oak, laminated, 7 riser stair	7.000	L.F.	.933	266	46	312
14 riser stair	14.000	L.F.	1.867	530	91.50	621.50
Stringers, fir, 2" x 10" 7 riser stair	21.000	L.F.	2.585	16.80	126	142.80
14 riser stair	42.000	L.F.	5.169	33.50	252	285.50
2" x 12", 7 riser stair	21.000	L.F.	2.585	24.50	126	150.50
14 riser stair	42.000	L.F.	5.169	49	252	301

Special Stairways	QUAN.	UNIT	LABOR HOURS	COST EACH		
				MAT.	INST.	TOTAL
Basement stairs, open risers	1.000	Flight	4.000	785	196	981
Spiral stairs, oak, 4'-6" diameter, prefabricated, 9' high	1.000	Flight	10.667	3,975	520	4,495
Aluminum, 5'-0" diameter stock unit	1.000	Flight	9.956	7,700	650	8,350
Custom unit	1.000	Flight	9.956	14,700	650	15,350
Cast iron, 4'-0" diameter, minimum	1.000	Flight	9.956	6,850	650	7,500
Maximum	1.000	Flight	17.920	9,375	1,175	10,550
Steel, industrial, pre-erected, 3'-6" wide, bar rail	1.000	Flight	7.724	7,000	740	7,740
Picket rail	1.000	Flight	7.724	7,850	740	8,590

213

Division 7
Specialties

Soffit Drywall — Soffit Framing — Top Cabinets — Counter Top — Bottom Cabinets

System Description	QUAN.	UNIT	LABOR HOURS	COST PER L.F.		
				MAT.	INST.	TOTAL
KITCHEN, ECONOMY GRADE						
Top cabinets, economy grade	1.000	L.F.	.171	51.52	8.32	59.84
Bottom cabinets, economy grade	1.000	L.F.	.256	77.28	12.48	89.76
Square edge, plastic face countertop	1.000	L.F.	.267	29	13.05	42.05
Blocking, wood, 2" x 4"	1.000	L.F.	.032	.27	1.57	1.84
Soffit, framing, wood, 2" x 4"	4.000	L.F.	.071	1.08	3.48	4.56
Soffit drywall	2.000	S.F.	.047	.70	2.32	3.02
Drywall painting	2.000	S.F.	.013	.10	.66	.76
TOTAL		L.F.	.857	159.95	41.88	201.83
AVERAGE GRADE						
Top cabinets, average grade	1.000	L.F.	.213	64.40	10.40	74.80
Bottom cabinets, average grade	1.000	L.F.	.320	96.60	15.60	112.20
Solid surface countertop, solid color	1.000	L.F.	.800	66	39	105
Blocking, wood, 2" x 4"	1.000	L.F.	.032	.27	1.57	1.84
Soffit framing, wood, 2" x 4"	4.000	L.F.	.071	1.08	3.48	4.56
Soffit drywall	2.000	S.F.	.047	.70	2.32	3.02
Drywall painting	2.000	S.F.	.013	.10	.66	.76
TOTAL		L.F.	1.496	229.15	73.03	302.18
CUSTOM GRADE						
Top cabinets, custom grade	1.000	L.F.	.256	138	12.60	150.60
Bottom cabinets, custom grade	1.000	L.F.	.384	207	18.90	225.90
Solid surface countertop, premium patterned color	1.000	L.F.	1.067	115	52	167
Blocking, wood, 2" x 4"	1.000	L.F.	.032	.27	1.57	1.84
Soffit framing, wood, 2" x 4"	4.000	L.F.	.071	1.08	3.48	4.56
Soffit drywall	2.000	S.F.	.047	.70	2.32	3.02
Drywall painting	2.000	S.F.	.013	.10	.66	.76
TOTAL		L.F.	1.870	462.15	91.53	553.68

Description	QUAN.	UNIT	LABOR HOURS	COST PER L.F.		
				MAT.	INST.	TOTAL

Kitchen Price Sheet	QUAN.	UNIT	LABOR HOURS	COST PER L.F.		
				MAT.	INST.	TOTAL
Top cabinets, economy grade	1.000	L.F.	.171	51.50	8.30	59.80
Average grade	1.000	L.F.	.213	64.50	10.40	74.90
Custom grade	1.000	L.F.	.256	138	12.60	150.60
Bottom cabinets, economy grade	1.000	L.F.	.256	77.50	12.50	90
Average grade	1.000	L.F.	.320	96.50	15.60	112.10
Custom grade	1.000	L.F.	.384	207	18.90	225.90
Counter top, laminated plastic, 7/8" thick, no splash	1.000	L.F.	.267	23	13.05	36.05
With backsplash	1.000	L.F.	.267	30	13.05	43.05
1-1/4" thick, no splash	1.000	L.F.	.286	34	14	48
With backsplash	1.000	L.F.	.286	33	14	47
Post formed, laminated plastic	1.000	L.F.	.267	11.80	13.05	24.85
Ceramic tile, with backsplash		L.F.	.427	17.05	7.85	24.90
Marble, with backsplash, minimum	1.000	L.F.	.471	42	22.50	64.50
Maximum	1.000	L.F.	.615	105	29.50	134.50
Maple, solid laminated, no backsplash	1.000	L.F.	.286	68.50	14	82.50
With backsplash	1.000	L.F.	.286	81.50	14	95.50
Solid Surface, with backsplash, minimum		L.F.	.842	72.50	41	113.50
Maximum		L.F.	1.067	115	52	167
Blocking, wood, 2" x 4"	1.000	L.F.	.032	.27	1.57	1.84
2" x 6"	1.000	L.F.	.036	.41	1.76	2.17
2" x 8"	1.000	L.F.	.040	.61	1.96	2.57
Soffit framing, wood, 2" x 3"	4.000	L.F.	.064	1.16	3.12	4.28
2" x 4"	4.000	L.F.	.071	1.08	3.48	4.56
Soffit, drywall, painted	2.000	S.F.	.060	.80	2.98	3.78
Paneling, standard	2.000	S.F.	.064	1.96	3.14	5.10
Deluxe	2.000	S.F.	.091	4.34	4.48	8.82
Sinks, porcelain on cast iron, single bowl, 21" x 24"	1.000	Ea.	10.334	580	525	1,105
21" x 30"	1.000	Ea.	10.334	630	525	1,155
Double bowl, 20" x 32"	1.000	Ea.	10.810	725	550	1,275
Stainless steel, single bowl, 16" x 20"	1.000	Ea.	10.334	910	525	1,435
22" x 25"	1.000	Ea.	10.334	980	525	1,505
Double bowl, 20" x 32"	1.000	Ea.	10.810	525	550	1,075

217

Kitchen Price Sheet	QUAN.	UNIT	LABOR HOURS	COST PER L.F. MAT.	COST PER L.F. INST.	COST PER L.F. TOTAL
Range, free standing, minimum	1.000	Ea.	3.600	470	165	635
Maximum	1.000	Ea.	6.000	2,200	252	2,452
Built-in, minimum	1.000	Ea.	3.333	840	179	1,019
Maximum	1.000	Ea.	10.000	1,750	495	2,245
Counter top range, 4-burner, minimum	1.000	Ea.	3.333	420	179	599
Maximum	1.000	Ea.	4.667	750	250	1,000
Compactor, built-in, minimum	1.000	Ea.	2.215	605	112	717
Maximum	1.000	Ea.	3.282	930	164	1,094
Dishwasher, built-in, minimum	1.000	Ea.	6.735	465	375	840
Maximum	1.000	Ea.	9.235	580	515	1,095
Garbage disposer, minimum	1.000	Ea.	2.810	184	158	342
Maximum	1.000	Ea.	2.810	315	158	473
Microwave oven, minimum	1.000	Ea.	2.615	143	140	283
Maximum	1.000	Ea.	4.615	480	247	727
Range hood, ducted, minimum	1.000	Ea.	4.658	91.50	235	326.50
Maximum	1.000	Ea.	5.991	930	300	1,230
Ductless, minimum	1.000	Ea.	2.615	100	133	233
Maximum	1.000	Ea.	3.948	940	199	1,139
Refrigerator, 16 cu.ft., minimum	1.000	Ea.	2.000	615	72.50	687.50
Maximum	1.000	Ea.	3.200	980	116	1,096
16 cu.ft. with icemaker, minimum	1.000	Ea.	4.210	840	189	1,029
Maximum	1.000	Ea.	5.410	1,200	233	1,433
19 cu.ft., minimum	1.000	Ea.	2.667	495	96.50	591.50
Maximum	1.000	Ea.	4.667	865	169	1,034
19 cu.ft. with icemaker, minimum	1.000	Ea.	5.143	725	223	948
Maximum	1.000	Ea.	7.143	1,100	295	1,395
Sinks, porcelain on cast iron single bowl, 21" x 24"	1.000	Ea.	10.334	580	525	1,105
21" x 30"	1.000	Ea.	10.334	630	525	1,155
Double bowl, 20" x 32"	1.000	Ea.	10.810	725	550	1,275
Stainless steel, single bowl 16" x 20"	1.000	Ea.	10.334	910	525	1,435
22" x 25"	1.000	Ea.	10.334	980	525	1,505
Double bowl, 20" x 32"	1.000	Ea.	10.810	525	550	1,075
Water heater, electric, 30 gallon	1.000	Ea.	3.636	635	205	840
40 gallon	1.000	Ea.	4.000	675	225	900
Gas, 30 gallon	1.000	Ea.	4.000	985	225	1,210
75 gallon	1.000	Ea.	5.333	1,350	300	1,650
Wall, packaged terminal heater/air conditioner cabinet, wall sleeve, louver, electric heat, thermostat, manual changeover, 208V		Ea.				
6000 BTUH cooling, 8800 BTU heating	1.000	Ea.	2.667	750	135	885
9000 BTUH cooling, 13,900 BTU heating	1.000	Ea.	3.200	865	162	1,027
12,000 BTUH cooling, 13,900 BTU heating	1.000	Ea.	4.000	935	202	1,137
15,000 BTUH cooling, 13,900 BTU heating	1.000	Ea.	5.333	1,000	269	1,269

System Description	QUAN.	UNIT	LABOR HOURS	COST EACH		
				MAT.	INST.	TOTAL
Curtain rods, stainless, 1″ diameter, 3′ long	1.000	Ea.	.615	38	30	68
5′ long	1.000	Ea.	.615	38	30	68
Grab bar, 1″ diameter, 12″ long	1.000	Ea.	.283	28.50	13.85	42.35
36″ long	1.000	Ea.	.340	32.50	16.65	49.15
1-1/4″ diameter, 12″ long	1.000	Ea.	.333	33.50	16.30	49.80
36″ long	1.000	Ea.	.400	38	19.60	57.60
1-1/2″ diameter, 12″ long	1.000	Ea.	.383	38.50	18.75	57.25
36″ long	1.000	Ea.	.460	43.50	22.50	66
Mirror, 18″ x 24″	1.000	Ea.	.400	62.50	19.60	82.10
72″ x 24″	1.000	Ea.	1.333	231	65.50	296.50
Medicine chest with mirror, 18″ x 24″	1.000	Ea.	.400	208	19.60	227.60
36″ x 24″	1.000	Ea.	.600	310	29.50	339.50
Toilet tissue dispenser, surface mounted, minimum	1.000	Ea.	.267	19.15	13.05	32.20
Maximum	1.000	Ea.	.400	28.50	19.60	48.10
Flush mounted, minimum	1.000	Ea.	.293	21	14.35	35.35
Maximum	1.000	Ea.	.427	30.50	21	51.50
Towel bar, 18″ long, minimum	1.000	Ea.	.278	35	13.65	48.65
Maximum	1.000	Ea.	.348	43.50	17.05	60.55
24″ long, minimum	1.000	Ea.	.313	39	15.35	54.35
Maximum	1.000	Ea.	.383	48	18.75	66.75
36″ long, minimum	1.000	Ea.	.381	123	18.65	141.65
Maximum	1.000	Ea.	.419	135	20.50	155.50

Chimney

Damper

Foundation

Footing

Mantle

Facing Brick

Firebox

Hearth

Cleanout

System Description	QUAN.	UNIT	LABOR HOURS	COST EACH		
				MAT.	INST.	TOTAL
MASONRY FIREPLACE						
Footing, 8″ thick, concrete, 4′ x 7′	.700	C.Y.	2.800	115.50	129.64	245.14
Foundation, concrete block, 32″ x 60″ x 4′ deep	1.000	Ea.	5.275	172.20	234.60	406.80
Fireplace, brick firebox, 30″ x 29″ opening	1.000	Ea.	40.000	590	1,750	2,340
Damper, cast iron, 30″ opening	1.000	Ea.	1.333	97.50	64.50	162
Facing brick, standard size brick, 6′ x 5′	30.000	S.F.	5.217	119.10	232.50	351.60
Hearth, standard size brick, 3′ x 6′	1.000	Ea.	8.000	217	350	567
Chimney, standard size brick, 8″ x 12″ flue, one story house	12.000	V.L.F.	12.000	444	522	966
Mantle, 4″ x 8″, wood	6.000	L.F.	1.333	45.60	65.40	111
Cleanout, cast iron, 8″ x 8″	1.000	Ea.	.667	41	32	73
TOTAL		Ea.	76.625	1,841.90	3,380.64	5,222.54

The costs in this system are on a cost each basis.

Description	QUAN.	UNIT	LABOR HOURS	COST EACH		
				MAT.	INST.	TOTAL

Masonry Fireplace Price Sheet	QUAN.	UNIT	LABOR HOURS	COST EACH		
				MAT.	INST.	TOTAL
Footing 8" thick, 3' x 6'	.440	C.Y.	1.326	72.50	81.50	154
4' x 7'	.700	C.Y.	2.110	116	130	246
5' x 8'	1.000	C.Y.	3.014	165	185	350
1' thick, 3' x 6'	.670	C.Y.	2.020	111	124	235
4' x 7'	1.030	C.Y.	3.105	170	191	361
5' x 8'	1.480	C.Y.	4.461	244	274	518
Foundation-concrete block, 24" x 48", 4' deep	1.000	Ea.	4.267	138	188	326
8' deep	1.000	Ea.	8.533	276	375	651
24" x 60", 4' deep	1.000	Ea.	4.978	161	219	380
8' deep	1.000	Ea.	9.956	320	440	760
32" x 48", 4' deep	1.000	Ea.	4.711	152	207	359
8' deep	1.000	Ea.	9.422	305	415	720
32" x 60", 4' deep	1.000	Ea.	5.333	172	235	407
8' deep	1.000	Ea.	10.845	350	475	825
32" x 72", 4' deep	1.000	Ea.	6.133	198	270	468
8' deep	1.000	Ea.	12.267	395	540	935
Fireplace, brick firebox 30" x 29" opening	1.000	Ea.	40.000	590	1,750	2,340
48" x 30" opening	1.000	Ea.	60.000	885	2,625	3,510
Steel fire box with registers, 25" opening	1.000	Ea.	26.667	1,075	1,175	2,250
48" opening	1.000	Ea.	44.000	1,800	1,950	3,750
Damper, cast iron, 30" opening	1.000	Ea.	1.333	97.50	64.50	162
36" opening	1.000	Ea.	1.556	114	75.50	189.50
Steel, 30" opening	1.000	Ea.	1.333	87.50	64.50	152
36" opening	1.000	Ea.	1.556	102	75.50	177.50
Facing for fireplace, standard size brick, 6' x 5'	30.000	S.F.	5.217	119	233	352
7' x 5'	35.000	S.F.	6.087	139	271	410
8' x 6'	48.000	S.F.	8.348	191	370	561
Fieldstone, 6' x 5'	30.000	S.F.	5.217	585	233	818
7' x 5'	35.000	S.F.	6.087	680	271	951
8' x 6'	48.000	S.F.	8.348	935	370	1,305
Sheetrock on metal, studs, 6' x 5'	30.000	S.F.	.980	21.50	48	69.50
7' x 5'	35.000	S.F.	1.143	25	56	81
8' x 6'	48.000	S.F.	1.568	34.50	77	111.50
Hearth, standard size brick, 3' x 6'	1.000	Ea.	8.000	217	350	567
3' x 7'	1.000	Ea.	9.280	252	405	657
3' x 8'	1.000	Ea.	10.640	289	465	754
Stone, 3' x 6'	1.000	Ea.	8.000	234	350	584
3' x 7'	1.000	Ea.	9.280	272	405	677
3' x 8'	1.000	Ea.	10.640	310	465	775
Chimney, standard size brick, 8" x 12" flue, one story house	12.000	V.L.F.	12.000	445	520	965
Two story house	20.000	V.L.F.	20.000	740	870	1,610
Mantle wood, beams, 4" x 8"	6.000	L.F.	1.333	45.50	65.50	111
4" x 10"	6.000	L.F.	1.371	84.50	67	151.50
Ornate, prefabricated, 6' x 3'-6" opening, minimum	1.000	Ea.	1.600	251	78.50	329.50
Maximum	1.000	Ea.	1.600	455	78.50	533.50
Cleanout, door and frame, cast iron, 8" x 8"	1.000	Ea.	.667	41	32	73
12" x 12"	1.000	Ea.	.800	50	38.50	88.50

Chimney, Flue, Fittings & Framing

Framing

Mantle

Facing Brick

Prefabricated Fireplace

Hearth

System Description	QUAN.	UNIT	LABOR HOURS	COST EACH		
				MAT.	INST.	TOTAL
PREFABRICATED FIREPLACE						
Prefabricated fireplace, metal, minimum	1.000	Ea.	6.154	1,325	300	1,625
Framing, 2" x 4" studs, 6' x 5'	35.000	L.F.	.509	9.45	24.85	34.30
Fire resistant gypsum drywall, unfinished	40.000	S.F.	.320	12.40	15.60	28
Drywall finishing adder	40.000	S.F.	.320	2	15.60	17.60
Facing, brick, standard size brick, 6' x 5'	30.000	S.F.	5.217	119.10	232.50	351.60
Hearth, standard size brick, 3' x 6'	1.000	Ea.	8.000	217	350	567
Chimney, one story house, framing, 2" x 4" studs	80.000	L.F.	1.164	21.60	56.80	78.40
Sheathing, plywood, 5/8" thick	32.000	S.F.	.758	85.44	37.12	122.56
Flue, 10" metal, insulated pipe	12.000	V.L.F.	4.000	444	193.20	637.20
Fittings, ceiling support	1.000	Ea.	.667	165	32	197
Fittings, joist shield	1.000	Ea.	.667	94.50	32	126.50
Fittings, roof flashing	1.000	Ea.	.667	198	32	230
Mantle beam, wood, 4" x 8"	6.000	L.F.	1.333	45.60	65.40	111
TOTAL		Ea.	29.776	2,739.09	1,387.07	4,126.16

The costs in this system are on a cost each basis.

Description	QUAN.	UNIT	LABOR HOURS	COST EACH		
				MAT.	INST.	TOTAL

Prefabricated Fireplace Price Sheet	QUAN.	UNIT	LABOR HOURS	COST EACH		
				MAT.	INST.	TOTAL
Prefabricated fireplace, minimum	1.000	Ea.	6.154	1,325	300	1,625
Average	1.000	Ea.	8.000	1,850	390	2,240
Maximum	1.000	Ea.	8.889	3,700	435	4,135
Framing, 2″ x 4″ studs, fireplace, 6′ x 5′	35.000	L.F.	.509	9.45	25	34.45
7′ x 5′	40.000	L.F.	.582	10.80	28.50	39.30
8′ x 6′	45.000	L.F.	.655	12.15	32	44.15
Sheetrock, 1/2″ thick, fireplace, 6′ x 5′	40.000	S.F.	.640	14.40	31	45.40
7′ x 5′	45.000	S.F.	.720	16.20	35	51.20
8′ x 6′	50.000	S.F.	.800	18	39	57
Facing for fireplace, brick, 6′ x 5′	30.000	S.F.	5.217	119	233	352
7′ x 5′	35.000	S.F.	6.087	139	271	410
8′ x 6′	48.000	S.F.	8.348	191	370	561
Fieldstone, 6′ x 5′	30.000	S.F.	5.217	630	233	863
7′ x 5′	35.000	S.F.	6.087	735	271	1,006
8′ x 6′	48.000	S.F.	8.348	1,000	370	1,370
Hearth, standard size brick, 3′ x 6′	1.000	Ea.	8.000	217	350	567
3′ x 7′	1.000	Ea.	9.280	252	405	657
3′ x 8′	1.000	Ea.	10.640	289	465	754
Stone, 3′ x 6′	1.000	Ea.	8.000	234	350	584
3′ x 7′	1.000	Ea.	9.280	272	405	677
3′ x 8′	1.000	Ea.	10.640	310	465	775
Chimney, framing, 2″ x 4″, one story house	80.000	L.F.	1.164	21.50	57	78.50
Two story house	120.000	L.F.	1.746	32.50	85	117.50
Sheathing, plywood, 5/8″ thick	32.000	S.F.	.758	85.50	37	122.50
Stucco on plywood	32.000	S.F.	1.125	46	53	99
Flue, 10″ metal pipe, insulated, one story house	12.000	V.L.F.	4.000	445	193	638
Two story house	20.000	V.L.F.	6.667	740	320	1,060
Fittings, ceiling support	1.000	Ea.	.667	165	32	197
Fittings joist sheild, one story house	1.000	Ea.	.667	94.50	32	126.50
Two story house	2.000	Ea.	1.333	189	64	253
Fittings roof flashing	1.000	Ea.	.667	198	32	230
Mantle, wood beam, 4″ x 8″	6.000	L.F.	1.333	45.50	65.50	111
4″ x 10″	6.000	L.F.	1.371	84.50	67	151.50
Ornate prefabricated, 6′ x 3′-6″ opening, minimum	1.000	Ea.	1.600	251	78.50	329.50
Maximum	1.000	Ea.	1.600	455	78.50	533.50

System Description	QUAN.	UNIT	LABOR HOURS	COST EACH		
				MAT.	INST.	TOTAL
Economy, lean to, shell only, not including 2' stub wall, fndtn, flrs, heat						
4' x 16'	1.000	Ea.	26.212	2,050	1,275	3,325
4' x 24'	1.000	Ea.	30.259	2,375	1,475	3,850
6' x 10'	1.000	Ea.	16.552	2,525	810	3,335
6' x 16'	1.000	Ea.	23.034	3,500	1,125	4,625
6' x 24'	1.000	Ea.	29.793	4,525	1,450	5,975
8' x 10'	1.000	Ea.	22.069	3,350	1,075	4,425
8' x 16'	1.000	Ea.	38.400	5,850	1,875	7,725
8' x 24'	1.000	Ea.	49.655	7,550	2,425	9,975
Free standing, 8' x 8'	1.000	Ea.	17.356	2,650	850	3,500
8' x 16'	1.000	Ea.	30.211	4,625	1,475	6,100
8' x 24'	1.000	Ea.	39.051	5,975	1,900	7,875
10' x 10'	1.000	Ea.	18.824	2,950	920	3,870
10' x 16'	1.000	Ea.	24.095	3,775	1,175	4,950
10' x 24'	1.000	Ea.	31.624	4,950	1,550	6,500
14' x 10'	1.000	Ea.	20.741	3,575	1,025	4,600
14' x 16'	1.000	Ea.	24.889	4,275	1,225	5,500
14' x 24'	1.000	Ea.	33.349	5,750	1,625	7,375
Standard, lean to, shell only, not incl. 2' stub wall, fndtn, flrs, heat 4'x10'	1.000	Ea.	28.235	2,225	1,375	3,600
4' x 16'	1.000	Ea.	39.341	3,100	1,925	5,025
4' x 24'	1.000	Ea.	45.412	3,575	2,225	5,800
6' x 10'	1.000	Ea.	24.827	3,775	1,225	5,000
6' x 16'	1.000	Ea.	34.538	5,250	1,700	6,950
6' x 24'	1.000	Ea.	44.689	6,800	2,175	8,975
8' x 10'	1.000	Ea.	33.103	5,050	1,625	6,675
8' x 16'	1.000	Ea.	57.600	8,775	2,825	11,600
8' x 24'	1.000	Ea.	74.482	11,300	3,650	14,950
Free standing, 8' x 8'	1.000	Ea.	26.034	3,975	1,275	5,250
8' x 16'	1.000	Ea.	45.316	6,925	2,225	9,150
8' x 24'	1.000	Ea.	58.577	8,975	2,850	11,825
10' x 10'	1.000	Ea.	28.236	4,425	1,375	5,800
10' x 16'	1.000	Ea.	36.142	5,675	1,775	7,450
10' x 24'	1.000	Ea.	47.436	7,425	2,325	9,750
14' x 10'	1.000	Ea.	31.112	5,350	1,525	6,875
14' x 16'	1.000	Ea.	37.334	6,425	1,825	8,250
14' x 24'	1.000	Ea.	50.030	8,600	2,450	11,050
Deluxe, lean to, shell only, not incl. 2' stub wall, fndtn, flrs or heat, 4'x10'	1.000	Ea.	20.645	3,400	1,025	4,425
4' x 16'	1.000	Ea.	33.032	5,450	1,625	7,075
4' x 24'	1.000	Ea.	49.548	8,150	2,450	10,600
6' x 10'	1.000	Ea.	30.968	5,100	1,525	6,625
6' x 16'	1.000	Ea.	49.548	8,150	2,450	10,600
6' x 24'	1.000	Ea.	74.323	12,200	3,675	15,875
8' x 10'	1.000	Ea.	41.290	6,800	2,050	8,850
8' x 16'	1.000	Ea.	66.065	10,900	3,275	14,175
8' x 24'	1.000	Ea.	99.097	16,300	4,900	21,200
Freestanding, 8' x 8'	1.000	Ea.	18.618	5,600	910	6,510
8' x 16'	1.000	Ea.	37.236	11,200	1,825	13,025
8' x 24'	1.000	Ea.	55.855	16,800	2,725	19,525
10' x 10'	1.000	Ea.	29.091	8,750	1,425	10,175
10' x 16'	1.000	Ea.	46.546	14,000	2,275	16,275
10' x 24'	1.000	Ea.	69.818	21,000	3,425	24,425
14' x 10'	1.000	Ea.	40.727	12,300	2,000	14,300
14' x 16'	1.000	Ea.	65.164	19,600	3,200	22,800
14' x 24'	1.000	Ea.	97.746	29,400	4,800	34,200

System Description	QUAN.	UNIT	LABOR HOURS	COST EACH		
				MAT.	INST.	TOTAL
Swimming pools, vinyl lined, metal sides, sand bottom, 12' x 28'	1.000	Ea.	50.177	4,100	2,575	6,675
12' x 32'	1.000	Ea.	55.366	4,525	2,825	7,350
12' x 36'	1.000	Ea.	60.061	4,900	3,075	7,975
16' x 32'	1.000	Ea.	66.798	5,450	3,425	8,875
16' x 36'	1.000	Ea.	71.190	5,825	3,650	9,475
16' x 40'	1.000	Ea.	74.703	6,100	3,850	9,950
20' x 36'	1.000	Ea.	77.860	6,350	4,000	10,350
20' x 40'	1.000	Ea.	82.135	6,700	4,225	10,925
20' x 44'	1.000	Ea.	90.348	7,375	4,625	12,000
24' x 40'	1.000	Ea.	98.562	8,050	5,075	13,125
24' x 44'	1.000	Ea.	108.418	8,850	5,575	14,425
24' x 48'	1.000	Ea.	118.274	9,650	6,075	15,725
Vinyl lined, concrete sides, 12' x 28'	1.000	Ea.	79.447	6,500	4,075	10,575
12' x 32'	1.000	Ea.	88.818	7,250	4,575	11,825
12' x 36'	1.000	Ea.	97.656	7,975	5,000	12,975
16' x 32'	1.000	Ea.	111.393	9,100	5,700	14,800
16' x 36'	1.000	Ea.	121.354	9,925	6,225	16,150
16' x 40'	1.000	Ea.	130.445	10,700	6,675	17,375
28' x 36'	1.000	Ea.	140.585	11,500	7,225	18,725
20' x 40'	1.000	Ea.	149.336	12,200	7,650	19,850
20' x 44'	1.000	Ea.	164.270	13,400	8,450	21,850
24' x 40'	1.000	Ea.	179.203	14,600	9,200	23,800
24' x 44'	1.000	Ea.	197.124	16,100	10,100	26,200
24' x 48'	1.000	Ea.	215.044	17,600	11,000	28,600
Gunite, bottom and sides, 12' x 28'	1.000	Ea.	129.767	9,575	6,650	16,225
12' x 32'	1.000	Ea.	142.164	10,500	7,275	17,775
12' x 36'	1.000	Ea.	153.028	11,300	7,850	19,150
16' x 32'	1.000	Ea.	167.743	12,400	8,600	21,000
16' x 36'	1.000	Ea.	176.421	13,000	9,050	22,050
16' x 40'	1.000	Ea.	182.368	13,500	9,350	22,850
20' x 36'	1.000	Ea.	187.949	13,900	9,650	23,550
20' x 40'	1.000	Ea.	179.200	18,400	9,175	27,575
20' x 44'	1.000	Ea.	197.120	20,200	10,100	30,300
24' x 40'	1.000	Ea.	215.040	22,100	11,000	33,100
24' x 44'	1.000	Ea.	273.244	20,200	14,000	34,200
24' x 48'	1.000	Ea.	298.077	22,000	15,300	37,300

System Description	QUAN.	UNIT	LABOR HOURS	COST PER S.F.		
				MAT.	INST.	TOTAL
8′ X 12′ DECK, PRESSURE TREATED LUMBER, JOISTS 16″ O.C.						
Decking, 2″ x 6″ lumber	2.080	L.F.	.027	.85	1.31	2.16
Lumber preservative	2.080	L.F.		.35		.35
Joists, 2″ x 8″, 16″ O.C.	1.000	L.F.	.015	.61	.71	1.32
Lumber preservative	1.000	L.F.		.23		.23
Girder, 2″ x 10″	.125	L.F.	.002	.10	.11	.21
Lumber preservative	.125	L.F.		.04		.04
Hand excavation for footings	.250	L.F.	.006		.22	.22
Concrete footings	.250	L.F.	.008	.33	.37	.70
4″ x 4″ Posts	.250	L.F.	.010	.43	.50	.93
Lumber preservative	.250	L.F.		.06		.06
Framing, pressure treated wood stairs, 3′ wide, 8 closed risers	1.000	Set	.080	1.51	3.90	5.41
Railings, 2″ x 4″	1.000	L.F.	.026	.27	1.26	1.53
Lumber preservative	1.000	L.F.		.11		.11
TOTAL		S.F.	.174	4.89	8.38	13.27
12′ X 16′ DECK, PRESSURE TREATED LUMBER, JOISTS 24″ O.C.						
Decking, 2″ x 6″	2.080	L.F.	.027	.85	1.31	2.16
Lumber preservative	2.080	L.F.		.35		.35
Joists, 2″ x 10″, 24″ O.C.	.800	L.F.	.014	.64	.70	1.34
Lumber preservative	.800	L.F.		.23		.23
Girder, 2″ x 10″	.083	L.F.	.001	.07	.07	.14
Lumber preservative	.083	L.F.		.02		.02
Hand excavation for footings	.122	L.F.	.006		.22	.22
Concrete footings	.122	L.F.	.008	.33	.37	.70
4″ x 4″ Posts	.122	L.F.	.005	.21	.25	.46
Lumber preservative	.122	L.F.		.03		.03
Framing, pressure treated wood stairs, 3′ wide, 8 closed risers	1.000	Set	.040	.76	1.95	2.71
Railings, 2″ x 4″	.670	L.F.	.017	.18	.84	1.02
Lumber preservative	.670	L.F.		.07		.07
TOTAL		S.F.	.118	3.74	5.71	9.45
12′ X 24′ DECK, REDWOOD OR CEDAR, JOISTS 16″ O.C.						
Decking, 2″ x 6″ redwood	2.080	L.F.	.027	7.78	1.31	9.09
Joists, 2″ x 10″, 16″ O.C.	1.000	L.F.	.018	8.30	.87	9.17
Girder, 2″ x 10″	.083	L.F.	.001	.69	.07	.76
Hand excavation for footings	.111	L.F.	.006		.22	.22
Concrete footings	.111	L.F.	.008	.33	.37	.70
Lumber preservative	.111	L.F.		.03		.03
Post, 4″ x 4″, including concrete footing	.111	L.F.	.009	7.33	.44	7.77
Framing, redwood or cedar stairs, 3′ wide, 8 closed risers	1.000	Set	.028	1.37	1.37	2.74
Railings, 2″ x 4″	.540	L.F.	.005	1.35	.23	1.58
TOTAL		S.F.	.102	27.18	4.88	32.06

The costs in this system are on a square foot basis.

Wood Deck Price Sheet	QUAN.	UNIT	LABOR HOURS	COST PER S.F.		
				MAT.	INST.	TOTAL
Decking, treated lumber, 1" x 4"	3.430	L.F.	.031	2.84	1.54	4.38
1" x 6"	2.180	L.F.	.033	2.98	1.62	4.60
2" x 4"	3.200	L.F.	.041	1.23	2.02	3.25
2" x 6"	2.080	L.F.	.027	1.20	1.31	2.51
Redwood or cedar,, 1" x 4"	3.430	L.F.	.035	3.31	1.69	5
1" x 6"	2.180	L.F.	.036	3.46	1.77	5.23
2" x 4"	3.200	L.F.	.028	8.25	1.39	9.64
2" x 6"	2.080	L.F.	.027	7.80	1.31	9.11
Joists for deck, treated lumber, 2" x 8", 16" O.C.	1.000	L.F.	.015	.84	.71	1.55
24" O.C.	.800	L.F.	.012	.67	.57	1.24
2" x 10", 16" O.C.	1.000	L.F.	.018	1.08	.87	1.95
24" O.C.	.800	L.F.	.014	.87	.70	1.57
Redwood or cedar, 2" x 8", 16" O.C.	1.000	L.F.	.015	4.98	.71	5.69
24" O.C.	.800	L.F.	.012	3.98	.57	4.55
2" x 10", 16" O.C.	1.000	L.F.	.018	8.30	.87	9.17
24" O.C.	.800	L.F.	.014	6.65	.70	7.35
Girder for joists, treated lumber, 2" x 10", 8' x 12' deck	.125	L.F.	.002	.14	.11	.25
12' x 16' deck	.083	L.F.	.001	.09	.07	.16
12' x 24' deck	.083	L.F.	.001	.09	.07	.16
Redwood or cedar, 2" x 10", 8' x 12' deck	.125	L.F.	.002	1.04	.11	1.15
12' x 16' deck	.083	L.F.	.001	.69	.07	.76
12' x 24' deck	.083	L.F.	.001	.69	.07	.76
Posts, 4" x 4", including concrete footing, 8' x 12' deck	.250	S.F.	.022	.82	1.09	1.91
12' x 16' deck	.122	L.F.	.017	.57	.84	1.41
12' x 24' deck	.111	L.F.	.017	.55	.81	1.36
Stairs 2" x 10" stringers, treated lumber, 8' x 12' deck	1.000	Set	.020	1.51	3.90	5.41
12' x 16' deck	1.000	Set	.012	.76	1.95	2.71
12' x 24' deck	1.000	Set	.008	.53	1.37	1.90
Redwood or cedar, 8' x 12' deck	1.000	Set	.040	3.90	3.90	7.80
12' x 16' deck	1.000	Set	.020	1.95	1.95	3.90
12' x 24' deck	1.000	Set	.012	1.37	1.37	2.74
Railings 2" x 4", treated lumber, 8' x 12' deck	1.000	L.F.	.026	.38	1.26	1.64
12' x 16' deck	.670	L.F.	.017	.25	.84	1.09
12' x 24' deck	.540	L.F.	.014	.21	.68	.89
Redwood or cedar, 8' x 12' deck	1.000	L.F.	.009	2.51	.42	2.93
12' x 16' deck	.670	L.F.	.006	1.65	.28	1.93
12' x 24' deck	.540	L.F.	.005	1.35	.23	1.58

Division 8
Mechanical

System Description	QUAN.	UNIT	LABOR HOURS	COST EACH		
				MAT.	INST.	TOTAL
LAVATORY INSTALLED WITH VANITY, PLUMBING IN 2 WALLS						
Water closet, floor mounted, 2 piece, close coupled, white	1.000	Ea.	3.019	284	153	437
Rough-in, vent, 2" diameter DWV piping	1.000	Ea.	.955	32.40	48.40	80.80
Waste, 4" diameter DWV piping	1.000	Ea.	.828	43.65	42	85.65
Supply, 1/2" diameter type "L" copper supply piping	1.000	Ea.	.593	16.44	33.30	49.74
Lavatory, 20" x 18", P.E. cast iron white	1.000	Ea.	2.500	286	127	413
Rough-in, vent, 1-1/2" diameter DWV piping	1.000	Ea.	.901	31	45.60	76.60
Waste, 2" diameter DWV piping	1.000	Ea.	.955	32.40	48.40	80.80
Supply, 1/2" diameter type "L" copper supply piping	1.000	Ea.	.988	27.40	55.50	82.90
Piping, supply, 1/2" diameter type "L" copper supply piping	10.000	L.F.	.988	27.40	55.50	82.90
Waste, 4" diameter DWV piping	7.000	L.F.	1.931	101.85	98	199.85
Vent, 2" diameter DWV piping	12.000	L.F.	2.866	97.20	145.20	242.40
Vanity base cabinet, 2 door, 30" wide	1.000	Ea.	1.000	288	49	337
Vanity top, plastic & laminated, square edge	2.670	L.F.	.712	97.46	34.84	132.30
TOTAL		Ea.	18.236	1,365.20	935.74	2,300.94
LAVATORY WITH WALL-HUNG LAVATORY, PLUMBING IN 2 WALLS						
Water closet, floor mounted, 2 piece close coupled, white	1.000	Ea.	3.019	284	153	437
Rough-in, vent, 2" diameter DWV piping	1.000	Ea.	.955	32.40	48.40	80.80
Waste, 4" diameter DWV piping	1.000	Ea.	.828	43.65	42	85.65
Supply, 1/2" diameter type "L" copper supply piping	1.000	Ea.	.593	16.44	33.30	49.74
Lavatory, 20" x 18", P.E. cast iron, wall hung, white	1.000	Ea.	2.000	390	101	491
Rough-in, vent, 1-1/2" diameter DWV piping	1.000	Ea.	.901	31	45.60	76.60
Waste, 2" diameter DWV piping	1.000	Ea.	.955	32.40	48.40	80.80
Supply, 1/2" diameter type "L" copper supply piping	1.000	Ea.	.988	27.40	55.50	82.90
Piping, supply, 1/2" diameter type "L" copper supply piping	10.000	L.F.	.988	27.40	55.50	82.90
Waste, 4" diameter DWV piping	7.000	L.F.	1.931	101.85	98	199.85
Vent, 2" diameter DWV piping	12.000	L.F.	2.866	97.20	145.20	242.40
Carrier, steel for studs, no arms	1.000	Ea.	1.143	78	64.50	142.50
TOTAL		Ea.	17.167	1,161.74	890.40	2,052.14

Description	QUAN.	UNIT	LABOR HOURS	COST EACH		
				MAT.	INST.	TOTAL

Two Fixture Lavatory Price Sheet	QUAN.	UNIT	LABOR HOURS	COST EACH		
				MAT.	INST.	TOTAL
Water closet, close coupled standard 2 piece, white	1.000	Ea.	3.019	284	153	437
Color	1.000	Ea.	3.019	380	153	533
One piece elongated bowl, white	1.000	Ea.	3.019	590	153	743
Color	1.000	Ea.	3.019	850	153	1,003
Low profile, one piece elongated bowl, white	1.000	Ea.	3.019	1,025	153	1,178
Color	1.000	Ea.	3.019	1,350	153	1,503
Rough-in for water closet						
1/2" copper supply, 4" cast iron waste, 2" cast iron vent	1.000	Ea.	2.376	92.50	124	216.50
4" PVC waste, 2" PVC vent	1.000	Ea.	2.678	47.50	139	186.50
4" copper waste , 2" copper vent	1.000	Ea.	2.520	210	136	346
3" cast iron waste, 1-1/2" cast iron vent	1.000	Ea.	2.244	81	117	198
3" PVC waste, 1-1/2" PVC vent	1.000	Ea.	2.388	40	129	169
3" copper waste, 1-1/2" copper vent	1.000	Ea.	2.524	198	131	329
1/2" PVC supply, 4" PVC waste, 2" PVC vent	1.000	Ea.	2.974	52.50	156	208.50
3" PVC waste, 1-1/2" PVC vent	1.000	Ea.	2.684	45.50	146	191.50
1/2" steel supply, 4" cast iron waste, 2" cast iron vent	1.000	Ea.	2.545	110	133	243
4" cast iron waste, 2" steel vent	1.000	Ea.	2.590	154	136	290
4" PVC waste, 2" PVC vent	1.000	Ea.	2.847	65	149	214
Lavatory, vanity top mounted, P.E. on cast iron 20" x 18" white	1.000	Ea.	2.500	286	127	413
Color	1.000	Ea.	2.500	286	127	413
Steel, enameled 10" x 17" white	1.000	Ea.	2.759	203	140	343
Color	1.000	Ea.	2.500	211	127	338
Vitreous china 20" x 16", white	1.000	Ea.	2.963	305	150	455
Color	1.000	Ea.	2.963	305	150	455
Wall hung, P.E. on cast iron, 20" x 18", white	1.000	Ea.	2.000	390	101	491
Color	1.000	Ea.	2.000	385	101	486
Vitreous china 19" x 17", white	1.000	Ea.	2.286	217	116	333
Color	1.000	Ea.	2.286	241	116	357
Rough-in supply waste and vent for lavatory						
1/2" copper supply, 2" cast iron waste, 1-1/2" cast iron vent	1.000	Ea.	2.844	91	150	241
2" PVC waste, 1-1/2" PVC vent	1.000	Ea.	2.962	47	161	208
2" copper waste, 1-1/2" copper vent	1.000	Ea.	2.308	123	130	253
1-1/2" PVC waste, 1-1/4" PVC vent	1.000	Ea.	2.639	45	148	193
1-1/2" copper waste, 1-1/4" copper vent	1.000	Ea.	2.114	111	119	230
1/2" PVC supply, 2" PVC waste, 1-1/2" PVC vent	1.000	Ea.	3.456	55.50	189	244.50
1-1/2" PVC waste, 1-1/4" PVC vent	1.000	Ea.	3.133	53.50	176	229.50
1/2" steel supply, 2" cast iron waste, 1-1/2" cast iron vent	1.000	Ea.	3.126	120	166	286
2" cast iron waste, 2" steel vent	1.000	Ea.	3.225	165	171	336
2" PVC waste, 1-1/2" PVC vent	1.000	Ea.	3.244	76	177	253
1-1/2" PVC waste, 1-1/4" PVC vent	1.000	Ea.	2.921	74	164	238
Piping, supply, 1/2" copper, type "L"	10.000	L.F.	.988	27.50	55.50	83
1/2" steel	10.000	L.F.	1.270	56.50	71.50	128
1/2" PVC	10.000	L.F.	1.482	36	83.50	119.50
Waste, 4" cast iron	7.000	L.F.	1.931	102	98	200
4" copper	7.000	L.F.	2.800	320	144	464
4" PVC	7.000	L.F.	2.333	47.50	118	165.50
Vent, 2" cast iron	12.000	L.F.	2.866	97	145	242
2" copper	12.000	L.F.	2.182	166	123	289
2" PVC	12.000	L.F.	3.254	32	165	197
2" steel	12.000	Ea.	3.000	228	152	380
Vanity base cabinet, 2 door, 24" x 30"	1.000	Ea.	1.000	288	49	337
24" x 36"	1.000	Ea.	1.200	385	59	444
Vanity top, laminated plastic, square edge 25" x 32"	2.670	L.F.	.712	97.50	35	132.50
25" x 38"	3.170	L.F.	.845	116	41.50	157.50
Post formed, laminated plastic, 25" x 32"	2.670	L.F.	.712	31.50	35	66.50
25" x 38"	3.170	L.F.	.845	37.50	41.50	79
Cultured marble, 25" x 32" with bowl	1.000	Ea.	2.500	262	127	389
25" x 38" with bowl	1.000	Ea.	2.500	283	127	410
Carrier for lavatory, steel for studs	1.000	Ea.	1.143	78	64.50	142.50
Wood 2" x 8" blocking	1.330	L.F.	.053	.81	2.61	3.42

System Description	QUAN.	UNIT	LABOR HOURS	COST EACH		
				MAT.	INST.	TOTAL
BATHROOM INSTALLED WITH VANITY						
Water closet, floor mounted, 2 piece, close coupled, white	1.000	Ea.	3.019	284	153	437
Rough-in, waste, 4" diameter DWV piping	1.000	Ea.	.828	43.65	42	85.65
Vent, 2" diameter DWV piping	1.000	Ea.	.955	32.40	48.40	80.80
Supply, 1/2" diameter type "L" copper supply piping	1.000	Ea.	.593	16.44	33.30	49.74
Lavatory, 20" x 18", P.E. cast iron with accessories, white	1.000	Ea.	2.500	286	127	413
Rough-in, supply, 1/2" diameter type "L" copper supply piping	1.000	Ea.	.988	27.40	55.50	82.90
Waste, 1-1/2" diameter DWV piping	1.000	Ea.	1.803	62	91.20	153.20
Bathtub, P.E. cast iron, 5' long with accessories, white	1.000	Ea.	3.636	1,050	184	1,234
Rough-in, waste, 4" diameter DWV piping	1.000	Ea.	.828	43.65	42	85.65
Vent, 1-1/2" diameter DWV piping	1.000	Ea.	.593	40.80	33.40	74.20
Supply, 1/2" diameter type "L" copper supply piping	1.000	Ea.	.988	27.40	55.50	82.90
Piping, supply, 1/2" diameter type "L" copper supply piping	20.000	L.F.	1.975	54.80	111	165.80
Waste, 4" diameter DWV piping	9.000	L.F.	2.483	130.95	126	256.95
Vent, 2" diameter DWV piping	6.000	L.F.	1.500	114	75.90	189.90
Vanity base cabinet, 2 door, 30" wide	1.000	Ea.	1.000	288	49	337
Vanity top, plastic laminated square edge	2.670	L.F.	.712	77.43	34.84	112.27
TOTAL		Ea.	24.401	2,578.92	1,262.04	3,840.96
BATHROOM WITH WALL HUNG LAVATORY						
Water closet, floor mounted, 2 piece, close coupled, white	1.000	Ea.	3.019	284	153	437
Rough-in, vent, 2" diameter DWV piping	1.000	Ea.	.955	32.40	48.40	80.80
Waste, 4" diameter DWV piping	1.000	Ea.	.828	43.65	42	85.65
Supply, 1/2" diameter type "L" copper supply piping	1.000	Ea.	.593	16.44	33.30	49.74
Lavatory, 20" x 18" P.E. cast iron, wall hung, white	1.000	Ea.	2.000	390	101	491
Rough-in, waste, 1-1/2" diameter DWV piping	1.000	Ea.	1.803	62	91.20	153.20
Supply, 1/2" diameter type "L" copper supply piping	1.000	Ea.	.988	27.40	55.50	82.90
Bathtub, P.E. cast iron, 5' long with accessories, white	1.000	Ea.	3.636	1,050	184	1,234
Rough-in, waste, 4" diameter DWV piping	1.000	Ea.	.828	43.65	42	85.65
Supply, 1/2" diameter type "L" copper supply piping	1.000	Ea.	.988	27.40	55.50	82.90
Vent, 1-1/2" diameter DWV piping	1.000	Ea.	1.482	102	83.50	185.50
Piping, supply, 1/2" diameter type "L" copper supply piping	20.000	L.F.	1.975	54.80	111	165.80
Waste, 4" diameter DWV piping	9.000	L.F.	2.483	130.95	126	256.95
Vent, 2" diameter DWV piping	6.000	L.F.	1.500	114	75.90	189.90
Carrier, steel, for studs, no arms	1.000	Ea.	1.143	78	64.50	142.50
TOTAL		Ea.	24.221	2,456.69	1,266.80	3,723.49

The costs in this system are a cost each basis, all necessary piping is included.

Three Fixture Bathroom Price Sheet

Three Fixture Bathroom Price Sheet	QUAN.	UNIT	LABOR HOURS	COST EACH		
				MAT.	INST.	TOTAL
Water closet, close coupled standard 2 piece, white	1.000	Ea.	3.019	284	153	437
Color	1.000	Ea.	3.019	380	153	533
One piece, elongated bowl, white	1.000	Ea.	3.019	590	153	743
Color	1.000	Ea.	3.019	850	153	1,003
Low profile, one piece elongated bowl, white	1.000	Ea.	3.019	1,025	153	1,178
Color	1.000	Ea.	3.019	1,350	153	1,503
Rough-in, for water closet						
1/2" copper supply, 4" cast iron waste, 2" cast iron vent	1.000	Ea.	2.376	92.50	124	216.50
4" PVC/DWV waste, 2" PVC vent	1.000	Ea.	2.678	47.50	139	186.50
4" copper waste, 2" copper vent	1.000	Ea.	2.520	210	136	346
3" cast iron waste, 1-1/2" cast iron vent	1.000	Ea.	2.244	81	117	198
3" PVC waste, 1-1/2" PVC vent	1.000	Ea.	2.388	40	129	169
3" copper waste, 1-1/2" copper vent	1.000	Ea.	2.014	135	109	244
1/2" PVC supply, 4" PVC waste, 2" PVC vent	1.000	Ea.	2.974	52.50	156	208.50
3" PVC waste, 1-1/2" PVC supply	1.000	Ea.	2.684	45.50	146	191.50
1/2" steel supply, 4" cast iron waste, 2" cast iron vent	1.000	Ea.	2.545	110	133	243
4" cast iron waste, 2" steel vent	1.000	Ea.	2.590	154	136	290
4" PVC waste, 2" PVC vent	1.000	Ea.	2.847	65	149	214
Lavatory, wall hung, P.E. cast iron 20" x 18", white	1.000	Ea.	2.000	390	101	491
Color	1.000	Ea.	2.000	385	101	486
Vitreous china 19" x 17", white	1.000	Ea.	2.286	217	116	333
Color	1.000	Ea.	2.286	241	116	357
Lavatory, for vanity top, P.E. cast iron 20" x 18"", white	1.000	Ea.	2.500	286	127	413
Color	1.000	Ea.	2.500	286	127	413
Steel, enameled 20" x 17", white	1.000	Ea.	2.759	203	140	343
Color	1.000	Ea.	2.500	211	127	338
Vitreous china 20" x 16", white	1.000	Ea.	2.963	305	150	455
Color	1.000	Ea.	2.963	305	150	455
Rough-in, for lavatory						
1/2" copper supply, 1-1/2" C.I. waste, 1-1/2" C.I. vent	1.000	Ea.	2.791	89.50	147	236.50
1-1/2" PVC waste, 1-1/4" PVC vent	1.000	Ea.	2.639	45	148	193
1/2" steel supply, 1-1/4" cast iron waste, 1-1/4" steel vent	1.000	Ea.	2.890	136	154	290
1-1/4" PVC@ waste, 1-1/4" PVC vent	1.000	Ea.	2.794	74	157	231
1/2" PVC supply, 1-1/2" PVC waste, 1-1/2" PVC vent	1.000	Ea.	3.260	53.50	184	237.50
Bathtub, P.E. cast iron, 5' long corner with fittings, white	1.000	Ea.	3.636	1,050	184	1,234
Color	1.000	Ea.	3.636	1,300	184	1,484
Rough-in, for bathtub						
1/2" copper supply, 4" cast iron waste, 1-1/2" copper vent	1.000	Ea.	2.409	112	131	243
4" PVC waste, 1-1/2" PVC vent	1.000	Ea.	2.877	56.50	156	212.50
1/2" steel supply, 4" cast iron waste, 1-1/2" steel vent	1.000	Ea.	2.898	157	154	311
4" PVC waste, 1-1/2" PVC vent	1.000	Ea.	3.159	85.50	172	257.50
1/2" PVC supply, 4" PVC waste, 1-1/2" PVC vent	1.000	Ea.	3.371	65	184	249
Piping, supply 1/2" copper	20.000	L.F.	1.975	55	111	166
1/2" steel	20.000	L.F.	2.540	113	143	256
1/2" PVC	20.000	L.F.	2.963	72	167	239
Piping, waste, 4" cast iron no hub	9.000	L.F.	2.483	131	126	257
4" PVC/DWV	9.000	L.F.	3.000	61	152	213
4" copper/DWV	9.000	L.F.	3.600	415	185	600
Piping, vent 2" cast iron no hub	6.000	L.F.	1.433	48.50	72.50	121
2" copper/DWV	6.000	L.F.	1.091	83	61.50	144.50
2" PVC/DWV	6.000	L.F.	1.627	15.90	82.50	98.40
2" steel, galvanized	6.000	L.F.	1.500	114	76	190
Vanity base cabinet, 2 door, 24" x 30"	1.000	Ea.	1.000	288	49	337
24" x 36"	1.000	Ea.	1.200	385	59	444
Vanity top, laminated plastic square edge 25" x 32"	2.670	L.F.	.712	77.50	35	112.50
25" x 38"	3.160	L.F.	.843	91.50	41	132.50
Cultured marble, 25" x 32", with bowl	1.000	Ea.	2.500	262	127	389
25" x 38", with bowl	1.000	Ea.	2.500	283	127	410
Carrier, for lavatory, steel for studs, no arms	1.000	Ea.	1.143	78	64.50	142.50
Wood, 2" x 8" blocking	1.300	L.F.	.052	.79	2.55	3.34

System Description	QUAN.	UNIT	LABOR HOURS	COST EACH		
				MAT.	INST.	TOTAL
BATHROOM WITH LAVATORY INSTALLED IN VANITY						
Water closet, floor mounted, 2 piece, close coupled, white	1.000	Ea.	3.019	284	153	437
Rough-in, waste, 4" diameter DWV piping	1.000	Ea.	.828	43.65	42	85.65
Vent, 2" diameter DWV piping	1.000	Ea.	.955	32.40	48.40	80.80
Supply, 1/2" diameter type "L" copper supply piping	1.000	Ea.	.593	16.44	33.30	49.74
Lavatory, 20" x 18", P.E. cast iron with accessories, white	1.000	Ea.	2.500	286	127	413
Rough-in, waste, 1-1/2" diameter DWV piping	1.000	Ea.	1.803	62	91.20	153.20
Supply, 1/2" diameter type "L" copper supply piping	1.000	Ea.	.988	27.40	55.50	82.90
Bathtub, P.E. cast iron 5' long with accessories, white	1.000	Ea.	3.636	1,050	184	1,234
Rough-in, waste, 4" diameter DWV piping	1.000	Ea.	.828	43.65	42	85.65
Vent, 1-1/2" diameter DWV piping	1.000	Ea.	.593	40.80	33.40	74.20
Supply, 1/2" diameter type "L" copper supply piping	1.000	Ea.	.988	27.40	55.50	82.90
Piping, supply, 1/2" diameter type "L" copper supply piping	10.000	L.F.	.988	27.40	55.50	82.90
Waste, 4" diameter DWV piping	6.000	L.F.	1.655	87.30	84	171.30
Vent, 2" diameter DWV piping	6.000	L.F.	1.500	114	75.90	189.90
Vanity base cabinet, 2 door, 30" wide	1.000	Ea.	1.000	288	49	337
Vanity top, plastic laminated square edge	2.670	L.F.	.712	77.43	34.84	112.27
TOTAL		Ea.	22.586	2,507.87	1,164.54	3,672.41
BATHROOM WITH WALL HUNG LAVATORY						
Water closet, floor mounted, 2 piece, close coupled, white	1.000	Ea.	3.019	284	153	437
Rough-in, vent, 2" diameter DWV piping	1.000	Ea.	.955	32.40	48.40	80.80
Waste, 4" diameter DWV piping	1.000	Ea.	.828	43.65	42	85.65
Supply, 1/2" diameter type "L" copper supply piping	1.000	Ea.	.593	16.44	33.30	49.74
Lavatory, 20" x 18" P.E. cast iron, wall hung, white	1.000	Ea.	2.000	390	101	491
Rough-in, waste, 1-1/2" diameter DWV piping	1.000	Ea.	1.803	62	91.20	153.20
Supply, 1/2" diameter type "L" copper supply piping	1.000	Ea.	.988	27.40	55.50	82.90
Bathtub, P.E. cast iron, 5' long with accessories, white	1.000	Ea.	3.636	1,050	184	1,234
Rough-in, waste, 4" diameter DWV piping	1.000	Ea.	.828	43.65	42	85.65
Supply, 1/2" diameter type "L" copper supply piping	1.000	Ea.	.988	27.40	55.50	82.90
Vent, 1-1/2" diameter DWV piping	1.000	Ea.	.593	40.80	33.40	74.20
Piping, supply, 1/2" diameter type "L" copper supply piping	10.000	L.F.	.988	27.40	55.50	82.90
Waste, 4" diameter DWV piping	6.000	L.F.	1.655	87.30	84	171.30
Vent, 2" diameter DWV piping	6.000	L.F.	1.500	114	75.90	189.90
Carrier, steel, for studs, no arms	1.000	Ea.	1.143	78	64.50	142.50
TOTAL		Ea.	21.517	2,324.44	1,119.20	3,443.64

The costs in this system are on a cost each basis. All necessary piping is included.

Three Fixture Bathroom Price Sheet	QUAN.	UNIT	LABOR HOURS	COST EACH		
				MAT.	INST.	TOTAL
Water closet, close coupled standard 2 piece, white	1.000	Ea.	3.019	284	153	437
Color	1.000	Ea.	3.019	380	153	533
One piece elongated bowl, white	1.000	Ea.	3.019	590	153	743
Color	1.000	Ea.	3.019	850	153	1,003
Low profile, one piece elongated bowl, white	1.000	Ea.	3.019	1,025	153	1,178
Color	1.000	Ea.	3.019	1,350	153	1,503
Rough-in for water closet						
1/2" copper supply, 4" cast iron waste, 2" cast iron vent	1.000	Ea.	2.376	92.50	124	216.50
4" PVC/DWV waste, 2" PVC vent	1.000	Ea.	2.678	47.50	139	186.50
4" carrier waste, 2" copper vent	1.000	Ea.	2.520	210	136	346
3" cast iron waste, 1-1/2" cast iron vent	1.000	Ea.	2.244	81	117	198
3" PVC waste, 1-1/2" PVC vent	1.000	Ea.	2.388	40	129	169
3" copper waste, 1-1/2" copper vent	1.000	Ea.	2.014	135	109	244
1/2" PVC supply, 4" PVC waste, 2" PVC vent	1.000	Ea.	2.974	52.50	156	208.50
3" PVC waste, 1-1/2" PVC supply	1.000	Ea.	2.684	45.50	146	191.50
1/2" steel supply, 4" cast iron waste, 2" cast iron vent	1.000	Ea.	2.545	110	133	243
4" cast iron waste, 2" steel vent	1.000	Ea.	2.590	154	136	290
4" PVC waste, 2" PVC vent	1.000	Ea.	2.847	65	149	214
Lavatory, wall hung, PE cast iron 20" x 18", white	1.000	Ea.	2.000	390	101	491
Color	1.000	Ea.	2.000	385	101	486
Vitreous china 19" x 17", white	1.000	Ea.	2.286	217	116	333
Color	1.000	Ea.	2.286	241	116	357
Lavatory, for vanity top, PE cast iron 20" x 18", white	1.000	Ea.	2.500	286	127	413
Color	1.000	Ea.	2.500	286	127	413
Steel enameled 20" x 17", white	1.000	Ea.	2.759	203	140	343
Color	1.000	Ea.	2.500	211	127	338
Vitreous china 20" x 16", white	1.000	Ea.	2.963	305	150	455
Color	1.000	Ea.	2.963	305	150	455
Rough-in for lavatory						
1/2" copper supply, 1-1/2" cast iron waste, 1-1/2" cast iron vent	1.000	Ea.	2.791	89.50	147	236.50
1-1/2" PVC waste, 1-1/4" PVC vent	1.000	Ea.	2.639	45	148	193
1/2" steel supply, 1-1/4" cast iron waste, 1-1/4" steel vent	1.000	Ea.	2.890	136	154	290
1-1/4" PVC waste, 1-1/4" PVC vent	1.000	Ea.	2.794	74	157	231
1/2" PVC supply, 1-1/2" PVC waste, 1-1/2" PVC vent	1.000	Ea.	3.260	53.50	184	237.50
Bathtub, PE cast iron, 5' long corner with fittings, white	1.000	Ea.	3.636	1,050	184	1,234
Color	1.000	Ea.	3.636	1,300	184	1,484
Rough-in for bathtub						
1/2" copper supply, 4" cast iron waste, 1-1/2" copper vent	1.000	Ea.	2.409	112	131	243
4" PVC waste, 1/2" PVC vent	1.000	Ea.	2.877	56.50	156	212.50
1/2" steel supply, 4" cast iron waste, 1-1/2" steel vent	1.000	Ea.	2.898	157	154	311
4" PVC waste, 1-1/2" PVC vent	1.000	Ea.	3.159	85.50	172	257.50
1/2" PVC supply, 4" PVC waste, 1-1/2" PVC vent	1.000	Ea.	3.371	65	184	249
Piping supply, 1/2" copper	10.000	L.F.	.988	27.50	55.50	83
1/2" steel	10.000	L.F.	1.270	56.50	71.50	128
1/2" PVC	10.000	L.F.	1.482	36	83.50	119.50
Piping waste, 4" cast iron no hub	6.000	L.F.	1.655	87.50	84	171.50
4" PVC/DWV	6.000	L.F.	2.000	40.50	101	141.50
4" copper/DWV	6.000	L.F.	2.400	276	123	399
Piping vent 2" cast iron no hub	6.000	L.F.	1.433	48.50	72.50	121
2" copper/DWV	6.000	L.F.	1.091	83	61.50	144.50
2" PVC/DWV	6.000	L.F.	1.627	15.90	82.50	98.40
2" steel, galvanized	6.000	L.F.	1.500	114	76	190
Vanity base cabinet, 2 door, 24" x 30"	1.000	Ea.	1.000	288	49	337
24" x 36"	1.000	Ea.	1.200	385	59	444
Vanity top, laminated plastic square edge 25" x 32"	2.670	L.F.	.712	77.50	35	112.50
25" x 38"	3.160	L.F.	.843	91.50	41	132.50
Cultured marble, 25" x 32", with bowl	1.000	Ea.	2.500	262	127	389
25" x 38", with bowl	1.000	Ea.	2.500	283	127	410
Carrier, for lavatory, steel for studs, no arms	1.000	Ea.	1.143	78	64.50	142.50
Wood, 2" x 8" blocking	1.300	L.F.	.052	.79	2.55	3.34

System Description	QUAN.	UNIT	LABOR HOURS	COST EACH MAT.	COST EACH INST.	COST EACH TOTAL
BATHROOM WITH LAVATORY INSTALLED IN VANITY						
Water closet, floor mounted, 2 piece, close coupled, white	1.000	Ea.	3.019	284	153	437
Rough-in, vent, 2″ diameter DWV piping	1.000	Ea.	.955	32.40	48.40	80.80
Waste, 4″ diameter DWV piping	1.000	Ea.	.828	43.65	42	85.65
Supply, 1/2″ diameter type "L" copper supply piping	1.000	Ea.	.593	16.44	33.30	49.74
Lavatory, 20″ x 18″, PE cast iron with accessories, white	1.000	Ea.	2.500	286	127	413
Rough-in, vent, 1-1/2″ diameter DWV piping	1.000	Ea.	1.803	62	91.20	153.20
Supply, 1/2″ diameter type "L" copper supply piping	1.000	Ea.	.988	27.40	55.50	82.90
Bathtub, P.E. cast iron, 5′ long with accessories, white	1.000	Ea.	3.636	1,050	184	1,234
Rough-in, waste, 4″ diameter DWV piping	1.000	Ea.	.828	43.65	42	85.65
Supply, 1/2″ diameter type "L" copper supply piping	1.000	Ea.	.988	27.40	55.50	82.90
Vent, 1-1/2″ diameter DWV piping	1.000	Ea.	.593	40.80	33.40	74.20
Piping, supply, 1/2″ diameter type "L" copper supply piping	32.000	L.F.	3.161	87.68	177.60	265.28
Waste, 4″ diameter DWV piping	12.000	L.F.	3.310	174.60	168	342.60
Vent, 2″ diameter DWV piping	6.000	L.F.	1.500	114	75.90	189.90
Vanity base cabinet, 2 door, 30″ wide	1.000	Ea.	1.000	288	49	337
Vanity top, plastic laminated square edge	2.670	L.F.	.712	77.43	34.84	112.27
TOTAL		Ea.	26.414	2,655.45	1,370.64	4,026.09
BATHROOM WITH WALL HUNG LAVATORY						
Water closet, floor mounted, 2 piece, close coupled, white	1.000	Ea.	3.019	284	153	437
Rough-in, vent, 2″ diameter DWV piping	1.000	Ea.	.955	32.40	48.40	80.80
Waste, 4″ diameter DWV piping	1.000	Ea.	.828	43.65	42	85.65
Supply, 1/2″ diameter type "L" copper supply piping	1.000	Ea.	.593	16.44	33.30	49.74
Lavatory, 20″ x 18″ P.E. cast iron, wall hung, white	1.000	Ea.	2.000	390	101	491
Rough-in, waste, 1-1/2″ diameter DWV piping	1.000	Ea.	1.803	62	91.20	153.20
Supply, 1/2″ diameter type "L" copper supply piping	1.000	Ea.	.988	27.40	55.50	82.90
Bathtub, P.E. cast iron, 5′ long with accessories, white	1.000	Ea.	3.636	1,050	184	1,234
Rough-in, waste, 4″ diameter DWV piping	1.000	Ea.	.828	43.65	42	85.65
Supply, 1/2″ diameter type "L" copper supply piping	1.000	Ea.	.988	27.40	55.50	82.90
Vent, 1-1/2″ diameter DWV piping	1.000	Ea.	.593	40.80	33.40	74.20
Piping, supply, 1/2″ diameter type "L" copper supply piping	32.000	L.F.	3.161	87.68	177.60	265.28
Waste, 4″ diameter DWV piping	12.000	L.F.	3.310	174.60	168	342.60
Vent, 2″ diameter DWV piping	6.000	L.F.	1.500	114	75.90	189.90
Carrier steel, for studs, no arms	1.000	Ea.	1.143	78	64.50	142.50
TOTAL		Ea.	25.345	2,472.02	1,325.30	3,797.32

The costs in this system are on a cost each basis. All necessary piping is included.

Three Fixture Bathroom Price Sheet	QUAN.	UNIT	LABOR HOURS	COST EACH		
				MAT.	INST.	TOTAL
Water closet, close coupled, standard 2 piece, white	1.000	Ea.	3.019	284	153	437
Color	1.000	Ea.	3.019	380	153	533
One piece, elongated bowl, white	1.000	Ea.	3.019	590	153	743
Color	1.000	Ea.	3.019	850	153	1,003
Low profile, one piece, elongated bowl, white	1.000	Ea.	3.019	1,025	153	1,178
Color	1.000	Ea.	3.019	1,350	153	1,503
Rough-in, for water closet						
1/2" copper supply, 4" cast iron waste, 2" cast iron vent	1.000	Ea.	2.376	92.50	124	216.50
4" PVC/DWV waste, 2" PVC vent	1.000	Ea.	2.678	47.50	139	186.50
4" copper waste, 2" copper vent	1.000	Ea.	2.520	210	136	346
3" cast iron waste, 1-1/2" cast iron vent	1.000	Ea.	2.244	81	117	198
3" PVC waste, 1-1/2" PVC vent	1.000	Ea.	2.388	40	129	169
3" copper waste, 1-1/2" copper vent	1.000	Ea.	2.014	135	109	244
1/2" PVC supply, 4" PVC waste, 2" PVC vent	1.000	Ea.	2.974	52.50	156	208.50
3" PVC waste, 1-1/2" PVC supply	1.000	Ea.	2.684	45.50	146	191.50
1/2" steel supply, 4" cast iron waste, 2" cast iron vent	1.000	Ea.	2.545	110	133	243
4" cast iron waste, 2" steel vent	1.000	Ea.	2.590	154	136	290
4" PVC waste, 2" PVC vent	1.000	Ea.	2.847	65	149	214
Lavatory wall hung, P.E. cast iron, 20" x 18", white	1.000	Ea.	2.000	390	101	491
Color	1.000	Ea.	2.000	385	101	486
Vitreous china, 19" x 17", white	1.000	Ea.	2.286	217	116	333
Color	1.000	Ea.	2.286	241	116	357
Lavatory, for vanity top, P.E., cast iron, 20" x 18", white	1.000	Ea.	2.500	286	127	413
Color	1.000	Ea.	2.500	286	127	413
Steel, enameled, 20" x 17", white	1.000	Ea.	2.759	203	140	343
Color	1.000	Ea.	2.500	211	127	338
Vitreous china, 20" x 16", white	1.000	Ea.	2.963	305	150	455
Color	1.000	Ea.	2.963	305	150	455
Rough-in, for lavatory						
1/2" copper supply, 1-1/2" C.I. waste, 1-1/2" C.I. vent	1.000	Ea.	2.791	89.50	147	236.50
1-1/2" PVC waste, 1-1/4" PVC vent	1.000	Ea.	2.639	45	148	193
1/2" steel supply, 1-1/4" cast iron waste, 1-1/4" steel vent	1.000	Ea.	2.890	136	154	290
1-1/4" PVC waste, 1-1/4" PVC vent	1.000	Ea.	2.794	74	157	231
1/2" PVC supply, 1-1/2" PVC waste, 1-1/2" PVC vent	1.000	Ea.	3.260	53.50	184	237.50
Bathtub, P.E. cast iron, 5' long corner with fittings, white	1.000	Ea.	3.636	1,050	184	1,234
Color	1.000	Ea.	3.636	1,300	184	1,484
Rough-in, for bathtub						
1/2" copper supply, 4" cast iron waste, 1-1/2" copper vent	1.000	Ea.	2.409	112	131	243
4" PVC waste, 1/2" PVC vent	1.000	Ea.	2.877	56.50	156	212.50
1/2" steel supply, 4" cast iron waste, 1-1/2" steel vent	1.000	Ea.	2.898	157	154	311
4" PVC waste, 1-1/2" PVC vent	1.000	Ea.	3.159	85.50	172	257.50
1/2" PVC supply, 4" PVC waste, 1-1/2" PVC vent	1.000	Ea.	3.371	65	184	249
Piping, supply, 1/2" copper	32.000	L.F.	3.161	87.50	178	265.50
1/2" steel	32.000	L.F.	4.063	181	229	410
1/2" PVC	32.000	L.F.	4.741	115	267	382
Piping, waste, 4" cast iron no hub	12.000	L.F.	3.310	175	168	343
4" PVC/DWV	12.000	L.F.	4.000	81	203	284
4" copper/DWV	12.000	L.F.	4.800	550	246	796
Piping, vent, 2" cast iron no hub	6.000	L.F.	1.433	48.50	72.50	121
2" copper/DWV	6.000	L.F.	1.091	83	61.50	144.50
2" PVC/DWV	6.000	L.F.	1.627	15.90	82.50	98.40
2" steel, galvanized	6.000	L.F.	1.500	114	76	190
Vanity base cabinet, 2 door, 24" x 30"	1.000	Ea.	1.000	288	49	337
24" x 36"	1.000	Ea.	1.200	385	59	444
Vanity top, laminated plastic square edge, 25" x 32"	2.670	L.F.	.712	77.50	35	112.50
25" x 38"	3.160	L.F.	.843	91.50	41	132.50
Cultured marble, 25" x 32", with bowl	1.000	Ea.	2.500	262	127	389
25" x 38", with bowl	1.000	Ea.	2.500	283	127	410
Carrier, for lavatory, steel for studs, no arms	1.000	Ea.	1.143	78	64.50	142.50
Wood, 2" x 8" blocking	1.300	L.F.	.052	.79	2.55	3.34

Corner Bathtub

Water Closet

Lavatory

Vanity Top

Vanity Base Cabinet

System Description	QUAN.	UNIT	LABOR HOURS	COST EACH		
				MAT.	INST.	TOTAL
BATHROOM WITH LAVATORY INSTALLED IN VANITY						
Water closet, floor mounted, 2 piece, close coupled, white	1.000	Ea.	3.019	284	153	437
Rough-in, vent, 2" diameter DWV piping	1.000	Ea.	.955	32.40	48.40	80.80
Waste, 4" diameter DWV piping	1.000	Ea.	.828	43.65	42	85.65
Supply, 1/2" diameter type "L" copper supply piping	1.000	Ea.	.593	16.44	33.30	49.74
Lavatory, 20" x 18", P.E. cast iron with fittings, white	1.000	Ea.	2.500	286	127	413
Rough-in, waste, 1-1/2" diameter DWV piping	1.000	Ea.	1.803	62	91.20	153.20
Supply, 1/2" diameter type "L" copper supply piping	1.000	Ea.	.988	27.40	55.50	82.90
Bathtub, P.E. cast iron, corner with fittings, white	1.000	Ea.	3.636	2,375	184	2,559
Rough-in, waste, 4" diameter DWV piping	1.000	Ea.	.828	43.65	42	85.65
Supply, 1/2" diameter type "L" copper supply piping	1.000	Ea.	.988	27.40	55.50	82.90
Vent, 1-1/2" diameter DWV piping	1.000	Ea.	.593	40.80	33.40	74.20
Piping, supply, 1/2" diameter type "L" copper supply piping	32.000	L.F.	3.161	87.68	177.60	265.28
Waste, 4" diameter DWV piping	12.000	L.F.	3.310	174.60	168	342.60
Vent, 2" diameter DWV piping	6.000	L.F.	1.500	114	75.90	189.90
Vanity base cabinet, 2 door, 30" wide	1.000	Ea.	1.000	288	49	337
Vanity top, plastic laminated, square edge	2.670	L.F.	.712	97.46	34.84	132.30
TOTAL		Ea.	26.414	4,000.48	1,370.64	5,371.12
BATHROOM WITH WALL HUNG LAVATORY						
Water closet, floor mounted, 2 piece, close coupled, white	1.000	Ea.	3.019	284	153	437
Rough-in, vent, 2" diameter DWV piping	1.000	Ea.	.955	32.40	48.40	80.80
Waste, 4" diameter DWV piping	1.000	Ea.	.828	43.65	42	85.65
Supply, 1/2" diameter type "L" copper supply piping	1.000	Ea.	.593	16.44	33.30	49.74
Lavatory, 20" x 18", P.E. cast iron, with fittings, white	1.000	Ea.	2.000	390	101	491
Rough-in, waste, 1-1/2" diameter DWV piping	1.000	Ea.	1.803	62	91.20	153.20
Supply, 1/2" diameter type "L" copper supply piping	1.000	Ea.	.988	27.40	55.50	82.90
Bathtub, P.E. cast iron, corner, with fittings, white	1.000	Ea.	3.636	2,375	184	2,559
Rough-in, waste, 4" diameter DWV piping	1.000	Ea.	.828	43.65	42	85.65
Supply, 1/2" diameter type "L" copper supply piping	1.000	Ea.	.988	27.40	55.50	82.90
Vent, 1-1/2" diameter DWV piping	1.000	Ea.	.593	40.80	33.40	74.20
Piping, supply, 1/2" diameter type "L" copper supply piping	32.000	L.F.	3.161	87.68	177.60	265.28
Waste, 4" diameter DWV piping	12.000	L.F.	3.310	174.60	168	342.60
Vent, 2" diameter DWV piping	6.000	L.F.	1.500	114	75.90	189.90
Carrier, steel, for studs, no arms	1.000	Ea.	1.143	78	64.50	142.50
TOTAL		Ea.	25.345	3,797.02	1,325.30	5,122.32

The costs in this system are on a cost each basis. All necessary piping is included.

Three Fixture Bathroom Price Sheet	QUAN.	UNIT	LABOR HOURS	COST EACH		
				MAT.	INST.	TOTAL
Water closet, close coupled, standard 2 piece, white	1.000	Ea.	3.019	284	153	437
Color	1.000	Ea.	3.019	380	153	533
One piece elongated bowl, white	1.000	Ea.	3.019	590	153	743
Color	1.000	Ea.	3.019	850	153	1,003
Low profile, one piece elongated bowl, white	1.000	Ea.	3.019	1,025	153	1,178
Color	1.000	Ea.	3.019	1,350	153	1,503
Rough-in, for water closet						
1/2" copper supply, 4" cast iron waste, 2" cast iron vent	1.000	Ea.	2.376	92.50	124	216.50
4" PVC/DWV waste, 2" PVC vent	1.000	Ea.	2.678	47.50	139	186.50
4" copper waste, 2" copper vent	1.000	Ea.	2.520	210	136	346
3" cast iron waste, 1-1/2" cast iron vent	1.000	Ea.	2.244	81	117	198
3" PVC waste, 1-1/2" PVC vent	1.000	Ea.	2.388	40	129	169
3" copper waste, 1-1/2" copper vent	1.000	Ea.	2.014	135	109	244
1/2" PVC supply, 4" PVC waste, 2" PVC vent	1.000	Ea.	2.974	52.50	156	208.50
3" PVC waste, 1-1/2" PVC supply	1.000	Ea.	2.684	45.50	146	191.50
1/2" steel supply, 4" cast iron waste, 2" cast iron vent	1.000	Ea.	2.545	110	133	243
4" cast iron waste, 2" steel vent	1.000	Ea.	2.590	154	136	290
4" PVC waste, 2" PVC vent	1.000	Ea.	2.847	65	149	214
Lavatory, wall hung P.E. cast iron 20" x 18", white	1.000	Ea.	2.000	390	101	491
Color	1.000	Ea.	2.000	385	101	486
Vitreous china 19" x 17", white	1.000	Ea.	2.286	217	116	333
Color	1.000	Ea.	2.286	241	116	357
Lavatory, for vanity top, P.E., cast iron, 20" x 18", white	1.000	Ea.	2.500	286	127	413
Color	1.000	Ea.	2.500	286	127	413
Steel enameled 20" x 17", white	1.000	Ea.	2.759	203	140	343
Color	1.000	Ea.	2.500	211	127	338
Vitreous china 20" x 16", white	1.000	Ea.	2.963	305	150	455
Color	1.000	Ea.	2.963	305	150	455
Rough-in, for lavatory						
1/2" copper supply, 1-1/2" cast iron waste, 1-1/2" cast iron vent	1.000	Ea.	2.791	89.50	147	236.50
1-1/2" PVC waste, 1-1/4" PVC vent	1.000	Ea.	2.639	45	148	193
1/2" steel supply, 1-1/4" cast iron waste, 1-1/4" steel vent	1.000	Ea.	2.890	136	154	290
1-1/4" PVC waste, 1-1/4" PVC vent	1.000	Ea.	2.794	74	157	231
1/2" PVC supply, 1-1/2" PVC waste, 1-1/2" PVC vent	1.000	Ea.	3.260	53.50	184	237.50
Bathtub, P.E. cast iron, corner with fittings, white	1.000	Ea.	3.636	2,375	184	2,559
Color	1.000	Ea.	4.000	2,675	203	2,878
Rough-in, for bathtub						
1/2" copper supply, 4" cast iron waste, 1-1/2" copper vent	1.000	Ea.	2.409	112	131	243
4" PVC waste, 1-1/2" PVC vent	1.000	Ea.	2.877	56.50	156	212.50
1/2" steel supply, 4" cast iron waste, 1-1/2" steel vent	1.000	Ea.	2.898	157	154	311
4" PVC waste, 1-1/2" PVC vent	1.000	Ea.	3.159	85.50	172	257.50
1/2" PVC supply, 4" PVC waste, 1-1/2" PVC vent	1.000	Ea.	3.371	65	184	249
Piping, supply, 1/2" copper	32.000	L.F.	3.161	87.50	178	265.50
1/2" steel	32.000	L.F.	4.063	181	229	410
1/2" PVC	32.000	L.F.	4.741	115	267	382
Piping, waste, 4" cast iron, no hub	12.000	L.F.	3.310	175	168	343
4" PVC/DWV	12.000	L.F.	4.000	81	203	284
4" copper/DWV	12.000	L.F.	4.800	550	246	796
Piping, vent 2" cast iron, no hub	6.000	L.F.	1.433	48.50	72.50	121
2" copper/DWV	6.000	L.F.	1.091	83	61.50	144.50
2" PVC/DWV	6.000	L.F.	1.627	15.90	82.50	98.40
2" steel, galvanized	6.000	L.F.	1.500	114	76	190
Vanity base cabinet, 2 door, 24" x 30"	1.000	Ea.	1.000	288	49	337
24" x 36"	1.000	Ea.	1.200	385	59	444
Vanity top, laminated plastic square edge 25" x 32"	2.670	L.F.	.712	97.50	35	132.50
25" x 38"	3.160	L.F.	.843	115	41	156
Cultured marble, 25" x 32", with bowl	1.000	Ea.	2.500	262	127	389
25" x 38", with bowl	1.000	Ea.	2.500	283	127	410
Carrier, for lavatory, steel for studs, no arms	1.000	Ea.	1.143	78	64.50	142.50
Wood, 2" x 8" blocking	1.300	L.F.	.053	.81	2.61	3.42

Lavatory

Vanity Top

Vanity Base
Cabinet

Shower

Water Closet

System Description	QUAN.	UNIT	LABOR HOURS	COST EACH		
				MAT.	INST.	TOTAL
BATHROOM WITH SHOWER, LAVATORY INSTALLED IN VANITY						
Water closet, floor mounted, 2 piece, close coupled, white	1.000	Ea.	3.019	284	153	437
Rough-in, vent, 2" diameter DWV piping	1.000	Ea.	.955	32.40	48.40	80.80
Waste, 4" diameter DWV piping	1.000	Ea.	.828	43.65	42	85.65
Supply, 1/2" diameter type "L" copper supply piping	1.000	Ea.	.593	16.44	33.30	49.74
Lavatory, 20" x 18" P.E. cast iron with fittings, white	1.000	Ea.	2.500	286	127	413
Rough-in, waste, 1-1/2" diameter DWV piping	1.000	Ea.	1.803	62	91.20	153.20
Supply, 1/2" diameter type "L" copper supply piping	1.000	Ea.	.988	27.40	55.50	82.90
Shower, steel enameled, stone base, corner, white	1.000	Ea.	3.200	975	162	1,137
Shower mixing valve	1.000	Ea.	1.333	156	75	231
Shower door	1.000	Ea.	1.000	259	53.50	312.50
Rough-in, vent, 1-1/2" diameter DWV piping	1.000	Ea.	.225	7.75	11.40	19.15
Waste, 2" diameter DWV piping	1.000	Ea.	1.433	48.60	72.60	121.20
Supply, 1/2" diameter type "L" copper supply piping	1.000	Ea.	1.580	43.84	88.80	132.64
Piping, supply, 1/2" diameter type "L" copper supply piping	36.000	L.F.	4.148	115.08	233.10	348.18
Waste, 4" diameter DWV piping	7.000	L.F.	2.759	145.50	140	285.50
Vent, 2" diameter DWV piping	6.000	L.F.	2.250	171	113.85	284.85
Vanity base 2 door, 30" wide	1.000	Ea.	1.000	288	49	337
Vanity top, plastic laminated, square edge	2.170	L.F.	.712	80.10	34.84	114.94
TOTAL		Ea.	30.326	3,041.76	1,584.49	4,626.25
BATHROOM WITH SHOWER, WALL HUNG LAVATORY						
Water closet, floor mounted, close coupled	1.000	Ea.	3.019	284	153	437
Rough-in, vent, 2" diameter DWV piping	1.000	Ea.	.955	32.40	48.40	80.80
Waste, 4" diameter DWV piping	1.000	Ea.	.828	43.65	42	85.65
Supply, 1/2" diameter type "L" copper supply piping	1.000	Ea.	.593	16.44	33.30	49.74
Lavatory, 20" x 18" P.E. cast iron with fittings, white	1.000	Ea.	2.000	390	101	491
Rough-in, waste, 1-1/2" diameter DWV piping	1.000	Ea.	1.803	62	91.20	153.20
Supply, 1/2" diameter type "L" copper supply piping	1.000	Ea.	.988	27.40	55.50	82.90
Shower, steel enameled, stone base, white	1.000	Ea.	3.200	975	162	1,137
Mixing valve	1.000	Ea.	1.333	156	75	231
Shower door	1.000	Ea.	1.000	259	53.50	312.50
Rough-in, vent, 1-1/2" diameter DWV piping	1.000	Ea.	.225	7.75	11.40	19.15
Waste, 2" diameter DWV piping	1.000	Ea.	1.433	48.60	72.60	121.20
Supply, 1/2" diameter type "L" copper supply piping	1.000	Ea.	1.580	43.84	88.80	132.64
Piping, supply, 1/2" diameter type "L" copper supply piping	36.000	L.F.	4.148	115.08	233.10	348.18
Waste, 4" diameter DWV piping	7.000	L.F.	2.759	145.50	140	285.50
Vent, 2" diameter DWV piping	6.000	L.F.	2.250	171	113.85	284.85
Carrier, steel, for studs, no arms	1.000	Ea.	1.143	78	64.50	142.50
TOTAL		Ea.	29.257	2,855.66	1,539.15	4,394.81

The costs in this system are on a cost each basis. All necessary piping
is included.

Three Fixture Bathroom Price Sheet	QUAN.	UNIT	LABOR HOURS	COST EACH		
				MAT.	INST.	TOTAL
Water closet, close coupled, standard 2 piece, white	1.000	Ea.	3.019	284	153	437
Color	1.000	Ea.	3.019	380	153	533
One piece elongated bowl, white	1.000	Ea.	3.019	590	153	743
Color	1.000	Ea.	3.019	850	153	1,003
Low profile, one piece elongated bowl, white	1.000	Ea.	3.019	1,025	153	1,178
Color	1.000	Ea.	3.019	1,350	153	1,503
Rough-in, for water closet						
1/2" copper supply, 4" cast iron waste, 2" cast iron vent	1.000	Ea.	2.376	92.50	124	216.50
4" PVC/DWV waste, 2" PVC vent	1.000	Ea.	2.678	47.50	139	186.50
4" copper waste, 2" copper vent	1.000	Ea.	2.520	210	136	346
3" cast iron waste, 1-1/2" cast iron vent	1.000	Ea.	2.244	81	117	198
3" PVC waste, 1-1/2" PVC vent	1.000	Ea.	2.388	40	129	169
3" copper waste, 1-1/2" copper vent	1.000	Ea.	2.014	135	109	244
1/2" PVC supply, 4" PVC waste, 2" PVC vent	1.000	Ea.	2.974	52.50	156	208.50
3" PVC waste, 1-1/2" PVC supply	1.000	Ea.	2.684	45.50	146	191.50
1/2" steel supply, 4" cast iron waste, 2" cast iron vent	1.000	Ea.	2.545	110	133	243
4" cast iron waste, 2" steel vent	1.000	Ea.	2.590	154	136	290
4" PVC waste, 2" PVC vent	1.000	Ea.	2.847	65	149	214
Lavatory, wall hung, P.E. cast iron 20" x 18", white	1.000	Ea.	2.000	390	101	491
Color	1.000	Ea.	2.000	385	101	486
Vitreous china 19" x 17", white	1.000	Ea.	2.286	217	116	333
Color	1.000	Ea.	2.286	241	116	357
Lavatory, for vanity top, P.E. cast iron 20" x 18", white	1.000	Ea.	2.500	286	127	413
Color	1.000	Ea.	2.500	286	127	413
Steel enameled 20" x 17", white	1.000	Ea.	2.759	203	140	343
Color	1.000	Ea.	2.500	211	127	338
Vitreous china 20" x 16", white	1.000	Ea.	2.963	305	150	455
Color	1.000	Ea.	2.963	305	150	455
Rough-in, for lavatory						
1/2" copper supply, 1-1/2" cast iron waste, 1-1/2" cast iron vent	1.000	Ea.	2.791	89.50	147	236.50
1-1/2" PVC waste, 1-1/2" PVC vent	1.000	Ea.	2.639	45	148	193
1/2" steel supply, 1-1/4" cast iron waste, 1-1/4" steel vent	1.000	Ea.	2.890	136	154	290
1-1/4" PVC waste, 1-1/4" PVC vent	1.000	Ea.	2.921	74	164	238
1/2" PVC supply, 1-1/2" PVC waste, 1-1/2" PVC vent	1.000	Ea.	3.260	53.50	184	237.50
Shower, steel enameled stone base, 32" x 32", white	1.000	Ea.	8.000	975	162	1,137
Color	1.000	Ea.	7.822	1,425	149	1,574
36" x 36" white	1.000	Ea.	8.889	1,575	169	1,744
Color	1.000	Ea.	8.889	1,625	169	1,794
Rough-in, for shower						
1/2" copper supply, 4" cast iron waste, 1-1/2" copper vent	1.000	Ea.	3.238	100	173	273
4" PVC waste, 1-1/2" PVC vent	1.000	Ea.	3.429	62	184	246
1/2" steel supply, 4" cast iron waste, 1-1/2" steel vent	1.000	Ea.	3.665	153	197	350
4" PVC waste, 1-1/2" PVC vent	1.000	Ea.	3.881	109	209	318
1/2" PVC supply, 4" PVC waste, 1-1/2" PVC vent	1.000	Ea.	4.219	75.50	229	304.50
Piping, supply, 1/2" copper	36.000	L.F.	4.148	115	233	348
1/2" steel	36.000	L.F.	5.333	237	300	537
1/2" PVC	36.000	L.F.	6.222	151	350	501
Piping, waste, 4" cast iron no hub	7.000	L.F.	2.759	146	140	286
4" PVC/DWV	7.000	L.F.	3.333	67.50	169	236.50
4" copper/DWV	7.000	L.F.	4.000	460	205	665
Piping, vent, 2" cast iron no hub	6.000	L.F.	2.149	73	109	182
2" copper/DWV	6.000	L.F.	1.636	124	92.50	216.50
2" PVC/DWV	6.000	L.F.	2.441	24	124	148
2" steel, galvanized	6.000	L.F.	2.250	171	114	285
Vanity base cabinet, 2 door, 24" x 30"	1.000	Ea.	1.000	288	49	337
24" x 36"	1.000	Ea.	1.200	385	59	444
Vanity top, laminated plastic square edge, 25" x 32"	2.170	L.F.	.712	80	35	115
25" x 38"	2.670	L.F.	.845	95	41.50	136.50
Carrier, for lavatory, steel for studs, no arms	1.000	Ea.	1.143	78	64.50	142.50
Wood, 2" x 8" blocking	1.300	L.F.	.052	.79	2.55	3.34

241

Shower →
Water Closet →
Lavatory
Vanity Top
Vanity Base Cabinet

System Description	QUAN.	UNIT	LABOR HOURS	COST EACH		
				MAT.	INST.	TOTAL
BATHROOM WITH LAVATORY INSTALLED IN VANITY						
Water closet, floor mounted, 2 piece, close coupled, white	1.000	Ea.	3.019	284	153	437
Rough-in, vent, 2″ diameter DWV piping	1.000	Ea.	.955	32.40	48.40	80.80
Waste, 4″ diameter DWV piping	1.000	Ea.	.828	43.65	42	85.65
Supply, 1/2″ diameter type "L" copper supply piping	1.000	Ea.	.593	16.44	33.30	49.74
Lavatory, 20″ x 18″, P.E. cast iron with fittings, white	1.000	Ea.	2.500	286	127	413
Rough-in, waste, 1-1/2″ diameter DWV piping	1.000	Ea.	1.803	62	91.20	153.20
Supply, 1/2″ diameter type "L" copper supply piping	1.000	Ea.	.988	27.40	55.50	82.90
Shower, steel enameled, stone base, corner, white	1.000	Ea.	3.200	975	162	1,137
Mixing valve	1.000	Ea.	1.333	156	75	231
Shower door	1.000	Ea.	1.000	259	53.50	312.50
Rough-in, vent, 1-1/2″ diameter DWV piping	1.000	Ea.	.225	7.75	11.40	19.15
Waste, 2″ diameter DWV piping	1.000	Ea.	1.433	48.60	72.60	121.20
Supply, 1/2″ diameter type "L" copper supply piping	1.000	Ea.	1.580	43.84	88.80	132.64
Piping, supply, 1/2″ diameter type "L" copper supply piping	36.000	L.F.	3.556	98.64	199.80	298.44
Waste, 4″ diameter DWV piping	7.000	L.F.	1.931	101.85	98	199.85
Vent, 2″ diameter DWV piping	6.000	L.F.	1.500	114	75.90	189.90
Vanity base, 2 door, 30″ wide	1.000	Ea.	1.000	288	49	337
Vanity top, plastic laminated, square edge	2.670	L.F.	.712	77.43	34.84	112.27
TOTAL		Ea.	28.156	2,922	1,471.24	4,393.24
BATHROOM, WITH WALL HUNG LAVATORY						
Water closet, floor mounted, 2 piece, close coupled, white	1.000	Ea.	3.019	284	153	437
Rough-in, vent, 2″ diameter DWV piping	1.000	Ea.	.955	32.40	48.40	80.80
Waste, 4″ diameter DWV piping	1.000	Ea.	.828	43.65	42	85.65
Supply, 1/2″ diameter type "L" copper supply piping	1.000	Ea.	.593	16.44	33.30	49.74
Lavatory, wall hung, 20″ x 18″ P.E. cast iron with fittings, white	1.000	Ea.	2.000	390	101	491
Rough-in, waste, 1-1/2″ diameter DWV piping	1.000	Ea.	1.803	62	91.20	153.20
Supply, 1/2″ diameter type "L" copper supply piping	1.000	Ea.	.988	27.40	55.50	82.90
Shower, steel enameled, stone base, corner, white	1.000	Ea.	3.200	975	162	1,137
Mixing valve	1.000	Ea.	1.333	156	75	231
Shower door	1.000	Ea.	1.000	259	53.50	312.50
Rough-in, waste, 1-1/2″ diameter DWV piping	1.000	Ea.	.225	7.75	11.40	19.15
Waste, 2″ diameter DWV piping	1.000	Ea.	1.433	48.60	72.60	121.20
Supply, 1/2″ diameter type "L" copper supply piping	1.000	Ea.	1.580	43.84	88.80	132.64
Piping, supply, 1/2″ diameter type "L" copper supply piping	36.000	L.F.	3.556	98.64	199.80	298.44
Waste, 4″ diameter DWV piping	7.000	L.F.	1.931	101.85	98	199.85
Vent, 2″ diameter DWV piping	6.000	L.F.	1.500	114	75.90	189.90
Carrier, steel, for studs, no arms	1.000	Ea.	1.143	78	64.50	142.50
TOTAL		Ea.	27.087	2,738.57	1,425.90	4,164.47

The costs in this system are on a cost each basis. All necessary piping is included.

Three Fixture Bathroom Price Sheet	QUAN.	UNIT	LABOR HOURS	COST EACH		
				MAT.	INST.	TOTAL
Water closet, close coupled, standard 2 piece, white	1.000	Ea.	3.019	284	153	437
Color	1.000	Ea.	3.019	380	153	533
One piece elongated bowl, white	1.000	Ea.	3.019	590	153	743
Color	1.000	Ea.	3.019	850	153	1,003
Low profile one piece elongated bowl, white	1.000	Ea.	3.019	1,025	153	1,178
Color	1.000	Ea.	3.623	1,350	153	1,503
Rough-in, for water closet						
1/2" copper supply, 4" cast iron waste, 2" cast iron vent	1.000	Ea.	2.376	92.50	124	216.50
4" P.V.C./DWV waste, 2" PVC vent	1.000	Ea.	2.678	47.50	139	186.50
4" copper waste, 2" copper vent	1.000	Ea.	2.520	210	136	346
3" cast iron waste, 1-1/2" cast iron vent	1.000	Ea.	2.244	81	117	198
3" PVC waste, 1-1/2" PVC vent	1.000	Ea.	2.388	40	129	169
3" copper waste, 1-1/2" copper vent	1.000	Ea.	2.014	135	109	244
1/2" P.V.C. supply, 4" P.V.C. waste, 2" P.V.C. vent	1.000	Ea.	2.974	52.50	156	208.50
3" P.V.C. waste, 1-1/2" P.V.C. vent	1.000	Ea.	2.684	45.50	146	191.50
1/2" steel supply, 4" cast iron waste, 2" cast iron vent	1.000	Ea.	2.545	110	133	243
4" cast iron waste, 2" steel vent	1.000	Ea.	2.590	154	136	290
4" P.V.C. waste, 2" P.V.C. vent	1.000	Ea.	2.847	65	149	214
Lavatory, wall hung P.E. cast iron 20" x 18", white	1.000	Ea.	2.000	390	101	491
Color	1.000	Ea.	2.000	385	101	486
Vitreous china 19" x 17", white	1.000	Ea.	2.286	217	116	333
Color	1.000	Ea.	2.286	241	116	357
Lavatory, for vanity top P.E. cast iron 20" x 18", white	1.000	Ea.	2.500	286	127	413
Color	1.000	Ea.	2.500	286	127	413
Steel enameled 20" x 17", white	1.000	Ea.	2.759	203	140	343
Color	1.000	Ea.	2.500	211	127	338
Vitreous china 20" x 16", white	1.000	Ea.	2.963	305	150	455
Color	1.000	Ea.	2.963	305	150	455
Rough-in, for lavatory						
1/2" copper supply, 1-1/2" cast iron waste, 1-1/2" cast iron vent	1.000	Ea.	2.791	89.50	147	236.50
1-1/2" P.V.C. waste, 1-1/2" P.V.C. vent	1.000	Ea.	2.639	45	148	193
1/2" steel supply, 1-1/2" cast iron waste, 1-1/4" steel vent	1.000	Ea.	2.890	136	154	290
1-1/2" P.V.C. waste, 1-1/4" P.V.C. vent	1.000	Ea.	2.921	74	164	238
1/2" P.V.C. supply, 1-1/2" P.V.C. waste, 1-1/2" P.V.C. vent	1.000	Ea.	3.260	53.50	184	237.50
Shower, steel enameled stone base, 32" x 32", white	1.000	Ea.	8.000	975	162	1,137
Color	1.000	Ea.	7.822	1,425	149	1,574
36" x 36", white	1.000	Ea.	8.889	1,575	169	1,744
Color	1.000	Ea.	8.889	1,625	169	1,794
Rough-in, for shower						
1/2" copper supply, 2" cast iron waste, 1-1/2" copper vent	1.000	Ea.	3.161	103	170	273
2" P.V.C. waste, 1-1/2" P.V.C. vent	1.000	Ea.	3.429	62	184	246
1/2" steel supply, 2" cast iron waste, 1-1/2" steel vent	1.000	Ea.	3.887	192	209	401
2" P.V.C. waste, 1-1/2" P.V.C. vent	1.000	Ea.	3.881	109	209	318
1/2" P.V.C. supply, 2" P.V.C. waste, 1-1/2" P.V.C. vent	1.000	Ea.	4.219	75.50	229	304.50
Piping, supply, 1/2" copper	36.000	L.F.	3.556	98.50	200	298.50
1/2" steel	36.000	L.F.	4.571	203	257	460
1/2" P.V.C.	36.000	L.F.	5.333	130	300	430
Waste, 4" cast iron, no hub	7.000	L.F.	1.931	102	98	200
4" P.V.C./DWV	7.000	L.F.	2.333	47.50	118	165.50
4" copper/DWV	7.000	L.F.	2.800	320	144	464
Vent, 2" cast iron, no hub	6.000	L.F.	1.091	83	61.50	144.50
2" copper/DWV	6.000	L.F.	1.091	83	61.50	144.50
2" P.V.C./DWV	6.000	L.F.	1.627	15.90	82.50	98.40
2" steel, galvanized	6.000	L.F.	1.500	114	76	190
Vanity base cabinet, 2 door, 24" x 30"	1.000	Ea.	1.000	288	49	337
24" x 36"	1.000	Ea.	1.200	385	59	444
Vanity top, laminated plastic square edge, 25" x 32"	2.670	L.F.	.712	77.50	35	112.50
25" x 38"	3.170	L.F.	.845	92	41.50	133.50
Carrier , for lavatory, steel, for studs, no arms	1.000	Ea.	1.143	78	64.50	142.50
Wood, 2" x 8" blocking	1.300	L.F.	.052	.79	2.55	3.34

Shower
Bathtub
Lavatory
Vanity Top
Vanity Base
Water Closet

System Description	QUAN.	UNIT	LABOR HOURS	COST EACH		
				MAT.	INST.	TOTAL
BATHROOM WITH LAVATORY INSTALLED IN VANITY						
Water closet, floor mounted, 2 piece, close coupled, white	1.000	Ea.	3.019	284	153	437
Rough-in, vent, 2" diameter DWV piping	1.000	Ea.	.955	32.40	48.40	80.80
Waste, 4" diameter DWV piping	1.000	Ea.	.828	43.65	42	85.65
Supply, 1/2" diameter type "L" copper supply piping	1.000	Ea.	.593	16.44	33.30	49.74
Lavatory, 20" x 18" P.E. cast iron with fittings, white	1.000	Ea.	2.500	286	127	413
Shower, steel, enameled, stone base, corner, white	1.000	Ea.	3.333	1,825	169	1,994
Mixing valve	1.000	Ea.	1.333	156	75	231
Shower door	1.000	Ea.	1.000	259	53.50	312.50
Rough-in, waste, 1-1/2" diameter DWV piping	2.000	Ea.	4.507	155	228	383
Supply, 1/2" diameter type "L" copper supply piping	2.000	Ea.	3.161	87.68	177.60	265.28
Bathtub, P.E. cast iron, 5' long with fittings, white	1.000	Ea.	3.636	1,050	184	1,234
Rough-in, waste, 4" diameter DWV piping	1.000	Ea.	.828	43.65	42	85.65
Supply, 1/2" diameter type "L" copper supply piping	1.000	Ea.	.988	27.40	55.50	82.90
Vent, 1-1/2" diameter DWV piping	1.000	Ea.	.593	40.80	33.40	74.20
Piping, supply, 1/2" diameter type "L" copper supply piping	42.000	L.F.	4.148	115.08	233.10	348.18
Waste, 4" diameter DWV piping	10.000	L.F.	2.759	145.50	140	285.50
Vent, 2" diameter DWV piping	13.000	L.F.	3.250	247	164.45	411.45
Vanity base, 2 doors, 30" wide	1.000	Ea.	1.000	288	49	337
Vanity top, plastic laminated, square edge	2.670	L.F.	.712	77.43	34.84	112.27
TOTAL		Ea.	39.143	5,180.03	2,043.09	7,223.12
BATHROOM WITH WALL HUNG LAVATORY						
Water closet, floor mounted, 2 piece, close coupled, white	1.000	Ea.	3.019	284	153	437
Rough-in, vent, 2" diameter DWV piping	1.000	Ea.	.955	32.40	48.40	80.80
Waste, 4" diameter DWV piping	1.000	Ea.	.828	43.65	42	85.65
Supply, 1/2" diameter type "L" copper supply piping	1.000	Ea.	.593	16.44	33.30	49.74
Lavatory, 20" x 18" P.E. cast iron with fittings, white	1.000	Ea.	2.000	390	101	491
Shower, steel enameled, stone base, corner, white	1.000	Ea.	3.333	1,825	169	1,994
Mixing valve	1.000	Ea.	1.333	156	75	231
Shower door	1.000	Ea.	1.000	259	53.50	312.50
Rough-in, waste, 1-1/2" diameter DWV piping	2.000	Ea.	4.507	155	228	383
Supply, 1/2" diameter type "L" copper supply piping	2.000	Ea.	3.161	87.68	177.60	265.28
Bathtub, P.E. cast iron, 5' long with fittings, white	1.000	Ea.	3.636	1,050	184	1,234
Rough-in, waste, 4" diameter DWV piping	1.000	Ea.	.828	43.65	42	85.65
Supply, 1/2" diameter type "L" copper supply piping	1.000	Ea.	.988	27.40	55.50	82.90
Vent, 1-1/2" diameter copper DWV piping	1.000	Ea.	.593	40.80	33.40	74.20
Piping, supply, 1/2" diameter type "L" copper supply piping	42.000	L.F.	4.148	115.08	233.10	348.18
Waste, 4" diameter DWV piping	10.000	L.F.	2.759	145.50	140	285.50
Vent, 2" diameter DWV piping	13.000	L.F.	3.250	247	164.45	411.45
Carrier, steel, for studs, no arms	1.000	Ea.	1.143	78	64.50	142.50
TOTAL		Ea.	38.074	4,996.60	1,997.75	6,994.35

The costs in this system are on a cost each basis. All necessary piping is included.

Four Fixture Bathroom Price Sheet	QUAN.	UNIT	LABOR HOURS	COST EACH		
				MAT.	INST.	TOTAL
Water closet, close coupled, standard 2 piece, white	1.000	Ea.	3.019	284	153	437
Color	1.000	Ea.	3.019	380	153	533
One piece elongated bowl, white	1.000	Ea.	3.019	590	153	743
Color	1.000	Ea.	3.019	850	153	1,003
Low profile, one piece elongated bowl, white	1.000	Ea.	3.019	1,025	153	1,178
Color	1.000	Ea.	3.019	1,350	153	1,503
1/2" copper supply, 4" cast iron waste, 2" cast iron vent	1.000	Ea.	2.376	92.50	124	216.50
4" PVC/DWV waste, 2" PVC vent	1.000	Ea.	2.678	47.50	139	186.50
4" copper waste, 2" copper vent	1.000	Ea.	2.520	210	136	346
3" cast iron waste, 1-1/2" cast iron vent	1.000	Ea.	2.244	81	117	198
3" P.V.C. waste, 1-1/2" P.V.C. vent	1.000	Ea.	2.388	40	129	169
3" copper waste, 1-1/2" copper vent	1.000	Ea.	2.014	135	109	244
1/2" P.V.C. supply, 4" P.V.C. waste, 2" P.V.C. vent	1.000	Ea.	2.974	52.50	156	208.50
3" P.V.C. waste, 1-1/2" P.V.C. vent	1.000	Ea.	2.684	45.50	146	191.50
1/2" steel supply, 4" cast iron waste, 2" cast iron vent	1.000	Ea.	2.545	110	133	243
4" cast iron waste, 2" steel vent	1.000	Ea.	2.590	154	136	290
4" P.V.C. waste, 2" P.V.C. vent	1.000	Ea.	2.847	65	149	214
Lavatory, wall hung P.E. cast iron 20" x 18", white	1.000	Ea.	2.000	390	101	491
Color	1.000	Ea.	2.000	385	101	486
Vitreous china 19" x 17", white	1.000	Ea.	2.286	217	116	333
Color	1.000	Ea.	2.286	241	116	357
Lavatory for vanity top, P.E. cast iron 20" x 18", white	1.000	Ea.	2.500	286	127	413
Color	1.000	Ea.	2.500	286	127	413
Steel enameled, 20" x 17", white	1.000	Ea.	2.759	203	140	343
Color	1.000	Ea.	2.500	211	127	338
Vitreous china 20" x 16", white	1.000	Ea.	2.963	305	150	455
Color	1.000	Ea.	2.963	305	150	455
Shower, steel enameled stone base, 36" square, white	1.000	Ea.	8.889	1,825	169	1,994
Color	1.000	Ea.	8.889	1,900	169	2,069
Rough-in, for lavatory or shower						
1/2" copper supply, 1-1/2" cast iron waste, 1-1/2" cast iron vent	1.000	Ea.	3.834	121	203	324
1-1/2" P.V.C. waste, 1-1/4" P.V.C. vent	1.000	Ea.	3.675	66	207	273
1/2" steel supply, 1-1/4" cast iron waste, 1-1/4" steel vent	1.000	Ea.	4.103	185	219	404
1-1/4" P.V.C. waste, 1-1/4" P.V.C. vent	1.000	Ea.	3.937	112	221	333
1/2" P.V.C. supply, 1-1/2" P.V.C. waste, 1-1/2" P.V.C. vent	1.000	Ea.	4.592	79.50	259	338.50
Bathtub, P.E. cast iron, 5' long with fittings, white	1.000	Ea.	3.636	1,050	184	1,234
Color	1.000	Ea.	3.636	1,300	184	1,484
Steel, enameled 5' long with fittings, white	1.000	Ea.	2.909	460	147	607
Color	1.000	Ea.	2.909	460	147	607
Rough-in, for bathtub						
1/2" copper supply, 4" cast iron waste, 1-1/2" copper vent	1.000	Ea.	2.409	112	131	243
4" P.V.C. waste, 1-1/2" P.V.C. vent	1.000	Ea.	2.877	56.50	156	212.50
1/2" steel supply, 4" cast iron waste, 1-1/2" steel vent	1.000	Ea.	2.898	157	154	311
4" P.V.C. waste, 1-1/2" P.V.C. vent	1.000	Ea.	3.159	85.50	172	257.50
1/2" P.V.C. supply, 4" P.V.C. waste, 1-1/2" P.V.C. vent	1.000	Ea.	3.371	65	184	249
Piping, supply, 1/2" copper	42.000	L.F.	4.148	115	233	348
1/2" steel	42.000	L.F.	5.333	237	300	537
1/2" P.V.C.	42.000	L.F.	6.222	151	350	501
Waste, 4" cast iron, no hub	10.000	L.F.	2.759	146	140	286
4" P.V.C./DWV	10.000	L.F.	3.333	67.50	169	236.50
4" copper/DWV	10.000	Ea.	4.000	460	205	665
Vent 2" cast iron, no hub	13.000	L.F.	3.105	105	157	262
2" copper/DWV	13.000	L.F.	2.364	179	133	312
2" P.V.C./DWV	13.000	L.F.	3.525	34.50	179	213.50
2" steel, galvanized	13.000	L.F.	3.250	247	164	411
Vanity base cabinet, 2 doors, 30" wide	1.000	Ea.	1.000	288	49	337
Vanity top, plastic laminated, square edge	2.670	L.F.	.712	77.50	35	112.50
Carrier, steel for studs, no arms	1.000	Ea.	1.143	78	64.50	142.50
Wood, 2" x 8" blocking	1.300	L.F.	.052	.79	2.55	3.34

System Description	QUAN.	UNIT	LABOR HOURS	COST EACH		
				MAT.	INST.	TOTAL
BATHROOM WITH LAVATORY INSTALLED IN VANITY						
Water closet, floor mounted, 2 piece, close coupled, white	1.000	Ea.	3.019	284	153	437
Rough-in, vent, 2" diameter DWV piping	1.000	Ea.	.955	32.40	48.40	80.80
Waste, 4" diameter DWV piping	1.000	Ea.	.828	43.65	42	85.65
Supply, 1/2" diameter type "L" copper supply piping	1.000	Ea.	.593	16.44	33.30	49.74
Lavatory, 20" x 18" P.E. cast iron with fittings, white	1.000	Ea.	2.500	286	127	413
Shower, steel, enameled, stone base, corner, white	1.000	Ea.	3.333	1,825	169	1,994
Mixing valve	1.000	Ea.	1.333	156	75	231
Shower door	1.000	Ea.	1.000	259	53.50	312.50
Rough-in, waste, 1-1/2" diameter DWV piping	2.000	Ea.	4.507	155	228	383
Supply, 1/2" diameter type "L" copper supply piping	2.000	Ea.	3.161	87.68	177.60	265.28
Bathtub, P.E. cast iron, 5' long with fittings, white	1.000	Ea.	3.636	1,050	184	1,234
Rough-in, waste, 4" diameter DWV piping	1.000	Ea.	.828	43.65	42	85.65
Supply, 1/2" diameter type "L" copper supply piping	1.000	Ea.	.988	27.40	55.50	82.90
Vent, 1-1/2" diameter DWV piping	1.000	Ea.	.593	40.80	33.40	74.20
Piping, supply, 1/2" diameter type "L" copper supply piping	42.000	L.F.	4.939	137	277.50	414.50
Waste, 4" diameter DWV piping	10.000	L.F.	4.138	218.25	210	428.25
Vent, 2" diameter DWV piping	13.000	L.F.	4.500	342	227.70	569.70
Vanity base, 2 doors, 30" wide	1.000	Ea.	1.000	288	49	337
Vanity top, plastic laminated, square edge	2.670	L.F.	.712	80.10	34.84	114.94
TOTAL		Ea.	42.563	5,372.37	2,220.74	7,593.11
BATHROOM WITH WALL HUNG LAVATORY						
Water closet, floor mounted, 2 piece, close coupled, white	1.000	Ea.	3.019	284	153	437
Rough-in, vent, 2" diameter DWV piping	1.000	Ea.	.955	32.40	48.40	80.80
Waste, 4" diameter DWV piping	1.000	Ea.	.828	43.65	42	85.65
Supply, 1/2" diameter type "L" copper supply piping	1.000	Ea.	.593	16.44	33.30	49.74
Lavatory, 20" x 18" P.E. cast iron with fittings, white	1.000	Ea.	2.000	390	101	491
Shower, steel enameled, stone base, corner, white	1.000	Ea.	3.333	1,825	169	1,994
Mixing valve	1.000	Ea.	1.333	156	75	231
Shower door	1.000	Ea.	1.000	259	53.50	312.50
Rough-in, waste, 1-1/2" diameter DWV piping	2.000	Ea.	4.507	155	228	383
Supply, 1/2" diameter type "L" copper supply piping	2.000	Ea.	3.161	87.68	177.60	265.28
Bathtub, P.E. cast iron, 5" long with fittings, white	1.000	Ea.	3.636	1,050	184	1,234
Rough-in, waste, 4" diameter DWV piping	1.000	Ea.	.828	43.65	42	85.65
Supply, 1/2" diameter type "L" copper supply piping	1.000	Ea.	.988	27.40	55.50	82.90
Vent, 1-1/2" diameter DWV piping	1.000	Ea.	.593	40.80	33.40	74.20
Piping, supply, 1/2" diameter type "L" copper supply piping	42.000	L.F.	4.939	137	277.50	414.50
Waste, 4" diameter DWV piping	10.000	L.F.	4.138	218.25	210	428.25
Vent, 2" diameter DWV piping	13.000	L.F.	4.500	342	227.70	569.70
Carrier, steel for studs, no arms	1.000	Ea.	1.143	78	64.50	142.50
TOTAL		Ea.	41.494	5,186.27	2,175.40	7,361.67

The costs in this system are on a cost each basis. All necessary piping is included.

Four Fixture Bathroom Price Sheet	QUAN.	UNIT	LABOR HOURS	COST EACH		
				MAT.	INST.	TOTAL
Water closet, close coupled, standard 2 piece, white	1.000	Ea.	3.019	284	153	437
Color	1.000	Ea.	3.019	380	153	533
One piece, elongated bowl, white	1.000	Ea.	3.019	590	153	743
Color	1.000	Ea.	3.019	850	153	1,003
Low profile, one piece elongated bowl, white	1.000	Ea.	3.019	1,025	153	1,178
Color	1.000	Ea.	3.019	1,350	153	1,503
Rough-in, for water closet						
1/2" copper supply, 4" cast iron waste, 2" cast iron vent	1.000	Ea.	2.376	92.50	124	216.50
4" PVC/DWW waste, 2" PVC vent	1.000	Ea.	2.678	47.50	139	186.50
4" copper waste, 2" copper vent	1.000	Ea.	2.520	210	136	346
3" cast iron waste, 1-1/2" cast iron vent	1.000	Ea.	2.244	81	117	198
3" PVC waste, 1-1/2" PVC vent	1.000	Ea.	2.388	40	129	169
3" PVC waste, 1-1/2" PVC vent	1.000	Ea.	2.014	135	109	244
1/2" PVC supply, 4" PVC waste, 2" PVC vent	1.000	Ea.	2.974	52.50	156	208.50
3" PVC waste, 1-1/2" PVC vent	1.000	Ea.	2.684	45.50	146	191.50
1/2" steel supply, 4" cast iron waste, 2" cast iron vent	1.000	Ea.	2.545	110	133	243
4" cast iron waste, 2" steel vent	1.000	Ea.	2.590	154	136	290
4" PVC waste, 2" PVC vent	1.000	Ea.	2.847	65	149	214
Lavatory wall hung, P.E. cast iron 20" x 18", white	1.000	Ea.	2.000	390	101	491
Color	1.000	Ea.	2.000	385	101	486
Vitreous china 19" x 17", white	1.000	Ea.	2.286	217	116	333
Color	1.000	Ea.	2.286	241	116	357
Lavatory for vanity top, P.E. cast iron, 20" x 18", white	1.000	Ea.	2.500	286	127	413
Color	1.000	Ea.	2.500	286	127	413
Steel, enameled 20" x 17", white	1.000	Ea.	2.759	203	140	343
Color	1.000	Ea.	2.500	211	127	338
Vitreous china 20" x 16", white	1.000	Ea.	2.963	305	150	455
Color	1.000	Ea.	2.963	305	150	455
Shower, steel enameled, stone base 36" square, white	1.000	Ea.	8.889	1,825	169	1,994
Color	1.000	Ea.	8.889	1,900	169	2,069
Rough-in, for lavatory and shower						
1/2" copper supply, 1-1/2" cast iron waste, 1-1/2" cast iron vent	1.000	Ea.	7.668	243	405	648
1-1/2" PVC waste, 1-1/4" PVC vent	1.000	Ea.	7.352	132	415	547
1/2" steel supply, 1-1/4" cast iron waste, 1-1/4" steel vent	1.000	Ea.	8.205	370	440	810
1-1/4" PVC waste, 1-1/4" PVC vent	1.000	Ea.	7.873	225	445	670
1/2" PVC supply, 1-1/2" PVC waste, 1-1/2" PVC vent	1.000	Ea.	9.185	159	515	674
Bathtub, P.E. cast iron, 5' long with fittings, white	1.000	Ea.	3.636	1,050	184	1,234
Color	1.000	Ea.	3.636	1,300	184	1,484
Steel enameled, 5' long with fittings, white	1.000	Ea.	2.909	460	147	607
Color	1.000	Ea.	2.909	460	147	607
Rough-in, for bathtub						
1/2" copper supply, 4" cast iron waste, 1-1/2" copper vent	1.000	Ea.	2.409	112	131	243
4" PVC waste, 1-1/2" PVC vent	1.000	Ea.	2.877	56.50	156	212.50
1/2" steel supply, 4" cast iron waste, 1-1/2" steel vent	1.000	Ea.	2.898	157	154	311
4" PVC waste, 1-1/2" PVC vent	1.000	Ea.	3.159	85.50	172	257.50
1/2" PVC supply, 4" PVC waste, 1-1/2" PVC vent	1.000	Ea.	3.371	65	184	249
Piping supply, 1/2" copper	42.000	L.F.	4.148	115	233	348
1/2" steel	42.000	L.F.	5.333	237	300	537
1/2" PVC	42.000	L.F.	6.222	151	350	501
Piping, waste, 4" cast iron, no hub	10.000	L.F.	3.586	189	182	371
4" PVC/DWV	10.000	L.F.	4.333	88	220	308
4" copper/DWV	10.000	L.F.	5.200	600	267	867
Piping, vent, 2" cast iron, no hub	13.000	L.F.	3.105	105	157	262
2" copper/DWV	13.000	L.F.	2.364	179	133	312
2" PVC/DWV	13.000	L.F.	3.525	34.50	179	213.50
2" steel, galvanized	13.000	L.F.	3.250	247	164	411
Vanity base cabinet, 2 doors, 30" wide	1.000	Ea.	1.000	288	49	337
Vanity top, plastic laminated, square edge	3.160	L.F.	.843	91.50	41	132.50
Carrier, steel, for studs, no arms	1.000	Ea.	1.143	78	64.50	142.50
Wood, 2" x 8" blocking	1.300	L.F.	.052	.79	2.55	3.34

247

System Description	QUAN.	UNIT	LABOR HOURS	COST EACH		
				MAT.	INST.	TOTAL
BATHROOM WITH SHOWER, BATHTUB, LAVATORIES IN VANITY						
Water closet, floor mounted, 1 piece, white	1.000	Ea.	3.019	1,025	153	1,178
Rough-in, vent, 2″ diameter DWV piping	1.000	Ea.	.955	32.40	48.40	80.80
Waste, 4″ diameter DWV piping	1.000	Ea.	.828	43.65	42	85.65
Supply, 1/2″ diameter type "L" copper supply piping	1.000	Ea.	.593	16.44	33.30	49.74
Lavatory, 20″ x 16″, vitreous china oval, with fittings, white	2.000	Ea.	5.926	610	300	910
Shower, steel enameled, stone base, corner, white	1.000	Ea.	3.333	1,825	169	1,994
Mixing valve	1.000	Ea.	1.333	156	75	231
Shower door	1.000	Ea.	1.000	259	53.50	312.50
Rough-in, waste, 1-1/2″ diameter DWV piping	3.000	Ea.	5.408	186	273.60	459.60
Supply, 1/2″ diameter type "L" copper supply piping	3.000	Ea.	2.963	82.20	166.50	248.70
Bathtub, P.E. cast iron, 5′ long with fittings, white	1.000	Ea.	3.636	1,050	184	1,234
Rough-in, waste, 4″ diameter DWV piping	1.000	Ea.	1.103	58.20	56	114.20
Supply, 1/2″ diameter type "L" copper supply piping	1.000	Ea.	.988	27.40	55.50	82.90
Vent, 1-1/2″ diameter copper DWV piping	1.000	Ea.	.593	40.80	33.40	74.20
Piping, supply, 1/2″ diameter type "L" copper supply piping	42.000	L.F.	4.148	115.08	233.10	348.18
Waste, 4″ diameter DWV piping	10.000	L.F.	2.759	145.50	140	285.50
Vent, 2″ diameter DWV piping	13.000	L.F.	3.250	247	164.45	411.45
Vanity base, 2 door, 24″ x 48″	1.000	Ea.	1.400	460	68.50	528.50
Vanity top, plastic laminated, square edge	4.170	L.F.	1.112	120.93	54.42	175.35
TOTAL		Ea.	44.347	6,500.60	2,303.67	8,804.27

The costs in this system are on a cost each basis. All necessary piping is included.

Description	QUAN.	UNIT	LABOR HOURS	COST EACH		
				MAT.	INST.	TOTAL

Five Fixture Bathroom Price Sheet	QUAN.	UNIT	LABOR HOURS	COST EACH		
				MAT.	INST.	TOTAL
Water closet, close coupled, standard 2 piece, white	1.000	Ea.	3.019	284	153	437
Color	1.000	Ea.	3.019	380	153	533
One piece elongated bowl, white	1.000	Ea.	3.019	590	153	743
Color	1.000	Ea.	3.019	850	153	1,003
Low profile, one piece elongated bowl, white	1.000	Ea.	3.019	1,025	153	1,178
Color	1.000	Ea.	3.019	1,350	153	1,503
Rough-in, supply, waste and vent for water closet						
1/2" copper supply, 4" cast iron waste, 2" cast iron vent	1.000	Ea.	2.376	92.50	124	216.50
4" P.V.C./DWV waste, 2" P.V.C. vent	1.000	Ea.	2.678	47.50	139	186.50
4" copper waste, 2" copper vent	1.000	Ea.	2.520	210	136	346
3" cast iron waste, 1-1/2" cast iron vent	1.000	Ea.	2.244	81	117	198
3" P.V.C. waste, 1-1/2" P.V.C. vent	1.000	Ea.	2.388	40	129	169
3" copper waste, 1-1/2" copper vent	1.000	Ea.	2.014	135	109	244
1/2" P.V.C. supply, 4" P.V.C. waste, 2" P.V.C. vent	1.000	Ea.	2.974	52.50	156	208.50
3" P.V.C. waste, 1-1/2" P.V.C. supply	1.000	Ea.	2.684	45.50	146	191.50
1/2" steel supply, 4" cast iron waste, 2" cast iron vent	1.000	Ea.	2.545	110	133	243
4" cast iron waste, 2" steel vent	1.000	Ea.	2.590	154	136	290
4" P.V.C. waste, 2" P.V.C. vent	1.000	Ea.	2.847	65	149	214
Lavatory, wall hung, P.E. cast iron 20" x 18", white	2.000	Ea.	4.000	780	202	982
Color	2.000	Ea.	4.000	770	202	972
Vitreous china, 19" x 17", white	2.000	Ea.	4.571	435	232	667
Color	2.000	Ea.	4.571	480	232	712
Lavatory, for vanity top, P.E. cast iron, 20" x 18", white	2.000	Ea.	5.000	570	254	824
Color	2.000	Ea.	5.000	570	254	824
Steel enameled 20" x 17", white	2.000	Ea.	5.517	405	280	685
Color	2.000	Ea.	5.000	420	254	674
Vitreous china 20" x 16", white	2.000	Ea.	5.926	610	300	910
Color	2.000	Ea.	5.926	610	300	910
Shower, steel enameled, stone base 36" square, white	1.000	Ea.	8.889	1,825	169	1,994
Color	1.000	Ea.	8.889	1,900	169	2,069
Rough-in, for lavatory or shower						
1/2" copper supply, 1-1/2" cast iron waste, 1-1/2" cast iron vent	3.000	Ea.	8.371	268	440	708
1-1/2" P.V.C. waste, 1-1/4" P.V.C. vent	3.000	Ea.	7.916	135	445	580
1/2" steel supply, 1-1/4" cast iron waste, 1-1/4" steel vent	3.000	Ea.	8.670	405	460	865
1-1/4" P.V.C. waste, 1-1/4" P.V.C. vent	3.000	Ea.	8.381	222	470	692
1/2" P.V.C. supply, 1-1/2" P.V.C. waste, 1-1/2" P.V.C. vent	3.000	Ea.	9.778	161	550	711
Bathtub, P.E. cast iron 5' long with fittings, white	1.000	Ea.	3.636	1,050	184	1,234
Color	1.000	Ea.	3.636	1,300	184	1,484
Steel, enameled 5' long with fittings, white	1.000	Ea.	2.909	460	147	607
Color	1.000	Ea.	2.909	460	147	607
Rough-in, for bathtub						
1/2" copper supply, 4" cast iron waste, 1-1/2" copper vent	1.000	Ea.	2.684	126	145	271
4" P.V.C. waste, 1-1/2" P.V.C. vent	1.000	Ea.	3.210	63	173	236
1/2" steel supply, 4" cast iron waste, 1-1/2" steel vent	1.000	Ea.	3.173	172	168	340
4" P.V.C. waste, 1-1/2" P.V.C. vent	1.000	Ea.	3.492	92.50	189	281.50
1/2" P.V.C. supply, 4" P.V.C. waste, 1-1/2" P.V.C. vent	1.000	Ea.	3.704	72	201	273
Piping, supply, 1/2" copper	42.000	L.F.	4.148	115	233	348
1/2" steel	42.000	L.F.	5.333	237	300	537
1/2" P.V.C.	42.000	L.F.	6.222	151	350	501
Piping, waste, 4" cast iron, no hub	10.000	L.F.	2.759	146	140	286
4" P.V.C./DWV	10.000	L.F.	3.333	67.50	169	236.50
4" copper/DWV	10.000	L.F.	4.000	460	205	665
Piping, vent, 2" cast iron, no hub	13.000	L.F.	3.105	105	157	262
2" copper/DWV	13.000	L.F.	2.364	179	133	312
2" P.V.C./DWV	13.000	L.F.	3.525	34.50	179	213.50
2" steel, galvanized	13.000	L.F.	3.250	247	164	411
Vanity base cabinet, 2 doors, 24" x 48"	1.000	Ea.	1.400	460	68.50	528.50
Vanity top, plastic laminated, square edge	4.170	L.F.	1.112	121	54.50	175.50
Carrier, steel, for studs, no arms	1.000	Ea.	1.143	78	64.50	142.50
Wood, 2" x 8" blocking	1.300	L.F.	.052	.79	2.55	3.34

Floor Registers
Lateral Ducts
Return Air Grille
Register Elbows
Return Air Duct
Supply Duct
Plenum
Furnace

System Description	QUAN.	UNIT	LABOR HOURS	COST PER SYSTEM		
				MAT.	INST.	TOTAL
HEATING ONLY, GAS FIRED HOT AIR, ONE ZONE, 1200 S.F. BUILDING						
Furnace, gas, up flow	1.000	Ea.	5.000	765	241	1,006
Intermittent pilot	1.000	Ea.		165		165
Supply duct, rigid fiberglass	176.000	S.F.	12.068	149.60	603.68	753.28
Return duct, sheet metal, galvanized	158.000	Lb.	16.137	82.16	805.80	887.96
Lateral ducts, 6" flexible fiberglass	144.000	L.F.	8.862	377.28	427.68	804.96
Register, elbows	12.000	Ea.	3.200	354	154.20	508.20
Floor registers, enameled steel	12.000	Ea.	3.000	342	160.80	502.80
Floor grille, return air	2.000	Ea.	.727	52	39	91
Thermostat	1.000	Ea.	1.000	48	53.50	101.50
Plenum	1.000	Ea.	1.000	88	48	136
TOTAL		System	50.994	2,423.04	2,533.66	4,956.70
HEATING/COOLING, GAS FIRED FORCED AIR, ONE ZONE, 1200 S.F. BUILDING						
Furnace, including plenum, compressor, coil	1.000	Ea.	14.720	5,037	708.40	5,745.40
Intermittent pilot	1.000	Ea.		165		165
Supply duct, rigid fiberglass	176.000	S.F.	12.068	149.60	603.68	753.28
Return duct, sheet metal, galvanized	158.000	Lb.	16.137	82.16	805.80	887.96
Lateral duct, 6" flexible fiberglass	144.000	L.F.	8.862	377.28	427.68	804.96
Register elbows	12.000	Ea.	3.200	354	154.20	508.20
Floor registers, enameled steel	12.000	Ea.	3.000	342	160.80	502.80
Floor grille return air	2.000	Ea.	.727	52	39	91
Thermostat	1.000	Ea.	1.000	48	53.50	101.50
Refrigeration piping, 25 ft. (pre-charged)	1.000	Ea.		259		259
TOTAL		System	59.714	6,866.04	2,953.06	9,819.10

The costs in these systems are based on complete system basis. For larger buildings use the price sheet on the opposite page.

Description	QUAN.	UNIT	LABOR HOURS	COST PER SYSTEM		
				MAT.	INST.	TOTAL

Gas Heating/Cooling Price Sheet	QUAN.	UNIT	LABOR HOURS	COST EACH		
				MAT.	INST.	TOTAL
Furnace, heating only, 100 MBH, area to 1200 S.F.	1.000	Ea.	5.000	765	241	1,006
120 MBH, area to 1500 S.F.	1.000	Ea.	5.000	765	241	1,006
160 MBH, area to 2000 S.F.	1.000	Ea.	5.714	775	276	1,051
200 MBH, area to 2400 S.F.	1.000	Ea.	6.154	2,650	297	2,947
Heating/cooling, 100 MBH heat, 36 MBH cool, to 1200 S.F.	1.000	Ea.	16.000	5,475	770	6,245
120 MBH heat, 42 MBH cool, to 1500 S.F.	1.000	Ea.	18.462	5,850	925	6,775
144 MBH heat, 47 MBH cool, to 2000 S.F.	1.000	Ea.	20.000	6,750	1,000	7,750
200 MBH heat, 60 MBH cool, to 2400 S.F.	1.000	Ea.	34.286	7,100	1,725	8,825
Intermittent pilot, 100 MBH furnace	1.000	Ea.		165		165
200 MBH furnace	1.000	Ea.		165		165
Supply duct, rectangular, area to 1200 S.F., rigid fiberglass	176.000	S.F.	12.068	150	605	755
Sheet metal insulated	228.000	Lb.	31.331	251	1,525	1,776
Area to 1500 S.F., rigid fiberglass	176.000	S.F.	12.068	150	605	755
Sheet metal insulated	228.000	Lb.	31.331	251	1,525	1,776
Area to 2400 S.F., rigid fiberglass	205.000	S.F.	14.057	174	705	879
Sheet metal insulated	271.000	Lb.	37.048	295	1,800	2,095
Round flexible, insulated 6″ diameter, to 1200 S.F.	156.000	L.F.	9.600	410	465	875
To 1500 S.F.	184.000	L.F.	11.323	480	545	1,025
8″ diameter, to 2000 S.F.	269.000	L.F.	23.911	890	1,150	2,040
To 2400 S.F.	248.000	L.F.	22.045	820	1,075	1,895
Return duct, sheet metal galvanized, to 1500 S.F.	158.000	Lb.	16.137	82	805	887
To 2400 S.F.	191.000	Lb.	19.507	99.50	975	1,074.50
Lateral ducts, flexible round 6″ insulated, to 1200 S.F.	144.000	L.F.	8.862	375	430	805
To 1500 S.F.	172.000	L.F.	10.585	450	510	960
To 2000 S.F.	261.000	L.F.	16.062	685	775	1,460
To 2400 S.F.	300.000	L.F.	18.462	785	890	1,675
Spiral steel insulated, to 1200 S.F.	144.000	L.F.	20.067	450	940	1,390
To 1500 S.F.	172.000	L.F.	23.952	535	1,125	1,660
To 2000 S.F.	261.000	L.F.	36.352	815	1,700	2,515
To 2400 S.F.	300.000	L.F.	41.825	935	1,950	2,885
Rectangular sheet metal galvanized insulated, to 1200 S.F.	228.000	Lb.	39.056	375	1,875	2,250
To 1500 S.F.	344.000	Lb.	53.966	490	2,625	3,115
To 2000 S.F.	522.000	Lb.	81.926	740	3,975	4,715
To 2400 S.F.	600.000	Lb.	94.189	850	4,575	5,425
Register elbows, to 1500 S.F.	12.000	Ea.	3.200	355	154	509
To 2400 S.F.	14.000	Ea.	3.733	415	180	595
Floor registers, enameled steel w/damper, to 1500 S.F.	12.000	Ea.	3.000	340	161	501
To 2400 S.F.	14.000	Ea.	4.308	460	231	691
Return air grille, area to 1500 S.F. 12″ x 12″	2.000	Ea.	.727	52	39	91
Area to 2400 S.F. 8″ x 16″	2.000	Ea.	.444	36	24	60
Area to 2400 S.F. 8″ x 16″	2.000	Ea.	.727	49	39	88
16″ x 16″	1.000	Ea.	.364	35	19.50	54.50
Thermostat, manual, 1 set back	1.000	Ea.	1.000	48	53.50	101.50
Electric, timed, 1 set back	1.000	Ea.	1.000	36.50	53.50	90
2 set back	1.000	Ea.	1.000	157	53.50	210.50
Plenum, heating only, 100 M.B.H.	1.000	Ea.	1.000	88	48	136
120 MBH	1.000	Ea.	1.000	88	48	136
160 MBH	1.000	Ea.	1.000	88	48	136
200 MBH	1.000	Ea.	1.000	88	48	136
Refrigeration piping, 3/8″	25.000	L.F.		27.50		27.50
3/4″	25.000	L.F.		63		63
7/8″	25.000	L.F.		73.50		73.50
Refrigerant piping, 25 ft. (precharged)	1.000	Ea.		259		259
Diffusers, ceiling, 6″ diameter, to 1500 S.F.	10.000	Ea.	4.444	255	240	495
To 2400 S.F.	12.000	Ea.	6.000	330	325	655
Floor, aluminum, adjustable, 2-1/4″ x 12″ to 1500 S.F.	12.000	Ea.	3.000	246	161	407
To 2400 S.F.	14.000	Ea.	3.500	287	188	475
Side wall, aluminum, adjustable, 8″ x 4″, to 1500 S.F.	12.000	Ea.	3.000	565.	161	726
5″ x 10″ to 2400 S.F.	12.000	Ea.	3.692	760	198	958

System Description	QUAN.	UNIT	LABOR HOURS	COST PER SYSTEM		
				MAT.	INST.	TOTAL
HEATING ONLY, OIL FIRED HOT AIR, ONE ZONE, 1200 S.F. BUILDING						
Furnace, oil fired, atomizing gun type burner	1.000	Ea.	4.571	2,050	220	2,270
3/8" diameter copper supply pipe	1.000	Ea.	2.759	62.10	156	218.10
Shut off valve	1.000	Ea.	.333	11.85	18.75	30.60
Oil tank, 275 gallon, on legs	1.000	Ea.	3.200	410	162	572
Supply duct, rigid fiberglass	176.000	S.F.	12.068	149.60	603.68	753.28
Return duct, sheet metal, galvanized	158.000	Lb.	16.137	82.16	805.80	887.96
Lateral ducts, 6" flexible fiberglass	144.000	L.F.	8.862	377.28	427.68	804.96
Register elbows	12.000	Ea.	3.200	354	154.20	508.20
Floor register, enameled steel	12.000	Ea.	3.000	342	160.80	502.80
Floor grille, return air	2.000	Ea.	.727	52	39	91
Thermostat	1.000	Ea.	1.000	48	53.50	101.50
TOTAL		System	55.857	3,938.99	2,801.41	6,740.40
HEATING/COOLING, OIL FIRED, FORCED AIR, ONE ZONE, 1200 S.F. BUILDING						
Furnace, including plenum, compressor, coil	1.000	Ea.	16.000	5,850	770	6,620
3/8" diameter copper supply pipe	1.000	Ea.	2.759	62.10	156	218.10
Shut off valve	1.000	Ea.	.333	11.85	18.75	30.60
Oil tank, 275 gallon on legs	1.000	Ea.	3.200	410	162	572
Supply duct, rigid fiberglass	176.000	S.F.	12.068	149.60	603.68	753.28
Return duct, sheet metal, galvanized	158.000	Lb.	16.137	82.16	805.80	887.96
Lateral ducts, 6" flexible fiberglass	144.000	L.F.	8.862	377.28	427.68	804.96
Register elbows	12.000	Ea.	3.200	354	154.20	508.20
Floor registers, enameled steel	12.000	Ea.	3.000	342	160.80	502.80
Floor grille, return air	2.000	Ea.	.727	52	39	91
Refrigeration piping (precharged)	25.000	L.F.		259		259
TOTAL		System	66.286	7,949.99	3,297.91	11,247.90

Description	QUAN.	UNIT	LABOR HOURS	COST EACH		
				MAT.	INST.	TOTAL

Oil Fired Heating/Cooling	QUAN.	UNIT	LABOR HOURS	COST EACH		
				MAT.	INST.	TOTAL
Furnace, heating, 95.2 MBH, area to 1200 S.F.	1.000	Ea.	4.706	2,075	227	2,302
123.2 MBH, area to 1500 S.F.	1.000	Ea.	5.000	2,150	241	2,391
151.2 MBH, area to 2000 S.F.	1.000	Ea.	5.333	2,500	257	2,757
200 MBH, area to 2400 S.F.	1.000	Ea.	6.154	2,550	297	2,847
Heating/cooling, 95.2 MBH heat, 36 MBH cool, to 1200 S.F.	1.000	Ea.	16.000	5,850	770	6,620
112 MBH heat, 42 MBH cool, to 1500 S.F.	1.000	Ea.	24.000	8,775	1,150	9,925
151 MBH heat, 47 MBH cool, to 2000 S.F.	1.000	Ea.	20.800	7,600	1,000	8,600
184.8 MBH heat, 60 MBH cool, to 2400 S.F.	1.000	Ea.	24.000	2,700	1,200	3,900
Oil piping to furnace, 3/8" dia., copper	1.000	Ea.	3.412	191	190	381
Oil tank, on legs above ground, 275 gallons	1.000	Ea.	3.200	410	162	572
550 gallons	1.000	Ea.	5.926	2,475	299	2,774
Below ground, 275 gallons	1.000	Ea.	3.200	410	162	572
550 gallons	1.000	Ea.	5.926	2,475	299	2,774
1000 gallons	1.000	Ea.	6.400	3,125	325	3,450
Supply duct, rectangular, area to 1200 S.F., rigid fiberglass	176.000	S.F.	12.068	150	605	755
Sheet metal, insulated	228.000	Lb.	31.331	251	1,525	1,776
Area to 1500 S.F., rigid fiberglass	176.000	S.F.	12.068	150	605	755
Sheet metal, insulated	228.000	Lb.	31.331	251	1,525	1,776
Area to 2400 S.F., rigid fiberglass	205.000	S.F.	14.057	174	705	879
Sheet metal, insulated	271.000	Lb.	37.048	295	1,800	2,095
Round flexible, insulated, 6" diameter to 1200 S.F.	156.000	L.F.	9.600	410	465	875
To 1500 S.F.	184.000	L.F.	11.323	480	545	1,025
8" diameter to 2000 S.F.	269.000	L.F.	23.911	890	1,150	2,040
To 2400 S.F.	269.000	L.F.	22.045	820	1,075	1,895
Return duct, sheet metal galvanized, to 1500 S.F.	158.000	Lb.	16.137	82	805	887
To 2400 S.F.	191.000	Lb.	19.507	99.50	975	1,074.50
Lateral ducts, flexible round, 6", insulated to 1200 S.F.	144.000	L.F.	8.862	375	430	805
To 1500 S.F.	172.000	L.F.	10.585	450	510	960
To 2000 S.F.	261.000	L.F.	16.062	685	775	1,460
To 2400 S.F.	300.000	L.F.	18.462	785	890	1,675
Spiral steel, insulated to 1200 S.F.	144.000	L.F.	20.067	450	940	1,390
To 1500 S.F.	172.000	L.F.	23.952	535	1,125	1,660
To 2000 S.F.	261.000	L.F.	36.352	815	1,700	2,515
To 2400 S.F.	300.000	L.F.	41.825	935	1,950	2,885
Rectangular sheet metal galvanized insulated, to 1200 S.F.	288.000	Lb.	45.183	410	2,200	2,610
To 1500 S.F.	344.000	Lb.	53.966	490	2,625	3,115
To 2000 S.F.	522.000	Lb.	81.926	740	3,975	4,715
To 2400 S.F.	600.000	Lb.	94.189	850	4,575	5,425
Register elbows, to 1500 S.F.	12.000	Ea.	3.200	355	154	509
To 2400 S.F.	14.000	Ea.	3.733	415	180	595
Floor registers, enameled steel w/damper, to 1500 S.F.	12.000	Ea.	3.000	340	161	501
To 2400 S.F.	14.000	Ea.	4.308	460	231	691
Return air grille, area to 1500 S.F., 12" x 12"	2.000	Ea.	.727	52	39	91
12" x 24"	1.000	Ea.	.444	36	24	60
Area to 2400 S.F., 8" x 16"	2.000	Ea.	.727	49	39	88
16" x 16"	1.000	Ea.	.364	35	19.50	54.50
Thermostat, manual, 1 set back	1.000	Ea.	1.000	48	53.50	101.50
Electric, timed, 1 set back	1.000	Ea.	1.000	36.50	53.50	90
2 set back	1.000	Ea.	1.000	157	53.50	210.50
Refrigeration piping, 3/8"	25.000	L.F.		27.50		27.50
3/4"	25.000	L.F.		63		63
Diffusers, ceiling, 6" diameter, to 1500 S.F.	10.000	Ea.	4.444	255	240	495
To 2400 S.F.	12.000	Ea.	6.000	330	325	655
Floor, aluminum, adjustable, 2-1/4" x 12" to 1500 S.F.	12.000	Ea.	3.000	246	161	407
To 2400 S.F.	14.000	Ea.	3.500	287	188	475
Side wall, aluminum, adjustable, 8" x 4", to 1500 S.F.	12.000	Ea.	3.000	565	161	726
5" x 10" to 2400 S.F.	12.000	Ea.	3.692	760	198	958

System Description	QUAN.	UNIT	LABOR HOURS	COST EACH		
				MAT.	INST.	TOTAL
OIL FIRED HOT WATER HEATING SYSTEM, AREA TO 1200 S.F.						
Boiler package, oil fired, 97 MBH, area to 1200 S.F. building	1.000	Ea.	15.000	1,900	730	2,630
3/8" diameter copper supply pipe	1.000	Ea.	2.759	62.10	156	218.10
Shut off valve	1.000	Ea.	.333	11.85	18.75	30.60
Oil tank, 275 gallon, with black iron filler pipe	1.000	Ea.	3.200	410	162	572
Supply piping, 3/4" copper tubing	176.000	L.F.	18.526	740.96	1,047.20	1,788.16
Supply fittings, copper 3/4"	36.000	Ea.	15.158	129.60	846	975.60
Supply valves, 3/4"	2.000	Ea.	.800	204	45	249
Baseboard radiation, 3/4"	106.000	L.F.	35.333	526.82	1,786.10	2,312.92
Zone valve	1.000	Ea.	.400	172	22.50	194.50
TOTAL		Ea.	91.509	4,157.33	4,813.55	8,970.88
OIL FIRED HOT WATER HEATING SYSTEM, AREA TO 2400 S.F.						
Boiler package, oil fired, 225 MBH, area to 2400 S.F. building	1.000	Ea.	25.105	6,100	1,225	7,325
3/8" diameter copper supply pipe	1.000	Ea.	2.759	62.10	156	218.10
Shut off valve	1.000	Ea.	.333	11.85	18.75	30.60
Oil tank, 550 gallon, with black iron pipe filler pipe	1.000	Ea.	5.926	2,475	299	2,774
Supply piping, 3/4" copper tubing	228.000	L.F.	23.999	959.88	1,356.60	2,316.48
Supply fittings, copper	46.000	Ea.	19.368	165.60	1,081	1,246.60
Supply valves	2.000	Ea.	.800	204	45	249
Baseboard radiation	212.000	L.F.	70.666	1,053.64	3,572.20	4,625.84
Zone valve	1.000	Ea.	.400	172	22.50	194.50
TOTAL		Ea.	149.356	11,204.07	7,776.05	18,980.12

The costs in this system are on a cost each basis. The costs represent
total cost for the system based on a gross square foot of plan area.

Description	QUAN.	UNIT	LABOR HOURS	COST EACH		
				MAT.	INST.	TOTAL

Hot Water Heating Price Sheet	QUAN.	UNIT	LABOR HOURS	COST EACH MAT.	COST EACH INST.	COST EACH TOTAL
Boiler, oil fired, 97 MBH, area to 1200 S.F.	1.000	Ea.	15.000	1,900	730	2,630
118 MBH, area to 1500 S.F.	1.000	Ea.	16.506	2,000	805	2,805
161 MBH, area to 2000 S.F.	1.000	Ea.	18.405	2,225	895	3,120
215 MBH, area to 2400 S.F.	1.000	Ea.	19.704	3,525	1,900	5,425
Oil piping, (valve & filter), 3/8" copper	1.000	Ea.	3.289	74	175	249
1/4" copper	1.000	Ea.	3.242	93	182	275
Oil tank, filler pipe and cap on legs, 275 gallon	1.000	Ea.	3.200	410	162	572
550 gallon	1.000	Ea.	5.926	2,475	299	2,774
Buried underground, 275 gallon	1.000	Ea.	3.200	410	162	572
550 gallon	1.000	Ea.	5.926	2,475	299	2,774
1000 gallon	1.000	Ea.	6.400	3,125	325	3,450
Supply piping copper, area to 1200 S.F., 1/2" tubing	176.000	L.F.	17.384	480	975	1,455
3/4" tubing	176.000	L.F.	18.526	740	1,050	1,790
Area to 1500 S.F., 1/2" tubing	186.000	L.F.	18.371	510	1,025	1,535
3/4" tubing	186.000	L.F.	19.578	785	1,100	1,885
Area to 2000 S.F., 1/2" tubing	204.000	L.F.	20.149	560	1,125	1,685
3/4" tubing	204.000	L.F.	21.473	860	1,225	2,085
Area to 2400 S.F., 1/2" tubing	228.000	L.F.	22.520	625	1,275	1,900
3/4" tubing	228.000	L.F.	23.999	960	1,350	2,310
Supply pipe fittings copper, area to 1200 S.F., 1/2"	36.000	Ea.	14.400	57.50	810	867.50
3/4"	36.000	Ea.	15.158	130	845	975
Area to 1500 S.F., 1/2"	40.000	Ea.	16.000	64	900	964
3/4"	40.000	Ea.	16.842	144	940	1,084
Area to 2000 S.F., 1/2"	44.000	Ea.	17.600	70.50	990	1,060.50
3/4"	44.000	Ea.	18.526	158	1,025	1,183
Area to 2400, S.F., 1/2"	46.000	Ea.	18.400	73.50	1,025	1,098.50
3/4"	46.000	Ea.	19.368	166	1,075	1,241
Supply valves, 1/2" pipe size	2.000	Ea.	.667	151	37.50	188.50
3/4"	2.000	Ea.	.800	204	45	249
Baseboard radiation, area to 1200 S.F., 1/2" tubing	106.000	L.F.	28.267	880	1,425	2,305
3/4" tubing	106.000	L.F.	35.333	525	1,775	2,300
Area to 1500 S.F., 1/2" tubing	134.000	L.F.	35.734	1,100	1,800	2,900
3/4" tubing	134.000	L.F.	44.666	665	2,250	2,915
Area to 2000 S.F., 1/2" tubing	178.000	L.F.	47.467	1,475	2,400	3,875
3/4" tubing	178.000	L.F.	59.333	885	3,000	3,885
Area to 2400 S.F., 1/2" tubing	212.000	L.F.	56.534	1,750	2,850	4,600
3/4" tubing	212.000	L.F.	70.666	1,050	3,575	4,625
Zone valves, 1/2" tubing	1.000	Ea.	.400	172	22.50	194.50
3/4" tubing	1.000	Ea.	.400	173	22.50	195.50

255

System Description	QUAN.	UNIT	LABOR HOURS	COST EACH		
				MAT.	INST.	TOTAL
ROOFTOP HEATING/COOLING UNIT, AREA TO 2000 S.F.						
Rooftop unit, single zone, electric cool, gas heat, to 2000 S.F.	1.000	Ea.	28.521	5,350	1,450	6,800
Gas piping	34.500	L.F.	5.207	238.05	293.25	531.30
Duct, supply and return, galvanized steel	38.000	Lb.	3.881	19.76	193.80	213.56
Insulation, ductwork	33.000	S.F.	1.508	24.75	68.97	93.72
Lateral duct, flexible duct 12" diameter, insulated	72.000	L.F.	11.520	345.60	554.40	900
Diffusers	4.000	Ea.	4.571	1,160	246	1,406
Return registers	1.000	Ea.	.727	101	39	140
TOTAL		Ea.	55.935	7,239.16	2,845.42	10,084.58
ROOFTOP HEATING/COOLING UNIT, AREA TO 5000 S.F.						
Rooftop unit, single zone, electric cool, gas heat, to 5000 S.F.	1.000	Ea.	42.032	16,500	2,050	18,550
Gas piping	86.250	L.F.	13.019	595.13	733.13	1,328.26
Duct supply and return, galvanized steel	95.000	Lb.	9.702	49.40	484.50	533.90
Insulation, ductwork	82.000	S.F.	3.748	61.50	171.38	232.88
Lateral duct, flexible duct, 12" diameter, insulated	180.000	L.F.	28.800	864	1,386	2,250
Diffusers	10.000	Ea.	11.429	2,900	615	3,515
Return registers	3.000	Ea.	2.182	303	117	420
TOTAL		Ea.	110.912	21,273.03	5,557.01	26,830.04

Description	QUAN.	UNIT	LABOR HOURS	COST EACH		
				MAT.	INST.	TOTAL

Rooftop Price Sheet	QUAN.	UNIT	LABOR HOURS	COST EACH		
				MAT.	INST.	TOTAL
Rooftop unit, single zone, electric cool, gas heat to 2000 S.F.	1.000	Ea.	28.521	5,350	1,450	6,800
Area to 3000 S.F.	1.000	Ea.	35.982	11,600	1,750	13,350
Area to 5000 S.F.	1.000	Ea.	42.032	16,500	2,050	18,550
Area to 10000 S.F.	1.000	Ea.	68.376	28,100	3,450	31,550
Gas piping, area 2000 through 4000 S.F.	34.500	L.F.	5.207	238	293	531
Area 5000 to 10000 S.F.	86.250	L.F.	13.019	595	735	1,330
Duct, supply and return, galvanized steel, to 2000 S.F.	38.000	Lb.	3.881	19.75	194	213.75
Area to 3000 S.F.	57.000	Lb.	5.821	29.50	291	320.50
Area to 5000 S.F.	95.000	Lb.	9.702	49.50	485	534.50
Area to 10000 S.F.	190.000	Lb.	19.405	99	970	1,069
Rigid fiberglass, area to 2000 S.F.	33.000	S.F.	2.263	28	113	141
Area to 3000 S.F.	49.000	S.F.	3.360	41.50	168	209.50
Area to 5000 S.F.	82.000	S.F.	5.623	69.50	281	350.50
Area to 10000 S.F.	164.000	S.F.	11.245	139	565	704
Insulation, supply and return, blanket type, area to 2000 S.F.	33.000	S.F.	1.508	25	69	94
Area to 3000 S.F.	49.000	S.F.	2.240	37	102	139
Area to 5000 S.F.	82.000	S.F.	3.748	61.50	171	232.50
Area to 10000 S.F.	164.000	S.F.	7.496	123	345	468
Lateral ducts, flexible round, 12" insulated, to 2000 S.F.	72.000	L.F.	11.520	345	555	900
Area to 3000 S.F.	108.000	L.F.	17.280	520	830	1,350
Area to 5000 S.F.	180.000	L.F.	28.800	865	1,375	2,240
Area to 10000 S.F.	360.000	L.F.	57.600	1,725	2,775	4,500
Rectangular, galvanized steel, to 2000 S.F.	239.000	Lb.	24.409	124	1,225	1,349
Area to 3000 S.F.	360.000	Lb.	36.767	187	1,825	2,012
Area to 5000 S.F.	599.000	Lb.	61.176	310	3,050	3,360
Area to 10000 S.F.	998.000	Lb.	101.926	520	5,100	5,620
Diffusers, ceiling, 1 to 4 way blow, 24" x 24", to 2000 S.F.	4.000	Ea.	4.571	1,150	246	1,396
Area to 3000 S.F.	6.000	Ea.	6.857	1,750	370	2,120
Area to 5000 S.F.	10.000	Ea.	11.429	2,900	615	3,515
Area to 10000 S.F.	20.000	Ea.	22.857	5,800	1,225	7,025
Return grilles, 24" x 24", to 2000 S.F.	1.000	Ea.	.727	101	39	140
Area to 3000 S.F.	2.000	Ea.	1.455	202	78	280
Area to 5000 S.F.	3.000	Ea.	2.182	305	117	422
Area to 10000 S.F.	5.000	Ea.	3.636	505	195	700

Division 9
Electrical

Weather Cap

Service Entrance Cable

Meter Socket

Panelboard, Including Breakers

Ground Cable

Ground Rod with Clamp

System Description	QUAN.	UNIT	LABOR HOURS	COST EACH		
				MAT.	INST.	TOTAL
100 AMP SERVICE						
Weather cap	1.000	Ea.	.667	14.30	35.50	49.80
Service entrance cable	10.000	L.F.	.762	39.70	40.70	80.40
Meter socket	1.000	Ea.	2.500	48.50	134	182.50
Ground rod with clamp	1.000	Ea.	1.455	18.40	78	96.40
Ground cable	5.000	L.F.	.250	10.65	13.35	24
Panel board, 12 circuit	1.000	Ea.	6.667	277	355	632
TOTAL		Ea.	12.301	408.55	656.55	1,065.10
200 AMP SERVICE						
Weather cap	1.000	Ea.	1.000	39.50	53.50	93
Service entrance cable	10.000	L.F.	1.143	62.50	61	123.50
Meter socket	1.000	Ea.	4.211	81.50	225	306.50
Ground rod with clamp	1.000	Ea.	1.818	40	97	137
Ground cable	10.000	L.F.	.500	21.30	26.70	48
3/4" EMT	5.000	L.F.	.308	5.30	16.45	21.75
Panel board, 24 circuit	1.000	Ea.	12.308	630	555	1,185
TOTAL		Ea.	21.288	880.10	1,034.65	1,914.75
400 AMP SERVICE						
Weather cap	1.000	Ea.	2.963	490	158	648
Service entrance cable	180.000	L.F.	5.760	658.80	307.80	966.60
Meter socket	1.000	Ea.	4.211	81.50	225	306.50
Ground rod with clamp	1.000	Ea.	2.000	101	107	208
Ground cable	20.000	L.F.	.485	46.40	26	72.40
3/4" greenfield	20.000	L.F.	1.000	17.20	53.40	70.60
Current transformer cabinet	1.000	Ea.	6.154	231	330	561
Panel board, 42 circuit	1.000	Ea.	33.333	3,275	1,775	5,050
TOTAL		Ea.	55.906	4,900.90	2,982.20	7,883.10

Thermostat

Electric Baseboard

System Description	QUAN.	UNIT	LABOR HOURS	COST EACH		
				MAT.	INST.	TOTAL
4' BASEBOARD HEATER						
Electric baseboard heater, 4' long	1.000	Ea.	1.194	59.50	64	123.50
Thermostat, integral	1.000	Ea.	.500	33	26.50	59.50
Romex, 12-3 with ground	40.000	L.F.	1.600	21.20	85.60	106.80
Panel board breaker, 20 Amp	1.000	Ea.	.300	11.55	16.05	27.60
TOTAL		Ea.	3.594	125.25	192.15	317.40
6' BASEBOARD HEATER						
Electric baseboard heater, 6' long	1.000	Ea.	1.600	81.50	85.50	167
Thermostat, integral	1.000	Ea.	.500	33	26.50	59.50
Romex, 12-3 with ground	40.000	I.F.	1.600	21.20	85.60	106.80
Panel board breaker, 20 Amp	1.000	Ea.	.400	15.40	21.40	36.80
TOTAL		Ea.	4.100	151.10	219	370.10
8' BASEBOARD HEATER						
Electric baseboard heater, 8' long	1.000	Ea.	2.000	101	107	208
Thermostat, integral	1.000	Ea.	.500	33	26.50	59.50
Romex, 12-3 with ground	40.000	L.F.	1.600	21.20	85.60	106.80
Panel board breaker, 20 Amp	1.000	Ea.	.500	19.25	26.75	46
TOTAL		Ea.	4.600	174.45	245.85	420.30
10' BASEBOARD HEATER						
Electric baseboard heater, 10' long	1.000	Ea.	2.424	212	130	342
Thermostat, integral	1.000	Ea.	.500	33	26.50	59.50
Romex, 12-3 with ground	40.000	L.F.	1.600	21.20	85.60	106.80
Panel board breaker, 20 Amp	1.000	Ea.	.750	28.88	40.13	69.01
TOTAL		Ea.	5.274	295.08	282.23	577.31

The costs in this system are on a cost each basis and include all necessary conduit fittings.

Description	QUAN.	UNIT	LABOR HOURS	COST EACH		
				MAT.	INST.	TOTAL

System Description	QUAN.	UNIT	LABOR HOURS	COST EACH		
				MAT.	INST.	TOTAL
Air conditioning receptacles						
Using non-metallic sheathed cable	1.000	Ea.	.800	22	43	65
Using BX cable	1.000	Ea.	.964	39	51.50	90.50
Using EMT conduit	1.000	Ea.	1.194	48	64	112
Disposal wiring						
Using non-metallic sheathed cable	1.000	Ea.	.889	16.20	47.50	63.70
Using BX cable	1.000	Ea.	1.067	32.50	57	89.50
Using EMT conduit	1.000	Ea.	1.333	43.50	71.50	115
Dryer circuit						
Using non-metallic sheathed cable	1.000	Ea.	1.455	42	78	120
Using BX cable	1.000	Ea.	1.739	57.50	93	150.50
Using EMT conduit	1.000	Ea.	2.162	58	116	174
Duplex receptacles						
Using non-metallic sheathed cable	1.000	Ea.	.615	22	33	55
Using BX cable	1.000	Ea.	.741	39	39.50	78.50
Using EMT conduit	1.000	Ea.	.920	48	49	97
Exhaust fan wiring						
Using non-metallic sheathed cable	1.000	Ea.	.800	18.50	43	61.50
Using BX cable	1.000	Ea.	.964	35.50	51.50	87
Using EMT conduit	1.000	Ea.	1.194	45	64	109
Furnace circuit & switch						
Using non-metallic sheathed cable	1.000	Ea.	1.333	25.50	71.50	97
Using BX cable	1.000	Ea.	1.600	45	85.50	130.50
Using EMT conduit	1.000	Ea.	2.000	51	107	158
Ground fault						
Using non-metallic sheathed cable	1.000	Ea.	1.000	55.50	53.50	109
Using BX cable	1.000	Ea.	1.212	71	65	136
Using EMT conduit	1.000	Ea.	1.481	90	79	169
Heater circuits						
Using non-metallic sheathed cable	1.000	Ea.	1.000	28	53.50	81.50
Using BX cable	1.000	Ea.	1.212	37.50	65	102.50
Using EMT conduit	1.000	Ea.	1.481	46.50	79	125.50
Lighting wiring						
Using non-metallic sheathed cable	1.000	Ea.	.500	29	26.50	55.50
Using BX cable	1.000	Ea.	.602	38.50	32	70.50
Using EMT conduit	1.000	Ea.	.748	44	40	84
Range circuits						
Using non-metallic sheathed cable	1.000	Ea.	2.000	89	107	196
Using BX cable	1.000	Ea.	2.424	143	130	273
Using EMT conduit	1.000	Ea.	2.963	103	158	261
Switches, single pole						
Using non-metallic sheathed cable	1.000	Ea.	.500	18.50	26.50	45
Using BX cable	1.000	Ea.	.602	35.50	32	67.50
Using EMT conduit	1.000	Ea.	.748	45	40	85
Switches, 3-way						
Using non-metallic sheathed cable	1.000	Ea.	.667	23.50	35.50	59
Using BX cable	1.000	Ea.	.800	37.50	43	80.50
Using EMT conduit	1.000	Ea.	1.333	64.50	71.50	136
Water heater						
Using non-metallic sheathed cable	1.000	Ea.	1.600	30.50	85.50	116
Using BX cable	1.000	Ea.	1.905	56	102	158
Using EMT conduit	1.000	Ea.	2.353	52.50	126	178.50
Weatherproof receptacle						
Using non-metallic sheathed cable	1.000	Ea.	1.333	156	71.50	227.50
Using BX cable	1.000	Ea.	1.600	166	85.50	251.50
Using EMT conduit	1.000	Ea.	2.000	175	107	282

DESCRIPTION	QUAN.	UNIT	LABOR HOURS	COST EACH		
				MAT.	INST.	TOTAL
Fluorescent strip, 4' long, 1 light, average	1.000	Ea.	.941	34.50	50.50	85
Deluxe	1.000	Ea.	1.129	41.50	60.50	102
2 lights, average	1.000	Ea.	1.000	38	53.50	91.50
Deluxe	1.000	Ea.	1.200	45.50	64	109.50
8' long, 1 light, average	1.000	Ea.	1.194	52	64	116
Deluxe	1.000	Ea.	1.433	62.50	77	139.50
2 lights, average	1.000	Ea.	1.290	62.50	69	131.50
Deluxe	1.000	Ea.	1.548	75	83	158
Surface mounted, 4' x 1', economy	1.000	Ea.	.914	65	49	114
Average	1.000	Ea.	1.143	81.50	61	142.50
Deluxe	1.000	Ea.	1.371	98	73	171
4' x 2', economy	1.000	Ea.	1.208	83	64.50	147.50
Average	1.000	Ea.	1.509	104	80.50	184.50
Deluxe	1.000	Ea.	1.811	125	96.50	221.50
Recessed, 4'x 1', 2 lamps, economy	1.000	Ea.	1.123	47	60	107
Average	1.000	Ea.	1.404	59	75	134
Deluxe	1.000	Ea.	1.684	71	90	161
4' x 2', 4' lamps, economy	1.000	Ea.	1.362	57.50	73	130.50
Average	1.000	Ea.	1.702	72	91	163
Deluxe	1.000	Ea.	2.043	86.50	109	195.50
Incandescent, exterior, 150W, single spot	1.000	Ea.	.500	33.50	26.50	60
Double spot	1.000	Ea.	1.167	104	62	166
Recessed, 100W, economy	1.000	Ea.	.800	61.50	43	104.50
Average	1.000	Ea.	1.000	77	53.50	130.50
Deluxe	1.000	Ea.	1.200	92.50	64	156.50
150W, economy	1.000	Ea.	.800	89.50	43	132.50
Average	1.000	Ea.	1.000	112	53.50	165.50
Deluxe	1.000	Ea.	1.200	134	64	198
Surface mounted, 60W, economy	1.000	Ea.	.800	48	43	91
Average	1.000	Ea.	1.000	54	53.50	107.50
Deluxe	1.000	Ea.	1.194	76	64	140
Metal halide, recessed 2' x 2' 250W	1.000	Ea.	2.500	340	134	474
2' x 2', 400W	1.000	Ea.	2.759	395	147	542
Surface mounted, 2' x 2', 250W	1.000	Ea.	2.963	370	158	528
2' x 2', 400W	1.000	Ea.	3.333	435	178	613
High bay, single, unit, 400W	1.000	Ea.	3.478	445	186	631
Twin unit, 400W	1.000	Ea.	5.000	885	267	1,152
Low bay, 250W	1.000	Ea.	2.500	390	134	524

Location Factors

Costs shown in *RSMeans Residential Cost Data* are based on national averages for materials and installation. To adjust these costs to a specific location, simply multiply the base cost by the factor for that city. The data is arranged alphabetically by state and postal zip code numbers. For a city not listed, use the factor for a nearby city with similar economic characteristics.

STATE	CITY	Residential
ALABAMA		
350-352	Birmingham	.86
354	Tuscaloosa	.77
355	Jasper	.72
356	Decatur	.77
357-358	Huntsville	.83
359	Gadsden	.74
360-361	Montgomery	.75
362	Anniston	.77
363	Dothan	.75
364	Evergreen	.73
365-366	Mobile	.81
367	Selma	.72
368	Phenix City	.73
369	Butler	.73
ALASKA		
995-996	Anchorage	1.26
997	Fairbanks	1.27
998	Juneau	1.25
999	Ketchikan	1.29
ARIZONA		
850,853	Phoenix	.86
851,852	Mesa/Tempe	.81
855	Globe	.77
856-857	Tucson	.84
859	Show Low	.79
860	Flagstaff	.84
863	Prescott	.77
864	Kingman	.81
865	Chambers	.77
ARKANSAS		
716	Pine Bluff	.79
717	Camden	.67
718	Texarkana	.72
719	Hot Springs	.68
720-722	Little Rock	.83
723	West Memphis	.77
724	Jonesboro	.76
725	Batesville	.73
726	Harrison	.75
727	Fayetteville	.70
728	Russellville	.75
729	Fort Smith	.76
CALIFORNIA		
900-902	Los Angeles	1.08
903-905	Inglewood	1.01
906-908	Long Beach	1.00
910-912	Pasadena	1.00
913-916	Van Nuys	1.03
917-918	Alhambra	1.04
919-921	San Diego	1.03
922	Palm Springs	1.00
923-924	San Bernardino	1.01
925	Riverside	1.07
926-927	Santa Ana	1.02
928	Anaheim	1.07
930	Oxnard	1.08
931	Santa Barbara	1.07
932-933	Bakersfield	1.06
934	San Luis Obispo	1.03
935	Mojave	1.01
936-938	Fresno	1.09
939	Salinas	1.11
940-941	San Francisco	1.26
942,956-958	Sacramento	1.12
943	Palo Alto	1.14
944	San Mateo	1.22
945	Vallejo	1.15
946	Oakland	1.22
947	Berkeley	1.20
948	Richmond	1.23
949	San Rafael	1.21
950	Santa Cruz	1.14
951	San Jose	1.21
952	Stockton	1.08
953	Modesto	1.08

STATE	CITY	Residential
CALIFORNIA (CONT'D)		
954	Santa Rosa	1.16
955	Eureka	1.10
959	Marysville	1.09
960	Redding	1.09
961	Susanville	1.09
COLORADO		
800-802	Denver	.92
803	Boulder	.89
804	Golden	.87
805	Fort Collins	.86
806	Greeley	.76
807	Fort Morgan	.89
808-809	Colorado Springs	.87
810	Pueblo	.89
811	Alamosa	.85
812	Salida	.87
813	Durango	.87
814	Montrose	.84
815	Grand Junction	.88
816	Glenwood Springs	.87
CONNECTICUT		
060	New Britain	1.09
061	Hartford	1.09
062	Willimantic	1.10
063	New London	1.09
064	Meriden	1.09
065	New Haven	1.10
066	Bridgeport	1.10
067	Waterbury	1.10
068	Norwalk	1.10
069	Stamford	1.11
D.C.		
200-205	Washington	.96
DELAWARE		
197	Newark	1.03
198	Wilmington	1.04
199	Dover	1.02
FLORIDA		
320,322	Jacksonville	.81
321	Daytona Beach	.88
323	Tallahassee	.78
324	Panama City	.75
325	Pensacola	.82
326,344	Gainesville	.81
327-328,347	Orlando	.89
329	Melbourne	.88
330-332,340	Miami	.88
333	Fort Lauderdale	.87
334,349	West Palm Beach	.87
335-336,346	Tampa	.92
337	St. Petersburg	.79
338	Lakeland	.89
339,341	Fort Myers	.87
342	Sarasota	.90
GEORGIA		
300-303,399	Atlanta	.88
304	Statesboro	.71
305	Gainesville	.77
306	Athens	.76
307	Dalton	.75
308-309	Augusta	.82
310-312	Macon	.80
313-314	Savannah	.80
315	Waycross	.79
316	Valdosta	.74
317,398	Albany	.77
318-319	Columbus	.81
HAWAII		
967	Hilo	1.19
968	Honolulu	1.21

Location Factors

STATE	CITY	Residential
STATES & POSS.		
969	Guam	.94
IDAHO		
832	Pocatello	.84
833	Twin Falls	.71
834	Idaho Falls	.73
835	Lewiston	.94
836-837	Boise	.84
838	Coeur d'Alene	.92
ILLINOIS		
600-603	North Suburban	1.20
604	Joliet	1.22
605	South Suburban	1.20
606-608	Chicago	1.22
609	Kankakee	1.12
610-611	Rockford	1.11
612	Rock Island	.98
613	La Salle	1.09
614	Galesburg	1.03
615-616	Peoria	1.05
617	Bloomington	1.03
618-619	Champaign	1.04
620-622	East St. Louis	1.02
623	Quincy	1.02
624	Effingham	1.03
625	Decatur	1.03
626-627	Springfield	1.02
628	Centralia	1.02
629	Carbondale	.99
INDIANA		
460	Anderson	.90
461-462	Indianapolis	.92
463-464	Gary	1.04
465-466	South Bend	.90
467-468	Fort Wayne	.89
469	Kokomo	.90
470	Lawrenceburg	.87
471	New Albany	.86
472	Columbus	.92
473	Muncie	.91
474	Bloomington	.92
475	Washington	.90
476-477	Evansville	.90
478	Terre Haute	.91
479	Lafayette	.92
IOWA		
500-503,509	Des Moines	.86
504	Mason City	.74
505	Fort Dodge	.74
506-507	Waterloo	.76
508	Creston	.78
510-511	Sioux City	.82
512	Sibley	.70
513	Spencer	.72
514	Carroll	.72
515	Council Bluffs	.80
516	Shenandoah	.72
520	Dubuque	.83
521	Decorah	.73
522-524	Cedar Rapids	.90
525	Ottumwa	.81
526	Burlington	.83
527-528	Davenport	.93
KANSAS		
660-662	Kansas City	.98
664-666	Topeka	.77
667	Fort Scott	.85
668	Emporia	.73
669	Belleville	.77
670-672	Wichita	.77
673	Independence	.82
674	Salina	.75
675	Hutchinson	.77
676	Hays	.79
677	Colby	.81
678	Dodge City	.79
679	Liberal	.78
KENTUCKY		
400-402	Louisville	.90
403-405	Lexington	.87

STATE	CITY	Residential
KENTUCKY (CONT'D)		
406	Frankfort	.83
407-409	Corbin	.74
410	Covington	.96
411-412	Ashland	.93
413-414	Campton	.75
415-416	Pikeville	.82
417-418	Hazard	.70
420	Paducah	.88
421-422	Bowling Green	.88
423	Owensboro	.85
424	Henderson	.90
425-426	Somerset	.74
427	Elizabethtown	.86
LOUISIANA		
700-701	New Orleans	.85
703	Thibodaux	.81
704	Hammond	.76
705	Lafayette	.79
706	Lake Charles	.81
707-708	Baton Rouge	.83
710-711	Shreveport	.77
712	Monroe	.72
713-714	Alexandria	.73
MAINE		
039	Kittery	.91
040-041	Portland	.90
042	Lewiston	.90
043	Augusta	.93
044	Bangor	.89
045	Bath	.91
046	Machias	.91
047	Houlton	.92
048	Rockland	.92
049	Waterville	.91
MARYLAND		
206	Waldorf	.83
207-208	College Park	.90
209	Silver Spring	.85
210-212	Baltimore	.90
214	Annapolis	.83
215	Cumberland	.87
216	Easton	.66
217	Hagerstown	.86
218	Salisbury	.72
219	Elkton	.85
MASSACHUSETTS		
010-011	Springfield	1.05
012	Pittsfield	1.05
013	Greenfield	1.03
014	Fitchburg	1.11
015-016	Worcester	1.13
017	Framingham	1.15
018	Lowell	1.15
019	Lawrence	1.15
020-022, 024	Boston	1.21
023	Brockton	1.15
025	Buzzards Bay	1.12
026	Hyannis	1.12
027	New Bedford	1.14
MICHIGAN		
480,483	Royal Oak	1.01
481	Ann Arbor	1.02
482	Detroit	1.06
484-485	Flint	.97
486	Saginaw	.94
487	Bay City	.94
488-489	Lansing	.96
490	Battle Creek	.94
491	Kalamazoo	.93
492	Jackson	.93
493,495	Grand Rapids	.84
494	Muskegon	.90
496	Traverse City	.84
497	Gaylord	.81
498-499	Iron mountain	.91
MINNESOTA		
550-551	Saint Paul	1.14
553-555	Minneapolis	1.16
556-558	Duluth	1.10

STATE	CITY	Residential
MINNESOTA (CONT'd)		
559	Rochester	1.06
560	Mankato	1.02
561	Windom	.82
562	Willmar	.84
563	St. Cloud	1.10
564	Brainerd	1.00
565	Detroit Lakes	.95
566	Bemidji	.97
567	Thief River Falls	.96
MISSISSIPPI		
386	Clarksdale	.76
387	Greenville	.83
388	Tupelo	.77
389	Greenwood	.78
390-392	Jackson	.83
393	Meridian	.82
394	Laurel	.78
395	Biloxi	.80
396	Mccomb	.76
397	Columbus	.77
MISSOURI		
630-631	St. Louis	1.02
633	Bowling Green	.93
634	Hannibal	.84
635	Kirksville	.79
636	Flat River	.92
637	Cape Girardeau	.86
638	Sikeston	.81
639	Poplar Bluff	.81
640-641	Kansas City	1.03
644-645	St. Joseph	.91
646	Chillicothe	.84
647	Harrisonville	.94
648	Joplin	.81
650-651	Jefferson City	.86
652	Columbia	.89
653	Sedalia	.83
654-655	Rolla	.88
656-658	Springfield	.86
MONTANA		
590-591	Billings	.87
592	Wolf Point	.82
593	Miles City	.85
594	Great Falls	.87
595	Havre	.82
596	Helena	.86
597	Butte	.86
598	Missoula	.85
599	Kalispell	.83
NEBRASKA		
680-681	Omaha	.89
683-685	Lincoln	.85
686	Columbus	.85
687	Norfolk	.90
688	Grand Island	.90
689	Hastings	.92
690	Mccook	.83
691	North Platte	.90
692	Valentine	.84
693	Alliance	.83
NEVADA		
889-891	Las Vegas	1.05
893	Ely	.84
894-895	Reno	.92
897	Carson City	.92
898	Elko	.88
NEW HAMPSHIRE		
030	Nashua	.94
031	Manchester	.94
032-033	Concord	.92
034	Keene	.73
035	Littleton	.79
036	Charleston	.72
037	Claremont	.73
038	Portsmouth	.94

STATE	CITY	Residential
NEW JERSEY		
070-071	Newark	1.12
072	Elizabeth	1.14
073	Jersey City	1.11
074-075	Paterson	1.12
076	Hackensack	1.11
077	Long Branch	1.11
078	Dover	1.11
079	Summit	1.12
080,083	Vineland	1.09
081	Camden	1.10
082,084	Atlantic City	1.12
085-086	Trenton	1.10
087	Point Pleasant	1.09
088-089	New Brunswick	1.12
NEW MEXICO		
870-872	Albuquerque	.84
873	Gallup	.84
874	Farmington	.84
875	Santa Fe	.85
877	Las Vegas	.84
878	Socorro	.84
879	Truth/Consequences	.83
880	Las Cruces	.82
881	Clovis	.84
882	Roswell	.84
883	Carrizozo	.84
884	Tucumcari	.85
NEW YORK		
100-102	New York	1.39
103	Staten Island	1.32
104	Bronx	1.33
105	Mount Vernon	1.16
106	White Plains	1.19
107	Yonkers	1.20
108	New Rochelle	1.20
109	Suffern	1.16
110	Queens	1.32
111	Long Island City	1.34
112	Brooklyn	1.36
113	Flushing	1.34
114	Jamaica	1.33
115,117,118	Hicksville	1.21
116	Far Rockaway	1.33
119	Riverhead	1.22
120-122	Albany	.97
123	Schenectady	.98
124	Kingston	1.06
125-126	Poughkeepsie	1.20
127	Monticello	1.08
128	Glens Falls	.88
129	Plattsburgh	.94
130-132	Syracuse	.96
133-135	Utica	.93
136	Watertown	.93
137-139	Binghamton	.94
140-142	Buffalo	1.04
143	Niagara Falls	1.01
144-146	Rochester	.98
147	Jamestown	.90
148-149	Elmira	.88
NORTH CAROLINA		
270,272-274	Greensboro	.81
271	Winston-Salem	.81
275-276	Raleigh	.83
277	Durham	.82
278	Rocky Mount	.72
279	Elizabeth City	.73
280	Gastonia	.82
281-282	Charlotte	.83
283	Fayetteville	.81
284	Wilmington	.79
285	Kinston	.72
286	Hickory	.77
287-288	Asheville	.80
289	Murphy	.71
NORTH DAKOTA		
580-581	Fargo	.76
582	Grand Forks	.73
583	Devils Lake	.76
584	Jamestown	.71
585	Bismarck	.76

Location Factors

STATE	CITY	Residential
NORTH DAKOTA (CONT'D)		
586	Dickinson	.74
587	Minot	.79
588	Williston	.74
OHIO		
430-432	Columbus	.94
433	Marion	.88
434-436	Toledo	.99
437-438	Zanesville	.87
439	Steubenville	.93
440	Lorain	.96
441	Cleveland	1.00
442-443	Akron	.96
444-445	Youngstown	.94
446-447	Canton	.92
448-449	Mansfield	.92
450	Hamilton	.91
451-452	Cincinnati	.91
453-454	Dayton	.90
455	Springfield	.92
456	Chillicothe	.94
457	Athens	.88
458	Lima	.89
OKLAHOMA		
730-731	Oklahoma City	.78
734	Ardmore	.77
735	Lawton	.80
736	Clinton	.76
737	Enid	.76
738	Woodward	.75
739	Guymon	.65
740-741	Tulsa	.76
743	Miami	.80
744	Muskogee	.70
745	Mcalester	.73
746	Ponca City	.76
747	Durant	.76
748	Shawnee	.75
749	Poteau	.77
OREGON		
970-972	Portland	.98
973	Salem	.96
974	Eugene	.97
975	Medford	.96
976	Klamath Falls	.96
977	Bend	.98
978	Pendleton	.96
979	Vale	.94
PENNSYLVANIA		
150-152	Pittsburgh	.98
153	Washington	.95
154	Uniontown	.92
155	Bedford	.88
156	Greensburg	.95
157	Indiana	.92
158	Dubois	.90
159	Johnstown	.90
160	Butler	.94
161	New Castle	.93
162	Kittanning	.95
163	Oil City	.90
164-165	Erie	.93
166	Altoona	.88
167	Bradford	.90
168	State College	.91
169	Wellsboro	.92
170-171	Harrisburg	.95
172	Chambersburg	.89
173-174	York	.93
175-176	Lancaster	.92
177	Williamsport	.85
178	Sunbury	.93
179	Pottsville	.93
180	Lehigh Valley	1.04
181	Allentown	1.05
182	Hazleton	.93
183	Stroudsburg	.93
184-185	Scranton	.98
186-187	Wilkes-Barre	.95
188	Montrose	.92
189	Doylestown	1.08

STATE	CITY	Residential
PENNSYLVANIA (CONT'D)		
190-191	Philadelphia	1.17
193	Westchester	1.13
194	Norristown	1.12
195-196	Reading	.98
PUERTO RICO		
009	San Juan	.73
RHODE ISLAND		
028	Newport	1.08
029	Providence	1.08
SOUTH CAROLINA		
290-292	Columbia	.82
293	Spartanburg	.82
294	Charleston	.85
295	Florence	.78
296	Greenville	.81
297	Rock Hill	.80
298	Aiken	.99
299	Beaufort	.80
SOUTH DAKOTA		
570-571	Sioux Falls	.77
572	Watertown	.74
573	Mitchell	.75
574	Aberdeen	.76
575	Pierre	.75
576	Mobridge	.74
577	Rapid City	.76
TENNESSEE		
370-372	Nashville	.84
373-374	Chattanooga	.81
375,380-381	Memphis	.81
376	Johnson City	.70
377-379	Knoxville	.74
382	Mckenzie	.71
383	Jackson	.73
384	Columbia	.72
385	Cookeville	.70
TEXAS		
750	Mckinney	.74
751	Waxahackie	.76
752-753	Dallas	.83
754	Greenville	.70
755	Texarkana	.74
756	Longview	.69
757	Tyler	.75
758	Palestine	.68
759	Lufkin	.72
760-761	Fort Worth	.82
762	Denton	.75
763	Wichita Falls	.78
764	Eastland	.72
765	Temple	.75
766-767	Waco	.78
768	Brownwood	.68
769	San Angelo	.72
770-772	Houston	.85
773	Huntsville	.68
774	Wharton	.70
775	Galveston	.83
776-777	Beaumont	.82
778	Bryan	.74
779	Victoria	.73
780	Laredo	.72
781-782	San Antonio	.78
783-784	Corpus Christi	.77
785	Mc Allen	.75
786-787	Austin	.78
788	Del Rio	.66
789	Giddings	.69
790-791	Amarillo	.79
792	Childress	.77
793-794	Lubbock	.76
795-796	Abilene	.75
797	Midland	.76
798-799,885	El Paso	.75
UTAH		
840-841	Salt Lake City	.79
842,844	Ogden	.77
843	Logan	.77

STATE	CITY	Residential
UTAH (CONT'D)		
845	Price	.68
846-847	Provo	.78
VERMONT		
050	White River Jct.	.74
051	Bellows Falls	.78
052	Bennington	.79
053	Brattleboro	.80
054	Burlington	.80
056	Montpelier	.81
057	Rutland	.80
058	St. Johnsbury	.76
059	Guildhall	.76
VIRGINIA		
220-221	Fairfax	1.03
222	Arlington	1.04
223	Alexandria	1.07
224-225	Fredericksburg	.93
226	Winchester	.89
227	Culpeper	.98
228	Harrisonburg	.88
229	Charlottesville	.89
230-232	Richmond	.97
233-235	Norfolk	.99
236	Newport News	.98
237	Portsmouth	.91
238	Petersburg	.95
239	Farmville	.87
240-241	Roanoke	.95
242	Bristol	.84
243	Pulaski	.81
244	Staunton	.89
245	Lynchburg	.94
246	Grundy	.82
WASHINGTON		
980-981,987	Seattle	1.03
982	Everett	1.03
983-984	Tacoma	1.01
985	Olympia	1.00
986	Vancouver	.94
988	Wenatchee	.89
989	Yakima	.95
990-992	Spokane	.96
993	Richland	.95
994	Clarkston	.94
WEST VIRGINIA		
247-248	Bluefield	.88
249	Lewisburg	.89
250-253	Charleston	.95
254	Martinsburg	.88
255-257	Huntington	.97
258-259	Beckley	.90
260	Wheeling	.92
261	Parkersburg	.90
262	Buckhannon	.91
263-264	Clarksburg	.90
265	Morgantown	.92
266	Gassaway	.91
267	Romney	.89
268	Petersburg	.91
WISCONSIN		
530,532	Milwaukee	1.08
531	Kenosha	1.01
534	Racine	1.01
535	Beloit	.97
537	Madison	.98
538	Lancaster	.95
539	Portage	.94
540	New Richmond	.97
541-543	Green Bay	.99
544	Wausau	.94
545	Rhinelander	.93
546	La Crosse	.93
547	Eau Claire	.96
548	Superior	.96
549	Oshkosh	.93
WYOMING		
820	Cheyenne	.80
821	Yellowstone Nat. Pk.	.73
822	Wheatland	.73

STATE	CITY	Residential
WYOMING (CONT'D)		
823	Rawlins	.73
824	Worland	.72
825	Riverton	.72
826	Casper	.75
827	Newcastle	.72
828	Sheridan	.77
829-831	Rock Springs	.76
CANADIAN FACTORS (reflect Canadian currency)		
ALBERTA		
	Calgary	1.11
	Edmonton	1.10
	Fort McMurray	1.12
	Lethbridge	1.09
	Lloydminster	1.04
	Medicine Hat	1.04
	Red Deer	1.04
BRITISH COLUMBIA		
	Kamloops	1.02
	Prince George	1.03
	Vancouver	1.04
	Victoria	.98
MANITOBA		
	Brandon	1.00
	Portage la Prairie	.99
	Winnipeg	.99
NEW BRUNSWICK		
	Bathurst	.92
	Dalhousie	.92
	Fredericton	.99
	Moncton	.93
	Newcastle	.92
	St. John	.99
NEWFOUNDLAND		
	Corner Brook	.94
	St Johns	.95
NORTHWEST TERRITORIES	Yellowknife	1.05
NOVA SCOTIA		
	Bridgewater	.95
	Dartmouth	.95
	Halifax	.98
	New Glasgow	.95
	Sydney	.94
	Truro	.95
	Yarmouth	.95
ONTARIO		
	Barrie	1.10
	Brantford	1.12
	Cornwall	1.11
	Hamilton	1.13
	Kingston	1.11
	Kitchener	1.07
	London	1.11
	North Bay	1.08
	Oshawa	1.10
	Ottawa	1.12
	Owen Sound	1.09
	Peterborough	1.09
	Sarnia	1.12
	Sault Ste Marie	1.05
	St. Catharines	1.07
	Sudbury	1.05
	Thunder Bay	1.09
	Timmins	1.08
	Toronto	1.15
	Windsor	1.09
PRINCE EDWARD ISLAND		
	Charlottetown	.90
	Summerside	.90
QUEBEC		
	Cap-de-la-Madeleine	1.10
	Charlesbourg	1.10
	Chicoutimi	1.13
	Gatineau	1.09
	Granby	1.09

Location Factors

STATE	CITY	Residential
QUEBEC (CONT'D)		
	Hull	1.09
	Joliette	1.10
	Laval	1.09
	Montreal	1.15
	Quebec	1.15
	Rimouski	1.13
	Rouyn-Noranda	1.09
	Saint Hyacinthe	1.09
	Sherbrooke	1.09
	Sorel	1.10
	St Jerome	1.09
	Trois Rivieres	1.10
SASKATCHEWAN		
	Moose Jaw	.92
	Prince Albert	.91
	Regina	.94
	Saskatoon	.92
YUKON		
	Whitehorse	.91

Abbreviations

A	Area Square Feet; Ampere	BTUH	BTU per Hour	Cwt.	100 Pounds
ABS	Acrylonitrile Butadiene Stryrene; Asbestos Bonded Steel	B.U.R.	Built-up Roofing	C.W.X.	Cool White Deluxe
A.C.	Alternating Current; Air-Conditioning; Asbestos Cement; Plywood Grade A & C	BX	Interlocked Armored Cable	C.Y.	Cubic Yard (27 cubic feet)
		°C	degree centegrade	C.Y./Hr.	Cubic Yard per Hour
		c	Conductivity, Copper Sweat	Cyl.	Cylinder
		C	Hundred; Centigrade	d	Penny (nail size)
A.C.I.	American Concrete Institute	C/C	Center to Center, Cedar on Cedar	D	Deep; Depth; Discharge
AD	Plywood, Grade A & D	C-C	Center to Center	Dis., Disch.	Discharge
Addit.	Additional	Cab.	Cabinet	Db.	Decibel
Adj.	Adjustable	Cair.	Air Tool Laborer	Dbl.	Double
af	Audio-frequency	Calc	Calculated	DC	Direct Current
A.G.A.	American Gas Association	Cap.	Capacity	DDC	Direct Digital Control
Agg.	Aggregate	Carp.	Carpenter	Demob.	Demobilization
A.H.	Ampere Hours	C.B.	Circuit Breaker	d.f.u.	Drainage Fixture Units
A hr.	Ampere-hour	C.C.A.	Chromate Copper Arsenate	D.H.	Double Hung
A.H.U.	Air Handling Unit	C.C.F.	Hundred Cubic Feet	DHW	Domestic Hot Water
A.I.A.	American Institute of Architects	cd	Candela	DI	Ductile Iron
AIC	Ampere Interrupting Capacity	cd/sf	Candela per Square Foot	Diag.	Diagonal
Allow.	Allowance	CD	Grade of Plywood Face & Back	Diam., Dia	Diameter
alt.	Altitude	CDX	Plywood, Grade C & D, exterior glue	Distrib.	Distribution
Alum.	Aluminum	Cefi.	Cement Finisher	Div.	Division
a.m.	Ante Meridiem	Cem.	Cement	Dk.	Deck
Amp.	Ampere	CF	Hundred Feet	D.L.	Dead Load; Diesel
Anod.	Anodized	C.F.	Cubic Feet	DLH	Deep Long Span Bar Joist
Approx.	Approximate	CFM	Cubic Feet per Minute	Do.	Ditto
Apt.	Apartment	c.g.	Center of Gravity	Dp.	Depth
Asb.	Asbestos	CHW	Chilled Water; Commercial Hot Water	D.P.S.T.	Double Pole, Single Throw
A.S.B.C.	American Standard Building Code			Dr.	Drive
Asbe.	Asbestos Worker	C.I.	Cast Iron	Drink.	Drinking
ASCE.	American Society of Civil Engineers	C.I.P.	Cast in Place	D.S.	Double Strength
A.S.H.R.A.E.	American Society of Heating, Refrig. & AC Engineers	Circ.	Circuit	D.S.A.	Double Strength A Grade
		C.L.	Carload Lot	D.S.B.	Double Strength B Grade
		Clab.	Common Laborer	Dty.	Duty
A.S.M.E.	American Society of Mechanical Engineers	Clam	Common maintenance laborer	DWV	Drain Waste Vent
		C.L.F.	Hundred Linear Feet	DX	Deluxe White, Direct Expansion
A.S.T.M.	American Society for Testing and Materials	CLF	Current Limiting Fuse	dyn	Dyne
		CLP	Cross Linked Polyethylene	e	Eccentricity
Attchmt.	Attachment	cm	Centimeter	E	Equipment Only; East
Avg., Ave.	Average	CMP	Corr. Metal Pipe	Ea.	Each
A.W.G.	American Wire Gauge	C.M.U.	Concrete Masonry Unit	E.B.	Encased Burial
AWWA	American Water Works Assoc.	CN	Change Notice	Econ.	Economy
Bbl.	Barrel	Col.	Column	E.C.Y	Embankment Cubic Yards
B&B	Grade B and Better; Balled & Burlapped	CO₂	Carbon Dioxide	EDP	Electronic Data Processing
		Comb.	Combination	EIFS	Exterior Insulation Finish System
B.&S.	Bell and Spigot	Compr.	Compressor	E.D.R.	Equiv. Direct Radiation
B.&W.	Black and White	Conc.	Concrete	Eq.	Equation
b.c.c.	Body-centered Cubic	Cont.	Continuous; Continued, Container	EL	elevation
B.C.Y.	Bank Cubic Yards	Corr.	Corrugated	Elec.	Electrician; Electrical
BE	Bevel End	Cos	Cosine	Elev.	Elevator; Elevating
B.F.	Board Feet	Cot	Cotangent	EMT	Electrical Metallic Conduit; Thin Wall Conduit
Bg. cem.	Bag of Cement	Cov.	Cover		
BHP	Boiler Horsepower; Brake Horsepower	C/P	Cedar on Paneling	Eng.	Engine, Engineered
		CPA	Control Point Adjustment	EPDM	Ethylene Propylene Diene Monome
B.I.	Black Iron	Cplg.	Coupling	EPS	Expanded Polystyrene
Bit., Bitum.	Bituminous	C.P.M.	Critical Path Method	Eqhv.	Equip. Oper., Heavy
Bit., Conc.	Bituminous Concrete	CPVC	Chlorinated Polyvinyl Chloride	Eqlt.	Equip. Oper., Light
Bk.	Backed	C.Pr.	Hundred Pair	Eqmd.	Equip. Oper., Medium
Bkrs.	Breakers	CRC	Cold Rolled Channel	Eqmm.	Equip. Oper., Master Mechanic
Bldg.	Building	Creos.	Creosote	Eqol.	Equip. Oper., Oilers
Blk.	Block	Crpt.	Carpet & Linoleum Layer	Equip.	Equipment
Bm.	Beam	CRT	Cathode-ray Tube	ERW	Electric Resistance Welded
Boil.	Boilermaker	CS	Carbon Steel, Constant Shear Bar Joist	E.S.	Energy Saver
B.P.M.	Blows per Minute			Est.	Estimated
BR	Bedroom	Csc	Cosecant	esu	Electrostatic Units
Brg.	Bearing	C.S.F.	Hundred Square Feet	E.W.	Each Way
Brhe.	Bricklayer Helper	CSI	Construction Specifications Institute	EWT	Entering Water Temperature
Bric.	Bricklayer	C.T.	Current Transformer	Excav.	Excavation
Brk.	Brick	CTS	Copper Tube Size	Exp.	Expansion, Exposure
Brng.	Bearing	Cu	Copper, Cubic	Ext.	Exterior
Brs.	Brass	Cu. Ft.	Cubic Foot	Extru.	Extrusion
Brz.	Bronze	cw	Continuous Wave	f.	Fiber stress
Bsn.	Basin	C.W.	Cool White; Cold Water	F	Fahrenheit; Female; Fill
Btr.	Better			Fab.	Fabricated
Btu	British Thermal Unit				

Abbreviations

FBGS	Fiberglass	H.P.	Horsepower; High Pressure	LE	Lead Equivalent
F.C.	Footcandles	H.P.F.	High Power Factor	LED	Light Emitting Diode
f.c.c.	Face-centered Cubic	Hr.	Hour	L.F.	Linear Foot
f'c.	Compressive Stress in Concrete; Extreme Compressive Stress	Hrs./Day	Hours per Day	L.F. Nose	Linear Foot of Stair Nosing
		HSC	High Short Circuit	L.F. Rsr	Linear Foot of Stair Riser
F.E.	Front End	Ht.	Height	Lg.	Long; Length; Large
FEP	Fluorinated Ethylene Propylene (Teflon)	Htg.	Heating	L & H	Light and Heat
		Htrs.	Heaters	LH	Long Span Bar Joist
F.G.	Flat Grain	HVAC	Heating, Ventilation & Air-Conditioning	L.H.	Labor Hours
F.H.A.	Federal Housing Administration			L.L.	Live Load
Fig.	Figure	Hvy.	Heavy	L.L.D.	Lamp Lumen Depreciation
Fin.	Finished	HW	Hot Water	lm	Lumen
Fixt.	Fixture	Hyd.;Hydr.	Hydraulic	lm/sf	Lumen per Square Foot
Fl. Oz.	Fluid Ounces	Hz.	Hertz (cycles)	lm/W	Lumen per Watt
Flr.	Floor	I.	Moment of Inertia	L.O.A.	Length Over All
F.M.	Frequency Modulation; Factory Mutual	IBC	International Building Code	log	Logarithm
		I.C.	Interrupting Capacity	L-O-L	Lateralolet
Fmg.	Framing	ID	Inside Diameter	long.	longitude
Fdn.	Foundation	I.D.	Inside Dimension; Identification	L.P.	Liquefied Petroleum; Low Pressure
Fori.	Foreman, Inside	I.F.	Inside Frosted	L.P.F.	Low Power Factor
Foro.	Foreman, Outside	I.M.C.	Intermediate Metal Conduit	LR	Long Radius
Fount.	Fountain	In.	Inch	L.S.	Lump Sum
fpm	Feet per Minute	Incan.	Incandescent	Lt.	Light
FPT	Female Pipe Thread	Incl.	Included; Including	Lt. Ga.	Light Gauge
Fr.	Frame	Int.	Interior	L.T.L.	Less than Truckload Lot
F.R.	Fire Rating	Inst.	Installation	Lt. Wt.	Lightweight
FRK	Foil Reinforced Kraft	Insul.	Insulation/Insulated	L.V.	Low Voltage
FRP	Fiberglass Reinforced Plastic	I.P.	Iron Pipe	M	Thousand; Material; Male; Light Wall Copper Tubing
FS	Forged Steel	I.P.S.	Iron Pipe Size		
FSC	Cast Body; Cast Switch Box	I.P.T.	Iron Pipe Threaded	M²CA	Meters Squared Contact Area
Ft.	Foot; Feet	I.W.	Indirect Waste	m/hr.; M.H.	Man-hour
Ftng.	Fitting	J	Joule	mA	Milliampere
Ftg.	Footing	J.I.C.	Joint Industrial Council	Mach.	Machine
Ft lb.	Foot Pound	K	Thousand; Thousand Pounds; Heavy Wall Copper Tubing, Kelvin	Mag. Str.	Magnetic Starter
Furn.	Furniture			Maint.	Maintenance
FVNR	Full Voltage Non-Reversing	K.A.H.	Thousand Amp. Hours	Marb.	Marble Setter
FXM	Female by Male	KCMIL	Thousand Circular Mils	Mat; Mat'l.	Material
Fy.	Minimum Yield Stress of Steel	KD	Knock Down	Max.	Maximum
g	Gram	K.D.A.T.	Kiln Dried After Treatment	MBF	Thousand Board Feet
G	Gauss	kg	Kilogram	MBH	Thousand BTU's per hr.
Ga.	Gauge	kG	Kilogauss	MC	Metal Clad Cable
Gal., gal.	Gallon	kgf	Kilogram Force	M.C.F.	Thousand Cubic Feet
gpm, GPM	Gallon per Minute	kHz	Kilohertz	M.C.F.M.	Thousand Cubic Feet per Minute
Galv.	Galvanized	Kip.	1000 Pounds	M.C.M.	Thousand Circular Mils
Gen.	General	KJ	Kiljoule	M.C.P.	Motor Circuit Protector
G.F.I.	Ground Fault Interrupter	K.L.	Effective Length Factor	MD	Medium Duty
Glaz.	Glazier	K.L.F.	Kips per Linear Foot	M.D.O.	Medium Density Overlaid
GPD	Gallons per Day	Km	Kilometer	Med.	Medium
GPH	Gallons per Hour	K.S.F.	Kips per Square Foot	MF	Thousand Feet
GPM	Gallons per Minute	K.S.I.	Kips per Square Inch	M.F.B.M.	Thousand Feet Board Measure
GR	Grade	kV	Kilovolt	Mfg.	Manufacturing
Gran.	Granular	kVA	Kilovolt Ampere	Mfrs.	Manufacturers
Grnd.	Ground	K.V.A.R.	Kilovar (Reactance)	mg	Milligram
H	High Henry	KW	Kilowatt	MGD	Million Gallons per Day
H.C.	High Capacity	KWh	Kilowatt-hour	MGPH	Thousand Gallons per Hour
H.D.	Heavy Duty; High Density	L	Labor Only; Length; Long; Medium Wall Copper Tubing	MH, M.H.	Manhole; Metal Halide; Man-Hour
H.D.O.	High Density Overlaid			MHz	Megahertz
H.D.P.E.	high density polyethelene	Lab.	Labor	Mi.	Mile
Hdr.	Header	lat	Latitude	MI	Malleable Iron; Mineral Insulated
Hdwe.	Hardware	Lath.	Lather	mm	Millimeter
Help.	Helper Average	Lav.	Lavatory	Mill.	Millwright
HEPA	High Efficiency Particulate Air Filter	lb.; #	Pound	Min., min.	Minimum, minute
Hg	Mercury	L.B.	Load Bearing; L Conduit Body	Misc.	Miscellaneous
HIC	High Interrupting Capacity	L. & E.	Labor & Equipment	ml	Milliliter, Mainline
HM	Hollow Metal	lb./hr.	Pounds per Hour	M.L.F.	Thousand Linear Feet
HMWPE	high molecular weight polyethylene	lb./L.F.	Pounds per Linear Foot	Mo.	Month
H.O.	High Output	lbf/sq.in.	Pound-force per Square Inch	Mobil.	Mobilization
Horiz.	Horizontal	L.C.L.	Less than Carload Lot	Mog.	Mogul Base
		L.C.Y.	Loose Cubic Yard	MPH	Miles per Hour
		Ld.	Load	MPT	Male Pipe Thread

271

MRT	Mile Round Trip	Pl.	Plate	S.F.C.A.	Square Foot Contact Area
ms	Millisecond	Plah.	Plasterer Helper	S.F. Flr.	Square Foot of Floor
M.S.F.	Thousand Square Feet	Plas.	Plasterer	S.F.G.	Square Foot of Ground
Mstz.	Mosaic & Terrazzo Worker	Pluh.	Plumbers Helper	S.F. Hor.	Square Foot Horizontal
M.S.Y.	Thousand Square Yards	Plum.	Plumber	S.F.R.	Square Feet of Radiation
Mtd., mtd.	Mounted	Ply.	Plywood	S.F. Shlf.	Square Foot of Shelf
Mthe.	Mosaic & Terrazzo Helper	p.m.	Post Meridiem	S4S	Surface 4 Sides
Mtng.	Mounting	Pntd.	Painted	Shee.	Sheet Metal Worker
Mult.	Multi; Multiply	Pord.	Painter, Ordinary	Sin.	Sine
M.V.A.	Million Volt Amperes	pp	Pages	Skwk.	Skilled Worker
M.V.A.R.	Million Volt Amperes Reactance	PP, PPL	Polypropylene	SL	Saran Lined
MV	Megavolt	P.P.M.	Parts per Million	S.L.	Slimline
MW	Megawatt	Pr.	Pair	Sldr.	Solder
MXM	Male by Male	P.E.S.B.	Pre-engineered Steel Building	SLH	Super Long Span Bar Joist
MYD	Thousand Yards	Prefab.	Prefabricated	S.N.	Solid Neutral
N	Natural; North	Prefin.	Prefinished	S-O-L	Socketolet
nA	Nanoampere	Prop.	Propelled	sp	Standpipe
NA	Not Available; Not Applicable	PSF, psf	Pounds per Square Foot	S.P.	Static Pressure; Single Pole; Self-Propelled
N.B.C.	National Building Code	PSI, psi	Pounds per Square Inch		
NC	Normally Closed	PSIG	Pounds per Square Inch Gauge	Spri.	Sprinkler Installer
N.E.M.A.	National Electrical Manufacturers Assoc.	PSP	Plastic Sewer Pipe	spwg	Static Pressure Water Gauge
		Pspr.	Painter, Spray	S.P.D.T.	Single Pole, Double Throw
NEHB	Bolted Circuit Breaker to 600V.	Psst.	Painter, Structural Steel	SPF	Spruce Pine Fir
N.L.B.	Non-Load-Bearing	P.T.	Potential Transformer	S.P.S.T.	Single Pole, Single Throw
NM	Non-Metallic Cable	P. & T.	Pressure & Temperature	SPT	Standard Pipe Thread
nm	Nanometer	Ptd.	Painted	Sq.	Square; 100 Square Feet
No.	Number	Ptns.	Partitions	Sq. Hd.	Square Head
NO	Normally Open	Pu	Ultimate Load	Sq. In.	Square Inch
N.O.C.	Not Otherwise Classified	PVC	Polyvinyl Chloride	S.S.	Single Strength; Stainless Steel
Nose.	Nosing	Pvmt.	Pavement	S.S.B.	Single Strength B Grade
N.P.T.	National Pipe Thread	Pwr.	Power	sst, ss	Stainless Steel
NQOD	Combination Plug-on/Bolt on Circuit Breaker to 240V.	Q	Quantity Heat Flow	Sswk.	Structural Steel Worker
		Qt.	Quart	Sswl.	Structural Steel Welder
N.R.C.	Noise Reduction Coefficient/ Nuclear Regulator Commission	Quan., Qty.	Quantity	St.;Stl.	Steel
		Q.C.	Quick Coupling	S.T.C.	Sound Transmission Coefficient
N.R.S.	Non Rising Stem	r	Radius of Gyration	Std.	Standard
ns	Nanosecond	R	Resistance	Stg.	Staging
nW	Nanowatt	R.C.P.	Reinforced Concrete Pipe	STK	Select Tight Knot
OB	Opposing Blade	Rect.	Rectangle	STP	Standard Temperature & Pressure
OC	On Center	Reg.	Regular	Stpi.	Steamfitter, Pipefitter
OD	Outside Diameter	Reinf.	Reinforced	Str.	Strength; Starter; Straight
O.D.	Outside Dimension	Req'd.	Required	Strd.	Stranded
ODS	Overhead Distribution System	Res.	Resistant	Struct.	Structural
O.G.	Ogee	Resi.	Residential	Sty.	Story
O.H.	Overhead	Rgh.	Rough	Subj.	Subject
O&P	Overhead and Profit	RGS	Rigid Galvanized Steel	Subs.	Subcontractors
Oper.	Operator	R.H.W.	Rubber, Heat & Water Resistant; Residential Hot Water	Surf.	Surface
Opng.	Opening			Sw.	Switch
Orna.	Ornamental	rms	Root Mean Square	Swbd.	Switchboard
OSB	Oriented Strand Board	Rnd.	Round	S.Y.	Square Yard
O.S.&Y.	Outside Screw and Yoke	Rodm.	Rodman	Syn.	Synthetic
Ovhd.	Overhead	Rofc.	Roofer, Composition	S.Y.P.	Southern Yellow Pine
OWG	Oil, Water or Gas	Rofp.	Roofer, Precast	Sys.	System
Oz.	Ounce	Rohe.	Roofer Helpers (Composition)	t.	Thickness
P.	Pole; Applied Load; Projection	Rots.	Roofer, Tile & Slate	T	Temperature; Ton
p.	Page	R.O.W.	Right of Way	Tan	Tangent
Pape.	Paperhanger	RPM	Revolutions per Minute	T.C.	Terra Cotta
P.A.P.R.	Powered Air Purifying Respirator	R.S.	Rapid Start	T & C	Threaded and Coupled
PAR	Parabolic Reflector	Rsr	Riser	T.D.	Temperature Difference
Pc., Pcs.	Piece, Pieces	RT	Round Trip	Tdd	Telecommunications Device for the Deaf
P.C.	Portland Cement; Power Connector	S.	Suction; Single Entrance; South		
P.C.F.	Pounds per Cubic Foot	SC	Screw Cover	T.E.M.	Transmission Electron Microscopy
P.C.M.	Phase Contrast Microscopy	SCFM	Standard Cubic Feet per Minute	TFE	Tetrafluoroethylene (Teflon)
P.E.	Professional Engineer; Porcelain Enamel; Polyethylene; Plain End	Scaf.	Scaffold	T. & G.	Tongue & Groove; Tar & Gravel
		Sch., Sched.	Schedule		
		S.C.R.	Modular Brick	Th., Thk.	Thick
Perf.	Perforated	S.D.	Sound Deadening	Thn.	Thin
PEX	Cross linked polyethylene	S.D.R.	Standard Dimension Ratio	Thrded	Threaded
Ph.	Phase	S.E.	Surfaced Edge	Tilf.	Tile Layer, Floor
P.I.	Pressure Injected	Sel.	Select	Tilh.	Tile Layer, Helper
Pile.	Pile Driver	S.E.R., S.E.U.	Service Entrance Cable	THHN	Nylon Jacketed Wire
Pkg.	Package	S.F.	Square Foot	THW.	Insulated Strand Wire

Abbreviations

THWN	Nylon Jacketed Wire
T.L.	Truckload
T.M.	Track Mounted
Tot.	Total
T-O-L	Threadolet
T.S.	Trigger Start
Tr.	Trade
Transf.	Transformer
Trhv.	Truck Driver, Heavy
Trlr	Trailer
Trlt.	Truck Driver, Light
TTY	Teletypewriter
TV	Television
T.W.	Thermoplastic Water Resistant Wire
UCI	Uniform Construction Index
UF	Underground Feeder
UGND	Underground Feeder
U.H.F.	Ultra High Frequency
U.I.	United Inch
U.L.	Underwriters Laboratory
Uld.	unloading
Unfin.	Unfinished
URD	Underground Residential Distribution
US	United States

USP	United States Primed
UTP	Unshielded Twisted Pair
V	Volt
V.A.	Volt Amperes
V.C.T.	Vinyl Composition Tile
VAV	Variable Air Volume
VC	Veneer Core
Vent.	Ventilation
Vert.	Vertical
V.F.	Vinyl Faced
V.G.	Vertical Grain
V.H.F.	Very High Frequency
VHO	Very High Output
Vib.	Vibrating
V.L.F.	Vertical Linear Foot
Vol.	Volume
VRP	Vinyl Reinforced Polyester
W	Wire; Watt; Wide; West
w/	With
W.C.	Water Column; Water Closet
W.F.	Wide Flange
W.G.	Water Gauge
Wldg.	Welding
W. Mile	Wire Mile
W-O-L	Weldolet
W.R.	Water Resistant

Wrck.	Wrecker
W.S.P.	Water, Steam, Petroleum
WT., Wt.	Weight
WWF	Welded Wire Fabric
XFER	Transfer
XFMR	Transformer
XHD	Extra Heavy Duty
XHHW,	Cross-Linked Polyethylene Wire
XLPE	Insulation
XLP	Cross-linked Polyethylene
Y	Wye
yd	Yard
yr	Year
Δ	Delta
%	Percent
~	Approximately
Ø	**Phase; diameter**
@	At
#	Pound; Number
<	Less Than
>	Greater Than
Z	zone

Index

For more information visit
the RSMeans Website at
www.rsmeans.com

Contractor's Pricing Guides

Contractor's Pricing Guide: Residential Detailed Costs 2010

Every aspect of residential construction, from overhead costs to residential lighting and wiring, is in here. All the detail you need to accurately estimate the costs of your work with or without markups—labor-hours, typical crews, and equipment are included as well. When you need a detailed estimate, this publication has all the costs to help you come up with a complete, on the money price you can rely on to win profitable work.

**Unit prices organized according to
the latest MasterFormat!**

$39.95 per copy
Available Dec. 2009
Catalog no. 60330

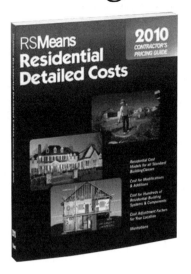

Contractor's Pricing Guide: Residential Repair & Remodeling Costs 2010

This book provides total unit price costs for every aspect of the most common repair and remodeling projects. Organized in the order of construction by component and activity, it includes demolition and installation, cleaning, painting, and more. With simplified estimating methods, clear, concise descriptions, and technical specifications for each component, the book is a valuable tool for contractors who want to speed up their estimating time, while making sure their costs are on target.

$39.95 per copy
Available Dec. 2009
Catalog no. 60340

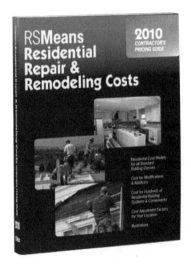

Contractor's Pricing Guide: Residential Square Foot Costs 2010

Now available in one concise volume, all you need to know to plan and budget the cost of new homes. If you are looking for a quick reference, the model home section contains costs for over 250 different sizes and types of residences, with hundreds of easily applied modifications. If you need even more detail, the Assemblies Section lets you build your own costs or modify the model costs further. Hundreds of graphics are provided, along with forms and procedures to help you get it right.

$39.95 per copy
Available Dec. 2009
Catalog no. 60320

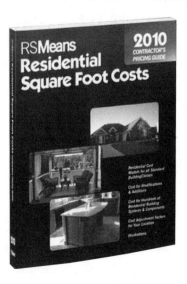

Annual Cost Guides

**For more information
visit the RSMeans website
at www.rsmeans.com**

RSMeans Building Construction Cost Data 2010

Offers you unchallenged unit price reliability in an easy-to-use format. Whether used for verifying complete, finished estimates or for periodic checks, it supplies more cost facts better and faster than any comparable source. Over 21,000 unit prices have been updated for 2010. The City Cost Indexes and Location Factors cover over 930 areas, for indexing to any project location in North America. Order and get *RSMeans Quarterly Update Service* FREE. You'll have year-long access to the RSMeans Estimating **HOTLINE** FREE with your subscription. Expert assistance when using RSMeans data is just a phone call away.

$169.95 per copy
Available Sept. 2009
Catalog no. 60010

**Unit prices organized according to
the latest MasterFormat!**

RSMeans Mechanical Cost Data 2010
- **HVAC**
- **Controls**

Total unit and systems price guidance for mechanical construction. . . materials, parts, fittings, and complete labor cost information. Includes prices for piping, heating, air conditioning, ventilation, and all related construction.

Plus new 2010 unit costs for:

- Thousands of installed HVAC/controls assemblies components
- "On-site" Location Factors for over 930 cities and towns in the U.S. and Canada
- Crews, labor, and equipment

$169.95 per copy
Available Oct. 2009
Catalog no. 60020

RSMeans Plumbing Cost Data 2010

Comprehensive unit prices and assemblies for plumbing, irrigation systems, commercial and residential fire protection, point-of-use water heaters, and the latest approved materials. This publication and its companion, *RSMeans Mechanical Cost Data*, provide full-range cost estimating coverage for all the mechanical trades.

Now contains updated costs for potable water and radiant heat systems and high efficiency fixtures.

$169.95 per copy
Available Oct. 2009
Catalog no. 60210

**Unit prices organized according to
the latest MasterFormat!**

RSMeans Facilities Construction Cost Data 2010

For the maintenance and construction of commercial, industrial, municipal, and institutional properties. Costs are shown for new and remodeling construction and are broken down into materials, labor, equipment, and overhead and profit. Special emphasis is given to sections on mechanical, electrical, furnishings, site work, building maintenance, finish work, and demolition.

More than 43,000 unit costs, plus assemblies costs and a comprehensive Reference Section are included.

$419.95 per copy
Available Nov. 2009
Catalog no. 60200

For more information
visit the RSMeans website
at www.rsmeans.com

Annual Cost Guides

RSMeans Square Foot Costs 2010

It's Accurate and Easy To Use!

- **Updated price information** based on nationwide figures from suppliers, estimators, labor experts, and contractors

- "How-to-Use" sections, with **clear examples** of commercial, residential, industrial, and institutional structures

- Realistic graphics, offering true-to-life illustrations of building projects

- Extensive information on using square foot cost data, including sample estimates and alternate pricing methods

$84.95 per copy
Available Oct. 2009
Catalog no. 60050

RSMeans Repair & Remodeling Cost Data 2010

Commercial/Residential

Use this valuable tool to estimate commercial and residential renovation and remodeling.

Includes: New costs for hundreds of unique methods, materials, and conditions that only come up in repair and remodeling, PLUS:

- Unit costs for over 15,000 construction components
- Installed costs for over 90 assemblies
- Over 930 "on-site" localization factors for the U.S. and Canada.

Unit prices organized according to the latest MasterFormat!

$144.95 per copy
Available Oct. 2009
Catalog no. 60040

RSMeans Electrical Cost Data 2010

Pricing information for every part of electrical cost planning. More than 9,000 unit and systems costs with design tables; clear specifications and drawings; engineering guides; illustrated estimating procedures; complete labor-hour and materials costs for better scheduling and procurement; and the latest electrical products and construction methods.

- A variety of special electrical systems including cathodic protection

- Costs for maintenance, demolition, HVAC/mechanical, specialties, equipment, and more

Unit prices organized according to the latest MasterFormat!

$99.95 per copy
Available Oct. 2009
Catalog no. 60030

RSMeans Electrical Change Order Cost Data 2010

RSMeans Electrical Change Order Cost Data provides you with electrical unit prices exclusively for pricing change orders—based on the recent, direct experience of contractors and suppliers. Analyze and check your own change order estimates against the experience others have had doing the same work. It also covers productivity analysis and change order cost justifications. With useful information for calculating the effects of change orders and dealing with their administration.

$169.95 per copy
Available Dec. 2009
Catalog no. 60230

RSMeans Assemblies Cost Data 2010

RSMeans Assemblies Cost Data takes the guesswork out of preliminary or conceptual estimates. Now you don't have to try to calculate the assembled cost by working up individual component costs. We've done all the work for you.

Presents detailed illustrations, descriptions, specifications, and costs for every conceivable building assembly—240 types in all—arranged in the easy-to-use UNIFORMAT II system. Each illustrated "assembled" cost includes a complete grouping of materials and associated installation costs, including the installing contractor's overhead and profit.

$279.95 per copy
Available Sept. 2009
Catalog no. 60060

RSMeans Open Shop Building Construction Cost Data 2010

The latest costs for accurate budgeting and estimating of new commercial and residential construction. . . renovation work. . . change orders. . . cost engineering.

RSMeans Open Shop "BCCD" will assist you to:
• Develop benchmark prices for change orders
• Plug gaps in preliminary estimates and budgets
• Estimate complex projects
• Substantiate invoices on contracts
• Price ADA-related renovations

Unit prices organized according to the latest MasterFormat!

$169.95 per copy
Available Dec. 2009
Catalog no. 60150

RSMeans Residential Cost Data 2010

Contains square foot costs for 30 basic home models with the look of today, plus hundreds of custom additions and modifications you can quote right off the page. With costs for the 100 residential systems you're most likely to use in the year ahead. Complete with blank estimating forms, sample estimates, and step-by-step instructions.

Now contains line items for cultured stone and brick, PVC trim lumber, and TPO roofing.

$144.95 per copy
Available Oct. 2009
Catalog no. 60170

Unit prices organized according to the latest MasterFormat!

RSMeans Site Work & Landscape Cost Data 2010

Includes unit and assemblies costs for earthwork, sewerage, piped utilities, site improvements, drainage, paving, trees & shrubs, street openings/repairs, underground tanks, and more. Contains 57 tables of assemblies costs for accurate conceptual estimates.

Includes:
• Estimating for infrastructure improvements
• Environmentally-oriented construction
• ADA-mandated handicapped access
• Hazardous waste line items

$169.95 per copy
Available Nov. 2009
Catalog no. 60280

RSMeans Facilities Maintenance & Repair Cost Data 2010

RSMeans Facilities Maintenance & Repair Cost Data gives you a complete system to manage and plan your facility repair and maintenance costs and budget efficiently. Guidelines for auditing a facility and developing an annual maintenance plan. Budgeting is included, along with reference tables on cost and management, and information on frequency and productivity of maintenance operations.

The only nationally recognized source of maintenance and repair costs. Developed in cooperation with the Civil Engineering Research Laboratory (CERL) of the Army Corps of Engineers.

$379.95 per copy
Available Nov. 2009
Catalog no. 60300

RSMeans Light Commercial Cost Data 2010

Specifically addresses the light commercial market which is a specialized niche in the construction industry. Aids you, the owner/designer/contractor, in preparing all types of estimates—from budgets to detailed bids. Includes new advances in methods and materials.

Assemblies Section allows you to evaluate alternatives in the early stages of design/planning.

Over 11,000 unit costs ensure that you have the prices you need. . . when you need them.

Unit prices organized according to the latest MasterFormat

$144.95 per copy
Available Nov. 2009
Catalog no. 60180

For more information
visit the RSMeans website
at www.rsmeans.com

Annual Cost Guides

RSMeans Concrete & Masonry Cost Data 2010

Provides you with cost facts for virtually all concrete/masonry estimating needs, from complicated formwork to various sizes and face finishes of brick and block—all in great detail. The comprehensive Unit Price Section contains more than 7,500 selected entries. Also contains an Assemblies [Cost] Section, and a detailed Reference Section that supplements the cost data.

Unit prices organized according to the latest MasterFormat !

154.95 per copy
Available Dec. 2009
Catalog no. 60110

RSMeans Labor Rates for the Construction Industry 2010

Complete information for estimating labor costs, making comparisons, and negotiating wage rates by trade for over 300 U.S. and Canadian cities. With 46 construction trades listed by local union number in each city, and historical wage rates included for comparison. Each city chart lists the county and is alphabetically arranged with handy visual flip tabs for quick reference.

$379.95 per copy
Available Dec. 2009
Catalog no. 60120

RSMeans Construction Cost Indexes 2010

What materials and labor costs will change unexpectedly this year? By how much?
Breakdowns for 316 major cities
National averages for 30 key cities
Expanded five major city indexes
Historical construction cost indexes

62.00 per year (subscription)
Catalog no. 50140

0.50 individual quarters
Catalog no. 60140 A,B,C,D

RSMeans Interior Cost Data 2010

Provides you with prices and guidance needed to make accurate interior work estimates. Contains costs on materials, equipment, hardware, custom installations, furnishings, and labor costs. . . for new and remodel commercial and industrial interior construction, including updated information on office furnishings, and reference information.

Unit prices organized according to the latest MasterFormat !

$169.95 per copy
Available Nov. 2009
Catalog no. 60090

RSMeans Heavy Construction Cost Data 2010

comprehensive guide to heavy construction costs. Includes costs for highly specialized projects such as tunnels, dams, highways, ports, and waterways. Information on labor es, equipment, and materials costs is included. tures unit price costs, systems costs, and merous reference tables for costs and design.

9.95 per copy
ailable Nov. 2009
talog no. 60160

Unit prices organized according to the latest MasterFormat!

Reference Books

**For more information
visit the RSMeans website
at www.rsmeans.com**

Value Engineering: Practical Applications

For Design, Construction, Maintenance & Operations

by Alphonse Dell'Isola, PE

A tool for immediate application—for engineers, architects, facility managers, owners, and contractors. Includes making the case for VE—the management briefing; integrating VE into planning, budgeting, and design; conducting life cycle costing; using VE methodology in design review and consultant selection; case studies; VE workbook; and a life cycle costing program on disk.

$79.95 per copy
**Over 450 pages, illustrated, softcover
Catalog no. 67319A**

Facilities Operations & Engineering Reference

by the Association for Facilities Engineering and RSMeans

An all-in-one technical reference for planning and managing facility projects and solving day-to-day operations problems. Selected as the official certified plant engineer reference, this handbook covers financial analysis, maintenance, HVAC and energy efficiency, and more.

$54.98 per copy
**Over 700 pages, illustrated, hardcover
Catalog no. 67318**

The Building Professional's Guide to Contract Documents

3rd Edition

by Waller S. Poage, AIA, CSI, CVS

A comprehensive reference for owners, design professionals, contractors, and students

- Structure your documents for maximum efficiency.
- Effectively communicate construction requirements.
- Understand the roles and responsibilities of construction professionals.
- Improve methods of project delivery.

$64.95 per copy, 400 pages
**Diagrams and construction forms, hardcover
Catalog no. 67261A**

Complete Book of Framing

by Scot Simpson

This straightforward, easy-to-learn method will help framers, carpenters, and handy homeowners build their skills in rough carpentry and framing. Shows how to frame all the parts of a house: floors, walls, roofs, door & window openings, and stairs—with hundreds of color photographs and drawings that show every detail.

The book gives beginners all the basics they need to go from zero framing knowledge to a journeyman level.

$29.95 per copy
**352 pages, softcover
Catalog no. 67353**

Cost Planning & Estimating for Facilities Maintenance

In this unique book, a team of facilities management authorities shares their expertise on:

- Evaluating and budgeting maintenance operations
- Maintaining and repairing key building components
- Applying *RSMeans Facilities Maintenance & Repair Cost Data* to your estimating

Covers special maintenance requirements of the ten major building types.

$89.95 per copy
**Over 475 pages, hardcover
Catalog no. 67314**

Life Cycle Costing for Facilities

by Alphonse Dell'Isola and Dr. Steven Kirk

Guidance for achieving higher quality design and construction projects at lower costs! Cost-cutting effort often sacrifice quality to yield the cheapest product. Life cycle costing enables building designers and owners to achieve both. The authors of this book show how LCC can work for a variety of projects — from roads to HVAC upgrades to different types of buildings.

$99.95 per copy
**450 pages, hardcover
Catalog no. 67341**

Planning & Managing Interior Projects 2nd Edition

by Carol E. Farren, CFM

Expert guidance on managing renovation & relocation projects

This book guides you through every step in relocating to a new space or renovating an old one. From initial meeting through design and construction, to post-project administration, it helps you get the most for your company or client. Includes sample forms, spec lists, agreements, drawings, and much more!

$34.98 per copy
**200 pages, softcover
Catalog no. 67245A**

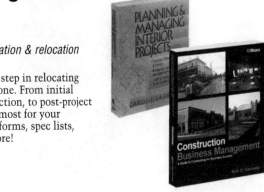

Construction Business Management

by Nick Ganaway

Only 43% of construction firms stay in business after four years. Make sure your company thrives with valuable guidance from a pro with 25 years of success a commercial contractor. Find out what it takes to buil all aspects of a business that is profitable, enjoyable, a enduring. With a bonus chapter on retail construction.

$49.95 per copy
**200 pages, softcover
Catalog no. 67352**

For more information
visit the RSMeans website
at www.rsmeans.com

Reference Books

Interior Home Improvement Costs 9th Edition

Updated estimates for the most popular remodeling and repair projects—from small, do-it-yourself jobs to major renovations and new construction. Includes: kitchens & baths; new living space from your attic, basement, or garage; new floors, paint, and wallpaper; tearing out or building new walls; closets, stairs, and fireplaces; new energy-saving improvements, home theaters, and more!

$24.95 per copy
50 pages, illustrated, softcover
Catalog no. 67308E

Exterior Home Improvement Costs 9th Edition

Updated estimates for the most popular remodeling and repair projects—from small, do-it-yourself jobs, to major renovations and new construction. Includes: curb appeal projects—landscaping, patios, porches, driveways, and walkways; new windows and doors; decks, greenhouses, and sunrooms; room additions and garages; roofing, siding, and painting; "green" improvements to save energy & water.

$24.95 per copy
Over 275 pages, illustrated, softcover
Catalog no. 67309E

Builder's Essentials: Plan Reading & Material Takeoff

For Residential and Light Commercial Construction

by Wayne J. DelPico

A valuable tool for understanding plans and specs, and accurately calculating material quantities. Step-by-step instructions and takeoff procedures based on a full set of working drawings.

$5.95 per copy
Over 420 pages, softcover
Catalog no. 67307

Means Unit Price Estimating Methods

New 4th Edition

This new edition includes up-to-date cost data and estimating examples, updated to reflect changes to the CSI numbering system and new features of RSMeans cost data. It describes the most productive, universally accepted ways to estimate, and uses checklists and forms to illustrate shortcuts and timesavers. A model estimate demonstrates procedures. A new chapter explores computer estimating alternatives.

$59.95 per copy
Over 350 pages, illustrated, softcover
Catalog no. 67303B

Total Productive Facilities Management

by Richard W. Sievert, Jr.

Today, facilities are viewed as strategic resources. . . elevating the facility manager to the role of asset manager supporting the organization's overall business goals. Now, Richard Sievert Jr., in this well-articulated guidebook, sets forth a new operational standard for the facility manager's emerging role. . . a comprehensive program for managing facilities as a true profit center.

$.98 per copy
pages, softcover
Catalog no. 67321

Green Building: Project Planning & Cost Estimating 2nd Edition

This new edition has been completely updated with the latest in green building technologies, design concepts, standards, and costs. Now includes a 2010 Green Building *CostWorks* CD with more than 300 green building assemblies and over 5,000 unit price line items for sustainable building. The new edition is also full-color with all new case studies—plus a new chapter on deconstruction, a key aspect of green building.

$129.95 per copy
350 pages, softcover
Catalog no. 67338A

Concrete Repair and Maintenance Illustrated

Peter Emmons

Hundreds of illustrations show users how to analyze, repair, clean, and maintain concrete structures for optimal performance and cost effectiveness. From parking garages to roads and bridges to structural concrete, this comprehensive book describes the causes, effects, and remedies for concrete wear and failure. Invaluable in planning jobs, selecting materials, and training employees, this book is a must-have for concrete specialists, general contractors, facility managers, civil and structural engineers, and architects.

$95 per copy
pages, illustrated, softcover
Catalog no. 67146

Means Illustrated Construction Dictionary Condensed, 2nd Edition

The best portable dictionary for office or field use—an essential tool for contractors, architects, insurance and real estate personnel, facility managers, homeowners, and anyone who needs quick, clear definitions for construction terms. The second edition has been further enhanced with updates and hundreds of new terms and illustrations . . . in keeping with the most recent developments in the construction industry.

Now with a quick-reference Spanish section. Includes tools and equipment, materials, tasks, and more!

$59.95 per copy
Over 500 pages, softcover
Catalog no. 67282A

Means Repair & Remodeling Estimating 4th Edition

By Edward B. Wetherill and RSMeans

This important reference focuses on the unique problems of estimating renovations of existing structures, and helps you determine the true costs of remodeling through careful evaluation of architectural details and a site visit.

New section on disaster restoration costs.

$69.95 per copy
Over 450 pages, illustrated, hardcover
Catalog no. 67265B

Facilities Planning & Relocation

by David D. Owen

A complete system for planning space needs and managing relocations. Includes step-by-step manual, over 50 forms, and extensive reference section on materials and furnishings.

New lower price and user-friendly format.

$49.98 per copy
Over 450 pages, softcover
Catalog no. 67301

Means Square Foot & UNIFORMAT Assemblies Estimating Methods 3rd Edition

Develop realistic square foot and assemblies costs for budgeting and construction funding. The new edition features updated guidance on square foot and assemblies estimating using UNIFORMAT II. An essential reference for anyone who performs conceptual estimates.

$69.95 per copy
Over 300 pages, illustrated, softcover
Catalog no. 67145B

Means Electrical Estimating Methods 3rd Edition

Expanded edition includes sample estimates and cost information in keeping with the latest version of the CSI MasterFormat and UNIFORMAT II. Complete coverage of fiber optic and uninterruptible power supply electrical systems, broken down by components, and explained in detail. Includes a new chapter on computerized estimating methods. A practical companion to *RSMeans Electrical Cost Data.*

$64.95 per copy
Over 325 pages, hardcover
Catalog no. 67230B

Means Mechanical Estimating Methods 4th Edition

Completely updated, this guide assists you in making a review of plans, specs, and bid packages, with suggestions for takeoff procedures, listings, substitutions, and pre-bid scheduling for all components of HVAC. Includes suggestions for budgeting labor and equipment usage. Compares materials and construction methods to allow you to select the best option.

$64.95 per copy
Over 350 pages, illustrated, softcover
Catalog no. 67294B

Means ADA Compliance Pricing Guide 2nd Edition

by Adaptive Environments and RSMeans

Completely updated and revised to the new 2004 *Americans with Disabilities Act Accessibility Guidelines,* this book features more than 70 of the most commonly needed modifications for ADA compliance. Projects range from installing ramps and walkways, widening doorways and entryways, and installing and refitting elevators, to relocating light switches and signage.

$79.95 per copy
Over 350 pages, illustrated, softcover
Catalog no. 67310A

Project Scheduling & Management for Construction 3rd Edition

by David R. Pierce, Jr.

A comprehensive yet easy-to-follow guide to construction project scheduling and control—from vital project management principles through the latest scheduling, tracking, and controlling techniques. The author is a leading authority on scheduling, with years of field and teaching experience at leading academic institutions. Spend a few hours with this book and come away with a solid understanding of this essential management topic.

$64.95 per copy
Over 300 pages, illustrated, hardcover
Catalog no. 67247B

more information
t the RSMeans website
www.rsmeans.com

Reference Books

e Practice of Cost egregation Analysis

Bruce A. Desrosiers and yne J. DelPico

expert guide walks you through the practice of cost egation analysis, which enables property owners to taxes and benefit from "accelerated cost recovery" gh depreciation deductions on assets that are properly tified and classified.

a glossary of terms, sample cost segregation nates for various building types, key information rces, and updates via a dedicated website, this book is tical resource for anyone involved in cost segregation sis.

95 per copy
r 225 pages
log no. 67345

Preventive Maintenance for Multi-Family Housing

by John C. Maciha

Prepared by one of the nation's leading experts on multi-family housing.

This complete PM system for apartment and condominium communities features expert guidance, checklists for buildings and grounds maintenance tasks and their frequencies, a reusable wall chart to track maintenance, and a dedicated website featuring customizable electronic forms. A must-have for anyone involved with multi-family housing maintenance and upkeep.

$89.95 per copy
225 pages
Catalog no. 67346

ow to Estimate with eans Data & CostWorks

3rd Edition

RSMeans and eh A. Mubarak, Ph.D.

3rd Edition—fully updated with new chapters, new CD with updated *CostWorks* cost data MasterFormat organization. Includes all major truction items—with more than 300 exercises wo sets of plans that show how to estimate for ad range of construction items and systems— ding general conditions and equipment costs.

95 per copy
pages, softcover
des CostWorks CD
log no. 67324B

Job Order Contracting

Expediting Construction Project Delivery

by Allen Henderson

Expert guidance to help you implement JOC—fast becoming the preferred project delivery method for repair and renovation, minor new construction, and maintenance projects in the public sector and in many states and municipalities. The author, a leading JOC expert and practitioner, shows how to:

- Establish a JOC program
- Evaluate proposals and award contracts
- Handle general requirements and estimating
- Partner for maximum benefits

$89.95 per copy
192 pages, illustrated, hardcover
Catalog no. 67348

ilder's Essentials: timating Building Costs

the Residential & Light mmercial Contractor

Wayne J. DelPico

by-step estimating methods for residential and commercial contractors. Includes a detailed at every construction specialty—explaining all omponents, takeoff units, and labor needed ell-organized, complete estimates. Covers correctly preting plans and specifications, and developing ate and complete labor and material costs.

95 per copy
400 pages, illustrated, softcover
log no. 67343

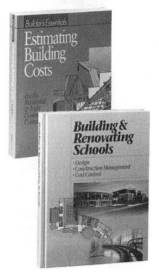

Building & Renovating Schools

This all-inclusive guide covers every step of the school construction process—from initial planning, needs assessment, and design, right through moving into the new facility. A must-have resource for anyone concerned with new school construction or renovation. With square foot cost models for elementary, middle, and high school facilities, and real-life case studies of recently completed school projects.

The contributors to this book—architects, construction project managers, contractors, and estimators who specialize in school construction—provide start-to-finish, expert guidance on the process.

$69.98 per copy
Over 425 pages, hardcover
Catalog no. 67342

The Homeowner's Guide to Mold By Michael Pugliese

Expert guidance to protect your health and your home.

Mold, whether caused by leaks, humidity or flooding, is a real health and financial issue—for homeowners and contractors. This full-color book explains:
- Construction and maintenance practices to prevent mold
- How to inspect for and remove mold
- Mold remediation procedures and costs
- What to do after a flood
- How to deal with insurance companies

$21.95 per copy
144 pages, softcover
Catalog no. 67344

Means Illustrated Construction Dictionary
Unabridged 3rd Edition, with CD-ROM

Long regarded as the industry's finest, *Means Illustrated Construction Dictionary* is now even better. With the addition of over 1,000 new terms and hundreds of new illustrations, it is the clear choice for the most comprehensive and current information. The companion CD-ROM that comes with this new edition adds many extra features: larger graphics, expanded definitions, and links to both CSI MasterFormat numbers and product information.

$99.95 per copy
Over 790 pages, illustrated, hardcover
Catalog no. 67292A

Means Landscape Estimating Methods

New 5th Edition

Answers questions about preparing competitive landscape construction estimates, with up-to-date cost estimates and the new MasterFormat classification system. Expanded and revised to address the latest materials and methods, including new coverage on approaches to green building. Includes:
- Step-by-step explanation of the estimating process
- Sample forms and worksheets that save time and prevent errors

$64.95 per copy
Over 350 pages, softcover
Catalog no. 67295C

Means Plumbing Estimating Methods 3rd Edition
by Joseph Galeno and Sheldon Greene

Updated and revised! This practical guide walks you through a plumbing estimate, from basic materials and installation methods through change order analysis. *Plumbing Estimating Methods* covers residential, commercial, industrial, and medical systems, and features sample takeoff and estimate forms and detailed illustrations of systems and components.

$29.98 per copy
330+ pages, softcover
Catalog no. 67283B

Understanding & Negotiating Construction Contracts
by Kit Werremeyer

Take advantage of the author's 30 years' experience in small-to-large (including international) construction projects. Learn how to identify, understand, and evaluate high risk terms and conditions typically found in all construction contracts—then negotiate to lower or eliminate the risk, improve terms of payment, and reduce exposure to claims and disputes. The author avoids "legalese" and gives real-life examples from actual projects.

$69.95 per copy
300 pages, softcover
Catalog no. 67350

The Gypsum Construction Handbook (Spanish)

The Gypsum Construction Handbook, Spanish edition is an illustrated, comprehensive, and authoritative guide on all facets of gypsum construction. You'll find comprehensive guidance on available products, installation methods, fire- and sound-rated construction information, illustrated framing-to-finish application instructions, estimating and planning information, and more.

$29.95 per copy
Over 450 pages, softcover
Catalog No. 67357S

Means Spanish/English Construction Dictionary 2nd Edition
by RSMeans and the International Code Council

This expanded edition features thousands of the most common words and useful phrases in the construction industry with easy-to-follow pronunciations in both Spanish and English. Over 800 new terms, phrases, and illustrations have been added. It also features a new stand-alone "Safety & Emergencies" section, with colored pages for quick access.

Unique to this dictionary are the systems illustrations showing the relationship of components in the most common building systems for all major trades.

$23.95 per copy
Over 400 pages
Catalog no. 67327A

How Your House Works
by Charlie Wing

A must-have reference for every homeowner, handyman, contractor—for repair, remodeling, and new construction. This book uncovers the mysteries behind just about every major appliance and building element in your house—from electrical, heating and AC, to plumbing, framing, foundations and appliances. Clear, "exploded" drawings show exactly how things should be put together and how they function—what to check if they don't work, and what you can do that might save you having to call in a professional.

$21.95 per copy
160 pages, softcover
Catalog no. 67351

For more information
visit the RSMeans website
at www.rsmeans.com

Professional Development

Means CostWorks® CD Training

This one-day course helps users become more familiar with the functionality of *Means CostWorks* program. Each menu, icon, screen, and function found in the program is explained in depth. Time is devoted to hands-on estimating exercises.

Some of what you'll learn:
- Searching the database utilizing all navigation methods
- Exporting RSMeans Data to your preferred spreadsheet format
- Viewing crews, assembly components, and much more!
- Automatically regionalizing the database

You are required to bring your own laptop computer for this course.

When you register for this course you will receive an outline for your laptop requirements.

Also offering web training for CostWorks CD!

Unit Price Estimating

This interactive *two-day* seminar teaches attendees how to interpret project information and process it into final, detailed estimates with the greatest accuracy level.

The most important credential an estimator can take to the job is the ability to visualize construction, and estimate accurately.

Some of what you'll learn:
- Interpreting the design in terms of cost
- The most detailed, time-tested methodology for accurate pricing
- Key cost drivers—material, labor, equipment, staging, and subcontracts
- Understanding direct and indirect costs for accurate job cost accounting and change order management

Who should attend: Corporate and government estimators and purchasers, architects, engineers… and others needing to produce accurate project estimates.

Square Foot & Assemblies Estimating

This *two-day* course teaches attendees how to quickly deliver accurate square foot estimates using limited budget and design information.

Some of what you'll learn:
- How square foot costing gets the estimate done faster
- Taking advantage of a "systems" or "assemblies" format
- The RSMeans "building assemblies/square foot cost approach"
- How to create a reliable preliminary systems estimate using bare-bones design information

Who should attend: Facilities managers, facilities engineers, estimators, planners, developers, construction finance professionals… and others needing to make quick, accurate construction cost estimates at commercial, government, educational, and medical facilities.

Repair & Remodeling Estimating

This *two-day* seminar emphasizes all the underlying considerations unique to repair/remodeling estimating and presents the correct methods for generating accurate, reliable R&R project costs using the unit price and assemblies methods.

Some of what you'll learn:
- Estimating considerations—like labor-hours, building code compliance, working within existing structures, purchasing materials in smaller quantities, unforeseen deficiencies
- Identifying problems and providing solutions to estimating building alterations
- Rules for factoring in minimum labor costs, accurate productivity estimates, and allowances for project contingencies
- R&R estimating examples calculated using unit price and assemblies data

Who should attend: Facilities managers, plant engineers, architects, contractors, estimators, builders… and others who are concerned with the proper preparation and/or evaluation of repair and remodeling estimates.

Mechanical & Electrical Estimating

This *two-day* course teaches attendees how to prepare more accurate and complete mechanical/electrical estimates, avoiding the pitfalls of omission and double-counting, while understanding the composition and rationale within the RSMeans Mechanical/Electrical database.

Some of what you'll learn:
- The unique way mechanical and electrical systems are interrelated
- M&E estimates–conceptual, planning, budgeting, and bidding stages
- Order of magnitude, square foot, assemblies, and unit price estimating
- Comparative cost analysis of equipment and design alternatives

Who should attend: Architects, engineers, facilities managers, mechanical and electrical contractors… and others needing a highly reliable method for developing, understanding, and evaluating mechanical and electrical contracts.

Green Building: Planning & Construction

In this *two-day* course, learn about tailoring a building and its placement on the site to the local climate, site conditions, culture, and community. Includes information to reduce resource consumption and augment resource supply.

Some of what you'll learn:
- Green technologies, materials, systems, and standards
- Modeling tools and how to use them
- Cost vs. value of green products over their life cycle
- Low-cost green strategies, and economic incentives and funding
- Health, comfort, and productivity

Who should attend: Contractors, project managers, building owners, building officials, healthcare and insurance professionals.

Facilities Maintenance & Repair Estimating

This *two-day* course teaches attendees how to plan, budget, and estimate the cost of ongoing and preventive maintenance and repair for existing buildings and grounds.

Some of what you'll learn:
- The most financially favorable maintenance, repair, and replacement scheduling and estimating
- Auditing and value engineering facilities
- Preventive planning and facilities upgrading
- Determining both in-house and contract-out service costs
- Annual, asset-protecting M&R plan

Who should attend: Facility managers, maintenance supervisors, buildings and grounds superintendents, plant managers, planners, estimators… and others involved in facilities planning and budgeting.

Practical Project Management for Construction Professionals

In this *two-day* course, acquire the essential knowledge and develop the skills to effectively and efficiently execute the day-to-day responsibilities of the construction project manager.

Covers:
- General conditions of the construction contract
- Contract modifications: change orders and construction change directives
- Negotiations with subcontractors and vendors
- Effective writing: notification and communications
- Dispute resolution: claims and liens

Who should attend: Architects, engineers, owner's representatives, project managers.

Facilities Construction Estimating

In this *two-day* course, professionals working in facilities management can get help with their daily challenges to establish budgets for all phase of a project

Some of what you'll learn:
- Determine the full scope of a project
- Identify the scope of risks & opportunities
- Creative solutions to estimating issues
- Organizing estimates for presentation & discussion
- Special techniques for repair/remodel and maintenance projects
- Negotiating project change orders

Who should attend: Facility managers, engineers, contractors, facility trades-people, planners & project managers

Professional Development

For more information visit the RSMeans website at www.rsmeans.com

Scheduling and Project Management

This *two-day* course teaches attendees the most current and proven scheduling and management techniques needed to bring projects in on time and on budget.

Some of what you'll learn:
- Crucial phases of planning and scheduling
- How to establish project priorities and develop realistic schedules and management techniques
- Critical Path and Precedence Methods
- Special emphasis on cost control

Who should attend: Construction project managers, supervisors, engineers, estimators, contractors... and others who want to improve their project planning, scheduling, and management skills.

Assessing Scope of Work for Facility Construction Estimating

This *two-day* practical training program addresses the vital importance of understanding the SCOPE of projects in order to produce accurate cost estimates for facility repair and remodeling.

Some of what you'll learn:
- Discussions of site visits, plans/specs, record drawings of facilities, and site-specific lists
- Review of CSI divisions, including means, methods, materials, and the challenges of scoping each topic
- Exercises in SCOPE identification and SCOPE writing for accurate estimating of projects
- Hands-on exercises that require SCOPE, take-off, and pricing

Who should attend: Corporate and government estimators, planners, facility managers, and others who need to produce accurate project estimates.

Site Work & Heavy Construction Estimating

This *two-day* course teaches attendees how to estimate earthwork, site utilities, foundations, and site improvements, using the assemblies and the unit price methods.

Some of what you'll learn:
- Basic site work and heavy construction estimating skills
- Estimating foundations, utilities, earthwork, and site improvements
- Correct equipment usage, quality control, and site investigation for estimating purposes

Who should attend: Project managers, design engineers, estimators, and contractors doing site work and heavy construction.

2010 RSMeans Seminar Schedule

Note: call for exact dates and details.

Location	Dates
Las Vegas, NV	March
Washington, DC	April
Denver, CO	May
San Francisco, CA	June
Washington, DC	September
Dallas, TX	September
Las Vegas, NV	October
Atlantic City, NJ	October
Orlando, FL	November
San Diego, CA	December

2010 Regional Seminar Schedule

Location	Dates	Location	Dates
Seattle, WA	January and August	St. Louis, MO	August
Dallas/Ft. Worth, TX	January	Houston, TX	October
Austin, TX	February	Colorado Springs, CO	October
Anchorage, AK	March and September	Baltimore, MD	November
Oklahoma City, OK	March	Sacramento, CA	November
Phoenix, AZ	March	San Antonio, TX	December
Aiea, HI	May	Raleigh, NC	December
Kansas City, MO	May		
Bethesda, MD	June		
Columbus, GA	June		
El Segundo, CA	August		

1-800-334-3509, ext. 511

For more information
visit the RSMeans website
at www.rsmeans.com

Professional Development

Registration Information

Register early... Save up to $100! Register 30 days before the start date of a seminar and save $100 off your total fee. *Note: This discount can be applied only once per order. It cannot be applied to team discount registrations or any other special offer.*

How to register Register by phone today! The RSMeans toll-free number for making reservations is **1-800-334-3509, ext. 5115.**

Individual seminar registration fee - $935. *Means CostWorks®* **training registration fee - $375.** To register by mail, complete the registration form and return, with your full fee, to: RSMeans Seminars, 63 Smiths Lane, Kingston, MA 02364.

Government pricing All federal government employees save off the regular seminar price. Other promotional discounts cannot be combined with the government discount.

Team discount program for two to four seminar registrations. Call for pricing: 1-800-334-3509, ext. 5115

Multiple course discounts When signing up for two or more courses, call for pricing.

Refund policy Cancellations will be accepted up to ten business days prior to the seminar start. There are no refunds for cancellations received later than ten working days prior to the first day of the seminar. A $150 processing fee will be applied for all cancellations. Written notice of cancellation is required. Substitutions can be made at any time before the session starts. **No-shows are subject to the full seminar fee.**

AACE approved courses Many seminars described and offered here have been approved for 14 hours (1.4 recertification credits) of credit by the AACE International Certification Board toward meeting the continuing education requirements for recertification as a Certified Cost Engineer/Certified Cost Consultant.

AIA Continuing Education We are registered with the AIA Continuing Education System (AIA/CES) and are committed to developing quality learning activities in accordance with the CES criteria. Many seminars meet the AIA/CES criteria for Quality Level 2. AIA members may receive (14) learning units (LUs) for each two-day RSMeans course.

Daily course schedule The first day of each seminar session begins at 8:30 a.m. and ends at 4:30 p.m. The second day begins at 8:00 a.m. and ends at 4:00 p.m. Participants are urged to bring a hand-held calculator, since many actual problems will be worked out in each session.

Continental breakfast Your registration includes the cost of a continental breakfast, and a morning and afternoon refreshment break. These informal segments allow you to discuss topics of mutual interest with other seminar attendees. (You are free to make your own lunch and dinner arrangements.)

Hotel/transportation arrangements RSMeans arranges to hold a block of rooms at most host hotels. To take advantage of special group rates when making your reservation, be sure to mention that you are attending the RSMeans seminar. You are, of course, free to stay at the lodging place of your choice. **(Hotel reservations and transportation arrangements should be made directly by seminar attendees.)**

Important Class sizes are limited, so please register as soon as possible.

Note: Pricing subject to change.

Registration Form

ADDS-1000

Call 1-800-334-3509, ext. 5115 to register or FAX this form 1-800-632-6732. Visit our Web site: www.rsmeans.com

Please register the following people for the RSMeans construction seminars as shown here. We understand that we must make our own hotel reservations if overnight stays are necessary.

Full payment of $_____ enclosed.

Bill me

Please print name of registrant(s)

(to appear on certificate of completion)

_____

_____

_____

_____

#: _____

GOVERNMENT AGENCIES MUST SUPPLY PURCHASE ORDER NUMBER OR TRAINING FORM.

Firm name_____

Address_____

City/State/Zip_____

Telephone no._____ Fax no._____

E-mail address_____

Charge registration(s) to: ☐ MasterCard ☐ VISA ☐ American Express

Account no._____ Exp. date_____

Cardholder's signature_____

Seminar name_____

Seminar City _____

Please mail check to: RSMeans Seminars, 63 Smiths Lane, P.O. Box 800, Kingston, MA 02364 USA

For more information
visit the RSMeans website
at www.rsmeans.com

New Titles

The Gypsum Construction Handbook by USG

An invaluable reference of construction procedures for gypsum drywall, cement board, veneer plaster, and conventional plaster. This new edition includes the newest product developments, installation methods, fire- and sound-rated construction information, illustrated framing-to-finish application instructions, estimating and planning information, and more. Great for architects and engineers; contractors, builders, and dealers; apprentices and training programs; building inspectors and code officials; and anyone interested in gypsum construction. Features information on tools and safety practices, a glossary of construction terms, and a list of important agencies and associations. Also available in Spanish.

$29.95
Over 575 pages, illustrated, softcover
Catalog no. 67357A

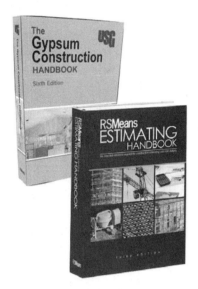

RSMeans Estimating Handbook, 3rd Edition

Widely used in the industry for tasks ranging from routine estimates to special cost analysis projects, this handbook has been completely updated and reorganized with new and expanded technical information.

RSMeans Estimating Handbook will help construction professionals:
- Evaluate architectural plans and specifications
- Prepare accurate quantity takeoffs
- Compare design alternatives and costs
- Perform value engineering
- Double-check estimates and quotes
- Estimate change orders

$99.95 per copy
Over 900 pages, hardcover
Catalog No. 67276B

BIM Handbook

A Guide to Building Information Modeling for Owners, Managers, Designers, Engineers and Contractors

by Chuck Eastman, Paul Teicholz, Rafael Sacks, Kathleen Liston

Building Information Modeling (BIM) is a new approach to design, construction, and facility management where a digital depiction of the building process is used to facilitate the exchange of information in digital format.

The BIM Handbook provides an in-depth understanding of BIM technologies, the business and organizational issues associated with its implementation, and the profound advantages that effective use of BIM can provide to all members of a project team. Also includes a rich set of informative real case studies.

$5.00
pages
Catalog no. 67356

Universal Design Ideas for Style, Comfort & Safety

by RSMeans and Lexicon Consulting, Inc.

Incorporating universal design when building or remodeling helps people of any age and physical ability more fully and safely enjoy their living spaces. This book shows how universal design can be artfully blended into the most attractive homes. It discusses specialized products like adjustable countertops and chair lifts, as well as simple ways to enhance a home's safety and comfort. With color photos and expert guidance, every area of the home is covered. Includes budget estimates that give an idea how much projects will cost.

$21.95
160 pages, illustrated, softcover
Catalog no. 67354

Green Home Improvement

by Daniel D. Chiras, PhD

With energy costs rising and environmental awareness increasing, many people are looking to make their homes greener. This book makes it easy, with 65 projects and actual costs and projected savings that will help homeowners prioritize their own improvements.

Projects range from simple water savers that cost just a few dollars, to bigger-ticket items such as efficient appliances and HVAC systems, green roofing, flooring, landscaping, and much more. With color photos and cost estimates, each project compares options and describes the work involved, the benefits, and the savings.

$24.95
pages, illustrated, softcover
Catalog no. 67355

Residential & Light Commercial Construction Standards, 3rd Edition, Updated

by RSMeans and contributing authors

This book provides authoritative requirements and recommendations compiled from leading professional associations, industry publications, and building code organizations. This all-in-one reference helps establish a standard for workmanship, quickly resolve disputes, and avoid defect claims. Updated third edition includes new coverage of green building, seismic, hurricane, and mold-resistant construction.

$59.95
Over 550 pages, illustrated, softcover
Catalog no. 67322B

2010 Order Form

Qty.	Book no.	COST ESTIMATING BOOKS	Unit Price	Total
	60060	Assemblies Cost Data 2010	$279.95	
	60010	Building Construction Cost Data 2010	169.95	
	60110	Concrete & Masonry Cost Data 2010	154.95	
	50140	Construction Cost Indexes 2010 (subscription)	362.00	
	60140A	Construction Cost Index–January 2010	90.50	
	60140B	Construction Cost Index–April 2010	90.50	
	60140C	Construction Cost Index–July 2010	90.50	
	60140D	Construction Cost Index–October 2010	90.50	
	60340	Contr. Pricing Guide: Resid. R & R Costs 2010	39.95	
	60330	Contr. Pricing Guide: Resid. Detailed 2010	39.95	
	60320	Contr. Pricing Guide: Resid. Sq. Ft. 2010	39.95	
	60230	Electrical Change Order Cost Data 2010	169.95	
	60030	Electrical Cost Data 2010	169.95	
	60200	Facilities Construction Cost Data 2010	419.95	
	60300	Facilities Maintenance & Repair Cost Data 2010	379.95	
	60160	Heavy Construction Cost Data 2010	169.95	
	60090	Interior Cost Data 2010	169.95	
	60120	Labor Rates for the Const. Industry 2010	379.95	
	60180	Light Commercial Cost Data 2010	144.95	
	60020	Mechanical Cost Data 2010	169.95	
	60150	Open Shop Building Const. Cost Data 2010	169.95	
	60210	Plumbing Cost Data 2010	169.95	
	60040	Repair & Remodeling Cost Data 2010	144.95	
	60170	Residential Cost Data 2010	144.95	
	60280	Site Work & Landscape Cost Data 2010	169.95	
	60050	Square Foot Costs 2010	184.95	
	62019	Yardsticks for Costing (2009)	154.95	
	62010	Yardsticks for Costing (2010)	169.95	
		REFERENCE BOOKS		
	67310A	ADA Compliance Pricing Guide, 2nd Ed.	79.95	
	67356	BIM Handbook	85.00	
	67330	Bldrs Essentials: Adv. Framing Methods	12.98	
	67329	Bldrs Essentials: Best Bus. Practices for Bldrs	29.95	
	67298A	Bldrs Essentials: Framing/Carpentry 2nd Ed.	15.98	
	67298AS	Bldrs Essentials: Framing/Carpentry Spanish	15.98	
	67307	Bldrs Essentials: Plan Reading & Takeoff	35.95	
	67342	Building & Renovating Schools	69.98	
	67339	Building Security: Strategies & Costs	44.98	
	67353	Complete Book of Framing	29.95	
	67146	Concrete Repair & Maintenance Illustrated	69.95	
	67352	Construction Business Management	49.95	
	67314	Cost Planning & Est. for Facil. Maint.	89.95	
	67328A	Designing & Building with the IBC, 2nd Ed.	99.95	
	67230B	Electrical Estimating Methods, 3rd Ed.	64.95	
	64777A	Environmental Remediation Est. Methods, 2nd Ed.	49.98	
	67343	Estimating Bldg. Costs for Resi. & Lt. Comm.	29.95	
	67276B	Estimating Handbook, 3rd Ed.	$99.95	
	67318	Facilities Operations & Engineering Reference	54.98	
	67301	Facilities Planning & Relocation	49.98	
	67338A	Green Building: Proj. Planning & Cost Est., 2nd Ed.	129.95	
	67355	Green Home Improvement	24.95	

Qty.	Book no.	REFERENCE BOOKS (Cont.)	Unit Price	Total
	67357A	The Gypsum Construction Handbook	29.95	
	67357S	The Gypsum Construction Handbook (Spanish)	29.95	
	67323	Historic Preservation: Proj. Planning & Est.	49.98	
	67308E	Home Improvement Costs–Int. Projects, 9th Ed.	24.95	
	67309E	Home Improvement Costs–Ext. Projects, 9th Ed.	24.95	
	67344	Homeowner's Guide to Mold	21.95	
	67324B	How to Est.w/Means Data & CostWorks, 3rd Ed.	59.95	
	67351	How Your House Works	21.95	
	67282A	Illustrated Const. Dictionary, Condensed, 2nd Ed.	59.95	
	67292A	Illustrated Const. Dictionary, w/CD-ROM, 3rd Ed.	99.95	
	67348	Job Order Contracting	89.95	
	67347	Kitchen & Bath Project Costs	19.98	
	67295C	Landscape Estimating Methods, 5th Ed.	64.95	
	67341	Life Cycle Costing for Facilities	99.95	
	67294B	Mechanical Estimating Methods, 4th Ed.	64.95	
	67245A	Planning & Managing Interior Projects, 2nd Ed.	34.98	
	67283B	Plumbing Estimating Methods, 3rd Ed.	29.98	
	67345	Practice of Cost Segregation Analysis	99.95	
	67337	Preventive Maint. for Higher Education Facilities	149.95	
	67346	Preventive Maint. for Multi-Family Housing	89.95	
	67326	Preventive Maint. Guidelines for School Facil.	149.95	
	67247B	Project Scheduling & Management for Constr. 3rd Ed.	64.95	
	67265B	Repair & Remodeling Estimating Methods, 4th Ed.	69.95	
	67322B	Resi. & Light Commercial Const. Stds., 3rd Ed.	59.95	
	67327A	Spanish/English Construction Dictionary, 2nd Ed.	23.95	
	67145B	Sq. Ft. & Assem. Estimating Methods, 3rd Ed.	69.95	
	67321	Total Productive Facilities Management	29.98	
	67350	Understanding and Negotiating Const. Contracts	69.95	
	67303B	Unit Price Estimating Methods, 4th Ed.	59.95	
	67354	Universal Design	21.95	
	67319A	Value Engineering: Practical Applications	79.95	

MA residents add 6.25% state sales tax

Shipping & Handling**

Total (U.S. Funds)*

Prices are subject to change and are for U.S. delivery only. *Canadian customers may call for current prices. **Shipping & handling charges: Add 7% of total order for check and credit card payments. Add 9% of total order for invoiced orders.

Send order to: **ADDV-1000**

Name (please print) _____

Company _____

☐ **Company**

☐ **Home Address** _____

_____

City/State/Zip _____

Phone # _____ P.O. # _____

(Must accompany all orders being billed

Mail to: RSMeans, P.O. Box 800, Kingston, MA 02364